CAMBRIDGE GREEK AN

CU00972041

LUCRETIUS

DE RERVM NATVRA

BOOK III

EDITED BY

E. J. KENNEY

Kennedy Professor Emeritus of Latin,
University of Cambridge

SECOND EDITION

CAMBRIDGE
UNIVERSITY PRESS

CAMBRIDGE
UNIVERSITY PRESS

University Printing House, Cambridge CB2 8BS, United Kingdom

Cambridge University Press is part of the University of Cambridge.

It furthers the University's mission by disseminating knowledge in the pursuit of education, learning and research at the highest international levels of excellence.

www.cambridge.org
Information on this title: www.cambridge.org/9780521173896

© Cambridge University Press 1971, 2014

First edition published 1971
Second edition published 2014

Printed in the United Kingdom by CPI Group Ltd, Croydon CR0 4YY

A catalogue record for this publication is available from the British Library

ISBN 978-1-107-00211-1 Hardback
ISBN 978-0-521-17389-6 Paperback

FOR ANNE

'Long life and good health to your honour,' said he as he turned away.

The Philosopher lit his pipe.

'We live as long as we are let,' said he, 'and we get the health we deserve. Your salutation embodies a reflection on death which is not philosophic. We must acquiesce in all logical progressions. The merging of opposites is completion. Life runs to death as to its goal, and we should go towards that next stage of experience either carelessly as to what must be, or with a good, honest curiosity as to what may be.'

'There's not much fun in being dead, sir', said Meehawl.

'How do you know?' said the Philosopher.

'I know well enough,' replied Meehawl.

(JAMES STEPHENS, *The crock of gold*)

[P]hysical matter is simultaneously indestructible and entirely transmutable . . . it can swap states drastically, from vegetable to mineral or from liquid to solid. To attempt to hold these two contradictory ideas, of permanence and mutability, in the brain at the same time is usefully difficult, for it makes the individual feel at once valuable and superfluous. You become aware of yourself as constituted of nothing more than endlessly convertible matter – but also of always being perpetuated in some form. Such knowledge grants us a kind of comfortless immortality: an understanding that our bodies belong to a limitless cycle of dispersal and reconstitution.

(ROBERT MACFARLANE, *The wild places*)

CONTENTS

PREFACE TO THE FIRST EDITION

The conscientious commentator will offer his work to the public in a mood of doubt and self-questioning. As an Editor of the series in which this edition appears I have felt a special duty to keep in the forefront of my mind its declared aim: 'to provide the student with the guidance that he needs for the interpretation and understanding of the book as a work of literature'. The amount of guidance here provided may, however, strike some readers as excessive. If so, it is because it has seemed to me that in the past Lucretius' interpreters have not always taken enough pains to disentangle and follow his argument as he intended it to be followed, and this, whatever shortcomings may be found in the execution, is what I have attempted to do. The *De Rerum Natura*, in spite of the lucid style of which the poet was rightly proud, is a difficult book, and I have often preferred the risk of telling the reader what he already knows to that of leaving him in the lurch – the besetting sin of commentators. It may also be felt that there is here too much expatiation on the poetical techniques of Lucretius. In this department the existing commentaries seem to leave much to be desired. In spite of the lead given by H. Sykes Davies in his *Criterion* article of 1931–2 and in spite of more recent contributions in this field such as Professor David West's excellent *The imagery and poetry of Lucretius* (1969), the conventional idea of Lucretius' art still persists: *ingenio maximus, arte rudis*. Cicero knew otherwise; but posterity has yet to be convinced. The student who finds some notes inordinately long may care to note that an effort has been made to, so to say, 'grade' their contents so that the essential information is usually presented at the beginning.

It would have been tedious in the extreme to record each and every debt to my predecessors. My general obligation to the commentaries of, in particular, Munro, Ernout–Robin and Bailey will be evident. I must make specific mention, however, of the way in which my approach to the understanding and exegesis of Book III has been influenced by the superb edition of Richard Heinze – unworthily neglected by Bailey, who makes quite inadequate use of it. I have not been able to bring myself to reproduce any existing text; in preparing my own I have relied principally on Bailey's reports of the manuscripts.

It is a pleasure to record my thanks, for help and advice of various kinds, to Dr M. Baltes, Dr H.-D. Blume, Dr R. D. Dawe, Dr G. E. R. Lloyd, Mr Roland G. Mayer, Dr D. O'Brien, Mr N. H. Reed and Professor H. Tränkle. I am particularly indebted to my editorial colleague Mrs Easterling for suggestions leading to a number of important improvements in both presentation and substance. Professor R. G. M. Nisbet kindly agreed to read the proofs, and a number of weaknesses have been exposed by his acute criticisms. I regret only that it was not possible to incorporate more of his suggestions. His and Mrs Easterling's vigilance has saved me from more errors than I care to remember; those that remain must be laid at my door, where they belong.

March 1971   E. J. K.

PREFACE TO THE SECOND EDITION

Two considerations have prompted the thought that a second edition of this book may not be unwelcome. As informed interest in Lucretius has continued to grow – a fact strikingly illustrated by the number of translations that continue to appear – so it must be accepted that students now come to him less well prepared linguistically than was the case in the 1970s. Accordingly the Commentary has been extensively revised and enlarged, with, it is hoped, due account taken of the comments of reviewers – though my old friend and critic Professor David West would now miss in the notes the 'brevity that comes close to wit' that he admired in the first edition.

Three passages in the Introduction to the first edition have called for reconsideration: what was said there about the 'middle' or 'florid' style of oratory, the discussion of the diatribe and what is said about the spelling of *seorsum*. These points are dealt with at p. 13 n. 51, p. 14 n. 55 and p. 18 n. 73 respectively. The section on the text has been rewritten in the light of subsequent work in that field, especially that of Professor Michael Reeve and Dr David Butterfield, to both of whom I am greatly indebted for help and advice generously given. The *apparatus criticus* has also been revised in accordance with Dr Butterfield's advice. Otherwise the Introduction is reprinted unaltered apart from a handful of additions to the footnotes in addition to the three noted above, and adjustment of the references to the secondary literature in conformity with current series style. In the Supplementary Introduction I have confined myself for the most part to comments on such post-1971 contributions to Lucretian studies (some of which are in any case noticed in the revised Commentary) as seem likely to be useful to readers of this book of the *De Rerum Natura*. I regret that it has not been possible to include references to all the important work of Professor Ferguson Smith on the Oenoanda inscription.

As the book passes through the press I take the opportunity of recording my grateful acknowledgements of the help I have received in the process of revising it for this new edition. Dr Monica Gale has generously taken time from the preparation of her eagerly expected edition of Catullus in this series to revise and amplify the Supplementary Introduction to its great benefit. Dr Robert Macfarlane has kindly permitted me to reproduce the passage from his fine book *The wild places* as a second epigraph, so providing the perfect rueful Epicurean gloss on the Irish peasant's dour verdict: 'There's not much fun in being dead.' Professor Roland Mayer volunteered of his goodness to read the proofs – an undertaking that cost him more time and wrestling with my type- and manuscript than either of us had initially bargained for. Finally I must thank and apologize to the members of the Production staff of the Cambridge University Press who were faced with the task of transforming copy presented in computer-unfriendly guise into what is now offered to the reader. I owe a special debt of gratitude to Dr Iveta Adams. Her searching scrutiny has detected and eliminated a great many loose ends, inconsistencies and authorial slips of pen, typewriter and attention, and many others have been revealed by the vigilance of my fellow editors. For any that may have eluded our joint efforts the responsibility rests with me. My wife has never spared herself in the labour of retrieving books from shelves now inaccessible to me, and this edition is dedicated to her in love and gratitude.

May 2014   E. J. K.

ABBREVIATIONS

CLE	*Carmina Latina epigraphica*, ed. F. Bücheler. 2 vols. Leipzig 1895–7. *Supplementum*, ed. E. Lommatzsch. Leipzig 1926.
CP	*The classical papers of A. E. Housman*, ed. J. Diggle and F. R. D. Goodyear. 3 vols. Cambridge 1972.
Ernout–Meillet	A. Ernout and A. Meillet, *Dictionnaire étymologique de la langue latine. Histoire des mots*. 4th edn. 2 vols. Paris 1959.
Ernout–Robin	Ernout, A. and L. Robin. *Lucrèce De Rerum Natura. Commentaire exégétique et critique*. 2nd edn. Paris 1962.
FLP	*The fragmentary Latin poets*, ed. E. Courtney. Oxford 1993.
G–L	B. L. Gildersleeve and G. Lodge, *Gildersleeve's Latin grammar*. 3rd edn. London 1895. (Cited by paragraph.)
GLK	*Grammatici Latini*, ed. H. Keil. 8 vols. Leipzig 1857–70. Reprinted Hildesheim 1961.
GP	*The Greek Anthology. The Garland of Philip and some contemporary epigrams*, ed. A. S. F. Gow and D. L. Page. 2 vols. Cambridge 1968.
HE	*The Greek Anthology. Hellenistic epigrams*, ed. A. S. F. Gow and D. L. Page. 2 vols. Cambridge 1965.
H–S	J. B. Hofmann and A. Szantyr, *Lateinische Syntax und Stilistik*. Munich 1965.
K–S	R. Kühner and C. Stegmann, *Ausführliche Grammatik der lateinischen Sprache*. 3. Auflage, ed. A. Thierfelder. 2 vols. Leverkusen 1955.
NLS	E. C. Woodcock, *A new Latin syntax*. London 1959. (Cited by paragraph.)
N–H	R. G. M. Nisbet and M. Hubbard, *A commentary on Horace: Odes Book I* 1970; *Book II* 1978. Oxford.
N–R	R. G. M. Nisbet and N. Rudd, *A commentary on Horace: Odes Book III*. Oxford 2004.
N–W	F. Neue and C. Wagener, *Formenlehre der lateinischen Sprache*. 3. Auflage. 4 vols. Leipzig and Berlin 1892–1905.
OCD[1]	*The Oxford Classical Dictionary*, ed. M. Cary *et al.* Oxford 1949.
OLD	*Oxford Latin Dictionary*, ed. P. G. W. Glare. Oxford 1982.

PLM   *Poetae Latini Minores*, ed. E. Baehrens. 5 vols. Leipzig
                   1879–83.
Roby   H. J. Roby, *A grammar of the Latin language from Plautus
                   to Suetonius*. Vol. II *Syntax*. London 1889. Reprinted
                   1896.
ROL   *Remains of Old Latin*, ed. and tr. E. H. Warmington.
                   4 vols. London and Cambridge, Mass. 1935–40.
TLL   *Thesaurus Linguae Latinae*. Munich 1900–.

NOTE. For full titles of works cited by author and date only see the
Bibliography.

INTRODUCTION

1. THE DOCTRINE

Ab Epicuro principium: Lucretius utters his allegiance in unambiguous terms (Comm. 1–4n. *primus*). Yet this allegiance was perhaps to an idea as much as to a man. Epicurus (341–271 BC) was no Socrates; and he lacked both the poetic gifts and the humour to be his own Plato. What excited Lucretius to produce the most passionate didactic poem ever written was the Epicurean philosophy itself. Diogenes Laertius (10.9) speaks of the 'siren-charms' of Epicurean doctrine; to Lucretius it seems to have come as a revelation, the only philosophical system which, by abolishing fear of the gods and of death, allowed mankind to achieve release from spiritual bondage. However, much of the appeal of the system must have derived from the character and personality of its founder. In the first place he was self-taught (D.L. 10.13), a fact which perhaps helps to explain the originality of his doctrines taken as a whole and their essentially practical nature.[1] He was also a man of blameless life and singular sweetness of disposition, as his letters to his disciples testify; it is small wonder that they venerated him. The Homeric heroes were honoured by their peoples 'as gods' (Hom. *Il.* 5.78, 10.33, 12.312, etc.); divine honours were on occasion paid to earthly rulers even before the Hellenistic period; and Empedocles had claimed that he walked among men 'as an immortal god, no longer mortal'.[2] Such were the precedents according to which it was natural that the followers of Epicurus should acclaim him as the true, the only Saviour, σωτήρ;[3] greater than the powers which, through sheer force of mind, he had vanquished: *deus ille fuit, deus* proclaims Lucretius (5.3); and the evangelistic fervour and single-minded impetus of the *De Rerum Natura* make it singularly tempting to see in the poem the document of a conversion. Certainly it is hardly an exaggeration to say that this self-styled enemy of religion was 'in the profounder sense that transcends creeds and

---

[1] Festugière 1968: 27–8; Martha (1867: 9) remarks that the Epicurean philosophy represents an attempt to systematize the temperament of a single individual: 'S'il est vrai que les doctrines font les mœurs, n'est-il pas vrai aussi que les mœurs font les doctrines?' The point is valid for most, if not all, ancient philosophies, but particularly so for the Epicurean. Cf. Boyancé 1963: 301.

[2] ἐγὼ δ' ὑμῖν θεὸς ἄμβροτος, οὐκέτι θνητός | πωλεῦμαι (31 B 112.4–5 D–K).

[3] Cf. Festugière 1968: 63 n. 1; for the growth of 'individual' religion and the quest for personal salvation in post-classical Greece see ibid., ch. 1 'Le fait religieux au seuil de l'ère hellénistique'; Tarn and Griffith 1952: ch. x 'Philosophy and Religion'; Dodds 1951: ch. viii 'The fear of freedom'; Murray 1935: ch. iv 'The failure of nerve'.

forms, the greatest religious mind of pagan Rome',[4] as he contemplated
the revelation achieved by reason with an awe that can only be called religious, *diuina uoluptas atque horror* (cf. Comm. 28–30n.). It has often been
remarked that the Epicurean school of philosophy (and the same is true of
the Stoic) had many of the characteristics of a church: 'a sacred founder,
and sacred books, and a credo of memory verses from those books',[5] con-
gregations of the faithful, and a tradition that was more concerned to
preserve and gloss than to build upon and develop the founder's doctrine.[6] Dogma and orthodoxy pervade the *DRN*. Lucretius' purpose was
to help men to attain happiness, which he describes (3.322) as *dignam dis
degere uitam*; but the godlike existence to which he encourages his readers
to aspire is closer to that of Epicurus than to the detached and ineffectual
gods of the *intermundia*. To those gods he owed of necessity a duty of formal
piety as exemplified by Epicurus himself (6.67–79),[7] but no more; their
appearance in Book III (18–24) serves not to introduce the contemplation
of their virtues, but to lend force (by way of contrast to the non-existence
of Hell) to the idea that inspires the poet's true religious feelings – the
operation of the laws of Nature, dictating inexorably the motions of the
atoms in the void, *quaecumque infra per inane geruntur* (27). The vehicle of
this revelation is the Epicurean doctrine, sprung – the analogy with the
mythical birth of Athena from the head of Zeus is unmistakably hinted
at – from the divine mind of Epicurus (3.14–15); and it is Epicurus, not
the gods of the *intermundia*, whom Lucretius invokes throughout the poem
in terms borrowed from, and clearly intended to recall, the conventional
invocation of deity. Here, not in the anthropomorphic figments of priests
and poets, was the true divinity.

In the *DRN* we are offered not an account of the Epicurean system (cf.
§3 below), but the personal testament of the poet. For a full exposition
of the Epicurean faith and of what it demanded of its adherents we must
look elsewhere.[8] However, if Book III is to be read with understanding,
certain preliminary points must be made. In particular the associations
that cling to the word 'Epicurean' in modern usage must be ignored. The
Epicurean philosophy was materialistic: its account of the universe, based
on the theories of the earlier atomists Democritus and Leucippus, taught

---

[4] Leonard and Smith 1965: 76. Cf. Mill 1924: 38: 'the best among [unbeliev-
ers]…are more genuinely religious, in the best sense of the word religion, than
those who exclusively arrogate to themselves the title'.

[5] Leonard and Smith 1965: 80.

[6] Cf. Martha 1867: 10–12, 346; Festugière 1968: 31 n. 2; and on the points of
resemblance between Epicurus and St Paul ibid. 36 n. 3.

[7] Cf. Festugière 1968: 74–5.

[8] See e.g. Martha 1867; DeWitt 1954; Schmid 1962; Leonard and Smith 1965:
36–55; Farrington 1967; Festugière 1968; Rist 1972.

that all phenomena are produced by the motions, according to certain laws, of solid and indestructible bodies (atoms) in the void. Nothing is created out of nothing; nothing is resolved into nothing; everything, except the individual atoms themselves, is subject to change. The human soul, like the human body, is composed of atoms and is mortal. The gods exist but do not regulate either natural phenomena or human affairs. There is no life after death; the business of man is to achieve happiness as best he can in this life, according to the dictates of reason. Happiness is defined as well-being of body and mind, and consists fundamentally in the avoidance of pain and anxiety (ἀπονία, ἀταραξία).[9] This bald summary may, it is hoped, assist comprehension of Lucretius, but it is totally inadequate to describe what Epicureanism really was and the part which it played in the lives of its devotees, particularly the emphasis, of which we hear little in the *DRN*, which was laid on friendship and a common life. Various features of the physical doctrines are open to criticism and were attacked in antiquity by rival schools, and in particular the self-centred gods of Epicurus were a favourite target; but the most vulnerable aspect of the system as a whole clearly lay in its emphasis on happiness and pleasure, as opposed to the Stoic insistence on virtue. It is this emphasis that, in trivialized and degraded forms, has come to be synonymous with Epicureanism in the minds of many, to whom of course 'pleasure' means something quite different from what it meant to Epicurus. This misunderstanding was already well established in Lucretius' day. Nothing in fact could be more misleading than the equation of Epicurean doctrine with mere hedonism. Rather the reverse is the case: the trouble with Epicureanism, and the main reason perhaps why it never enjoyed the general success of Stoicism, was not that it was too easy, but that it was too difficult, too austere, too unworldly.[10] It is hard for an ordinary man, at the same time as he is forbidden to pursue the usual goals of worldly ambition, to accept that he must live well now because there will be no other chance for him to live at all, and that the good life must be lived for its own sake without any prospect of either reward or punishment in the hereafter.[11] At its best the austerity and nobility of the Epicurean life as it was lived by

[9] Cf. the *Quadruple Remedy* (*Tetrapharmakon*) of Philodemus (cit. Festugière 1968: 46 n. 1): 'The gods are not to be feared, death is without danger, good is easy to possess, evil is easy to bear bravely.'

[10] Cf. the apology placed in the mouth of Torquatus by Cicero: *ut tollatur error omnis imperitorum intellegaturque ea quae uoluptuaria, delicata, mollis habeatur disciplina, quam grauis, quam continens, quam seuera sit* (*Fin.* 1.37).

[11] 'Here we have one of the deepest implications of the Epicurean doctrine of nihilism – the moral obligation laid upon us by the brief span of our existence to live a rich and abundant life of sense and spirit, of the body and of the soul, that one might withdraw, at the appointed hour, *plenus vitae conviva*, with equanimity, and even nobly and proudly' (Hadzsits 1935: 138–9).

the founder and by its highest representatives compels admiration; but it
was a style of life that, essentially, rejected life. 'There is a strange shadow
of sadness hanging over this wise and kindly faith, which proceeds from
the essential distrust of life that lies at its heart. The best that Epicurus
has really to say of the world is that if you are very wise and do not attract
its notice – Λάθε βιώσας – it will not hurt you. It is a philosophy not of
conquest but of escape.'[12] And admirable as certain aspects of Epicurean
ethics are, the connexion between the physical premisses of the system
and its moral conclusions is sometimes loose.[13] Lucretius has occasionally
been criticized for expending so much moral energy in the denunciation
of old wives' tales which the educated Romans of his day – for whom, as the
style of his poem shows, he must have been writing – could not conceivably have taken seriously; and, conversely, it has been regretted that he did
not devote some part of the poem to expounding Epicurean ethics.[14] Such
criticisms rest on a misconception of the poet's aims. In limiting himself to
a negative and destructive approach (based, it should be stressed, on positive physical teaching) Lucretius was both following the promptings of his
own nature and writing for the world and for posterity. He was anything but
a fool, and we are bound to assume that he was aware that his enlightened
contemporaries did not require to be undeceived about Hades. In attacking these popular notions he was attacking a particular manifestation of
something universal and eternal, or at all events coeval with the human
species: 'the poet is not so much concerned to refute a popular belief as
to point its moral, if rightly understood'.[15] An intelligent reader, trained
to draw general conclusions from particular cases, can see all the innu-
merable superstitions of the Hellenistic and Greco-Roman worlds imaged
in Lucretius' great diatribe;[16] but to convey his point forcefully it was necessary for him to choose examples that would carry emotional conviction
through their familiarity. Tantalus, Tityos, Sisyphus are demolished, not
because Memmius and his peers believed in them, but because other men
had believed in them, did believe in them – and would believe in them,
or in fresh variations of them, again.[17] The charge that Lucretius was

[12] Murray 1935: 110.
[13] '[I]n Epicureanism (as so commonly in other naturalistic or behaviorist sys-
tems), ideals of the good life are smuggled in from without the system – as it were,
even from the very folklore of ethics, those ancient notions of what is decent for
a true man, recorded long ago in Hesiod and Homer, and doubtless invoked even
by a Boeotian blacksmith when he praised or pummeled his neighbor' (Leonard
and Smith 1965: 44); cf. Festugière 1968: 52–3.
[14] See, for instance, Hadzsits 1935: 153.   [15] Sikes 1936: 127–8.
[16] Cf. Murray 1935: ch. IV 'The failure of nerve'; Leonard and Smith 1965: 73–4.
[17] 'Little could Lucretius…anticipate the diseased imaginations and the cru-
elties imposed upon later centuries by fears of everlasting punishment' (Hadzsits
1935: 141). Perhaps not; but these things would have confirmed his worst fears of

battering at an open door could with equal justice be levelled against each and every writer who in any age has attacked folly and superstition.[18]

2. THE POET

Little is known about Lucretius. This is by no means a disadvantage for the interpretation of his poem, which can and should be understood without reference to the personal circumstances of the poet.[19] Since however in Lucretius' case the biographical question has had a certain nuisance value it must receive some discussion. St Jerome has transmitted under the year 94 BC the following notice: *Titus Lucretius poeta nascitur, qui postea amatorio poculo in furorem uersus, cum aliquot libros per interualla insaniae conscripsisset quos postea Cicero emendauit, propria se manu interfecit anno aetatis XLIIII* (*Eusebii Pamphili Chronici Canones*, p. 231 Fotheringham). This would place Lucretius' death in 51 BC, a date which fails to square with a statement in the *Life* of Virgil ascribed to Donatus (but generally thought to be based on Suetonius' *De uiris illustribus*) that he died in the year in which Virgil, aged 17, assumed the *toga uirilis*, i.e. 53 BC. These and other inconsistencies make secure dating impossible: for the reader of the *DRN* it is enough to know that the poet was born in the 90s and died, a comparatively young man, in the late 50s of the first century BC.[20] A more intractable problem is posed by St Jerome's account of the love-philtre and the poet's madness and suicide. Few scholars have either accepted or rejected this tradition outright,[21] and even those who are disinclined to trust the unsupported word of a Christian saint in such a matter as the obviously edifying death of a pagan and a blasphemer are inclined to allow that some features of the *DRN* are consistent with what St Jerome tells us. Both Santayana and Bailey use the phrase 'strange vehemence' of Lucretius' manner in certain passages, and Bailey sees evidence of actual derangement in the famous excursus in Book v on the use of animals in warfare (1308-49). This line

what men will do to themselves once they have rejected the guidance of reason and true philosophy.

[18] Cf. Festugière 1968: 78 n. 1. One form of superstition (as Lucretius must have seen it) that flourished in the first century BC as it had flourished in Hellenistic Greece (cf. n. 3 above) was the romantic expectation of a political σωτήρ or Messiah: for contemporary exploitation of this idea see Norden 1966: 369 n. 26. For the period as one favourable to mysticism see also Dodds 1965: 100 n. 1. Lucretius' purpose was to declare the true Messiah: Epicurus.

[19] Cf. Cherniss 1943/1962.

[20] For a fuller discussion see Bailey 1947: 3-5; his favourable assessment of the *Vita Borgiana* should be discounted. There is no evidence as to Lucretius' birthplace. If, as seems not improbable, it was Rome, he was one of the very few Latin poets or men of letters not to hail from the provinces; cf. Watts 1971.

[21] See Bailey 1947: 8-12; Boyancé 1963: 18. On some of the weaknesses of the case against St Jerome's veracity see Gain 1969 (but see now Smith 1992: xix-xxvi; Kenney 1977b/1995: 4-5).

of argument, however, would hardly have been started if St Jerome's statement had not given a lead, and should be regarded sceptically.[22] The
'vehemence' remarked by Santayana and Bailey is real enough, but vehemence does not necessarily connote derangement; and in the *DRN* it is,
so far from being 'strange', an essential feature of the diatribe style (see
§4(*a*) below), as also of the poet's emotional involvement in the terrible
history of his country (Comm. 48–86n.). Nor is the 'high melancholy' of
which Santayana speaks evident to all readers of the poem who approach
it without preconceptions of the poet's manner. It is well over a century
since M. Patin in his *Études sur la poésie latine* (1868) launched the theory
of 'l'Antilucrèce dans Lucrèce': the idea that Lucretius is fundamentally
unconvinced by what he is saying and that a deep native pessimism is constantly breaking through the doctrinaire optimism that he is committed
to preaching. This theory is by no means universally discarded and still
colours some assessments of Lucretius; it is based in the main on the interpretation of selected passages taken out of their context in the argument
of the poem.[23]

A second problem is raised by St Jerome's reference to Cicero. It
must be read together with a well-known passage in Cicero's letters to his
brother Quintus, written in February of 54 BC: *Lucreti poemata, ut scribis,
ita sunt, multis luminibus ingeni, multae tamen artis (Q. F.* 2.10(9).3). The
stylistic judgement implied in this sentence is discussed below (§4(*b*)); it
is very difficult to deduce from it any reliable chronological or biographical data. It need not imply that Lucretius was dead when the words were
written,[24] and it certainly implies nothing about any editorial activity on
the part of either Cicero or his brother. The *DRN* was clearly left in an
unfinished state at the poet's death (§3 below); but the ancient practice
was always to allow incomplete but publishable work to appear with the
barest minimum of correction.[25] The term *emendo* was no doubt used by
St Jerome, who was well acquainted with the details of book production,
in its technical sense, which signified something not much more ambitious than proof-correcting in modern times: it amounted to little more
than the elimination of copying errors. Some such process would have

---

[22] This is not the place to expatiate on 5.1308–49; it is enough to say that the
verses, if read carefully in their context, offer no foundation whatever for any sus-
picions as to the poet's sanity. MacKay is right to suggest (MacKay 1964: 125) that
the vivid descriptions are based on Lucretius' experience of *uenationes*; but his
attempt (134) to fit the passage into the argument rests on a misunderstanding
of the (very carefully written) sequence 5.1341–9. See Schrijvers 1970: 296–305;
Kenney 1972: 19–24.

[23] See also Wormell 1960; de Saint Denis 1963; Kinsey 1964.

[24] See Bailey 1947: 4, repeating the important arguments of Sandbach 1940.

[25] The Virgilian half-lines are a striking example: see *Vit. Donat.* 41 *edidit...
auctore Augusto Varius, sed summatim emendata, ut qui uersus etiam imperfectos sicut erant
reliquerit.*

had to be carried out by the person, whoever he was, who 'published' the
DRN after the poet's death, but it is unlikely to have entailed anything that
a literate slave could not have managed; and in view of Cicero's outspoken contempt for Epicureanism it seems inherently unlikely that he would
have been willing to spend his own time performing the operation.[26] In
any event it is hazardous to use these two notices as evidence for the character of the relationship between Cicero and Lucretius; they could hardly
have been oblivious of each other's existence,[27] but more than that one
may hardly say.

The poem itself, as one might expect, offers no direct and very little
indirect information about the poet. It is dedicated to a certain Memmius who, whether or not he is identical with the well-known Gaius Memmius,[28] was certainly an aristocrat, as is shown by the terms in which he is
addressed: 1.26 *Memmiadae nostro*, 42 *Memmi clara propago*. This fact does
not of course entail that the poet was Memmius' social equal. On the
other hand the *DRN* is obviously the work of a well-educated man, widely
read in the literatures of both Greece and Rome, a 'lord of language',
who used Latin masterfully and as to the manner born, and who spoke
as a Roman to Romans. None of this proves anything about Lucretius'
birth or social status, but a comparison with the manner of Horace tempts
one to guess that the authority with which Lucretius addressed his fellow-
countrymen was rooted in something more than confidence in his role of
philosopher-poet. His repeated insistence on the hazards of ambition,
though a central feature of Epicurean doctrine, takes on added significance when viewed against the contemporary background of civil strife.
These read as the sentiments, not of a detached observer out of the *sapien-
tum templa serena* (2.8), but of a man who had witnessed and indeed been
a party to the demoralization of a class in whose fate he was deeply interested. The agonies he describes sound like those of his own friends and
kindred.[29]

3. THE POEM

(a) Scope

It is important to grasp at the outset the fact, already stressed, that the
DRN does not set out to present a complete account of the Epicurean

[26] It has been suggested (Giussani 1896: xvi) that Cicero accepted nominal
responsibility but entrusted the actual work to a secretary or to one of the staff of
copyists maintained by his friend Atticus. Why however should he have felt obliged
to become involved at all?

[27] Cicero was not above borrowing a striking phrase from Lucretius (Comm.
992–4n.).

[28] See Catull. 10.13 and Fordyce ad loc.

[29] Cf. Martha 1867: 25–9; Sellar 1889: 290–1; Hadzsits 1935: 5, drawing attention to 1.41, 5.36.

system. Lucretius' ultimate aim is positive, to put his readers in the way of achieving happiness: this is acknowledged, not, one feels, without a hint of irony – for such certainties were not for the poet of the *Aeneid* – in Virgil's famous apostrophe.[30] His immediate aim, however, is negative: to destroy the barriers that obstruct man's path to self-fulfilment, the illusions that stand between him and enlightenment – fear of the gods, fear of the after-life, fear of death. In order for these illusions to be destroyed they must be shown to be inconsistent with a correct understanding of the physical uni-verse (cf. Comm. 38–40n. *liquidam puramque*). Thus the physical doctrines, though they are fundamental and though the exposition of them occupies most of the poem, are in the design of Lucretius' great enterprise func-tionally subservient to its main end: the scientific argument provides the premiss for the destructive argument which in turn provides the premiss for the final positive ethical conclusions – the statements about how men ought to live. But those final conclusions are not drawn, the statements are not made: the last link in the chain of argument Lucretius takes as read or leaves for others to provide. Thus, though the argument often takes a particular Epicurean ethical position for granted, there is very little in the poem that may be called ethical doctrine.[31] This great omission has of course excited remark. It has been suggested that these limitations reflect a personal limitation of interest in Epicurean philosophy, which Lucretius saw less as a way of life than as the means to an end which was not precisely the end envisaged by the founder.[32] That the stimulus to write the *DRN* was personal and deeply felt is extremely probable, indeed is the overwhelm-ing impression that the poem makes on the great majority of readers; but it does not follow that Lucretius was not interested in the parts of the system which he does not choose to develop. It is important to emphasize that the *DRN* is a poem, for the fact carries certain implications. It belonged of necessity, according to ancient ways of thinking about literature, to a spe-cific genre (εἶδος, γένος, *genus*), that of the didactic epos (see §4(*a*) below), and that tradition, as represented in particular by Parmenides and Empe-docles (to whom Lucretius was obviously indebted), did not offer a model for the exposition of ethical doctrine. Hesiod, who stood at the head of the

---

[30] G. 2.490–2 *felix qui potuit rerum cognoscere causas | atque metus omnis et inexorabile fatum | subiecit pedibus strepitumque Acherontis auari.*
[31] Thus in the *DRN* the traditional subordination of Canonics (as the Epicure-ans called rational philosophy) and Physics (natural philosophy) to Ethics (moral philosophy) is reversed: cf. Hadzsits 1935: 11. On the other hand, as is shown by, for instance, the famous description of the sacrifice of Iphigenia (1.80–101), Lucretius' objections to religion were moral, as have been those of James Mill and indeed of all reflective unbelievers. Cf. Robinson 1964: 130.
[32] So Boyancé 1963: 301: 'Lucrèce n'a adhéré à l'épicurisme que parceque qu'il y a decouvert l'explication d'un mal dont l'importance ne pouvait lui apparaître que parce lui–même il en souffrait'.

whole tradition, has something to say in the *Works and Days* about Justice and of the rules which should govern the behaviour of men to the gods and to each other, but what he says is couched in the primitive style of 'wisdom-literature', not as systematic and constructive exposition. Is a metrical account of Epicurean ethics (which were fundamentally very simple) imaginable?[33] Poetry, especially poetry such as Lucretius', cannot thrive upon an unmixed diet of abstractions; it must have its roots in and be nourished by bodily images and concrete associations. On the other hand, the Epicurean cosmos, *machina mundi*, a complex but wholly material organization, provided a theme for which models already existed in the tradition and which was calculated to call forth the full force of Lucretius' unique creative powers. Moreover, it offered a great technical challenge. The importance of this point is apt to be overlooked by a modern reader; but ancient poets were from first to last preoccupied with technique, and Lucretius, though he should certainly not be pigeonholed *tout court* as a New Poet, was fully aware of the requirements of Alexandrian *doctrina* and all that they implied.[34] The scope of the *DRN* must be seen as conditioned by the tradition in which it was written: Lucretius' predecessors in that tradition – Hesiod, Parmenides, Empedocles – offered both models for didactic poetry of a certain kind, the exposition of complex cosmogonical and physical theory, and also an incentive to demonstrate superiority in this kind of writing. The Epicurean system itself, with its emphasis on phenomena and the evidence of the senses, afforded a splendid stimulus to Lucretius' superb powers of observation and description, both of what he could see and of what he could not see but could visualize – the minute but all-potent motions of the atoms. Generic influences can be seen at work also in another profoundly important characteristic of the poem, its satire, the roots of which we may trace as far back as Hesiod. 'We may see in the underlying moral earnestness [of Hesiod] the origins of a *mood* which pervaded the later masterpieces of didactic poetry and was perhaps an essential element in their success as works of art: for poetry seems most easily to combine with a didactic purpose when teaching rises to *preaching*.'[35] This potentiality for satire that was latent in the didactic and philosophical tradition had been exploited by Xenophanes, who was celebrated for the biting expression of his contempt for the views of his fellow-men, and by Democritus, known throughout antiquity as the Laughing Philosopher. Yet it was, it seems, Lucretius who first harnessed the power of satire and applied it to the systematic exposure of error, folly and superstition. The manner in which he did so will be discussed below (§4(*a*)); at present

---

[33] Lucilius' well-known fragment on Virtue (1326–38 M.) is as dull as ditchwater; and no writer is in general more lively and pungent.

[34] See Kenney 1970b/1986/2007.   [35] Cox 1969: 126.

it is sufficient to establish the point that the limitations in scope and intention of the *DRN* were designed by the poet, for the best, and that viewed in
the light of the tradition in which Lucretius found himself called to work
they make sense.[36] They are not necessarily to be taken, as they sometimes
are, as the index of a deficiency in Lucretius.

(b) Structure

Though on close investigation a good many complexities can be detected
the structure of the *DRN* in its broad outlines is simple:

| The atoms | { | I The atoms and the void; rival theories refuted |
| | | II The properties of atoms; their secondary qualities in combination |

| The soul | { | III The soul is proved to be mortal |
| | | IV Thought and sensation |

| The world | { | V The creation and history of the world |
| | | VI Celestial and terrestrial phenomena |

Various correspondences, thematic and formal, underline this symmetry.[37] The outermost pairs of books, I–II and V–VI, are linked in so far
as they demonstrate that all phenomena must be explained in material
terms and that no intervention of divine or supernatural agencies may be
postulated; hence these four books may be seen as directed, ultimately,
against the fear of the gods. This identity of purpose is explicitly recognized by the statement, repeated at the beginning of each book, that in
the Epicurean universe gods are not needed.[38] Books I and V, the first
of their pairs, are further linked by repetition of the *leitmotiv* 1.76–7 =
5.89–90,[39] with which may be compared the often-remarked correspondences in Virgil's *Aeneid* between the beginnings of Books I and VII. This
type of responsion was a standard device to articulate long poems. Within
this framework the two central books III–IV are directed against fear of the
afterlife; and once again the point is emphasized by correspondences at

---

[36] A qualification, however, may be admitted. These self-imposed limitations go
some way to explain why the poem had more influence on the history of Latin
poetry than on the history of philosophy. See Crawley 1963: 17–18.

[37] For further discussion of structure see Bailey 1947: 31–7; Boyancé 1963:
69–83; Minadeo 1965; Owen 1968–9; Farrell 2007. The details of these and other
schemata are open to question, but there can be no quarrelling with the general
conclusion that Lucretius planned and executed the poem with immense care,
though he died before he could complete the revision of Books IV–VI (Sedley
1998: 134–65). On the implications for the editorial treatment of the text as it has
come down to us see below, Section 6 'The Text'.

[38] 1.146–58, 2.167–81, 5.76–90, 6.50–79.

[39] Cf. also 1.80 *ne forte rearis* ~ 5.78 *ne forte... reamur*.

the beginning of each book.[40] Symmetrical disposition of this kind about a centre is 'natural' in the sense that it seems to suggest itself spontaneously in architecture and the visual arts, but in large-scale works of literature it can be achieved only through careful planning and execution. Other literary examples show that the principle of 'centrality' was deliberately cultivated.[41] Together with this static pattern of arrangement the poem exhibits a dynamic movement: in Books I and II the foundations are laid for the questions that are explored in Books III–IV, V–VI. Moreover the reappearances of Epicurus, progressively presented as man (1.66), father (3.9) and god (5.8), imply an articulation in three pairs of books and, connected with this articulation, a crescendo in the development of the poem.[42] This combination of symmetry and movement is characteristic of much Latin poetry.[43]

4. THE POETRY

(a) The two traditions and the two styles

Ancient writers, critics and readers were, as has already been indicated, used to thinking of literature in terms of established 'kinds' or types (εἴδη, γένη, genera: hence 'genre'). The DRN belonged formally to the genre of didactic epos, a 'high' and 'literary' genre. Epicurus was notoriously hostile to poetry, holding that the truth should be communicated in plain words (Comm. 133–4n.); hence Lucretius' choice of the poetical medium for his message has occasioned much comment and speculation.[44] It entailed not only the rejection of an Epicurean position, but a positive commitment: acceptance of the standards appropriate to the chosen genre and the continuance – not interpreted as slavish dependence – of the tradition established by the poet's predecessors. These predecessors fall into three groups: (1) Hesiod; (2) the philosophical poets, notably Parmenides and Empedocles; (3) Hellenistic didactic poets, above all Aratus. Lucretius' most obvious debt might seem to be to Empedocles' Περὶ Φύσεως (On Nature), and Empedocles is in fact eulogized at 1.716–33. However, in literary terms the influence of Hesiod and the Hellenistic poets is scarcely less important. This is less a matter of specific indebtedness in this or that detail[45] than of the poet's self-consciousness vis-à-vis his art and of his expressed sense of personal involvement. Such self-consciousness is a

---

[40] 3.31–40 ~ 4.26–44.   [41] Moritz 1968; Williams 1968: 233–9.
[42] Cox 1969: 135; Wormell 1965: 43.   [43] See Camps 1969: 51–60.
[44] Waszink 1954; Boyancé 1963: 57–68; Classen 1968/1986; Amory 1969.
[45] Among the numerous translations of Aratus' Phaenomena was one by Cicero, which Lucretius had evidently read and occasionally borrowed from: Bailey 1947: 29–30.

peculiarly Hellenistic trait, which manifests itself in such well-known passages as the Prologue to Callimachus' *Aetia;* but it derives ultimately from Hesiod. Lucretius' awareness of and participation in this and other aspects of the literary tradition can be seen in such passages as 1.926–50, which have been discussed elsewhere.[46] For the present purpose it is enough to emphasize that the *DRN* is a poem in the fullest sense: a literary production belonging in a literary tradition and written in complete awareness of the laws and conventions shaping the tradition. It appears, to judge at all events from the silence of our sources, that Lucretius was, so far as his philosophy went, a lone wolf: that is to say, he seems to have had no contact with contemporary Epicureanism,[47] of which he may indeed have disapproved. This isolation has no counterpart in the literary sphere: Lucretius did not live or write in a cultural vacuum, and his poem, because it is supremely original, is not therefore to be regarded as an oddity, a kind of literary 'sport'.

Another extremely potent influence, however, must be reckoned with; and it is precisely the combination of this second, subliterary (as it may be called), tradition with the main literary tradition of didactic epos that explains the peculiar character of the *DRN*. By this brilliant combinatory stroke Lucretius not only produced a profoundly original poem; he also laid the foundations of a tradition of satirical writing that has flourished down to modern times. One of the most striking features of the *DRN* is the discrepancy in tone and emotional impact between the scientific, or expository, and the non-expository passages. As has already been remarked, Epicurean physics provided the premises for Lucretius' views about the relationship of man to his environment, the universe, and to other men; and this fundamental role dictates that the exposition of the system should occupy a large part of the poem.[48] But these premises were subordinate to the conclusions which could be drawn from them, and it is when Lucretius confronts his readers with these great conclusions that the poem reaches its highest poetical and emotional levels. Nowhere is this better exemplified than in Book III: the elaborate exposition of the *animus* and *anima* that takes up most of the book is shown by the *igitur* of v. 830 (see §5(*a*) below) to have been preliminary to the real message, that death is not to be feared and that there is no life, and no punishment, after death. Thus it is not entirely appropriate to style passages of the non-expository type 'digressions' or 'excursuses'.[49] Neither type of passage is meaningful without the other; they are complementary to each other in the grand

---

[46] Kenney 1970b: 369–71/2007: 304–6.
[47] Boyancé 1963: 12; Crawley 1963: 11–12.
[48] It is clear, however, that the physics had fired his imagination and that he saw in this part of the doctrine much more than inevitable but somewhat tedious preliminaries: cf. Festugière 1968: 52–3; Amory 1969: 167–8.
[49] Sellar 1889: 322; Cox 1969: 134, also styling them 'calculated *intrusions*'.

strategy of the poem, and in both the poet is in full control of his aims and of the means which he has chosen to achieve those aims.

The fundamental characteristic that distinguishes the non-expository passages is their emotional effect, what ancient rhetoricians and critics called πάθος or τὸ παθητικόν. In contrast the expository passages, though occasionally enlivened by flashes of sarcastic wit at the expense of a rival viewpoint or by an odd stroke of satire, are for the most part rationally and logically argumentative; they are not devoid of emotion, but emotion is not the main driving force. These stylistic differences reflect a difference of ends: for rational persuasion a low-keyed style is suitable, for emotional conviction a highly charged style. The distinction was a basic one in ancient rhetorical theory, as expressed in the doctrine of the three styles of speaking, *genera dicendi*: a low, a middle, and a high, corresponding with the three chief aims of the orator, to instruct, to please, and to play on the emotions of his audience – *docere, delectare, mouere*.[50] In practice the so-called 'middle' or 'florid' style is of little importance: between two extremes it is pedantry to select any one intermediate position as more significant than the others, and it was the two extremes that provided the real points of reference.[51] These were the *genus tenue*, the 'slender' style suited to explanation and information; and the *genus grande* (*amplum, acre*), the grand style by which the hearer is swept off his feet and *compelled* to feel with the orator (or poet) by the sheer force and weight of the utterance. It was also standard doctrine that the accomplished speaker must be prepared to move from one stylistic level to another as his material required: *is est... eloquens, qui et humilia subtiliter et alta grauiter et mediocria temperate potest dicere* (Cic. *Or.* 100). Such a differentiation is exemplified even in the Elder Pliny's *Natural History*, where the moralizing excursuses (as Pliny's truly are) are consistently written in a much more elaborate and 'literary' Latin than the body of the work.[52] It is exemplified much more subtly, as might be expected, in the *Georgics*: the bulk of the poem, as with the *DRN*, is taken up by what purports to be technical instruction, but the full range of Virgil's poetical resources is reserved for the 'excursuses' in which, in fact, the real message of the poem, which is only formally about agriculture, is enshrined. In Virgil the distinction between the two types of passage is still perceptible, but much less sharply defined than in either Pliny or Lucretius.[53]

---

[50] See Douglas 1966: xxxiv–xxxv; Russell 1964: xxiv–xxvii; Kenney 2007: 92–3.

[51] This stands as originally written, but see now Kenney 2007: 93 n. 4, drawing attention to the emphasis placed by Lucretius at 1.935–50 (= 4.10–25) on the 'sweetness' of his poetry.

[52] A good example is *NH* 14.1, where the subject of trees leads into a representative specimen of the *locus communis de diuitiis*. On the combination of 'demonstration' and 'exhortation' in prose treatises see Michel 1962: 19.

[53] Wilkinson 1969: 183.

Among the means employed by Lucretius to convey his message satire
figures prominently, and the point has not gone unremarked.[54] What however has not been adequately assessed is the part that his poem played in
the foundation of the Roman satirical tradition, particularly by the incor-
poration in it of so many of the characteristics of the diatribe. In an often-
quoted passage (1.935–50 = 4.10–25) Lucretius compares the poetry in
which his message is conveyed to the honey which is smeared on a cup of
bitter medicine to induce a child to drink it. This type of homely comparison, which goes back at least to Plato's *Laws* (659e), is also used by Horace
(*Sat.* 1.1.25–6). Though Lucretius wrote for cultivated readers, who must
be prepared to take a good deal of trouble if they are to follow him, yet his
approach, on its higher level, is the same as that of more popular philosophers, in that it too relies heavily on a certain sweetening of the pill – in
his case the clothing of his message in poetry (for the 'honey' cannot be
taken to refer to the non-expository or 'pathetic' passages alone). There
is a closer relationship still with the popular tradition, however, which is
seen in Lucretius' use of stylistic devices and techniques drawn from that
tradition – in particular from the diatribe.

Diatribe, διατριβή, is defined by a writer on rhetoric as 'the expansion of
a brief moral thought',[55] but in practice it approached the status of a subliterary genre, one of a number of such genres of a generally homiletic type.
Its most famous exponent was one Bion of Borysthenes or Olbia (a Mile-
sian colony on the Black Sea), who lived from about 325 to 255 BC. Most
of what is known about him is to be found in Book IV of Diogenes Laertius'
Lives of the philosophers and in the few surviving fragments of his diatribes
which are embedded in the work of a later writer in the same field, Teles.[56]
Bion's status as what might be called the poor man's Socrates is well illustrated by the remark attributed to Eratosthenes that he was the first to dress
philosophy in brightly coloured clothes:[57] that is to say, he used all the

[54] Murley 1939; Waltz 1949; Dudley 1965b.
[55] Hermogenes, *Meth.* 5, p. 418 R. βραχέος διανοήματος ἠθικοῦ ἔκτασις. See, however, Jocelyn 1982, arguing that the term does not connote 'any particular manner
of philosophical discourse' (6); and for references to further discussions and a carefully balanced summary of conclusions Moles 1996: 464. *Pace* Jocelyn, there is after
all a good deal to be said for Kindstrand's view that 'so long as it is clearly realized
that the concept διατριβή, meaning popular philosophical discourse, is a modern
construction, I do not think that this use would do any harm, especially as the concept διατριβή seems to fill a need' (cit. Jocelyn ibid.). It is simply too useful a term to
discard. For a detailed discussion of the diatribe characteristics of 3.830–1094 see
Wallach 1976.
[56] See Hense 1909; a good many isolated *dicta* attributed to Bion are found in
Stobaeus. For further specimens of the genre see the texts edited by Martin 1959.
[57] D.L. 4.52 πρῶτος Βίων τὴν φιλοσοφίαν ἀνθινὰ ἐνέδυσεν. On Socrates cf. Cic. *Tusc.*
5.10 *primus philosophiam deuocauit e caelo et in urbibus collocauit et in domus etiam intro-
duxit et coegit de uita et moribus rebusque bonis et malis quaerere.*

resources of contemporary rhetoric to make philosophy palatable to the
common man.[58] He was not a philosopher as Plato or Zeno or Epicurus
were philosophers; in so far as he belonged to any school he was a Cynic,
but there was no exclusiveness in his doctrines. He was a travelling lecturer,
a communicator rather than an originator, the C. E. M. Joad of his day; his
philosophy aimed at helping the man in the street and 'treats of ordinary
human problems in a common-sense spirit'.[59] This entailed the constant
use of rhetorical and stylistic devices that were all designed to command
and retain, if necessary by shock tactics, the attention of audiences that
were all too vulnerable to any species of distraction. The style of the performance was semi-dramatic;[60] the interlocutor of the Platonic dialogues
survived in an attenuated form as an anonymous butt, whose objections,
invariably futile, were prefaced merely by a φησί, 'he says', and afforded
opportunities for the speaker to display his wit and sharpen his point. The
argument was illustrated by striking images drawn from the experience of
the audience; the tone was hectoring, relying more on pithy exhortation
than on urbane persuasion; the expression was vivid, pungent, sometimes
obscene. Formal logic and systematic arrangement were little regarded;
the intention of these sermons was to inculcate a few simple lessons of
conduct in memorable terms, and the speaker concentrated on enlisting
the sympathies of his audience, so that it should appear as clear to them as
it did to him that those who did not agree with the point of view expressed
were fools – *stultitiam arguit uulgi*, as the Horatian scholiast put it.[61]

Though Bion's own sympathies were fundamentally Cynic, the diatribe
was, as a vehicle for philosophy, non-sectarian: it was above all suited to
attack, to the deflation of folly and the destruction of error. Horace, who
refers (*Ep.* 2.2.60) to the 'biting wit of Bion's talks', *Bioneis sermonibus
et sale nigro*, was clearly influenced by the diatribe, as Lucilius had been
before him and as Seneca (a doctrinaire Stoic) was after him. The Christian sermon too was indebted to this popular homiletic tradition.[62] What
was original to Lucretius was the marriage of these techniques with the
high style that was mandatory for didactic epos so as to produce, in his
'pathetic' passages, a unique and individual fusion. The power of the satire

[58] For a sketch of Bion's life and work see Dudley 1938: 62–6.
[59] Dudley 1938: 65–6.
[60] The lecture as dramatic performance, a thing not indeed unknown in our own
day, was highly relished throughout antiquity. Seneca (*Ep.* 108.6) complains that
people came to philosophy lectures to be entertained rather than instructed, and
the substance of his complaint can be extensively documented from other sources.
[61] Ps.-Acro *ad* Hor. *Ep.* 2.2.60. On the diatribe see Oltramare 1926 (inadequate
on Lucretius); on its presence in Book III see Vallette 1940; Wallach 1976.
[62] Cf. Norden 1958: 556, drawing attention to diatribe-characteristics in the
Epistles of St Paul (1 Cor. 15:35–6, Rom. 9:19–20).

which resulted from this union was clearly appreciated by Horace (Comm.
1068–9n.), but it may be suggested that the most important outcome of
this Lucretian amalgamation of genres was the foundation of a new school
of satirical writing in the 'high' or 'tragic' vein. Horace, with his relatively
gentle and urbane approach to satire, contented himself with limited borrowing of specific motifs; it was left for Juvenal to exploit to the full the possibilities of this new type of satirical poetry. To return to Lucretius himself,
the point to be grasped is that he did not write satirically merely because his
mind had a satirical bent which would not be denied and had to be given
its head, even in a didactic poem; the satirical approach was suggested –
indeed dictated – by the work in hand, the attack on folly, error and superstition. *indignatio* – not 'indignation' but a refusal to acquiesce in popular
illusion – is not peculiar to Juvenal (1.79); it was precisely Lucretius' *indignatio* of what he had read and of what he saw and heard around him that
motivated the writing of the *DRN* in the first place.[63] If such very different
writers as Horace, Seneca and Juvenal all share certain satirical traits with
Lucretius, the explanation is not to be sought merely in temperamental
similarities, but is a matter of *generic* relationship: that is to say, all these
writers had more or less the same end in view, all were to a greater or
lesser extent indebted to the same tradition, and all adopted similar techniques belonging to that tradition to achieve their ends. It is only against
this historical background that the originality of Lucretius can be clearly
discerned.[64]

(b) *Language and metre*

Cicero's comment (p. 6 above) means: 'What you say in your letter is
quite right: Lucretius' poetry displays great originality, but also very careful
workmanship.'[65] *tamen* emphasizes what Cicero recognized as a paradox,
that Lucretius' work exemplified *both* original genius *and* literary crafts-
manship. Conventional assessments tended to emphasize either the *ars* or
the *ingenium* of a poet, yet here was one who displayed both; and Statius'
reference to *docti furor arduus Lucreti* (*Silv.* 2.7.76) appears to echo the
same judgement.[66] Any attempt to describe and evaluate Lucretius' poetry

---

[63] A loose fashion of writing ascribes to Juvenal and indeed to Lucretius (e.g.
Sikes 1936: 30; Dudley 1965a: 126; Leonard in Leonard and Smith 1965: 28) the
saeua indignatio that rightly belongs to Jonathan Swift.
[64] On the diatribe element in Lucretius see further, besides Oltramare 1926,
Vallette 1940, with particular reference to 3.870–1094.
[65] *luminibus ingeni* 'sparkling with natural genius' (Shackleton Bailey 1980:
190): the *lumina* are the 'high lights', the brilliantly original passages in the poem
(Sikes 1936: 38–9).
[66] Cf. Kenney 1970b: 366–7/2007: 300–1.

should begin by considering ends and means. Lucretius frequently insists
on the idea of clarity (cf. Comm. 1–4n. *tenebris*): at 1.933–4 he contrasts
the difficulty of his subject matter with the lucidity of his verse: ... *obscura
de re tam lucida pango | carmina, musaeo contingens cuncta lepore.* This claim is
on the whole justified: when all allowances have been made for numerous
and often thorny problems of interpretation, the preponderant impression of Lucretius' style is of its simplicity and clarity. These characteristics
were deliberately planned and achieved; they are the result of considered
stylistic decisions which were then executed with extreme care.[67] The style
which resulted is often labelled 'archaic'; and it is true that by comparison with Lucretius the didactic verse of his contemporary Cicero seems,
technically speaking, slick and 'modern' – modern, moreover, in the sense
that the Augustan poets appear to have followed the technical lead that
Cicero offered.[68] But a comparison which takes only means into account
and neglects ends is invalid. Cicero has in fact recorded, by implication, his
view of how didactic poetry should be written in the *De Oratore*: *etenim si constat inter doctos hominem ignarum astrologiae ornatissimis atque optimis uersibus
Aratum de caelo stellisque dixisse; si de rebus rusticis hominem ab agro remotis-
simum Nicandrum Colophonium poetica quadam facultate non rustica scripsisse
praeclare: quid est cur non orator de rebus eis eloquentissime dicat, quas ad certam
causam tempusque cognorit?* (1.69). Crassus, of whose speech this forms part,
goes on to say in so many words that poet and orator have the same ends in
view and, *mutatis mutandis*, employ the same means: *est enim finitimus oratori
poeta.* That the poet, like the orator, seeks to convince Lucretius must have
accepted; but the other implications of Cicero's argument he would have
rejected with contempt. The notion that a poet can and should be prepared to transmute any material whatsoever into polite literature belongs
to a different and less noble conception of life and poetry than Lucretius'.
It would have been technically feasible for him to sacrifice clarity to elegance of a Hellenistic sort, much as Cicero did himself in his didactic
poetry. Such a sacrifice would have entailed some loss of force, but that was
not the main reason for not making it. Lucretius would not and could not
compromise: his mission was too important. What was at stake was nothing
more nor less than personal salvation, and nothing could be suffered to
impair the clarity of the message; there must be no room for misunderstanding. If, after reading the *DRN*, a man declined to be saved, it should
not be said that it was because the call to salvation had been obscure. Thus,
when Bailey writes (1947: 117) that 'his rhythm is to a great extent dictated
by his vocabulary', this perfectly true remark is not to be interpreted as an

[67] Cf. 3.419 *conquisita diu dulcique reperta labore* and see Comm. ad loc.
[68] See Duckworth 1969: 43; his analysis is based on the distribution of dactyls
and spondees in the verse.

adverse criticism. This 'dictation' was something willed by the poet in the
interests of clarity – of that σαφήνεια which we are told Epicurus so much
prized (D.L. 10.13).[69] He was in fact by no means a helpless victim of that
patrii sermonis egestas of which he complains (1.892; 3.260: see n.): for it is
often overlooked that these complaints are made in the context of specific
technical problems and are not symptomatic of a general inability to cope
with the linguistic difficulties of his undertaking.

We must, then, be on our guard against what has been well described
as the 'heresy... of characterizing and estimating an author too much in
terms of his predecessors and, worse still, his successors, and too little
in terms of his own objectives and his chosen methods'.[70] If Lucretius'
style, compared with that of Cicero, seems 'archaic', that is no more than
a summary and somewhat misleading way of saying that he adhered to
certain usages and forms which were already being discarded in his own
day because by doing so he was able to communicate what he had to say
more directly and forcibly.[71] A well-known example is the practice of eliding final -*s* after a short vowel and before a consonant (cf. Comm. 51–4n.
manibu' diuis): this usage, described by Cicero (*Or.* 161) as 'countrified',
subrusticum, occurs in Cicero's own earlier poetry but is discarded in his
later work.[72] Similarly, to avoid circumlocution and paraphrase, Lucretius
allowed himself an amount of morphological variation which to Augustan
taste would have seemed excessive: thus in four verses (4.491–4) he uses
three different forms of the adverb *sorsum*, 'separately', obviously for metrical convenience.[73] The same considerations dictated his use of (for example) the archaic termination -*ai* for -*ae* (Comm. 83–4n. *amicitiai*). Again,
in the matter of repetition, Lucretius' practice was dictated partly by his

---

[69] This is a different matter from being 'forced' (Smith in Leonard and Smith
1965: 159) to use this or that form.

[70] Maguinness 1965: 71.

[71] '[H]istorically speaking there is no such thing as archaic literature; only
archaistic literature, that is, writings which are self-consciously old-fashioned at the
time of composition' (Bramble 1969: 3–4). See also Bramble's excellent remarks
on the pernicious influence of metaphors of growth, maturity and senility; of ascent
to and descent from a pinnacle; of cycles and ages of bronze, gold and silver. In the
Commentary 'archaic' is employed as a chronological term; it does not connote a
stylistic judgement.

[72] This point does not emerge clearly from Bailey's discussion; see Ewbank 1933:
70–1.

[73] *sorsum* (– –), admissible in several places in the verse; *seorsum* (◡ – –), fitting
best at the end; *sorsus* (– ◡), fitting in several places, most conveniently in the penul-
timate. Cf. Smith in Leonard and Smith 1965: 140–57, 159–66. Even among the
Augustans there is variance in such things from poet to poet: Virgil, for instance,
is more restrained than Ovid, who permits himself the variant forms *eburnus* and
eburneus in consecutive verses (*Met.* 10.275–6). Cf. Comm. 798–9n. and Index s.v.
variation. [This has been allowed to stand as originally written, but on *seorsum* see
now Comm. 282–7n.]

desire for clarity, but also by the need for emphasis.[74] We must accordingly beware of setting up an arbitrary norm and labelling deviations from it as either 'archaic' or 'decadent': each poet must to some extent be allowed to be a law unto himself. That Lucretius was technically capable when he wished of writing verse that is 'correct' by Ciceronian or Augustan standards is shown by the observation that in, for example, his famous description of the Sacrifice of Iphigenia (1.80–101), one of the most impassioned pieces of writing in the entire poem, there is not a single 'irregular' verse-ending. Bailey's remark, quoted above, applies predominantly to the expository parts of the poem, where the combination of technical subject matter and the need for clarity exercised a limiting influence. In the non-expository passages Lucretius could and did allow his genius a freer rein. It is in the light of these considerations that the indispensable catalogues of Lucretian usage compiled by modern investigators must be studied and evaluated.[75] The freedom with which Lucretius handled the Latin language and the great flexibility of choice which he allowed himself went too far for Augustan tastes, which emphasized above all balance, restraint and moderation.[76] Yet without Lucretius Augustan poetry could not have been what it was. From the immense range of possibilities that he opened up his successors chose at will; above all Ovid, who of all Roman poets alone approached and at times surpassed Lucretius in his experimental attitude to language.[77]

The fundamental stylistic problem in Latin hexameter poetry concerns the relationship between the metrical unit, the hexameter verse, and the units of discourse – phrase, clause, sentence and period. No Latin poet holds the balance with more perfect mastery than Virgil, and the history of the Latin hexameter during the first century BC may profitably be studied in terms of the evolution of a verse 'period' analogous to the period of artistic prose. However, such a study should not be conducted on deterministic premisses. Lucretius' treatment of the problem is not necessarily inferior because it is different from Virgil's. For him, in general, the individual verse and its main subdivisions coincide with and indeed constitute the units and the sub-units of discourse. This generalization is more consistently true of the expository than of the 'pathetic' parts of the *DRN*; in the latter enjambment, the carrying over of sense and construction from

---

[74] Cf. Maguinness 1965: 73–5. The practice of poets of all periods differs very widely: see Kenney 1959: 248 n. 1; and add Gildersleeve 1930: 161–2; Diggle 1970: 91–2.

[75] Bailey 1947: 72–171; Smith in Leonard and Smith 1965: 129–86; and the works listed by Boyancé 1963: 345–6.

[76] Well documented by Cupaiuolo 1966, and by Williams 1968.

[77] A single instance will make the point, that of Ovid's use of noun-formations in -*men* and -*tus*: cf. Bailey 1947: 134–5.

one verse to the next is considerably more frequent.[78] Moreover, within
the verse (more particularly in the expository passages) Lucretius is in
general much less preoccupied than Virgil or even Cicero with that bal-
ancing of complementary elements, such as the halves of adjective–noun
phrases, that distinguishes the developed Augustan hexameter.[79] This sort
of arrangement of the elements of the utterance has more than formal
value: it produces a feeling of suspense, a creation of expectancy in which
the reader is induced to look forward to the syntactical and semantic
dénouement of phrase, clause or sentence. The result is what we may call
'tension' in the writing. The principle is one that holds good in developed Latin prose writing, particularly that of Cicero.[80] It is a technique
that is essentially emotional – hence the Ciceronian employment of it in
oratory – but it does not necessarily assist, and may actually obscure, intellectual comprehension. To the orderly progress of the difficult argument
that Lucretius was faced with conducting, this sort of device, employed as
we meet it in Cicero or Virgil or Ovid, would have constituted an impedi-
ment. In the interests of his all-dominant desire for clarity he rejected this
style of writing: in the expository passages the movement of the utterance
is essentially 'linear', as we may call it,[81] accommodating itself closely to
the ends of the verses and to their main caesural divisions. This technique,
taken together with the repetitions which Lucretius employs to drive home
his points, as Sinker remarks (1937: x), 'intensifies the cumulative effect
of the arguments that he advances'. Criticism of style must spring from
an understanding of ends. The 'unperiodic' style of Lucretius is not to be
appraised as 'archaic' or undeveloped in comparison with Virgil's: the two
poets were attempting very different things.

   In its simplest form the Lucretian style of writing follows the structure
of the verse extremely closely: thus 6.356 *dissoluunt nodos omnis* ‖ *et uincla relaxant*, or 4.556 *seruat enim formaturam* ‖ *seruatque figuram*. But even
in cases such as these the apparent simplicity may be deceptive. In the
first instance there is chiasmus; and since *omnis*, though in grammatical

---

[78] See Bailey 1947: 120–3, summarizing the important work of Büchner 1936;
but see also the weighty criticisms of Schmid 1944.

[79] Conveniently illustrated by Pearce 1966: 162–6: thus verses of the type
'*sensifer* unde oritur primum per uiscera *motus*' (3. 272), with its variations, are
much fewer in Lucretius (about one in 225) than in Cicero's *Phaenomena* (about 1
in 34) or in Catull. 64 (about 1 in 15). Cf. also Maguinness 1965: 77–8.

[80] An excellent example is the first sentence of the *De Oratore*, where the role of
the 'enclosing' technique in engendering expectation is very clearly demonstrated.

[81] The distinction is made in Postgate 1907–8, a stimulating paper. His dictum
that 'the modern sentence, to put it roughly, is an arrangement in line, the ancient
one within a circle' (167) must be understood as referring principally to certain
kinds of poetry and artistic prose. It is not true, as the above discussion indicates,
of Lucretius.

agreement with *nodos*, also modifies *uincla* in sense (ἀπὸ κοινοῦ construction), there is in fact a stricter symmetry than at first appears:

dissoluunt nodos ‖ omnis ‖ et uincla relaxant.

This is not unsophisticated writing. In the second case the anaphora *seruat...seruatque* is effective, and the effect, as often in Lucretius, is reinforced by alliteration and assonance. The technique of 'theme and variation', particularly associated with Virgil,[82] was familiar to Lucretius: so at 5.980-1 ... *nec diffidere ne terras aeterna teneret | nox in perpetuum detracto lumine solis.* Here it will be seen that enjambment is discreetly used to diversify, as also at (for example) 3.136–9:

> nunc animum atque animam ‖ dico coniuncta teneri
> inter se ‖ atque unam naturam conficere ex se,
> sed caput esse quasi ‖ et dominari in corpore toto
> consilium ‖ quod nos ‖ animum mentemque uocamus.

The tendency to adjust the utterance to fill the verse is most clearly seen in duplicated phrases of the type *seiungi seque gregari* (1.452) or *disiectis disque sipatis* (1.651); but even in these phrases there is a significant amplification of the sense.[83]

The point that it is sought to make may emerge more clearly from a comparative analysis of two passages from Book III:

(i) *Expository style: 323–49*
In this 'paragraph' Lucretius demonstrates the indissoluble connexion of body and soul, and the stylistic texture must be seen as reflecting the movement of the argument. **323–4** Statement of thesis: theme (323) + variation, in the form of a statement of its converse (324: *est custos = tenet ~ 323 tenetur*). The syntax of 323 is 'linear' in the sense that it follows a simple order of subject – verb – adverbial phrase; and the structure of the variation is also simple (pair of nouns + dependent genitives), but the order is artful: emphatic *ipsa* beginning the verse and the twin phrases arranged chiastically, with the effect reinforced by alliteration. **325–6** First corroboration of thesis: positive theme (325) + negative variation (326). **327–30** Illustration: divided equally into

---

[82] See Henry 1873: 206–7, 745–51; it should be noted that Henry neither states nor implies that the technique was invented by Virgil (it is characteristic of the Psalms), indeed he emphasizes that it is 'almost inseparable from poetry' and is equally at home in prose (745–6, 750).
[83] Cf. Bailey 1947: 145–6, many of whose examples have been borrowed for the present discussion.

'protasis' (327–8) and 'apodosis' (329–30), each constructed in parallel fashion with substantized infinitive as subject + *quin*-clause. Monotony is avoided by a slight variation: whereas the subject phrase and predicate of the 'protasis' each occupy a whole verse, in the 'apodosis' *extrahere* is enjambed. **331–2** Resumption of the argument so far: statement of theme in atomic terms (*implexis...fiunt*) + metaphorical variation (see Comm.). **333–6** The impossibility of separate sensation by mind and body: theme (333–4) negatively expressed (*nec...sine...sorsum*) + variation positively expressed (*communibus...conflatur utrimque*). In the variation there is 'enclosing' word-order (*communibus...motibus*,[84] *accensus...sensus*[85]), perhaps designed to reinforce the idea of the atomic interconnexions (cf. Comm.). **337–8** The impossibility of the body's coming into being or existing after death by itself: simple tripartite enumeration, varied only by the metrical cliché *durare uidetur.* **339–43** Illustration, parallel to that of 327–30, but *ex conuerso*: the behaviour of water as an antitype of the behaviour of body and soul. The development is simply articulated (*non...ut...sed...non...sic...sed*; with the *sed* that prefaces each 'apodosis' beginning its verse), but there is enjambment between 339 and 340[86] and between 341 and 342; the period ends with a variation of the type already discussed, *pereunt conuulsi conque putrescunt*, reinforced by alliteration. **344–7** A virtual restatement of what has previously been said, but with emphasis on *ex ineunte aeuo*, so that *sic* is displaced from its obvious articulatory position at the beginning of the verse. The construction of 344–6 is perhaps slightly awkward, and the 'golden' line 345 is not typically Lucretian writing (see Comm.), but the development is still 'linear': 346 stands for a separate clause, i.e. the participial phrase = *'even when hidden'* (so that the verse expands and varies *ex ineunte aeuo*); and the conclusion has a verse to itself, strongly and simply articulated, *discidium ut nequeat ‖ fieri ‖ sine peste maloque.* **348–9** Summary: the last two verses of the 'paragraph', by a technique illustrated throughout the Commentary ('ring-composition'), repeat its doctrine and refer back to its beginning (*causa salutis...naturam ~ natura...causa salutis*). The syntax is simple, with the logical relationship between the *quoniam*-clause and its apodosis clearly marked by the repetition *coniunctast...coniunctam.*

(ii) *'Pathetic' style: 1025–52*
This passage is a harangue in terms indebted to the diatribe (Comm. 1024–52n.).[87] The argument is simple: 1025–44 convey the

---

[84] Cf. Pearce 1966: 163; he does not notice this instance.
[85] Pearce 1966: 307–10.
[86] Partial enjambment, in fact: the syntax of the half-clause *ut...uaporem* is complete, to the reader's ear, by the end of the verse.
[87] A good discussion by Conte 1965.

demonstrative premiss, that even great men have died; and 1045-52 the conclusion, that the person addressed has no call to chafe at the inevitability of death, especially as he has little to live for in any case. The logic is emotional rather than rational, and the style is correspondingly 'tense': specific points to note are the longer sentences, the greater frequency of enjambment, and the use of 'enclosing' word-order and syntactical anticipation. **1025-6** Exploitation of the separative possibilities of Latin word-order: *lumina... reliquit, multis... rebus* (with *tu... improbe* scornfully sandwiched between and the necessary but unexpressive *fuit* further sandwiched between *tu* and *improbe*). **1027-8** Enjambment and 'framing' of the verse by the sonorous perfect forms. **1029-33** A particularly impressive sentence: the subject *ille quoque ipse* is announced immediately, but is not completed by its predicate until 1033; the intervening 3+ verses enlarge the stature of the man – who is then shown to be as mortal as other men. The sentence-structure is designed to carry the reader on: *strauit iterque dedit... ac... docuit... et contempsit*; in detail note (1029-30) 'tension' (*uiam... strauit*) + enjambment, (1031) *pedibus* looking forward to *super ire, salsas* to *lacunas,*[88] (1032) *contempsit* to *murmura ponti,* (1033) *animam* to *fudit*. Nowhere can the reader pause at the main caesura with a complete syntactical sub-unit safely, so to say, negotiated; always he is drawn on. **1034-5** Momentarily 'linear' writing: subject in one verse, predicate in the next; but the structure of 1034 exemplifies a well-known rhetorical device, the 'tricolon crescendo': *Scipiadas* || *belli fulmen* || *Carthaginis horror*. **1036-8** Anaphora (*adde... adde*); enjambment + 'tension' (*eadem... quietest*). **1039-41** Enjambment + 'tension'; (1041) alliteration + assonance + enclosure (*sponte sua... ipse*). **1042-4** Enjambment + striking imagery (see Comm.). **1045-52** The harangue ends with a longer and fast-moving sentence: syntactically 1046-52 depend on 1045. Predominantly the effects are secured by enjambment, sometimes very strong (1050-1) and 'tension' (fully enclosing word-order at 1049 *sollicitam... mentem*); but monotony is carefully avoided, and the movement of 1047-9 is varied with some subtlety:

> qui *somno* PARTEM MAIOREM *conteris* AEVI (tension)
> et uigilans stertis || nec somnia cernere cessas ('linear'
>   articulation)
> *sollicitamque* geris CASSA FORMIDINE *mentem* (tension).

Within these larger developments attention is also paid to the smaller-scale effects, as in 1052, a very skilfully disposed verse:

> *incerto* FLVITANS *errore* VAGARIS.

---

[88] The effect here accentuated by the rhyme.

If the foregoing analyses are to be useful, their scope must be made clear. They have been chosen to represent two extreme cases: an expository passage in a low key is contrasted with a rhetorical harangue highly charged with feeling. Between these extremes there is a wide range of intermediate possibilities; and the analyses have shown that even in these two passages there is no rigid differentiation of style: enjambment occurs in the expository passage, 'linear' writing in the 'pathetic'. Thus there can be no question of a hard-and-fast distinction on stylistic grounds between different types of passage, no application of, so to say, a litmus-paper test, no 'either–or'. Analysis must always be based on the context and the end in view.

In conclusion something should be said about Lucretius' imagery. Commentators and interpreters have frequently remarked on his extraordinarily vivid powers of description and on his faculty (shared among modern writers only by Kipling) for transferring a sense of colour and movement to the written page. It is this faculty which gives Lucretius' images their peculiar quality. A full discussion is not necessary here: the subject has been well treated by West (1969/1994) and is dealt with at the appropriate places in the Commentary. What should be noted in the context of the matters discussed above is that in Lucretius both description and imagery, like all his other stylistic characteristics, are *functional*: they assist to carry conviction by illuminating the argument, and they are employed throughout the poem, in expository and 'pathetic' passages alike, for this purpose.[89] The illustrative role of simile and metaphor is of course their real *raison d'être*, and among Lucretius' predecessors Empedocles in particular was noted for his metaphors;[90] what is unique to Lucretius is the astonishing clarity and particularity of his vision and of its translation into words. In this respect the prophet of σαφήνεια was its actual embodiment.

5. BOOK III

(a) Subject, structure and argument

Books III and IV, as was said above (§3), are central in the structure, and hence in the argument, of the entire poem. There are two reasons why Book III seems to deserve special study. In the first place the problem that it poses is still as urgent and inescapable for humanity as it ever was, and perhaps never more so: for the second half of the twentieth century is a time

---

[89] This is what Dr C. J. Carter (in a letter to the editor) has strikingly called 'the pervasive community of metaphor'. See Sykes Davies 1931–2: 29–38/1986: 277–87.

[90] Cf. Longrigg 1970: Aristotle said of Empedocles that he was versed in the use of metaphor and all other poetical devices (D.L. 8.57).

when advances in the techniques of both the termination and the prolongation of life seem to have outstripped man's capacity to reckon with their ethical implications.[91] Some, admittedly, of the premisses of Lucretius' argument may seem to have lost whatever relevance they ever had: the gods in whose power he so passionately disbelieved are even more unreal to us than they must have been to the majority of his educated contemporaries. (Their place, however, has been taken by other gods and idols, not all obviously preferable.) In spite of such reservations the central problem persists: every human being must die, and nearly every human being fears to die. One of the means by which many people still try to come to terms with this fear is the concept of an afterlife, whether viewed with hope or with apprehension or with terror. The problem must be faced;[92] and Lucretius' solution to it deserves respect. It may in fact be judged to be no solution; but it is at least a beautiful, eloquent and courageous attempt. Secondly, of all the books of the *DRN*, Book III appears to be the most highly finished, neatly constructed, and the best able to stand on its own.[93] In its main structural outlines it follows a simple plan:

1–93	Introduction
94–829	Argument:
	94–416 the soul is material –
	417–829 and hence mortal
830–1094	Conclusion: death is not to be feared.[94]

This scheme is both intellectually and emotionally satisfying. The short Introduction is marked by the panegyric of Epicurus as signalling a fresh start in the development of the poem. In it Lucretius states concisely and powerfully the theme of the book. There then follows the Argument, a long and careful exposition of the scientific proofs of (i) the corporeal nature and action of the soul, (ii) its mortality and coduration with the body: this forms the great and ineluctable premiss on which the

[91] See Toynbee *et al.* 1968: *passim.*

[92] 'Si on considère le sujet, il n'en est pas capable d'émouvoir la pensée, plus digne d'être médité et plus entouré de mystères tristement séducteurs' (Martha 1867: 171).

[93] As an intellectual and imaginative achievement Book v must be awarded the palm.

[94] It was argued by Rand 1934 that Lucretius followed traditional rhetorical doctrine in the structure of Book III: thus 1–93 = *Prooemium,* 94–416 *Narratio,* 417–829 *Argumentatio,* 830–1094 *Peroratio.* The distinction between *Narratio* and *Argumentatio* is perhaps somewhat artificial. Owen 1968–9: 123–6 accepts Rand's argument and detects the same basic structure in every book of the poem. See however Farrell 2007: 80–2, identifying a 'triptych pattern' in each book, *Proem, Second Proem, Peroration.*

Conclusion of the book is founded.[95] The logical relationship between
these two great divisions of the book, Argument and Conclusion, is marked
by the simple but immensely pregnant *igitur* at line 830: in this one word
the whole preceding section is summed up. Their relationship is further
emphasized by a fundamental stylistic difference between them: the Argument is conducted in what we have called the 'expository' style, the Conclusion in the 'pathetic'. Though the discussion of the *animus* and *anima*
is essential to the argument, it is theoretical: the premiss must be established beyond all possibility of cavil, or the whole edifice of reasoning will
collapse, but passion, though Lucretius could not resist the occasional flirt
of irony or sarcasm, does not play a predominant part. The Conclusion,
by contrast, is essentially an essay in practical philosophy, couched in arguments whose validity of course depends on the doctrines established in the
first part of the book, but which are aimed at men's common sense and
humanity as much as at their intellects. Hence two connected phenomena: a rise in both emotional and poetic 'temperature' as Lucretius sets
himself to enforce, in the service of reason and humanity, the great truth
that death is not a thing to fear; and the change to a style of argument
appropriate to popular philosophical teaching and particularly indebted,
as explained above (§4(a)), to the diatribe. There is something peculiarly satisfying about this balance between the long, reasoned, comparatively passionless exposition and the relatively short but intense conclusion: neither element is complete without the other, and it is the success-
ful integration of the two that makes the reading of Book III a memorable
experience.

(b) The 'consolatio'

As was said above, the purpose of the Conclusion of Book III is practical:
Lucretius demonstrates, in the light of the facts now established, that death
is not to be feared. It has also been shown (§4(a)) that in such 'pathetic'
passages as this Lucretius drew freely on the popular homiletic tradition,
particularly on the diatribe. In Book III yet another extra-Epicurean influence may be seen at work, that of the *consolatio*.[96] This was a stock literary-
philosophical genre, designed to fortify men against the contingencies
of existence – particularly death and exile – by marshalling the available
arguments which might serve to console and comfort. Epicurus himself

---

[95] 'Toute cette physique lentement accumulée n'est qu'un immense ouvrage
de guerre, une sorte de savante circumvallation, par laquelle le poëte investit la
foule confuse de nos terreurs, qu'il va maintenant dissiper par quelques poétiques
assauts' (Martha 1867: 135).
[96] See *OCD*[1] s.v. *consolatio* for the connexion with the diatribe; and N–H 279–81.

seems to have made little use of this type of argument (which he possibly disdained?), and it is probable that Lucretius has imparted an Epicurean colouring to some treatise *On Death*, Περὶ Θανάτου, such as that which served as the basis of Plutarch's *Consolatio ad Apollonium*.[97] Be that as it may, his debt to the genre is unmistakable. Such treatises, artificial as they may now seem, had a strictly practical aim and were taken perfectly seriously, as can be seen from the witness of Cicero and Seneca. The Tenth Satire of Juvenal is a *consolatio*, and was praised as such by Byron: 'I should think it might be read with great effect to a man dying without much pain, in preference to all the stuff that ever was sung or said in churches.' Byron's qualification 'without much pain' is shrewd as well as sardonic, for it implies a fundamental question: how effective can formal consolatory writing ever be for those who stand most in need of it? The genre is little practised, if at all, today, but some effort must be made to criticize Lucretius' (or any other) *consolatio* in terms of its practical efficacy, for this was writing designed to serve a specific purpose. It should of course be acknowledged that the argument of the Conclusion of Book III is directed at the emotions and is conducted in emotional terms; such is the very essence of the *consolatio*. Considered then as emotional argument, how effective is it? It is difficult to improve on the answer given to this question by Santayana, who must be quoted *in extenso*:

Nothing could be more futile … than to marshal arguments against that fear of death which is merely another name for the energy of life, or the tendency to self-preservation. Arguments involve premises, and these premises, in the given case, express some particular form of the love of life; whence it is impossible to conclude that death is in no degree evil and not at all to be feared. For what is most dreaded is not the agony of dying, nor yet the strange impossibility that when we do not exist we should suffer for not existing. What is dreaded is the defeat of a present will directed upon life and its various undertakings. Such a present will cannot be argued away, but it may be weakened by contradictions arising within it, by the irony of experience, or by ascetic discipline. To introduce ascetic discipline, to bring out the irony of experience, to expose the self-contradictions of the will, would be the true means of mitigating the love of life; and if the love of life were extinguished, the fear of death, like smoke rising from that fire, would have vanished also.[98]

---

[97] Cf. Heinze 1897: 25.
[98] Santayana 1935: 52–3. Cf. Seneca, *Ep.* 82.15 (*mors*) *uidetur multa nobis bona eripere et nos ex hac cui assueuimus rerum copia educere.*

The same point is made, more briefly, by Cornford:

> Epicurus, it is true, abolished the terrors of hell; but he also abolished
> the joys of heaven . . . I do not know how common the horror of death
> may be among normal people; but, where it exists, is it not often the
> prospect of extinction that horrifies them? If so, the fear of death,
> which Epicurus claimed to have banished, is actually increased by
> the denial of immortality. Is it Plato's fault that Western humanity
> has, on the whole, rejected the Epicurean consolation?[99]

The fault, if there is one, belongs to Epicurus. If Lucretius is seen at his
greatest as a poet in Book III, the faith that he professes is here seen at
its weakest. For there are more questions still to be asked. When man has
cast out the fear of death – if he can – what is he left with? This question
Lucretius makes no real attempt to answer, and his failure to do so cannot
be attributed entirely to the limitations of his own enterprise. His readers
were bound to ask: death disposed of, what follows? The great paean of tri-
umph which concludes Book III contrasts strangely with the answer which
Lucretius would have had to give if to do so had lain within the scope of his
design: the promise of a cautious and muted happiness that awaited those
who had finally overcome superstition and fear. But for Lucretius the all-
important undertaking was the battle against ignorance and error: what
life might be like for mankind if the battle were ever to be won he does
not tell us and perhaps could not imagine. To say as much is not to admit
that after all Lucretius was a pessimist; the weakness was in the Epicurean
faith, and it was because of that weakness that 'the Lucretian argument
could not prevail over instinctive human hopes and, therefore, Platonic
reason, that supplanted that hope, Stoic persuasion and Christian faith
won the victory over the European heart and mind'.[100]

6. THE TEXT

Our knowledge of the text of the *DRN* depends principally on two MSS
now in the library of the University of Leiden, Oblongus (O) and Quadratus (Q), so called from their shapes.[101] They were written in Northern
France or Germany in the ninth century, and their texts go back, via one
or more intermediaries, to a common ancestor written in capital script and

---

[99] Cornford 1950: 136–7.   [100] Hadzsits 1935: 99.
[101] A number of carbonized scraps of papyrus from the library of Philodemus
at Herculaneum have been tentatively identified as fragments of a MS of the *DRN*
(Kleve 1989; 1997). Those attributed to Book III are of no textual significance; and
the identification of the fragments as Lucretian is in any case highly controversial
(Capasso 2003; Beer 2009).

dating from the end of classical antiquity.[102] O is the older and better of
the two, incorporating important supplements and corrections by the contemporary Irish scholar Dungal.[103] Fragments of another ninth-century
copy,[104] the so-called 'Schedae' (GVU), are preserved at Copenhagen and
Vienna: V contains *inter alia* lines 1–621 of Book III. All other copies date
from the fifteenth and sixteenth centuries and have been shown to derive
ultimately from O.[105] They are useful to the editor solely as a source of
humanist conjectures, to be evaluated on their merits. That being so, in
this edition, in the interests of simplicity, all such anonymous conjectures,
apart from those in OQ, are cited under the siglum 'c'. For a comprehensive account of the early history of the transmission of the text see
Butterfield 2013.

   In a class by itself is Munro's incisive and entertaining history of the
transmission and editing of the *DRN* down to his own time,[106] which was
to serve as the model for Housman's equally characteristic but considerably more outspoken prefaces to his monumental edition of Manilius.[107]
Munro's account of Lachmann's contribution, however, requires radical
reconsideration in the light of Sebastiano Timpanaro's analysis of the
centuries-long process that led step by step to the formulation of what has
been misleadingly termed 'the Lachmann method'; and in particular of
his demonstration that the credit for the systematic application of stem-
matics to the establishment of Lucretius' text must be shared with Hugo
Purmann and, in particular, Jacob Bernays, whom Lachmann described in
his edition 'with lofty condescension'[108] as 'adulescentes optime instituti'
but 'neque satis in Lucretii ingenio cognoscendo versati'.[109] In his survey
Munro also discussed at some length (Munro 1886: 16–14) the contributions to the establishment of Lucretius' text by the soldier-poet Michael
Marullus (1453–1500). Doubts on the extent of his contributions were
first raised by Reeve (1980: 44–8), and debate continues. However, the
name of Marullus has been allowed to stand in the critical notes of this edition, since 'the attribution was made by a Florentine contemporary [Petrus

---

[102] Lachmann's pioneering reconstruction of this MS, 'exemplar ceterorum
ARCHETYPON (ita appellare soleo)' (Lachmann 1850: 3), was subsequently ampli-
fied and revised by Goold 1958.
[103] The so-called 'corrector Saxonicus', now identified by Professor Bernhard
Bischoff (Reynolds 1983: 219 and n. 9).
[104] Reynolds 1983: 220 n. 11.
[105] Butterfield 2011: 156 n. 7. For the complex ramifications of the Italian tradition see Reeve 1980; 2005.
[106] Munro 1886: 12–3.   [107] Kenney 2009b: 256.
[108] Timpanaro 2005: 103.
[109] Lachmann 1850: 4. Bernays's modest Teubner edition appeared in 1852,
almost simultaneously with Lachmann's, and has been predictably eclipsed by it.

Candidus, editor of the Juntine edition, Florence 1512] and no other has
yet been suggested with plausibility' (Professor Reeve, *per litt.*).

It has been established beyond reasonable doubt that Lucretius died
leaving his poem lacking its final revision. To take two particularly compelling examples, it is difficult to believe, given the obvious importance
attached by writers conditioned, as Lucretius clearly was, by exposure to
Greek models, to perfection of literary form, that the duplication, with
variation of one phrase, of his triumphal affirmation of the originality of
what awaited his readers (1.926–50 = 4.1–25) could have been intended
to stand in the finished text; and the unredeemed promise of a full account
of the dwelling-place of the gods and of its nature at 5.155 *quae tibi posterius
largo sermone probabo* cannot be easily explained away.[110] That being so it
is only to be expected that there will be some authorial inconsistencies,
superfluous repetitions and loose ends in the argument which Lucretius,
had he lived long enough, would have set himself to tidy up. That does not
entitle his editors to do it for him. Few if any Latin or Greek books have
come down to us in texts free of unauthorized alterations and additions by
(more often than not well-meaning) interpolators, and the *DRN* is unlikely
to be an exception. However, the deletion and expulsion of verses judged
by critics and editors to be spurious may be thought to have got somewhat
out of hand when it is proposed to expel 368 verses out of a total of 7,417,
amounting to very nearly 5 per cent of the poem.[111] This is an area in
which editors do well to proceed with caution, and in this edition only a
handful of verses have been proposed, with varying degrees of conviction,
for expulsion from the text.[112]

[110] *Pace* Smith 1992: 390 n. b ad loc.; see Kenney 1998: 25–6.
[111] So Deufert 1996; on Konrad Müller's more modest total of 3 per cent cf.
Smith 1978: 31.
[112] See 474–5, 743, 763 and nn. On rejected proposals see 428–33, 806–18,
1029–33nn.; a number of others are passed over in silence.

SUPPLEMENTARY INTRODUCTION

During the forty-odd years since the publication of the first edition of this book, informed interest in Lucretius has continued to grow: a process reflected both by the continuing increase in the number of translations (Kenney 1985: i, x) and the proliferation of the scholarly literature (Gale, 'Addenda' in Kenney 1977b/1995; list of works cited in Gillespie and Hardie 2007). The volume on Lucretius in the series *Oxford Readings in Classical Studies* (Gale 2007a) has made a number of influential articles conveniently available.

That, 'as weapons in outer space threaten to move from science fiction to fact, Lucretius...seems more tragically contemporary than ever' (Segal 1990: 227), and that he has much of importance to say to today's politicians and scientists is strikingly argued in the concluding chapter, 'Wizards in bondage' (135–55), of W. R. Johnson's reading of the *DRN* as 'a powerful representation of classical antiquity's best and most influential effort to speculate on the material universe and the place and conditions of human beings in it' (Johnson 2000: ix). This is a welcome reminder of the fact that the *DRN* 'is the one didactic poem, ancient or modern which is both great poetry and good science' (Kenney 1998–9: 418).

In the revision of this edition P. M. Brown's translation and commentary (Brown 1997) has proved especially helpful. Other translations deserving of note are those of Esolen (1995), with Introduction and Notes; Melville (1997) (in verse), with Introduction and Notes by Don and Peta Fowler; Smith (2001), with Introduction and Notes; and Stallings (2007) (in verse), with Introduction by Richard Jenkyns and Notes by the translator.

Cicero's much-quoted characterization of Lucretius' style as distinguished by *multis luminibus ingenii, multae tamen artis* (*Q. F.* 15 (2.11 (10): 1 SB) – whether the rider in *tamen* is his own or Quintus' there is no knowing – shows that he 'found Lucretius' combination of genius and technique extraordinary' (Shackleton Bailey ad loc.), as indeed it is. Though inevitably drawing on the legacy of his poetical and philosophical predecessors (on his debt to Empedocles see below), it is uniquely his own, developed by him for the purpose in hand: the forceful and effective communication of the fundamentals of the Epicurean message, in a form which would not compromise the clarity (σαφήνεια) demanded by the Founder (D.L. 10.13). The discussions by Bailey and Smith of Lucretius' language and poetic usage provide what are in effect catalogues of grammatical and syntactical practice, indispensable but furnishing only the basic tools for interpretation (Bailey 1947: 72–108; Leonard and Smith 1965: 129–86). Recent work such as that of Dionigi (1988); Sedley (1998); and Farrell

(2001) has fruitfully explored the relationship of ends to means in the argument of the poem: how Lucretius developed and exploited his inherited linguistic resources to glorify and empower his message. Particularly rewarding are the discussions by Sedley (1998: ch. 2 'Two languages, two worlds', 35–61) on how he dealt with the problem of accommodating Greek technical jargon to the stylistic demands of Latin *epos*; and Farrell (2001: ch. 2 'The poverty of our ancestral speech', 28–51) on what must be understood as Lucretius' mock-apology for the 'poverty' of his linguistic inheritance, which takes the form of a demonstration of his ability to transcend it (Kenney 2007: 97). This point and much else is also covered in the full and thoughtful analysis of Lucretius' language as a medium of philosophical discourse by Dalzell (1996: 72–103).

The *DRN* is a striking example of what was famously described by Wilhelm Kroll as 'Kreuzung der Gattungen', generic crossbreeding. What has been generally overlooked is that though the poem is formally didactic, what propels and empowers Lucretius' argument is military imagery, sometimes extremely violent, as in the case of the scythed chariots in this book (642–56). He now sees things as the heir of Homer and Ennius, and the illustration is reworked in their manner. The case has been argued cogently (following a generally neglected article by Murley of 1947) by Mayer (1990).

In the *DRN* metaphor and imagery are not merely ornamental, but integral to the literary strategy, an essential and powerful weapon in the poet's argumentative armoury, pervading and informing the argument. The insistent physicality of his imagery is arrestingly brought out in Cristoph Catrein's groundbreaking exploration (Catrein 2003) of the part played by synaesthetic metaphor in Latin poetry, adventurously developing the line of enquiry embarked on some eighty years ago in the pioneering article of Sykes Davies (1931–2). However, for all its 'extreme versatility' (Volk 2002: 83), Lucretius' imagery is always under control, a point repeatedly brought out by Hardie (1986) and well illustrated by Volk's instructive comparison with the indiscriminate practice of Manilius (ibid. 233).

Though prefaced by rejection of his physical theories, Lucretius' fervent praise of Empedocles at 1.716–41 betokens a pervasive literary indebtedness, founded on a 'shared conviction that poetry in the high epic mode was an appropriate medium for the communication of philosophical truths' (Kenney 2006: 363; Piazzi 2005: 42–6). The question is comprehensively explored in Myrto Garani's *Empedocles redivivus: poetry and analogy in Lucretius* (Garani 2007). Particularly striking and taking up some two thirds of the book is Garani's demonstration of the Empedoclean character of the imagery that continually informs Lucretius' argument: on the image of the cracked or leaking vessel at 3.935, 1003–10 pp. 193–4 (cf. Comm. 434–9n.). The message of the book is that imagery and metaphor, along with personification, 'are all used as analogical tools with both demonstrative and probative force' (221). (See Index s.v. argument: from analogy).

Lucretius was a learned poet, both *doctus* in his command of poetic technique (Kenney 1970b/1986/2007; Brown 1982/2007), and *eruditus* as conversant with the whole range of Greek and Roman mythology as it had been handed down by generations of poets and scholars. Gale (1994) has illuminatingly focussed on his use of myth as 'an instrument of the poet's argument' (Costa 1995: 28) and an essential element in the creation of his own Epicurean poetic. He clearly took especial delight in the abrupt dismissal of fears and false beliefs grounded in the credulous acceptance of these tales of gods and monsters by a dash of ordinary common sense (Kenney 1981: 20; 2007: 101). For his allegorical interpretation of men's irrational dread of eternal punishment in an underground Hell (3.978–1023), as Gale has shown (1994: 37–8, 93–4), he drew expansively on the inherited store of mythological erudition to lead up to the single verse that disposes of the matter in a nutshell: *hic Acherusia fit stultorum denique uita. denique* does double duty = both 'in the end' and 'in short' (*OLD* 1, 3) – in Johnsonian phrase, 'there's an end on't' – and *stultorum* sums up in one word the reason for these collective delusions: those who hold these beliefs are ἄφρονες, lacking the philosophical enlightenment here on offer.

Charles Segal's *Lucretius on death and anxiety* (Segal 1990) offers a wide-ranging and perceptive discussion and analysis of Lucretius' treatment of the two themes that dominate Book III of the *De Rerum Natura*. Particularly pertinent to Lucretius' exploitation of myth to reinforce his argument is Segal's ch. 8, 'Generals, poets, and philosophers: death in the perspective of time and eternity' (171–80), in which he makes the interesting suggestion that the mythical examples of Tantalus, Tityos, Sisyphus and the Danaids 'are an obvious preparation' (171) for the parade of kings, captains, poets and philosophers that follows, 'a literary tour de force by Lucretius at his most *doctus*' (178), in which 'he is … taking on the whole of the literary tradition and (implicitly) declaring it superseded by the poetry of the *vera ratio*' 180). The ambivalence acutely detected by Segal is comprehensively explored by Gale (2007b) (with good bibliography), showing how 'through heavily qualified acknowledgement of a broad range of literary forebears, the *DRN* is able to present itself as at once critique and culmination of the Graeco–Roman literary canon' (74).

'Death therefore does not matter, is nothing to us' (3.830): the Epicurean position in the Founder's own words. But does the case so eloquently and passionately expounded stand up philosophically? James Warren's searching analysis in his *Facing death: Epicurus and his critics* (Warren 2004) has cogently exposed the flaws in the Epicurean position;

and Martha Nussbaum's subtly nuanced questioning in ch. 6, 'Mortal immortals: Lucretius on death and the voice of Nature', of her *The therapy of desire: theory and practice in Hellenistic ethics* (Nussbaum 1994: 193–238) casts further doubt on the efficacy of Epicurean 'therapy' as presented in the *De Rerum Natura*.

However, for contemporary readers of the poem hoping to find comfort in Lucretius' message, it is not the possible weaknesses in the philosophical argument that impair the therapeutic effect of the argument so much as his failure to recognize the incompatibility of the Epicurean position with fundamental characteristics of human nature (Introd. 27–8, Comm. 894–8, 904–8nn.). Moreover, and even more urgently in the light of current demographic trends, it is not death but dying that is the real bugbear. Many must have echoed the much-quoted words of Woody Allen: 'It's not that I'm afraid to die; I just don't want to be there when it happens.' Or, as Isaac Asimov has put it, 'Life is pleasant. Death is peaceful. It's the transition that's troublesome.' When Epicurus on his deathbed described the last day of his life as 'blissful' (μακαρίαν, D.L. 10.22), it was surely because it *was* the last, not because the process of dying from strangury and dysentery was enjoyable. 'Given the amount of time they spend discussing death, the Epicureans have surprisingly little to say about the ethical significance of dying' (Warren 2004: 13); or indeed about the physical experience. Lucretius too 'says nothing about the possibility that dying, the separation of soul and body, might be painful in itself' (Pearcy 2012: 213). It is, however, possible, as suggested by Pearcy, that his contemporary Philodemus drew on established medical theory to argue 'that separation of body and soul was painless, or at worst accompanied by only slight and bearable pain' (ibid. 222). If challenged, Lucretius could have answered that there was always a way out in the shape of suicide (Comm. 940–9n.). Not caring to weaken the single-minded impetus of his message, he leaves the question hanging in the air. With the ethics and legality of assisted suicide now the subject of earnest and indeed impassioned debate, that lingering uncertainty inevitably colours the response of a reflective reader to this great poem.

SIGLA

O = Leidensis Vossianus lat. F. 30 (Oblongus), saec. IX
    O^s = eiusdem 'corrector Saxonicus' (Dungal), saec. IX
    O^1 = eiusdem corrector, saec. IX uel X
    O^2 = eiusdem correctores recentiores
Q = Leidensis Vossianus lat. Q. 94 (Quadratus), saec. IX
    Q^1 = eiusdem corrector, saec. XV
V = Schedae Vindobonenses priores, saec. IX. Continent 2.642–3.621.
 c = corrector aliquis saec. XV

35

TITI LVCRETI CARI DE RERVM NATVRA
LIBER TERTIVS

TITI LVCRETI CARI DE RERVM NATVRA
LIBER TERTIVS

O TENEBRIS tantis tam clarum extollere lumen
qui primus potuisti illustrans commoda uitae,
te sequor, o Graiae gentis decus, inque tuis nunc
ficta pedum pono pressis uestigia signis,
non ita certandi cupidus quam propter amorem   5
quod te imitari aueo: quid enim contendat hirundo
cycnis, aut quidnam tremulis facere artubus haedi
consimile in cursu possint et fortis equi uis?
tu, pater, es rerum inuentor, tu patria nobis
suppeditas praecepta, tuisque ex, inclute, chartis,   10
floriferis ut apes in saltibus omnia libant,
omnia nos itidem depascimur aurea dicta,
aurea, perpetua semper dignissima uita.
nam simul ac ratio tua coepit uociferari
naturam rerum, diuina mente coorta,   15
diffugiunt animi terrores, moenia mundi
discedunt, totum uideo per inane geri res.
apparet diuum numen sedesque quietae,
quas neque concutiunt uenti nec nubila nimbis
aspergunt neque nix acri concreta pruina   20
cana cadens uiolat, semperque innubilus aether
integit et large diffuso lumine ridet.
omnia suppeditat porro natura, neque ulla
res animi pacem delibat tempore in ullo.
at contra nusquam apparent Acherusia templa   25
nec tellus obstat quin omnia dispiciantur,
sub pedibus quaecumque infra per inane geruntur.
his ibi me rebus quaedam diuina uoluptas
percipit atque horror, quod sic natura tua ui
tam manifesta patens ex omni parte retecta est.   30

---

1 o *OV*: *om. Q*: e *c*   11 libant *c*: limant *OQV*   15 coorta *Orelli*: coortam *O*: coartam *QV*   21 semperque *c*: semper *OQV*   22 ridet] rident *Lachmann*   28 ibi *Pontanus*: ubi *OQV*   29 sic natura *Auancius*: signatura *OQ*: signagtura *V*

Et quoniam docui cunctarum exordia rerum
qualia sint et quam uariis distantia formis
sponte sua uolitent aeterno percita motu
quoue modo possint res ex his quaeque creari,
hasce secundum res animi natura uidetur   35
atque animae claranda meis iam uersibus esse
et metus ille foras praeceps Acheruntis agendus,
funditus humanam qui uitam turbat ab imo
omnia suffundens mortis nigrore neque ullam
esse uoluptatem liquidam puramque relinquit.   40
nam quod saepe homines morbos magis esse timendos
infamemque ferunt uitam quam Tartara leti
et se scire animi naturam sanguinis esse
aut etiam uenti, si fert ita forte uoluntas,   [46]
nec prorsum quicquam nostrae rationis egere,   45 [44]
hinc licet aduertas animum magis omnia laudis   [45]
iactari causa quam quod res ipsa probetur:
extorres idem patria longeque fugati
conspectu ex hominum, foedati crimine turpi,
omnibus aerumnis affecti denique uiuunt   50
et quocumque tamen miseri uenere parentant
et nigras mactant pecudes et manibu' diuis
inferias mittunt multoque in rebus acerbis
acrius aduertunt animos ad religionem.
quo magis in dubiis hominem spectare periclis   55
conuenit aduersisque in rebus noscere qui sit:
nam uerae uoces tum demum pectore ab imo
eliciuntur et eripitur persona, manet res.
denique auarities et honorum caeca cupido
quae miseros homines cogunt transcendere finis   60
iuris et interdum socios scelerum atque ministros
noctes atque dies niti praestante labore
ad summas emergere opes, haec uulnera uitae
non minimam partem mortis formidine aluntur.
turpis enim ferme contemptus et acris egestas   65

31-4 = 4.45-8   33 aeterno *Naugerius*: alterno *OV*: alterna *Q*   43 animi *O*:
anime *QV*: animae *Wakefield*   44 [46] *post u.* 43 *transp. Bentley*   47 causa *O*^{s}
(*ut uid.*): causam *OQV*   53 inferias *Q*^{l}: inferis *OQV*   58 eliciuntur] eiciuntur
Gifanius   et *add. c*: om. *OQV*   manet res *c*: manare *OQV*   62-3 ~ 2.12-13

semota ab dulci uita stabilique uidentur
et quasi iam leti portas cunctarier ante:
unde homines dum se falso terrore coacti
effugisse uolunt longe longeque remosse,
sanguine ciuili rem conflant diuitiasque   70
conduplicant auidi, caedem caede accumulantes,
crudeles gaudent in tristi funere fratris
et consanguineum mensas odere timentque.
consimili ratione ab eodem saepe timore
macerat inuidia ante oculos illum esse potentem,   75
illum aspectari, claro qui incedit honore,
ipsi se in tenebris uolui caenoque queruntur.
intereunt partim statuarum et nominis ergo;
et saepe usque adeo mortis formidine uitae
percipit humanos odium lucisque uidendae   80
ut sibi consciscant maerenti pectore letum,
obliti fontem curarum hunc esse timorem,
hunc uexare pudorem, hunc uincula amicitiai
rumpere et in summa pietatem euertere fundo.
nam iam saepe homines patriam carosque parentis   85
prodiderunt, uitare Acherusia templa petentes.
nam ueluti pueri trepidant atque omnia caecis
in tenebris metuunt, sic nos in luce timemus
interdum nilo quae sunt metuenda magis quam
quae pueri in tenebris pauitant finguntque futura.   90
hunc igitur terrorem animi tenebrasque necessest
non radii solis neque lucida tela diei
discutiant, sed naturae species ratioque.

PRIMVM animum dico, mentem quam saepe uocamus,
in quo consilium uitae regimenque locatum est,   95
esse hominis partem nilo minus ac manus et pes
atque oculi partes animantis totius exstant.

.   .   .   .

66 uidentur *Lambinus*: uidetur *OQV*   72 fratris *Macrobius, Sat. 6.2.15*: fratres
OQV   77 ipsi] ipsos *Winckelmann, fort. recte*   78 statuarum *c*: statum *OQV*
81 consciscant *c*: coniciscant *OQV*   84 pietatem *c*: pietate *OV*: piaetate
Q   fundo *Lambinus*: suadet *OQV*: fraude *Lachmann*: clade *Bernays*: suesse
Merrill   e summa…sede *Bailey*   87–93 = 2.55–61, 6.35–41   91–3 =
1.146–8   94 quam *Charisius, GLK I 210.5*: quem *OQV*   95 locatum *Marullus*:
uocatum *OQV, nimirum ex u. 94*   97 *post hunc u. lacunam statuerunt edd. uett.*

sensum animi certa non esse in parte locatum,
uerum habitum quendam uitalem corporis esse,
harmoniam Grai quam dicunt, quod faciat nos   100
uiuere cum sensu, nulla cum in parte siet mens;
ut bona saepe ualetudo cum dicitur esse
corporis, et non est tamen haec pars ulla ualentis.
sic animi sensum non certa parte reponunt,
magno opere in quo mi diuersi errare uidentur.   105
saepe itaque in promptu corpus quod cernitur aegret,
cum tamen ex alia laetamur parte latenti;
et retro fit uti contra sit saepe uicissim,
cum miser ex animo laetatur corpore toto;
non alio pacto quam si, pes cum dolet aegri,   110
in nullo caput interea sit forte dolore.
praeterea molli cum somno dedita membra
effusumque iacet sine sensu corpus onustum,
est aliud tamen in nobis quod tempore in illo
multimodis agitatur et omnis accipit in se   115
laetitiae motus et curas cordis inanis.
nunc animam quoque ut in membris cognoscere possis
esse neque harmonia corpus sentire solere,
principio fit uti detracto corpore multo
saepe tamen nobis in membris uita moretur;   120
atque eadem rursum, cum corpora pauca caloris
diffugere forasque per os est editus aer,
deserit extemplo uenas atque ossa relinquit:
noscere ut hinc possis non aequas omnia partis
corpora habere neque ex aequo fulcire salutem,   125
sed magis haec, uenti quae sunt calidique uaporis
semina, curare in membris ut uita moretur.
est igitur calor ac uentus uitalis in ipso
corpore qui nobis moribundos deserit artus.
quapropter quoniam est animi natura reperta   130
atque animae quasi pars hominis, redde harmoniai

---

101 siet *O*: sit *QV*   106 promptu *O, Macrobius, GLK v 650.33*: prompto *Q*: prontu *V*   aegret *Macrobius, ibid.*: aegrum *OQV*   108 uti *Lambinus*: ubi *OQV*
113 onustum *c*: honustum *O¹*: honestum *OQV*   118 sentire *Cipelli, Wakefield*: interire *OQV*

nomen, ad organicos alto delatum Heliconi,
siue aliunde ipsi porro traxere et in illam
transtulerunt, proprio quae tum res nomine egebat.
quidquid id est, habeant; tu cetera percipe dicta.   135
   Nunc animum atque animam dico coniuncta teneri
inter se atque unam naturam conficere ex se,
sed caput esse quasi et dominari in corpore toto
consilium quod nos animum mentemque uocamus.
idque situm media regione in pectoris haeret.   140
hic exsultat enim pauor ac metus, haec loca circum
laetitiae mulcent, hic ergo mens animusquest.
cetera pars animae per totum dissita corpus
paret et ad numen mentis momenque mouetur.
idque sibi solum per se sapit, id sibi gaudet,   145
cum neque res animam neque corpus commouet ulla
et quasi, cum caput aut oculus temptante dolore
laeditur in nobis, non omni concruciamur
corpore, sic animus nonnumquam laeditur ipse
laetitiaque uiget, cum cetera pars animai   150
per membra atque artus nulla nouitate cietur.
uerum ubi uementi magis est commota metu mens,
consentire animam totam per membra uidemus
sudoresque ita palloremque exsistere toto
corpore et infringi linguam uocemque aboriri,   155
caligare oculos, sonere auris, succidere artus,
denique concidere ex animi terrore uidemus
saepe homines: facile ut quiuis hinc noscere possit
esse animam cum animo coniunctam, quae cum animi ui
percussast, exim corpus propellit et icit.   160
   Haec eadem ratio naturam animi atque animai
corpoream docet esse: ubi enim propellere membra,
corripere ex somno corpus mutareque uultum
atque hominem totum regere ac uersare uidetur,
quorum nil fieri sine tactu posse uidemus   165
nec tactum porro sine corpore, nonne fatendumst

135 id add. c: om. OQV   145 id alterum add. Wakefield: et add. c: om. OQV   146
ulla c: una OQV   154 ita palloremque c: itaque pallorem OQV   159 ui c: uis
Nonius Marcellus, p. 179 L.: om. OQV   160 perculsa est Nonius Marcellus, ibid.

corporea natura animum constare animamque?
praeterea pariter fungi cum corpore et una
consentire animum nobis in corpore cernis,
si minus offendit uitam uis horrida teli   170
ossibus ac neruis disclusis intus adacta,
at tamen insequitur languor terraeque petitus
suauis et in terra mentis qui gignitur aestus,
interdumque quasi exsurgendi incerta uoluntas.
ergo corpoream naturam animi esse necessest,   175
corporeis quoniam telis ictuque laborat.
   Is tibi nunc animus quali sit corpore et unde
constiterit pergam rationem reddere dictis.
principio esse aio persubtilem atque minutis
perquam corporibus factum constare. id ita esse   180
hinc licet aduertas animum ut pernoscere possis.
nil adeo fieri celeri ratione uidetur
quam sibi mens fieri proponit et incohat ipsa.
ocius ergo animus quam res se perciet ulla,
ante oculos quorum in promptu natura uidetur.   185
at quod mobile tanto operest, constare rutundis
perquam seminibus debet perquamque minutis,
momine uti paruo possint impulsa moueri.
namque mouetur aqua et tantillo momine flutat
quippe uolubilibus paruisque creata figuris.   190
at contra mellis constantior est natura
et pigri latices magis et cunctantior actus:
haeret enim inter se magis omnis materiai
copia, nimirum quia non tam leuibus exstat
corporibus neque tam subtilibus atque rutundis.   195
namque papaueris aura potest suspensa leuisque
cogere ut ab summo tibi diffluat altus aceruus,
at contra lapidum conlectum spicarumque
noenu potest. igitur paruissima corpora proquam
et leuissima sunt, ita mobilitate fruuntur,   200

170 teli *Marullus*: leti *OQV*   173 suauis] segnis *Munro*: *alii alia*   183 sibi
Wakefield: si OQV   194 leuibu' constat *Heinze*   198 conlectum *Marullus*:
coniectum *OQV*   spicarumque] cauru' mouere *Bernays*: spiritus acer *Lachmann*:
disicere umquam *Purmann*: ipse euru' mouere *Munro*

at contra quaecumque magis cum pondere magno
asperaque inueniuntur, eo stabilita magis sunt.
nunc igitur quoniam est animi natura reperta
mobilis egregie, perquam constare necessest
corporibus paruis et leuibus atque rutundis.   205
quae tibi cognita res in multis, o bone, rebus
utilis inuenietur et opportuna cluebit.
haec quoque res etiam naturam dedicat eius,
quam tenui constet textura quamque loco se
contineat paruo, si possit conglomerari,   210
quod simul atque hominem leti secura quies est
indepta atque animi natura animaeque recessit,
nil ibi libatum de toto corpore cernas
ad speciem, nil ad pondus: mors omnia praestat
uitalem praeter sensum calidumque uaporem.   215
ergo animam totam perparuis esse necessest
seminibus nexam per uenas uiscera neruos,
quatenus, omnis ubi e toto iam corpore cessit,
extima membrorum circumcaesura tamen se
incolumem praestat nec defit ponderis hilum.   220
quod genus est Bacchi cum flos euanuit aut cum
spiritus unguenti suauis diffugit in auras
aut aliquo cum iam sucus de corpore cessit:
nil oculis tamen esse minor res ipsa uidetur
propterea neque detractum de pondere quicquam,   225
nimirum quia multa minutaque semina sucos
efficiunt et odorem in toto corpore rerum.
quare etiam atque etiam mentis naturam animaeque
scire licet perquam pauxillis esse creatam
seminibus, quoniam fugiens nil ponderis aufert.   230
   Nec tamen haec simplex nobis natura putanda est.
tenuis enim quaedam moribundos deserit aura
mixta uapore, uapor porro trahit aera secum.
nec calor est quisquam, cui non sit mixtus et aer:
rara quod eius enim constat natura, necessest   235

---

203 est *add. c: om. OQV*   210 si *c:* se *OQV*   222 unguenti *c:* unguente *O:*
unguentes *Q:* umquentes *V*   224 nil *c:* nihil *OQV:* nilo *Heinsius*   226 multa]
pauca *Housman*

aeris inter eum primordia multa moueri.
iam triplex animi est igitur natura reperta,
nec tamen haec sat sunt ad sensum cuncta creandum,
nil horum quoniam recipit mens posse creare
sensiferos motus et quaecumque ipsa uolutat.   240
quarta quoque his igitur quaedam natura necessest
attribuatur. east omnino nominis expers,
qua neque mobilius quicquam neque tenuius exstat,
nec magis e paruis et leuibus est elementis,
sensiferos motus quae didit prima per artus.   245
prima cietur enim paruis perfecta figuris;
inde calor motus et uenti caeca potestas
accipit, inde aer; inde omnia mobilitantur,
concutitur sanguis, tum uiscera persentiscunt
omnia, postremis datur ossibus atque medullis   250
siue uoluptas est siue est contrarius ardor.
nec temere huc dolor usque potest penetrare neque acre
permanare malum, quin omnia perturbentur
usque adeo ut uitae desit locus atque animai
diffugiant partes per caulas corporis omnis.   255
sed plerumque fit in summo quasi corpore finis
motibus: hanc ob rem uitam retinere ualemus.
    Nunc ea quo pacto inter sese mixta quibusque
compta modis uigeant rationem reddere auentem
abstrahit inuitum patrii sermonis egestas;   260
sed tamen, ut potero summatim attingere, tangam.
inter enim cursant primordia principiorum
motibus inter se, nil ut secernier unum
possit nec spatio fieri diuisa potestas,
sed quasi multae uis unius corporis exstant.   265
quod genus in quouis animantum uiscere uulgo
est odor et quidam color et sapor, et tamen ex his
omnibus est unum perfectum corporis augmen:

---

236 multa moueri *O*[s]: multam quaeri *O*: multam queri *Q*: multam *V*   239
mens] res *Bernays*   240 et quaecumque ipsa *Saunders*: et mens quaecumque
Frerichs: quaedam quae mente *O*: quaedamque mente *QV*   244 c] est *c*   est
Cipelli, Wakefield: ex *OQV*   249 sanguis tum *Pontanus*: tum sanguis *OQV*   254
ut *add. Lambinus*: om. *OQV*   257 retinere *O*[s]: retinemus *OQV*   261 ut *Q*: ui *OV*
267 color *Lambinus*: calor *OQV*

sic calor atque aer et uenti caeca potestas
mixta creant unam naturam et mobilis illa   270
uis, initum motus ab se quae diuidit ollis,
sensifer unde oritur primum per uiscera motus.
nam penitus prorsum latet haec natura subestque,
nec magis hac infra quicquam est in corpore nostro,
atque anima est animae proporro totius ipsa.   275
quod genus in nostris membris et corpore toto
mixta latens animi uis est animaeque potestas,
corporibus quia de paruis paucisque creatast:
sic tibi nominis haec expers uis facta minutis
corporibus latet atque animae quasi totius ipsa   280
proporrost anima et dominatur corpore toto.
consimili ratione necessest uentus et aer
et calor inter se uigeant commixta per artus
atque aliis aliud subsit magis emineatque
ut quiddam fieri uideatur ab omnibus unum,   285
ni calor ac uentus seorsum seorsumque potestas
aeris interimant sensum diductaque soluant.
est etiam calor ille animo, quem sumit in ira,
cum feruescit et ex oculis micat acribus ardor.
est et frigida multa comes formidinis aura,   290
quae ciet horrorem membris et concitat artus.
est etiam quoque pacati status aeris ille,
pectore tranquillo qui fit uultuque sereno.
sed calidi plus est illis quibus acria corda
iracundaque mens facile efferuescit in iram.   295
quo genere in primis uis est uiolenta leonum,
pectora qui fremitu rumpunt plerumque gementes
nec capere irarum fluctus in pectore possunt.
at uentosa magis ceruorum frigida mens est
et gelidas citius per uiscera concitat auras,   300
quae tremulum faciunt membris exsistere motum.
at natura boum placido magis aere uiuit,

---

280 latet *Q¹*: late *OQV*   animae quasi] animai *Lambinus*   288 etiam] etenim
Faber, fort. recte   289 feruescit *c*: feruescat *O*: feruescet *QV*   acribus *Lambinus*:
acrius *OQV*   291 concitat *O²*: inconcitat *OQ*: incontat *V*: congelat *Housman*
293 qui fit *Marullus*: fit qui *OQV*   295 iram *Bentley*: ira *OQV*   298 *post u.* 295
transp. Lachmann

nec nimis irai fax umquam subdita percit
fumida, suffundens caecae caliginis umbra,
nec gelidis torpet telis perfixa pauoris: 305
interutrasque sitast, ceruos saeuosque leones.
sic hominum genus est: quamuis doctrina politos
constituat pariter quosdam, tamen illa relinquit
naturae cuiusque animi uestigia prima,
nec radicitus euelli mala posse putandumst,   310
quin procliuius hic iras decurrat ad acris,
ille metu citius paulo temptetur, at ille
tertius accipiat quaedam clementius aequo.
inque aliis rebus multis differre necessest
naturas hominum uarias moresque sequaces,   315
quorum ego nunc nequeo caecas exponere causas
nec reperire figurarum tot nomina quot sunt
principiis, unde haec oritur uariantia rerum.
illud in his rebus uideo firmare potesse,
usque adeo naturarum uestigia linqui   320
paruula quae nequeat ratio depellere nobis,
ut nil impediat dignam dis degere uitam.
    Haec igitur natura tenetur corpore ab omni
ipsaque corporis est custos et causa salutis:
nam communibus inter se radicibus haerent   325
nec sine pernicie diuelli posse uidentur.
quod genus e turis glaebis euellere odorem
haud facile est quin intereat natura quoque eius:
sic animi atque animae naturam corpore toto
extrahere haud facile est quin omnia dissoluantur.   330
implexis ita principiis ab origine prima
inter se fiunt consorti praedita uita.
nec sibi quaeque sine alterius ui posse uidetur

303 nimis *c*: minus *OQV*   304 umbra *Q*: umbram *OV*: umbras *c*   305
pauoris *O²*: uaporis *OQ*: uapori *V*   306 interutrasque] inter utrosque *Auancius*:
interutraque *Lachmann*   sitast *Auancius*: sitas *OQV*: secus *Lachmann*   309 naturae *Marullus*: natura *OQV*   317 quot *O¹*: quod *OQV*   319 firmare *O²*: formare
OQV   321 nobis *Cipelli, Lachmann*: noctis *O*: noctes *QV*: doctis *Lambinus*: mentis
Meurig Davies   325 = 5.554   332 fiunt consorti *O²*, *ut coni. Marullus*: consorti
fiunt *OQV*   uita *Q¹*: uitae *OQV*

corporis atque animi seorsum sentire potestas,
sed communibus inter eas conflatur utrimque   335
motibus accensus nobis per uiscera sensus.
praeterea corpus per se nec gignitur umquam
nec crescit neque post mortem durare uidetur.
non enim, ut umor aquae dimittit saepe uaporem
qui datus est neque ea causa conuellitur ipse,   340
sed manet incolumis, non, inquam, sic animai
discidium possunt artus perferre relicti,
sed penitus pereunt conuulsi conque putrescunt.
ex ineunte aeuo sic corporis atque animai
mutua uitalis discunt contagia motus   345
maternis etiam membris aluoque reposta,
discidium ut nequeat fieri sine peste maloque:
ut uideas, quoniam coniunctast causa salutis,
coniunctam quoque naturam consistere eorum.
    Quod superest, si quis corpus sentire refutat   350
atque animam credit permixtam corpore toto
suscipere hunc motum quem sensum nominitamus,
uel manifestas res contra uerasque repugnat.
quid sit enim corpus sentire quis adferet umquam,
si non ipsa palam quod res dedit ac docuit nos?   355
'at dimissa anima corpus caret undique sensu':
perdit enim quod non proprium fuit eius in aeuo,
multaque praeterea perdit cum expellitur aeuo.
dicere porro oculos nullam rem cernere posse,
sed per eos animum ut foribus spectare reclusis,   360
desiperest, contra cum sensus ducat eorum:
sensus enim trahit atque acies detrudit ad ipsas,
fulgida praesertim cum cernere saepe nequimus,
lumina luminibus quia nobis praepediuntur.
quod foribus non fit; neque enim, qua cernimus ipsi,   365
ostia suscipiunt ullum reclusa laborem.

335 eas *Lachmann*: eos OQV: se *Merrill*   346 reposta *c*: reposto OQV   347 ut *add. Marullus*: *om.* OQV   350 refutat] renutat *Lambinus, fort. recte*   358 perdit cum expellitur aeuo *c*: perditum expellitur aeuo quam OQV: perdit quam expellitur ante *Munro*   359 posse] per se *Butterfield, fort. recte*   361 desiperest *Lambinus*: difficile est OQV

praeterea si pro foribus sunt lumina nostra,
iam magis exemptis oculis debere uidetur
cernere res animus sublatis postibus ipsis.
   Illud in his rebus nequaquam sumere possis,   370
Democriti quod sancta uiri sententia ponit,
corporis atque animi primordia singula priuis
apposita alternis uariare ac nectere membra.
nam cum multo sunt animae elementa minora
quam quibus e corpus nobis et uiscera constant,   375
tum numero quoque concedunt et rara per artus
dissita sunt dumtaxat ut hoc promittere possis,
quantula prima queant nobis iniecta ciere
corpora sensiferos motus in corpore, tanta
interualla tenere exordia prima animai.   380
nam neque pulueris interdum sentimus adhaesum
corpore nec membris incussam sidere cretam,
nec nebulam noctu neque aranei tenuia fila
obuia sentimus, quando obretimur euntes,
nec supera caput eiusdem cecidisse uietam   385
uestem nec plumas auium papposque uolantis,
qui nimia leuitate cadunt plerumque grauatim,
nec repentis itum cuiusuiscumque animantis
sentimus nec priua pedum uestigia quaeque,
corpore quae in nostro culices et cetera ponunt.   390
usque adeo prius est in nobis multa ciendum
semina corporibus nostris immixta per artus,   393
quam primordia sentiscant concussa animai   392
et tantis interuallis tuditantia possint
concursare coire et dissultare uicissim.   395
   Et magis est animus uitai claustra coercens
et dominantior ad uitam quam uis animai.
nam sine mente animoque nequit residere per artus
temporis exiguam partem pars ulla animai,

371 = 5.622   372 priuis *Bentley*: primis *OQV*   374 elementa minora animai *Lachmann*   383 aranei *Marullus*: arani *OQV*   391 ciendum *V*: ciendo *OQ*
391–2 primordia multa ciendum | in nobis quam *Müller, ordine uu.* 392–3 *seruato*
393 *ante u.* 392 *transp. Marullus*   394 tantis *Wakefield*: quantis *OQV*: quam sis
Turnebus: quam in his *Lachmann*

sed comes insequitur facile et discedit in auras   400
et gelidos artus in leti frigore linquit.
at manet in uita cui mens animusque remansit:
quamuis est circum caesis lacer undique membris
truncus, adempta anima circum membrisque remota
uiuit et aetherias uitalis suscipit auras.   405
si non omnimodis, at magna parte animai
priuatus, tamen in uita cunctatur et haeret:
ut, lacerato oculo circum si pupula mansit
incolumis, stat cernundi uiuata potestas,
dummodo ne totum corrumpas luminis orbem   410
et circum caedas aciem solamque relinquas;
id quoque enim sine pernicie non fiet eorum.
at si tantula pars oculi media illa peresa est,
occidit extemplo lumen tenebraeque sequuntur,
incolumis quamuis alioqui splendidus orbis.   415
hoc anima atque animus uincti sunt foedere semper.

NVNC AGE, natiuos animantibus et mortalis
esse animos animasque leuis ut noscere possis,
conquisita diu dulcique reperta labore
digna tua pergam disponere carmina uita.   420
tu fac utrumque uno subiungas nomine eorum,
atque animam uerbi causa cum dicere pergam,
mortalem esse docens, animum quoque dicere credas,
quatenus est unum inter se coniunctaque res est.
   Principio quoniam tenuem constare minutis   425
corporibus docui multoque minoribus esse
principiis factam quam liquidus umor aquai
aut nebula aut fumus – nam longe mobilitate
praestat et a tenui causa magis icta mouetur:
quippe ubi imaginibus fumi nebulaeque mouetur,   430
quod genus in somnis sopiti ubi cernimus alte

400 et Q^1: e OQV   403 circum c: cretum OQV   404 remota Q^1: remot Q:
remotus OV: remotis c   405 aerias Lachmann   415 alioquist Kannengiesser
417 mortalis c: mortalibus OQV   420 uita] mente Müller: cultu Butterfield
430 mouetur Marullus: mouentur OQV   431 alte Lachmann: alta OQV

exhalare uaporem altaria ferreque fumum;
nam procul haec dubio nobis simulacra feruntur –
nunc igitur quoniam quassatis undique uasis
diffluere umorem et laticem discedere cernis   435
et nebula ac fumus quoniam discedit in auras,
crede animam quoque diffundi multoque perire
ocius et citius dissolui in corpora prima,
cum semel ex hominis membris ablata recessit.
quippe etenim corpus, quod uas quasi constitit eius,   440
cum cohibere nequit conquassatum ex aliqua re
ac rarefactum detracto sanguine uenis,
aere qui credas posse hanc cohiberier ullo,
corpore qui nostro rarus magis †incohibescit†?
    Praeterea gigni pariter cum corpore et una   445
crescere sentimus pariterque senescere mentem.
nam uelut infirmo pueri teneroque uagantur
corpore, sic animi sequitur sententia tenuis.
inde ubi robustis adoleuit uiribus aetas,
consilium quoque maius et auctior est animi uis.   450
post ubi iam ualidis quassatum est uiribus aeui
corpus et obtusis ceciderunt uiribus artus,
claudicat ingenium, delirat lingua, labat mens,
omnia deficiunt atque uno tempore desunt.
ergo dissolui quoque conuenit omnem animai   455
naturam, ceu fumus, in altas aeris auras:
quandoquidem gigni pariter pariterque uidemus
crescere et, ut docui, simul aeuo fessa fatisci.
    Huc accedit uti uideamus, corpus ut ipsum
suscipere immanis morbos durumque dolorem,   460
sic animum curas acris luctumque metumque:
quare participem leti quoque conuenit esse.
quin etiam morbis in corporis auius errat
saepe animus: dementit enim deliraque fatur

---

432 uaporem O^2: uapore OQV   433 haec] hinc *Bentley*   feruntur *Creech*: geruntur OQV: genuntur *Lachmann*   438 in *add.* Q^I: *om.* OQV   444 is cohibessit? *Lachmann*: incohibensquest *Bergk*: incohibens sit *Woltjer*: *alii alia*   450 auctior Q^I: auctor OQV   453 labat *add. Lachmann*: *om.* OQV: madet Q^I (*cf. u.* 479)   456 aeris *c*: acris OQV   458 ut *add.* Q^I: *om.* QQV   fatisci *c*: fatiscit Q^I: faetis OQ: fetis V

interdumque graui lethargo fertur in altum   465
aeternumque soporem oculis nutuque cadenti,
unde neque exaudit uoces nec noscere uultus
illorum potis est, ad uitam qui reuocantes
circumstant lacrimis rorantes ora genasque.
quare animum quoque dissolui fateare necessest,   470
quandoquidem penetrant in eum contagia morbi.
nam dolor ac morbus leti fabricator uterquest,
multorum exitio perdocti quod sumus ante.   473
denique cur, hominem cum uini uis penetrauit   476
acris et in uenas discessit diditus ardor,
consequitur grauitas membrorum, praepediuntur
crura uacillanti, tardescit lingua, madet mens,
nant oculi, clamor singultus iurgia gliscunt,   480
et iam cetera de genere hoc quaecumque sequuntur,
cur ea sunt, nisi quod uemens uiolentia uini
conturbare animam consueuit corpore in ipso?
at quaecumque queunt conturbari inque pediri,
significant, paulo si durior insinuarit   485
causa, fore ut pereant aeuo priuata futuro.
quin etiam subito ui morbi saepe coactus
ante oculos aliquis nostros, ut fulminis ictu,
concidit et spumas agit, ingemit et tremit artus,
desipit, extentat neruos, torquetur, anhelat   490
inconstanter, et in iactando membra fatigat.
nimirum quia ui morbi distracta per artus
turbat agens anima spumas, ut in aequore salso
uentorum ualidis feruescunt uiribus undae.
exprimitur porro gemitus, quia membra dolore   495
adficiuntur et omnino quod semina uocis
eiciuntur et ore foras glomerata feruntur
qua quasi consuerunt et sunt munita uiai.
desipientia fit, quia uis animi atque animai
conturbatur et, ut docui, diuisa seorsum   500

---

470 fateare *c*: fatere *OQV*   474–5 et quoniam mentem sanari corpus ut aegrum
(= 510) | et pariter mentem sanari corpus inani *del. c, Naugerius*   482 cur ea
c: curba *OQV*   492 quia *c*: qua *OQV*   ui *Brieger*: uis *OQV*   493 anima spumas
Tohte (animam spumas *iam Winckelmann*): animam spumans *OQV*: *alii alia*   ut *add.*
c: *om. OQV*   497 eiciuntur *Lambinus*: eliciuntur *OQV*   498 uiai *c*: uia *OQV*

disiectatur eodem illo distracta ueneno.
inde ubi iam morbi reflexit causa reditque
in latebras acer corrupti corporis umor,
tum quasi uaccillans primum consurgit et omnis
paulatim redit in sensus animamque receptat.   505
haec igitur tantis ubi morbis corpore in ipso
iactentur miserisque modis distracta laborent,
cur eadem credis sine corpore in aere aperto
cum ualidis uentis aetatem degere posse?
et quoniam mentem sanari, corpus ut aegrum,   510
cernimus et flecti medicina posse uidemus,
id quoque praesagit mortalem uiuere mentem.
addere enim partis aut ordine traiecere aequumst
aut aliquid prorsum de summa detrahere hilum,
commutare animum quicumque adoritur et infit   515
aut aliam quamuis naturam flectere quaerit.
at neque transferri sibi partis nec tribui uult
immortale quod est quicquam neque defluere hilum.
nam quodcumque suis mutatum finibus exit,
continuo hoc mors est illius quod fuit ante.   520
ergo animus siue aegrescit, mortalia signa
mittit, uti docui, seu flectitur a medicina:
usque adeo falsae rationi uera uidetur
res occurrere et effugium praecludere eunti
ancipitique refutatu conuincere falsum.   525
    Denique saepe hominem paulatim cernimus ire
et membratim uitalem deperdere sensum,
in pedibus primum digitos liuescere et unguis,
inde pedes et crura mori, post inde per artus
ire alios tractim gelidi uestigia leti.   530
scinditur †atque animo haec† quoniam natura nec uno

514 aliquid *OQV*: aliquod *Housman* (*dubitanter, ut uid.*): aliqui *Kenney*: aliqua
Butterfield   519–20 = 1.670–1, 792–3, 2.753–4   523 rationi *O²*, *sicut coni.*
Marullus: rationis *OQV*   525 refutatu *Q¹*: refutatur *OQV*   526–47 *post u.*
669 *transp. Giussani, fort. recte*   531 atque animo haec] atque animae *ed. Londin.*
1835 (*Gordon 120*), *Müller*: atque animae haec *Merrill, Martin*: atqui animae
Lambinus: aeque animi haec *Bernays*: itque animae huic *Winckelmann*: itque animae
hoc *Munro*: itque animae haec *Bailey*: aeque animae *Jessen*: atque animo *Büchner*:
haec animae *Clausen*: *an* ergo (*Heinze*) animae?

tempore sincera exsistit, mortalis habendast.
quod si forte putas ipsam se posse per artus
introrsum trahere et partis conducere in unum
atque ideo cunctis sensum deducere membris,   535
at locus ille tamen, quo copia tanta animai
cogitur, in sensu debet maiore uideri:
qui quoniam nusquamst, nimirum, ut diximus ante,
dilaniata foras dispargitur, interit ergo.
quin etiam si iam libeat concedere falsum   540
et dare posse animam glomerari in corpore eorum,
lumina qui linquunt moribundi particulatim,
mortalem tamen esse animam fateare necessest,
nec refert utrum pereat dispersa per auras
an contracta suis e partibus obbrutescat,   545
quando hominem totum magis ac magis undique sensus
deficit et uitae minus et minus undique restat.
     Et quoniam mens est hominis pars una, loco quae
fixa manet certo, uelut aures atque oculi sunt
atque alii sensus qui uitam cumque gubernant,   550
et ueluti manus atque oculus naresue seorsum
secreta ab nobis nequeunt sentire neque esse,
sed tamen in paruo liquuntur tempore tabe:
sic animus per se non quit sine corpore et ipso
esse homine, illius quasi quod uas esse uidetur   555
siue aliud quid uis potius coniunctius ei
fingere, quandoquidem conexu corpus adhaeret.
     Denique corporis atque animi uiuata potestas
inter se coniuncta ualent uitaque fruuntur:
nec sine corpore enim uitalis edere motus   560
sola potest animi per se natura nec autem
cassum anima corpus durare et sensibus uti.
scilicet auulsus radicibus ut nequit ullam

535 deducere *c*: diducere *OQV*   538 ante *add. c: om. OQV*   543 necessest *uel* necesse est *uett. edd.*: necesse *OQV*   548 quae *Lambinus*: que *OQV*
553 liquuntur…tabe *edd.* (liquuntur *c*, '*quidam doctus*' *ap. Lambinum*): licuntur
Munro…tabe *Lachmann in notis*: tabi *I. Vossius*: linguntur *OQV*…tale *V*: tali *OQ*
555 uas esse *c*: uasse *O*: uase *QV*

dispicere ipse oculus rem seorsum corpore toto,
sic anima atque animus per se nil posse uidetur.   565
nimirum quia per uenas et uiscera mixtim,
per neruos atque ossa, tenentur corpore ab omni
nec magnis interuallis primordia possunt
libera dissultare, ideo conclusa mouentur
sensiferos motus quos extra corpus in auras   570
aeris haud possunt post mortem eiecta moueri
propterea quia non simili ratione tenentur.
corpus enim atque animans erit aer, si cohibere
in se animam atque in eos poterit concludere motus
quos ante in neruis et in ipso corpore agebat.   575
quare etiam atque etiam resoluto corporis omni
tegmine et eiectis extra uitalibus auris
dissolui sensus animi fateare necessest
atque animam, quoniam coniunctast causa duobus.
  Denique cum corpus nequeat perferre animai   580
discidium quin in taetro tabescat odore,
quid dubitas quin ex imo penitusque coorta
emanarit uti fumus diffusa animae uis,
atque ideo tanta mutatum putre ruina
conciderit corpus, penitus quia mota loco sunt   585
fundamenta, foras anima emanante per artus
perque uiarum omnis flexus, in corpore qui sunt,
atque foramina? multimodis ut noscere possis
dispertitam animae naturam exisse per artus
et prius esse sibi distractam corpore in ipso   590
quam prolapsa foras enaret in aeris auras.
quin etiam finis dum uitae uertitur intra,
saepe aliqua tamen e causa labefacta uidetur
ire anima ac toto solui de corpore uelle

564 ipse oculus *c*: oculus ipse *O*ˢ: oculos ipse *OQV*   *an* seorsum a *legendum?*
566 per *add. c: om. OQV*   mixtim *c*: mixti *OV*: mixta *Q*   571 moueri *Lambinus*:
mouere *OQV*   573 animans erit *Lambinus*: animam serit *OQV*   574 in se animam *Wakefield*: sese anima *O*: esse anima *Q*: esse animam *V*   576 quare *Q*ᵗ: quae
O: que *Q: om. V*   582 ex imo *Q*ᵗ: ea imo *OQ*: e animo *V*   583 animae uis *c*:
anima eius *OQ*: animaei *V*   586 anima emanante *Wakefield*: manant animaeque
OQV: manante anima usque *Lachmann*   594 uelle *Lachmann*: partim *Butterfield*:
omnia membra *OQV*, nimirum e u. 596 *postquam corruptus est et ille*

et quasi supremo languescere tempore uultus   595
molliaque exsangui cadere omnia corpore membra.
quod genus est, animo male factum cum perhibetur
aut animam liquisse, ubi iam trepidatur et omnes
extremum cupiunt uitae reprehendere uinclum.
conquassatur enim tum mens animaeque potestas   600
omnis et haec ipso cum corpore collabefiunt,
ut grauior paulo possit dissoluere causa.
quid dubitas tandem quin extra prodita corpus
imbecilla foras, in aperto, tegmine dempto,
non modo non omnem possit durare per aeuom   605
sed minimum quoduis nequeat consistere tempus?
nec sibi enim quisquam moriens sentire uidetur
ire foras animam incolumem de corpore toto
nec prius ad iugulum et superas succedere fauces,
uerum deficere in certa regione locatam,   610
ut sensus alios in parti quemque sua scit
dissolui: quod si immortalis nostra foret mens,
non tam se moriens dissolui conquereretur,
sed magis ire foras uestemque relinquere, ut anguis.
   Denique cur animi numquam mens consiliumque   615
gignitur in capite aut pedibus manibusue, sed unis
sedibus et certis regionibus omnibus haeret,
si non certa loca ad nascendum reddita cuique
sunt et ubi quicquid possit durare creatum
atque ita multimodis partitis artubus esse,   620
membrorum ut numquam exsistat praeposterus ordo?
usque adeo sequitur res rem neque flamma creari
fluminibus solitast neque in igni gignier algor.
   Praeterea si immortalis natura animaist
et sentire potest secreta a corpore nostro,   625

596 cadere omnia corpore membra *c*: cadere omnia membra *OQV*: cadere omnia
membra colore *Winckelmann, fort. recte*: trunco cadere omnia membra *Lachmann*
597 peribetur *Q'*: peribet *QV*: periberet *O*   609 superas *Q'*: supera *OQ*: superae
V   611 alios *O*: alius *QV*: uarios *Winckelmann, fort. recte*   *post u.* 619 *lacunam statuit Munro*   620 ita *c*: ta *OQV*   partitis *Parrhasius, ut uid.*: pertotis *OQV*:
perfectis *Lachmann*   621 ut *O*: om. *QV*   *post hunc u. deficit V*   623 solitast
c: solita *OQ*   in igni *Q'*: insigni *OQ*   624 (= 670) immortalis *Q'*: mortalis
OQ   animaist *c, Q'*: animaest *OQ*

quinque, ut opinor, eam faciundum est sensibus auctam.
nec ratione alia nosmet proponere nobis
possumus infernas animas Acherunte uagari.
pictores itaque et scriptorum saecla priora
sic animas introduxerunt sensibus auctas.   630
at neque seorsum oculi neque nares nec manus ipsa
esse potest animae neque seorsum lingua neque aures:
haud igitur per se possunt sentire neque esse.
   Et quoniam toto sentimus corpore inesse
uitalem sensum et totum esse animale uidemus,   635
si subito medium celeri praeciderit ictu
uis aliqua ut seorsum partem secernat utramque,
dispertita procul dubio quoque uis animai
et discissa simul cum corpore dissicietur.
at quod scinditur et partis discedit in ullas,   640
scilicet aeternam sibi naturam abnuit esse.
falciferos memorant currus abscidere membra
saepe ita de subito permixta caede calentis,
ut tremere in terra uideatur ab artubus id quod
decidit abscisum, cum mens tamen atque hominis uis   645
mobilitate mali non quit sentire dolorem
et simul in pugnae studio quod dedita mens est:
corpore relicuo pugnam caedesque petessit,
nec tenet amissam laeuam cum tegmine saepe
inter equos abstraxe rotas falcesque rapaces,   650
nec cecidisse alius dextram, cum scandit et instat.
inde alius conatur adempto surgere crure,
cum digitos agitat propter moribundus humi pes,
et caput abscisum calido uiuenteque trunco
seruat humi uultum uitalem oculosque patentis,   655
donec reliquias animai reddidit omnis.
quin etiam tibi si lingua uibrante, minanti
serpentem cauda, procero corpore, utrimque

628 uagari *Gifanius*: uagare *Q¹*: uacare *OQ*   632 animae *Pius*: anima *OQ*
633 haud igitur *Lachmann*: auditum *OQ*   644 ab *Oˢ*: ad *OQ*   *post u.* 646 *dist.*
edd. nonnulli   650 rotas *c*: rote *OQ*   657 minanti *O*: *om. Q*: micanti *Lach-*
mann   658 serpentem…utrimque *Marullus*: serpentis…utrumque *OQ*: serpentem…toruum *Müller*   cauda *Oˢ* (*ut uid.*): caude *OQ*

sit libitum in multas partis discidere ferro,
omnia iam seorsum cernes ancisa recenti   660
uulnere tortari et terram conspargere tabo,
ipsam seque retro partem petere ore priorem
uulneris ardenti ut morsu premat icta dolore.
omnibus esse igitur totas dicemus in illis
particulis animas? at ea ratione sequetur   665
unam animantem animas habuisse in corpore multas.
ergo diuisast ea quae fuit una simul cum
corpore: quapropter mortale utrumque putandumst,
in multas quoniam partis disciditur aeque.
    Praeterea si immortalis natura animai   670
constat et in corpus nascentibus insinuatur,
cur super anteactam aetatem meminisse nequimus
nec uestigia gestarum rerum ulla tenemus?
nam si tanto operest animi mutata potestas
omnis ut actarum exciderit retinentia rerum,   675
non, ut opinor, id ab leto iam longiter errat:
quapropter fateare necessest quae fuit ante
interiisse et quae nunc est nunc esse creatam.
    Praeterea si iam perfecto corpore nobis
inferri solitast animi uiuata potestas   680
tum cum gignimur et uitae cum limen inimus,
haud ita conueniebat uti cum corpore et una
cum membris uideatur in ipso sanguine cresse,
sed uelut in cauea per se sibi uiuere solam
conuenit, ut sensu corpus tamen affluat omne.   685
quare etiam atque etiam neque originis esse putandumst
expertis animas nec leti lege solutas.
nam neque tanto opere adnecti potuisse putandumst
corporibus nostris extrinsecus insinuatas,

662 seque *c*: sequere *OQ*   663 ardentem *Brieger*   dolorem *Lachmann*   670
= 624   *post u.* 672 interisse et quae [*hactenus litteris uncialibus*] nunc est nunc
esse creatam (= 678) *O*: *spatium ii uu. relinquit Q*   674 operest animi *Marullus*:
opere animist *OQ*   676 a…longiter *Charisius, GLK I 204.14, Nonius Marcellus*
p. 828.17 L.: ab…longius *OQ*   680 solitast animi *c*: solita animist *OQ*: solitast
animae *Brieger, fort. recte*

quod fieri totum contra manifesta docet res: 690
namque ita conexa est per uenas uiscera neruos
ossaque, uti dentes quoque sensu participentur,
morbus ut indicat et gelidai stringor aquai
et lapis oppressus subito sub frugibus asper;
nec, tam contextae cum sint, exire uidentur   695
incolumes posse et saluas exsoluere sese
omnibus e neruis atque ossibus articulisque.
quod si forte putas extrinsecus insinuatam
permanare animam nobis per membra solere,
tanto quique magis cum corpore fusa peribit: 700
quod permanat enim dissoluitur, interit ergo.
dispertitus enim per caulas corporis omnis
ut cibus, in membra atque artus cum diditur omnis,
disperit atque aliam naturam sufficit ex se,
sic anima atque animus quamuis integra recens in   705
corpus eunt, tamen in manando dissoluuntur,
dum quasi per caulas omnis diduntur in artus
particulae quibus haec animi natura creatur,
quae nunc in nostro dominatur corpore nata
ex illa quae tunc periit partita per artus.   710
quapropter neque natali priuata uidetur
esse die natura animae nec funeris expers.
    Semina praeterea linquuntur necne animai
corpore in exanimo? quod si linquuntur et insunt,
haud erit ut merito immortalis possit haberi,   715
partibus amissis quoniam libata recessit.
sin ita sinceris membris ablata profugit
ut nullas partis in corpore liquerit ex se,
unde cadauera rancenti iam uiscere uermis
exspirant atque unde animantum copia tanta   720
exos et exsanguis tumidos perfluctuat artus?
quod si forte animas extrinsecus insinuari

690–4 *post u.* 685 *transp. Lachmann*   691 per uenas uiscera *Q¹*: uiscera per uenas
OQ   693 gelidai *c*: gelida *O*: gelidae *Q*   aquai *Q²*: aquae *OQ*   694 subito sub
MacKay: subsit si *A. C. Clark*: subsit si e *Bernays*: subitis e *OQ*   702 dispertitus
Lachmann: dispertitur *OQ*: dispertita *c*   enim *c*: ergo *OQ*   705 integra recens in
Marullus: est integra recens *Q¹*: est integra reces *OQ*   717 sinceris *OQ*: sincera
ex *Faber, Winckelmann, fort. recte*

uermibus et priuas in corpora posse uenire
credis nec reputas cur milia multa animarum
conueniant unde una recesserit, hoc tamen est ut   725
quaerendum uideatur et in discrimen agendum,
utrum tandem animae uenentur semina quaeque
uermiculorum ipsaeque sibi fabricentur ubi sint,
an quasi corporibus perfectis insinuentur.
at neque cur faciant ipsae quareue laborent   730
dicere suppeditat. neque enim, sine corpore cum sunt,
sollicitae uolitant morbis alguque fameque.
corpus enim magis his uitiis affine laborat
et mala multa animus contage fungitur eius.
sed tamen his esto quamuis facere utile corpus   735
cui subeant: at qua possint uia nulla uidetur.
haud igitur faciunt animae sibi corpora et artus.
nec tamen est utqui perfectis insinuentur
corporibus: neque enim poterunt subtiliter esse
conexae neque consensus contagia fient.   740
    Denique cur acris uiolentia triste leonum
seminium sequitur, uulpes dolus, et fuga ceruis
a patribus datur et patrius pauor incitat artus,
et iam cetera de genere hoc cur omnia membris
ex ineunte aeuo generascunt ingenioque,   745
si non certa suo quia semine seminioque
uis animi pariter crescit cum corpore quoque?
quod si immortalis foret et mutare soleret
corpora, permixtis animantes moribus essent,
effugeret canis Hyrcano de semine saepe   750
cornigeri incursum cerui tremeretque per auras
aeris accipiter fugiens ueniente columba,
desiperent homines, saperent fera saecla ferarum.
illud enim falsa fertur ratione, quod aiunt

---

723 priuas in *Nonius Marcellus p. 235.34 L.*, Q^I: priua si *OQ*   727 utrum *O*:
uerum *Q*   732 alguque *Nonius Marcellus p. 100.14 L.*: algoque *OQ*   734 contage e (*uel* ex) *dubitanter Wakefield*   736 cui *Bernays*: cum *OQ*: cur Q^I qua
Marullus: que *OQ*   738 utqui *Lambinus*: ut quicum *OQ*   740 consensus
Lachmann: consensu *OQ*   742 ceruis *c*: ceruos *OQ*   743 *del. 'doctus quidam'*
ap. Lambinum, seruato in u. 742 ceruos, *fort. recte*   patrius O^s, *ut uid.*: a patrius *OQ*
746 = 763, *q.u.*   747 quoque *O*: toto *Q*

immortalem animam mutato corpore flecti: 755
quod mutatur enim dissoluitur, interit ergo.
traiciuntur enim partes atque ordine migrant:
quare dissolui quoque debent posse per artus,
denique ut intereant una cum corpore cunctae.
sin animas hominum dicent in corpora semper   760
ire humana, tamen quaeram cur e sapienti
stulta queat fieri, nec prudens sit puer ullus   762
nec tam doctus equae pullus quam fortis equi uis.   764
scilicet in tenero tenerascere corpore mentem   765
confugient; quod si iam fit, fateare necessest
mortalem esse animam, quoniam mutata per artus
tanto opere amittit uitam sensumque priorem.
quoue modo poterit pariter cum corpore quoque
confirmata cupitum aetatis tangere florem   770
uis animi, nisi erit consors in origine prima?
quidue foras sibi uult membris exire senectis?
an metuit conclusa manere in corpore putri
et domus aetatis spatio ne fessa uetusto
obruat? at non sunt immortali ulla pericla.   775
    Denique conubia ad Veneris partusque ferarum
esse animas praesto deridiculum esse uidetur,
exspectare immortalis mortalia membra
innumero numero certareque praeproperanter
inter se quae prima potissimaque insinuetur;   780
si non forte ita sunt animarum foedera pacta
ut quae prima uolans aduenerit insinuetur
prima neque inter se contendant uiribus hilum.
    Denique in aethere non arbor, non aequore in alto
nubes esse queunt nec pisces uiuere in aruis   785
nec cruor in lignis neque saxis sucus inesse:
certum ac dispositumst ubi quicquid crescat et insit.
sic animi natura nequit sine corpore oriri
sola neque a neruis et sanguine longius esse.

759 *om. Q*   760 sin *Pontanus*: sic *OQ*   corpora *Q'*: corpore *OQ*   763 = 746,
del. Lachmann   764 pullus *c*: paulus *OQ*   770 ~ 5.847   775 immortali *O'*:
iam mortali *OQ*   784–96 = 5.128–40   784 in alto] salso *Lachmann, coll.* 5.128
789 longiter *Lambinus; cf. adn. ad u.* 676

quod si posset enim, multo prius ipsa animi uis   790
in capite aut umeris aut imis calcibus esse
posset et innasci quauis in parte soleret,
tandem in eodem homine atque in eodem uase manere.
quod quoniam in nostro quoque constat corpore certum
dispositumque uidetur ubi esse et crescere possit   795
seorsum anima atque animus, tanto magis infitiandum
totum posse extra corpus durare genique.
quare, corpus ubi interiit, periisse necessest
confiteare animam distractam in corpore toto.
quippe etenim mortale aeterno iungere et una   800
consentire putare et fungi mutua posse
desiperest. quid enim diuersius esse putandumst
aut magis inter se disiunctum discrepitansque,
quam mortale quod est immortali atque perenni
iunctum in concilio saeuas tolerare procellas?   805
praeterea quaecumque manent aeterna necessest
aut quia sunt solido cum corpore respuere ictus
nec penetrare pati sibi quicquam quod queat artas
dissociare intus partis, ut materiai
corpora sunt quorum naturam ostendimus ante;   810
aut ideo durare aetatem posse per omnem,
plagarum quia sunt expertia, sicut inanest
quod manet intactum neque ab ictu fungitur hilum;
aut etiam quia nulla loci fit copia circum,
quo quasi res possint discedere dissoluique,   815
sicuti summarum summast aeterna, neque extra
quis locus est quo diffugiant neque corpora sunt quae
possint incidere et ualida dissoluere plaga.
quod si forte ideo magis immortalis habendast,
quod uitalibus ab rebus munita tenetur,   820

790 quod] hoc *Marullus*   quid si posset enim? multo...*Lachmann*   792 et innasci *O*: enim nasci *Q*   794 in nostro *Lambinus*: nostro *OQ*   800 mortale *O⁵* (*ut uid.*): mortalem *OQ*   805 *om. Q*   saeuas *Marullus*: saluas *O*   806–18 = 5.351–63, *del. Bernays*   806 necessust 5.351   809 partis ut 5.354: partus et *O*: partusset *Q*   814 fit *ed. Bipont. 1782, Lachmann*: sit *OQ*   816 sicuti *OQ*: sicut (= 5.361) *c*   extra *Q¹*: exire *O*: ex ira *Q*   817 diffugiant] dissiliant 5.362   *post u.* 818 *lacunam statuerunt edd. nonnulli*   820 uitalibus] letalibus *Lambinus   post hunc u.* scilicet a uera longe ratione remota est *suppl. Marullus, post u.* 823 *Lambinus*: hoc fieri totum contra manifesta docet res *Bailey ex. gr. Cf.* 6.853

aut quia non ueniunt omnino aliena salutis
aut quia quae ueniunt aliqua ratione recedunt
pulsa prius quam quid noceant sentire queamus,

.   .   .   .

praeter enim quam quod morbis cum corporis aegret,
aduenit id quod eam de rebus saepe futuris   825
macerat inque metu male habet curisque fatigat,
praeteritisque male admissis peccata remordent.
adde furorem animi proprium atque obliuia rerum,
adde quod in nigras lethargi mergitur undas.

NIL IGITVR mors est ad nos neque pertinet hilum,   830
quandoquidem natura animi mortalis habetur.
et, uelut anteacto nil tempore sensimus aegri
ad confligendum uenientibus undique Poenis,
omnia cum belli trepido concussa tumultu
horrida contremuere sub altis aetheris oris   835
in dubioque fuere utrorum ad regna cadendum
omnibus humanis esset terraque marique,
sic, ubi non erimus, cum corporis atque animai
discidium fuerit quibus e sumus uniter apti,
scilicet haud nobis quicquam, qui non erimus tum,   840
accidere omnino poterit sensumque mouere,
non si terra mari miscebitur et mare caelo.
et, si iam nostro sentit de corpore postquam
distractast animi natura animaeque potestas,
nil tamen est ad nos qui comptu coniugioque   845
corporis atque animae consistimus uniter apti.
nec, si materiem nostram collegerit aetas
post obitum rursumque redegerit ut sita nunc est
atque iterum nobis fuerint data lumina uitae,
pertineat quicquam tamen ad nos id quoque factum,   850
interrupta semel cum sit repetentia nostri.

---

824 morbis *Auancius*: morbist *OQ*   aegret *Gifanius*: aegrit *OQ*   826 macerat
c: maceret *OQ*   835 oris *Gifanius*: auris *O*: auras *Q*   843 nostro sentit] sentit
nostro *Siebelis*   844 distracta est *c*: distractas *OQ*   851 repetentia *Q*: repentia
O: retinentia *Auancius, coll. u.* 675   nostri *Pius*: nostris *OQ*

et nunc nil ad nos de nobis attinet, ante
qui fuimus, neque iam de illis nos afficit angor.
nam cum respicias immensi temporis omne
praeteritum spatium, tum motus materiai   855
multimodis quam sint, facile hoc adcredere possis,
semina saepe in eodem, ut nunc sunt, ordine posta
haec eadem, quibus e nunc nos sumus, ante fuisse.   [865]
nec memori tamen id quimus reprehendere mente: [858]
inter enim iectast uitai pausa, uageque   860 [859]
deerrarunt passim motus ab sensibus omnes.   [860]
debet enim, misere si forte aegreque futurumst,   [861]
ipse quoque esse in eo tum tempore, cui male possit   [862]
accidere. id quoniam mors eximit esseque probet   [863]
illum cui possint incommoda conciliari,   865 [864]
scire licet nobis nil esse in morte timendum
nec miserum fieri, qui non est, posse neque hilum
differre an nullo fuerit iam tempore natus,
mortalem uitam mors cum immortalis ademit.

Proinde ubi se uideas hominem indignarier ipsum,   870
post mortem fore ut aut putescat corpore posto
aut flammis interfiat malisue ferarum,
scire licet non sincerum sonere atque subesse
caecum aliquem cordi stimulum, quamuis neget ipse
credere se quemquam sibi sensum in morte futurum.   875
non, ut opinor, enim dat quod promittit et unde
nec radicitus e uita se tollit et eicit,
sed facit esse sui quiddam super inscius ipse.
uiuus enim sibi cum proponit quisque futurum,
corpus uti uolucres lacerent in morte feraeque,   880
ipse sui miseret: neque enim se diuidit illim
nec remouet satis a proiecto corpore et illum
se fingit sensuque suo contaminat adstans.

852 et (&) *O*: te *Q*: ut *Susemihl, Heinze*   853 fuimus *c*: fumus *OQ*   neque *add.*
Lachmann: nec *Marullus*: om. *OQ*: nil *Merrill*: iam nil *García Calvo*: an nunc nil?
856 multimodis *c*: multimodi *OQ*   858 [865] *post u.* 857 *transp. Lachmann*
862 [861] misere si *Pontanus*: miserest *OQ*   864 [863] mors *Q¹*: mos *Q*: mox
O   probet *Lachmann*: prohibet *Turnebus*: prohibe *OQ*   868 an nullo *Pontanus*:
annullo anullo *O*: anullo anullo *Q*   871 putescat *c*: putes *OQ*: putrescat *c*   873
non *Q¹*: no *O*: nos *Q*   880 lacerent *c*: iacerent *OQ*   881 diuidit illim *O*: uidit
ilium *Q*

hinc indignatur se mortalem esse creatum
nec uidet in uera nullum fore morte alium se   885
qui possit uiuus sibi se lugere peremptum
stansque iacentem se lacerari uriue dolere.
nam si in morte malumst malis morsuque ferarum
tractari, non inuenio qui non sit acerbum
ignibus impositum calidis torrescere flammis   890
aut in melle situm suffocari atque rigere
frigore, cum summo gelidi cubat aequore saxi,
urgeriue superne obtritum pondere terrae.
'Iam iam non domus accipiet te laeta neque uxor
optima, nec dulces occurrent oscula nati   895
praeripere et tacita pectus dulcedine tangent.
non poteris factis florentibus esse tuisque
praesidium. misero misere' aiunt 'omnia ademit
una dies infesta tibi tot praemia uitae.'
illud in his rebus non addunt 'nec tibi earum   900
iam desiderium rerum super insidet una.'
quod bene si uideant animo dictisque sequantur,
dissoluant animi magno se angore metuque.
'tu quidem ut es leto sopitus, sic eris aeui
quod superest cunctis priuatu' doloribus aegris.   905
at nos horrifico cinefactum te prope busto
insatiabiliter defleuimus aeternumque
nulla dies nobis maerorem e pectore demet.'
illud ab hoc igitur quaerendum est, quid sit amari
tanto opere, ad somnum si res redit atque quietem,   910
cur quisquam aeterno possit tabescere luctu.
    Hoc etiam faciunt ubi discubuere tenentque
pocula saepe homines et inumbrant ora coronis,
ex animo ut dicant 'breuis hic est fructus homullis;

886 qui *c*: cui *OQ*   uiuus *O*ˢ (*ut uid.*): uibus *OQ*   887 se *add. c*: *om. OQ*: ipsum *Orth*   dolere *c*: dolore *O*: dolorem *Q*   893 obtritum *Marullus*: obrutum *OQ*   894 iam iam *c*: amiam *O*: uimiam *Q*   896 tangent *O*: tangunt *Q*   897 factis *Q*ʳ: facti *OQ*   901 ulla *Giussani, coll. u.* 922   902 quod *c*: quo *OQ*   905 *om. Q*   906 cinefactum *Nonius Marcellus p. 133 L.*: cinem factum *OQ*   907 deflebimus *ed. Brix. 1473*   908 e *Q*ʳ: et *OQ*   914 fructus *c*: fluctus *OQ*

iam fuerit neque post umquam reuocare licebit.'   915
tamquam in morte mali cum primis hoc sit eorum,
quod sitis exurat miseros atque arida torrat,
aut aliae cuius desiderium insideat rei.
nec sibi enim quisquam tum se uitamque requirit,
cum pariter mens et corpus sopita quiescunt: 920
nam licet aeternum per nos sic esse soporem,
nec desiderium nostri nos adficit ullum.
et tamen haudquaquam nostros tunc illa per artus
longe ab sensiferis primordia motibus errant,
cum correptus homo ex somno se colligit ipse.   925
multo igitur mortem minus ad nos esse putandumst,
si minus esse potest quam quod nil esse uidemus:
maior enim turba et disiectus materiai
consequitur leto, nec quisquam exspergitus exstat
frigida quem semel est uitai pausa secuta.   930
    Denique si uocem rerum natura repente
mittat et hoc alicui nostrum sic increpet ipsa
'quid tibi tanto operest, mortalis, quod nimis aegris
luctibus indulges? quid mortem congemis ac fles?
nam si grata fuit tibi uita anteacta priorque   935
et non omnia pertusum congesta quasi in uas
commoda perfluxere atque ingrata interiere,
cur non ut plenus uitae conuiua recedis
aequo animoque capis securam, stulte, quietem?
sin ea quae fructus cumque es periere profusa   940
uitaque in offensast, cur amplius addere quaeris,
rursum quod pereat male et ingratum occidat omne,
non potius uitae finem facis atque laboris?
nam tibi praeterea quod machiner inueniamque,
quod placeat, nil est; eadem sunt omnia semper.   945
si tibi non annis corpus iam marcet et artus
confecti languent, eadem tamen omnia restant,

---

917 torrat O^sQ: torret O: torres *Lachmann*: tortet *Romanes*   aridu' torror *Housman*:
torreat ardens *uel* arens *Butterfield*: torreat arda (*i.e.* arida) *Müller*   919 requirit
c: requiret OQ 921 soporem O: praemo Q 922 adficit *Lambinus*: adigit OQ
928 turba et *Goebel*: turbae OQ 935 si grata *Naugerius*: gratis OQ si gratis
fuit haec *Lachmann*   941 offensast *c*: offensost O^sQ: offensust *Lambinus*   942
male Q: mali O 943 facis *Auancius*: iacis OQ 945 placeat *c*: placet OQ

omnia si perges uiuendo uincere saecla,
atque etiam potius, si numquam sis moriturus':
quid respondemus, nisi iustam intendere litem   950
naturam et ueram uerbis exponere causam?
grandior hic uero si iam seniorque queratur   [955]
atque obitum lamentetur miser amplius aequo,   [952]
non merito inclamet magis et uoce increpet acri?   [953]
'aufer abhinc lacrimas, baratre, et compesce querellas.   955 [954]
omnia perfunctus uitai praemia marces;
sed quia semper aues quod abest, praesentia temnis,
imperfecta tibi elapsast ingrataque uita
et nec opinanti mors ad caput adstitit ante
quam satur ac plenus possis discedere rerum.   960
nunc aliena tua tamen aetate omnia mitte
aequo animoque annis agedum concede: necessest.'
iure, ut opinor, agat, iure increpet inciletque.
cedit enim rerum nouitate extrusa uetustas
semper, et ex aliis aliud reparare necessest,   965
nec quisquam in barathrum nec Tartara deditur atra;
materies opus est ut crescant postera saecla,
quae tamen omnia te uita perfuncta sequentur:
nec minus ergo antehac quam tu cecidere cadentque.
sic alid ex alio numquam desistet oriri   970
uitaque mancipio nulli datur, omnibus usu.
respice item quam nil ad nos anteacta uetustas
temporis aeterni fuerit quam nascimur ante:
hoc igitur speculum nobis natura futuri
temporis exponit post mortem denique nostram;   975
numquid ibi horribile apparet, num triste uidetur
quicquam, non omni somno securius exstat?
    Atque ea nimirum quaecumque Acherunte profundo
prodita sunt esse, in uita sunt omnia nobis.
nec miser impendens magnum timet aere saxum   980

---

948 pergas *Cipelli*   950 nisi *Marullus*: si *OQ*   952 [955] *post u.* 951 *transp.*
Lachmann   955 [954] baratre *OQ*: baratro *Naugerius*: barathro *Faber*: balatro
Turnebi amicus: blatero *dubitanter Merrill*: barde (*uett. edd.*) *uel* baro *M. F. Smith*
958 imperfecta *c*: imperfecte *OQ*   960 discedere *c*: discere *Q*: dicere *O*   962
annis agedum *Romanes*: agendum magnis *OQ*: agedum magnis *c*: *alii alia*   969
antehac *Cipelli, Heinze*: ante haec *OQ*

Tantalus, ut famast, cassa formidine torpens,
sed magis in uita diuum metus urget inanis
mortalis, casumque timent quem cuique ferat fors.
nec Tityon uolucres ineunt Acherunte iacentem
nec quod sub magno scrutentur pectore quicquam   985
perpetuam aetatem possunt reperire profecto:
quamlibet immani proiectu corporis exstet,
qui non sola nouem dispessis iugera membris
obtineat, sed qui terrai totius orbem,
non tamen aeternum poterit perferre dolorem   990
nec praebere cibum proprio de corpore semper.
sed Tityos nobis hic est, in amore iacentem
quem uolucres lacerant atque exest anxius angor
aut alia quauis scindunt cuppedine curae.
Sisyphus in uita quoque nobis ante oculos est   995
qui petere a populo fascis saeuasque securis
imbibit et semper uictus tristisque recedit.
nam petere imperium quod inanest nec datur umquam
atque in eo semper durum sufferre laborem,
hoc est aduerso nixantem trudere monte   1000
saxum, quod tamen e summo iam uertice rursum
uoluitur et plani raptim petit aequora campi.
deinde animi ingratam naturam pascere semper
atque explere bonis rebus satiareque numquam,
quod faciunt nobis annorum tempora circum   1005
cum redeunt fetusque ferunt uariosque lepores,
nec tamen explemur uitai fructibus umquam,
hoc, ut opinor, id est, aeuo florente puellas
quod memorant laticem pertusum congerere in uas,
quod tamen expleri nulla ratione potestur.   1010
Cerberus et Furiae iam uero et lucis egestas,

---

983 cuique *O*: cumque *Q*   985 quod *c*: quid *OQ*   988 dispessis *Turnebus*: dis-
persis *OQ*   992 est *Q¹*: es *OQ*   994 cuppedine *Pontanus*: cupedine *Q¹*: curpe-
dine *OQ*: turpedine *Oˢ*   995 quoque *O*: *om. Q*   997 tristisque *Q¹*: tristique *OQ*
999 sufferre laborem *Q¹*: laborem sufferre *OQ*   1001 e *add. c*: *om. OQ*   1007
uitai fructibus *O*: uita fructibus *c*: uitae runtibus *Q*   1008 ut *Q*: *om. O*   1009
congerere *Q¹*: cogere *OQ*   1010 nulla *c*: ulla *OQ*   *post hunc u. sunt qui Ixionis
mentionem desiderauerunt*   1011 egestas] egenus *ed. Ven. 1495*   *post hunc u. lacunam statuit Munro: post u.* 1012 *Bailey*

Tartarus horriferos eructans faucibus aestus,
qui neque sunt usquam nec possunt esse profecto.
sed metus in uita poenarum pro male factis
est insignibus insignis scelerisque luella,   1015
carcer et horribilis de saxo iactu' deorsum,
uerbera carnifices robur pix lammina taedae;
quae tamen etsi absunt, at mens sibi conscia facti
praemetuens adhibet stimulos torretque flagellis
nec uidet interea qui terminus esse malorum   1020
possit nec quae sit poenarum denique finis
atque eadem metuit magis haec ne in morte grauescant.
hic Acherusia fit stultorum denique uita.
   Hoc etiam tibi tute interdum dicere possis:
'lumina sis oculis etiam bonus Ancu' reliquit,   1025
qui melior multis quam tu fuit, improbe, rebus.
inde alii multi reges rerumque potentes
occiderunt, magnis qui gentibus imperitarunt.
ille quoque ipse, uiam qui quondam per mare magnum
strauit iterque dedit legionibus ire per altum   1030
ac pedibus salsas docuit super ire lacunas
et contempsit equis insultans murmura ponti,
lumine adempto animam moribundo corpore fudit.
Scipiadas, belli fulmen, Carthaginis horror,
ossa dedit terrae proinde ac famul infimus esset.   1035
adde repertores doctrinarum atque leporum,
adde Heliconiadum comites, quorum unus Homerus
sceptra potitus eadem aliis sopitu' quietest.
denique Democritum postquam matura uetustas
admonuit memores motus languescere mentis,   1040
sponte sua leto caput obuius obtulit ipse.
ipse Epicurus obit decurso lumine uitae,
qui genus humanum ingenio superauit et omnis

1013 qui] haec *Marullus*   1016 iactu' deorsum *Lambinus*: iactus eorum *OQ*:
iactu' reorum *Cipelli, Heinsius*   1017 lammina *Q¹*: iam mina *OQ*   1018 facti *c*:
factis *OQ*   1019 torretque *O*: torreto *Q*: torquetque *Heinsius*: terretque *c, Wallis*
(*sed u. comm.*), *Lachmann*   1031 *del. Lachmann*   super ire *OQ*: superare *c, fort.*
recte   lacunas *Q¹*: lucunas *OQ, rec. Lachmann*   1033 fudit *Pontanus*: fugit *OQ*
1038 potitus *c*: potius *OQ*   1039 matura *Q*: natura *O*   1041 leto] Leto *S. B.*
Smith   1042 obit *c*: obiit *OQ*   limite *Pius in notis*

restinxit, stellas exortus ut aetherius sol.
tu uero dubitabis et indignabere obire,   1045
mortua cui uita est prope iam uiuo atque uidenti,
qui somno partem maiorem conteris aeui
et uigilans stertis nec somnia cernere cessas
sollicitamque geris cassa formidine mentem
nec reperire potes tibi quid sit saepe mali, cum   1050
ebrius urgeris multis miser undique curis
atque animi incerto fluitans errore uagaris?'
   Si possent homines, proinde ac sentire uidentur
pondus inesse animo quod se grauitate fatiget,
e quibus id fiat causis quoque noscere et unde   1055
tanta mali tamquam moles in pectore constet,
haud ita uitam agerent ut nunc plerumque uidemus
quid sibi quisque uelit nescire et quaerere semper
commutare locum quasi onus deponere possit.
exit saepe foras magnis ex aedibus ille,   1060
esse domi quem pertaesumst, subitoque reuertit
quippe foris nilo melius qui sentiat esse.
currit agens mannos ad uillam praecipitanter,
auxilium tectis quasi ferre ardentibus instans;
oscitat extemplo, tetigit cum limina uillae,   1065
aut abit in somnum grauis atque obliuia quaerit
aut etiam properans urbem petit atque reuisit.
hoc se quisque modo fugit, at quem scilicet, ut fit,
effugere haud potis est, ingratis haeret et odit
propterea, morbi quia causam non tenet aeger;   1070
quam bene si uideat, iam rebus quisque relictis
naturam primum studeat cognoscere rerum,
temporis aeterni quoniam, non unius horae,
ambigitur status, in quo sit mortalibus omnis
aetas, post mortem quae restat cumque manenda.   1075

1050 potes tibi quid *c*: potest ibi quod *OQ*   1051 multis *O*: *om. Q*   1052 animi *Lambinus*: animo *OQ*   incertus *Bentley*   1061 quem *O¹*: per quem *OQ*   reuertit *Pomponius Laetus*: recurrit *Orth*: refert se *Butterfield*: *om. OQ*   1063 praecipitanter *c*: praecipiter *O*: praecepiter *Q*   1068 fugit at *O*: fugit ad *Q*: fugitat *Madvig (sed cf. Sen. De Tranqu. Animi 2.24)*   1069 ingratis *Lambinus*: ingratius *OQ*: ingratus *Q¹*: ingratiis *c*   1073 temporis aeterni *c*: aeterni temporis *Q*: aeternitatem corporis *O*   1075 manenda *Lambinus*: manendo *OQ*

Denique tanto opere in dubiis trepidare periclis
quae mala nos subigit uitai tanta cupido?
certa quidem finis uitae mortalibus adstat,
nec deuitari letum pote quin obeamus.
praeterea uersamur ibidem atque insumus usque   1080
nec noua uiuendo procuditur ulla uoluptas.
sed dum abest quod auemus, id exsuperare uidetur
cetera; post aliud, cum contigit illud, auemus,
et sitis aequa tenet uitai semper hiantis.
posteraque in dubiost fortunam quam uehat aetas,   1085
quidue ferat nobis casus quiue exitus instet.
nec prorsum uitam ducendo demimus hilum
tempore de mortis nec delibare ualemus
quo minus esse diu possimus forte perempti.
proinde licet quot uis uiuendo condere saecla: 1090
mors aeterna tamen nilo minus illa manebit,
nec minus ille diu iam non erit, ex hodierno
lumine qui finem uitai fecit, et ille
mensibus atque annis qui multis occidit ante.

1078 certa quidem *Auancius*: certe equidem *OQ*   1082, 1083 auemus *Q*: abe-
mus *O*: habemus *O^s*   1084 hiantis *c*: hientis *O*: hientes *Q*   1085 fortunam
c: fortuna *OQ*   1088 delibare *c*: deliberare *OQ*   1089 possimus *O^s* (*ut uid.*):
possumus *OQ*   sorte *ed. Aldina 1500*: morte *Lambinus*   1090 quot *c*: quod
OQ   condere *O*: ducere *Q*

COMMENTARY

I. INTRODUCTION

1–30

Prooemium. Lucretius begins each book of the poem in the high 'pathetic' style (*genus grande, amplum, acre* (Kenney 2007: 93)); here and in Books I, V and VI, it takes the form of a panegyric on Epicurus (Introd. 10–11). Only here is he addressed in the second person. For a sensitive analysis of the verbal structure and imagery of these lines see Stokes 1975. L. may intend to suggest a contrast with the false revelations of mystery religions, also expressed through images of light and darkness (Richardson 1974: 26–9). Whereas initiates in those cults were sworn to silence about what they had seen, the revelation offered by Epicurus is freely displayed in his teaching and writings and in L.'s verse.

1–4 These opening lines are carefully structured to create and then fulfil expectation. The apostrophe announced by *O* is deferred by the intervening *qui*-clause and so gains in weight; the grammatical and rhetorical structure is articulated by the sequence of monosyllables *o – qui – te*, each beginning a verse. This simple structure (characteristic of L.'s technique: Kenney 1977b/1995: 29; 2007: 103–4) is complicated and enriched by anticipation and enjambment (*extollere…potuisti, tuis…signis*) and by 'theme and variation', *sequor* being expanded in what follows. As throughout the Prooemium and indeed the whole poem the emotional impact is reinforced by alliteration. The whole style and feeling of L.'s address to Epicurus is hymnic, implicitly anticipating the explicit identification of 5.8 *deus ille fuit, deus.* Cf. 9–10nn.   **O:** this, the reading of OV, and not the humanist conjecture *e*, is certainly what L. wrote. The sonorous interjection matches the emotional tone of the passage better than the prosaic (indeed superfluous) preposition (Timpanaro 1960/1978) and imparts 'an elevated note appropriate to prayer' (N–H 364 on Hor. *C.* 1.32.13). In introducing his invocation of Epicurus L. was following normal poetic usage by prefacing it with *o* (Clarke 1977); he uses the word very sparingly elsewhere, either with a vocative, as at 206 *o bone* (n.) or exclamatory accusative, as at 2.14, 5.1194.   **tenebris** may be read as local or separative ablative, 'in/out of the midst of darkness', or dative of 'disadvantage', 'so as to put the darkness to flight' (not that a Roman reader would have stopped to ponder these alternatives); for the first possibility cf. Cic. *Sull.* 40 *in tantis tenebris erroris et inscientiae clarissimum lumen menti meae praetulistis.* This image was not Epicurean property, but L. deploys it with special emphasis, accentuated by the chiastic structure *tenebris tantis…clarum* *lumen.* If men could only be induced to think clearly they would *see* how baseless and irrational are their fears and hopes.   **primus:** it was Leucippus who was accounted the first of the atomists, but he is not mentioned in the *DRN*; it is Democritus who is honoured among the *repertores doctrinarum* along with the Master (1036–41); but it is Epicurus who ranks as *rerum inuentor* (9–10), completely laying bare the inmost secrets of Nature, and as the first mortal who dared to challenge superstition head on: *primum Graius homo mortalis tollere contra* | *est oculos ausus primusque obsistere contra* (1.66–7). *primus* connotes pre-eminence as well as chronological precedence (*OLD* 14a).   **illustrans:** the only other occurrence of the word in the poem is at 1.136–7 *nec me animi fallit Graiorum obscura reperta* | *difficile illustrare Latinis uersibus esse*; as Epicurus had shed light on the dark places of human ignorance and credulity, so L. aspires to illuminate the Master's often difficult teachings by his poetry: *obscura de re tam lucida pango* | *carmina* (1.933–4 = 4.8–9).

3–6 Graiae gentis decus: Epicurus is named only once in the poem (1042–4n.); the encomiastic periphrasis reflects the hymnic character of the Prooemium. *Graius,* not *Graecus,* is the form of the adjective preferred by the poets.   **ficta...signis** 'I plant my own footsteps firmly in the prints that you have made'; the phrases *ficta... uestigia* and *pressa... signa* are identical in meaning, emphasizing the fidelity with which L. will expound what Epicurus has taught. The image recurs at 5.55–7 *cuius ego ingressus uestigia dum rationis* | *persequor ac doceo...*; in his own mind's-eye exploration of the universe L. will follow him who *omne immensum peragrauit mente animoque* eqs. (1.74–9).   **ficta:** the original and correct form of the past participle (*OLD figo* headn.).   **non ita** 'less'. **quam...aueo:** i.e. *quam quod te propter amorem imitari aueo.*

6–8 The first of these comparisons would have been recognized by L.'s readers as originating in the literary tradition: Pindar (*Ol.* 2.87–8) compares rival poets to ravens screaming ineffectually at an eagle; and disparaging comparisons involving swans were a staple feature of Hellenistic interpoet polemic (Theoc. 5.136–7, 7.39–41, Antip. Sidon. *AP* 7.713.7–8 (*HE* 566–7)). Elsewhere in the poem L. uses a similar comparison, between a swan and a crane, to his own advantage (4.181; Kenney 1970b: 371–2/2007: 306). Here he chooses the swallow in self-disparagement, probably because for the Greeks the speech of barbarians (a category which for many would have included the Romans) seemed to resemble its twittering: χελιδονίζω = talk gibberish. The second comparison seems to be unique to L. Each is differently emphasized: the first by juxtaposing in enjambment the words *hirundo* | *cycnis,* the latter given additional emphasis by the metre, a spondaic word occupying the first foot of the verse (Bailey 1947: 111); the second by placing the key words *haedi* and

equi uis at the end of their verses.   **consimile ... et:** for the more usual
ac (*OLD et* 19a).   **fortis equi uis** (= 764) 'a mighty horse'; cf. 4.681,
6.1222 *canum uis*. The expression possibly suggested to L. by Cic. *Arat.*
57 *Equi uis*; but the model of Greek epic and tragic periphrases with βία
'strength' would have been familiar to him. Cf. 296, 645, 764, 790 and
nn.

9–10 tu ... tu ... tuisque: the repetition is characteristic of a hymn to a
deity, as in the invocation to Venus at 1.6–9 *te, dea, te fugiunt uenti, te nubila
caeli* | *aduentumque tuum, tibi suauis daedala tellus* | *summittit flores, tibi rident
aequora ponti*, Callim. *Hymn* 1.6–7 to Zeus. See N–H 131 on Hor. *C.* 1.10.9.
pater is best taken as vocative rather than as a predicate, as the text is
commonly punctuated: it is a traditional form of address to a god (Appel
1909: 101–3). Cf. Stokes 1975: 94 n. 5.   **rerum inuentor** 'discoverer of
truth': *res* is how things – the Universe, as in the title of the poem (*OLD*
4a) – really are.   **tuisque ... ex, inclute, chartis:** the word-order adjective – preposition – noun is common in poetry, but the separation by the
vocative is unusual: cf. Manil. 4.605 *usque canes ad, Scylla, tuos* and Housman ad loc., citing no other example but this.   **inclute:** Memmius is so
addressed at 5.8, but the word is more commonly reserved for the gods;
so at 1.40 for Venus.   **chartis:** the writings of Epicurus possessed for his
disciples the character of sacred books (Introd. 1–2); cf. 12 *aurea dicta*.
Most have been lost. The groundwork of his system was set out in his Περὶ
Φύσεως (*On Nature*), L.'s principal source (Sedley 1998: 134–65). There
is ample evidence in the *DRN* to show that L.'s studies were by no means
superficial.

11–13 The comparison of the poet to a bee was a commonplace,
here dignified by the substitution of the doctrines of Epicurus in
place of conventional sources of poetic inspiration. The repetitions
omnia ... omnia ... aurea ... aurea, in identical places in the verse, contribute
to the hymnic feeling of the passage. Syntactically and functionally, however, they differ: the first repetition makes the factual point that L. has
neglected no part of the Master's teaching, the second is rhetorically
expressive in a way that is analogous to the pathetic repetition of proper
names in epic, as at e.g. Hom. *Il.* 2.870–1, Virg. *Aen.* 7.649–51, 10.180–1;
cf. Bailey 1947: 156. The repetition of *aurea* also creates a pause after
the first foot of line 13, so lending weight to what follows, enhanced by
the enclosing word-order and the interplay of endings in long and short
a (cf. Pearce 1966: 162–4). Cf. 4.789–90, 5.950–1. On *aurea* as connoting luxury and 'characteristic in ancient poetry of the divine ambience',
leading to the climactic image of Epicurus' *diuina mente* (15), see Stokes
1975: 95 and n. 9.   **libant:** cf. Virg. *G.* 4.53–5 *illae* (*apes*) *continuo saltus
siluasque peragrant* | *pupureosque metunt flores et flumina libant* | *summa leues.*

This early correction of the transmitted *limant* has been generally accepted by editors. In defence of *limant* see Smith 1985: 220–3; 1992: 188–9 ad loc. The strongest argument against *libant* is its alleged incongruity with *depascimur* (see below) in the apodosis of the comparison. However, the word does not imply that L. had studied his sources in a 'casual and superficial manner' (Smith 1985: 222). Though usually translated 'sip' (Munro, Bailey, Smith), 'savour' (Brown), 'sample' (Stallings), along with *OLD* (3, citing this passage), the sense of the word here is rather 'cull', 'select' (*OLD* 5). The *DRN* was not designed to present a complete picture of Epicurean doctrine, and L.'s treatment was necessarily selective, concentrating on the atomic theory that formed its basis. The comparison with bees images his aspiration to transmute Epicurus' prose into poetic honey: *sic ego nunc, quoniam haec ratio plerumque uidetur | tristior esse quibus non est tractata retroque | uulgus abhorret ab hac, uolui tibi suauiloquenti | carmine Pierio rationem exponere nostram | et quasi musaeo dulci contingere melle* eqs. (1.943–50 = 4.18–24). *limant* conveys a quite inappropriate implication: as a literary-critical term the word connotes improvement, the removal of blemishes (*OLD* 1, 2), surely the last thing L. would want to suggest.   **depascimur** 'we graze right down', *de-* intensive (*OLD* s.v.).

14–15 ratio tua . . . diuina mente coorta 'your philosophy, sprung from a divine mind': Orelli's correction of the transmitted *coortam* restores a characteristic Lucretian ploy, the reinterpretation of poetic myth for Epicurean ends. That L. is alluding to the miraculous birth of Athena, goddess of wisdom, from the head of Zeus, is clearly signalled by *uociferari*: 'the first thing Athena did after the leap was to utter a great shout' (West 1972: 212, comparing *Hom. Hymn* 23.6–9, Pind. *Ol.* 7.26–8). As her shout astonished and alarmed the gods, so Epicurus' resounding challenge put superstition and ignorance to flight: a good example of what has been well described as 'the "predatory" nature of Lucretius' relationship to myth' (Gale 1994: 5). That the picture of Athena's birth from the head of Zeus is inconsistent with the general belief, shared by Epicurus, that the chest was the seat of the intellect (140–2n.) does not invalidate the interpretation offered here, as argued by Brown (1997: 93 ad loc.) and Sedley (1998: 71 n. 46). This, L. is saying, is the story that has been handed down to us, *scilicet ut ueteres Graium cecinere poetae* (5.405; cf. 2.600); but though wisdom did indeed spring from a 'divine mind', it was not quite in the way that the poets have told it. Elsewhere, as at 2.644–5, the correction may be immediate and explicit; here it is delayed to 5.4–5, where Epicurus is hailed as the man *qui talia nobis | pectore parta suo quaesitaque praemia liquit* (Duban 1979: 38). L. explains the myth while 'demythologizing' it (Kenney 2007: 98–9). For further discussion of L.'s glorification of Epicurus by this rhetorical ploy see Duban 1979, 1982; Gale 1994: 200–7, and cf. 1042–4n. Defenders of the transmitted *coortam* both miss the point and strain the language. Given the well-known propensity of copyists to work on one line at a time, the corruption, with *naturam* preceding, was almost inevitable.

16–17 The light of revelation (1–4n.) pierces intellectual darkness: the vision of Epicurean *ratio* passes through the surface of what is visible to the human eye and sees (*uideo*) the hidden workings of the universe. The image in what follows is of clouds parting: cf. Juv. 10.3–4 *remota | erroris nebula*, Val. Max. 7.2 *ext.* 1a (the sentiment ascribed to Socrates) *etenim densissimis tenebris inuoluta mortalium mens, in quam late patentem errorem caecas precationes tuas spargis!* The image is certainly as old as Plato (*Alc.* 2 150d–e). Again, alliteration lends emphasis. **diffugiunt...discedunt:** L. is given to emphasizing his points by such reiterations of prefixes, and *di*(*s*)- is a particular favourite: see 435–7, 477, 539, 638–9, 702–4, 802–3, 815; and for other prefixes see e.g. 70–1, 179–80, 253, 335, 343, 454, 502, 600–1, 740, 845–6, 925, 929, 958, 963. **animi terrores:** *religio*, groundless fear of the gods, banished by the tranquil vision that follows; and fear of punishment after death, shown to be groundless by the revelation of what is really happening below the earth (25–7). Conventional notions of Hell will be given the *coup de grâce* at length presently (978–1023). **moenia mundi:** the limits of our world, figured as ramparts stormed and carried by Epicurus in a magnificently aggressive series of images at 1.72–7 *ergo uiuida uis animi peruicit, et extra | processit longe flammantia moenia mundi | atque omne immensum peragrauit mente animoque* eqs. Cf. Sykes Davies 1931–2: 34; West 1969/1994: 57–63; Kenney 1974a: 19–24. **inane:** τὸ κενόν, the void; 'it is this knowledge that the universe depends on the eternal working of the atomic laws which refutes the belief in divine interference' (Bailey 1947: 1990 ad loc.).

18–22 According to the Epicureans, the gods lived in the spaces (μετακόσμια, *intermundia*) between the worlds (κόσμοι, *mundi*). There, in complete detachment, they exist beautifully; they do not and cannot interfere with the affairs of men. This is the first of the 'Sovereign Maxims' (Κύριαι Δόξαι) attributed to Epicurus (D.L. 10.139). Such influence as they do exert is passive, through a process over which they have no control, their appearance to men in dreams in the form of the *simulacra* (εἴδωλα), the atomic films constantly emitted from the surface of their bodies (5.1169–82). These self-sufficient gods were understandably much derided by rival schools. L. depicts their existence in a picture modelled on Homer's description of life on Olympus: *Od.* 6.42–6 ὅθι φασὶ θεῶν ἕδος ἀσφαλὲς αἰεὶ | ἔμμεναι· οὔτ' ἀνέμοισι τινάσσεται οὔτε ποτ' ὄμβρωι | δεύεται οὔτε χιὼν ἐπιπίλναται, ἀλλὰ μάλ' αἴθρη | πέπταται ἀνέφελος, λευκὴ δ' ἐπιδέδρομεν αἴγλη· | τῶι ἔνι τέρπονται μάκαρες θεοὶ ἤματα πάντα, 'where evermore they say the seat of the gods stays sure: for the winds shake it not, nor is it wetted by rain, nor approached by any snow. All around stretches the cloudless firmament, and a white glory of sunlight is diffused about its walls. There the blessed gods are happy all their days' (T. E. Lawrence). As at lines 14–15 (n.) L. draws on poetic myth to make an ironical point: the serene detachment of the (real) Epicurean gods contrasts pointedly with the turbulent life of Olympus as portrayed by Homer elsewhere and the (usually disastrous) interference of his gods in human affairs (Gale 1994: 111). **apparet** marks the culmination of the vision: 'l'apparition a quelque chose de miraculeux' (Ernout–Robin ad loc.).   **numen** suggests a paradox: it is the divine majesty (*OLD* 4) of these gods that is displayed, not their power to control (2, 3), for they have none.   **quietae:** more pointed than Homer's ἀσφαλές, 'immovable'; cf. 19–20.

19–22 Homer's picture is enriched and particularized by a series of vivid descriptive strokes heightened by alliteration, which throw into relief the serenity of these gods, secured against all such assaults (West 1969/1994: 31–3). The expansion of Homer's λευκή...αἴγλη, 'white splendour', into *large diffuso lumine ridet* picks the image which opens the poem (1–4n.) and returns to the idea, now literally illuminated, of the opening vision in *apparet*.   **semperque** 'but for ever', the metrically necessary *-que* adversative (Bömer on Ov. *Met.* 3.524).   **innubilus:** attested nowhere else and evidently coined by L. to render Homer's ἀνέφελος.   **integit...ridet:** on this type of enclosing word-order see Pearce 1966: 160; and for *ridet* cf. 1.9 (cit. 9–10n.), *OLD* 3. So in English we speak of a 'smiling' landscape.

23–4 An expansion in Epicurean terms of the Homeric τέρπονται, 'rejoice': these gods are self-sufficient, needing nothing and untouched by what happens in the *mundi*, which they neither inhabit nor frequent. **omnia suppeditat...natura** may hint that L. is skating round a problem with which he was presumably conversant, though extant Epicurean sources supply no specific solution: how, being themselves composed of atoms, do these gods achieve immunity from the effects of the ceaseless battering of other atoms to which all atomic compounds are exposed (819–29n.)? The problem is crisply summarized by Cotta at Cic. *ND* 1.114 *nec tamen uideo quo modo non uereatur iste deus beatus ne intereat, cum sine ulla intermissione pulsetur agiteturque atomorum incursione sempiterna, cumque ex ipso imagines semper afluant*; cf. Dyck ad loc. On suggested explanations see Rist 1972: 149–51. Such uncertainties exemplify the difficulties that Epicurus bequeathed to his successors by letting gods into his otherwise logical universe in the first place, albeit 'as suspicious characters and under promise of good behaviour' (Murray 1935: 129). Cf. Long and Sedley 1987: I 145–9, arguing that for him 'Gods, like giants, are thought-constructs', and Sedley 1998: 66 n. 2. Whether this was also what they were for L. does not appear from his text.

25–7 Epicurean *ratio* pierces downwards as well as upwards and outwards, and shows that there is no Underworld, only the regular workings of Nature as explained by the atomic theory.   **at contra nusquam appar-ent** 'what however does *not* appear anywhere…', picking up the open-ing word of the upward vision.   **Acherusia templa** (=1.120) 'the place of Acheron'. L. uses *templum* in a variety of senses (Bailey 1947: 620 on 1.120); here he seems to have borrowed from Ennius' *Andromacha, Sc.* 107–8 V.² (98 Jocelyn) *Acherusia templa alta Orci saluete infera*. Acheron (Latin *Acheruns*) was one of the rivers of the infernal geography, selected to signify the whole Underworld.

28–30 his…rebus (= 4.865) 'because of these things'; cf. 1.172 *hac re.* **ibi** 'then' (*OLD* 2a), sc. when I contemplate the vision of the universe as revealed by Epicurus.   **quaedam** 'what may be called' (*OLD quidam*¹ 3a), i.e. divine in the sense in which the word is used to describe or refer to Epicurus and his teaching, as at line 15 *diuina mente*. Cf. Giancotti 1989: 106.   **diuina uoluptas…atque horror:** a remarkable combina-tion. *diuina* may be felt as doing double duty, qualifying *horror* also; *uolup-tas*, unmixed pleasure, was the end of the Epicurean system (38–40n.), *horror* the awe inspired by manifestations of divinity (5.1165, *OLD* 6b). Cf. Boyancé 1963: 294, comparing a fragment of Aristotle on the θάμβος 'amazement' felt on contemplation of the ordered beauty of celestial phe-nomena. L.'s feelings are not those of a devotee in fear of the supposedly supernatural, but those of a rational being equipped with insight to pene-trate visible phenomena to a perception of the vast processes at work beneath. 'A man must be crass and unimaginative indeed if he can sim-ply study the intricacies of life, the movements of the stars, the intimate constitution of matter without feeling from time to time a sense of awe and astonishment…It would be difficult to find any great scientific man who had not been touched by this sense of wonder at the strangeness of things' (Huxley 1928: 269). In L.'s case, however, the qualification implied by *quaedam* is significant. The true pleasure which a disciple of Epicurus aims at achieving is engendered, not by unreflecting awe but by a cor-rect understanding of the natural laws that govern the workings of the universe, incidentally giving rise to the wonderful phenomena that stim-ulate curiosity. Gods have nothing to do with it.   **percipit…horror** 'a trembling seizes me'; cf. Plaut. *Amph.* 1118 *mihi horror membra mea percipit,* Pacuv. 224R.³ (*ROL* II 265) *horror percipit.*   **tua ui** (= 1.13): cf. 2.185, 5.206 *sua ui,* 1.728, 2.326 *uirum ui,* 5.252 *pedum ui.* L. ends a line with *uis* 17x. The metrical emphasis here reflects Epicurus' achievement in forc-ing Nature to reveal her secrets by the sheer power of his mind.   **mani-festa patens…retecta:** the pleonastic emphasis on revelation returns the reader to the point of departure at the beginning of the book, deploying the cyclic device of 'ring-composition', common in ancient literature from Homer onwards; L. habitually rounds off his paragraphs in this way: see e.g. 96 *hominis partem* ~ 131 *pars hominis*, 136 ~ 159, 161 ~ 175, *al.* This was an eminently practical technique in literatures which were intended to be heard – even when read silently – and it is not confined to poetry: see e.g. Ogilvie 1965: 769; Williams 1968: 808.

31–93

The subject of Book III is now announced: the fear of death and how to conquer it. This is the second of the *animi terrores*; the first, *religio*, has been dealt with in Books I and II (Introd. 10), the argument of which is summed up in lines 31–4. The fear of death can only be dispelled by a correct understanding of the nature of the soul (35–6), but it is on the destructive effects of this fear on human happiness that L. brings the full force of his emotional rhetoric to bear.

31–4 cunctarum exordia rerum [= 2.333, 4.45]; the atoms. L. rarely transliterates Greek technical terms (98–101n.); on the range of metaphorical paraphrases, shaped for metrical convenience (Kenney 2007: 95), to which he resorts (set forth at 1.54–61, though not including this one) cf. Sedley 1998: 38–9. The subject of the indirect question introduced by *qualia* in the next verse is brought forward: this is what the *DRN* is essentially about, the atoms. If their nature and behaviour is understood, the rest follows.   **sponte sua:** i.e. not through divine intervention but in accordance with their own laws as set out at 2.125–332.   **quoue =** *quoque*, as at 1.57. Commonly in early Latin and not infrequently in later writers -*ue* means 'and' rather than 'or' (H–S 505). Cf. 548–53n. *atque...* -*ue*, 147–51n. -*que*, 730–4n. *neque cur... quareue.*

35–7 hasce secundum res 'next', 'accordingly' (*OLD secundum²* 4, 5). **animi...animae** 'the mind...the vital principle'; the distinction will be developed at 94–116; see 94–7n.   **uidetur** 'it is clear that'; in L. *uideor* is generally to be read as passive, not deponent = 'seem', as at line 66 (n.). On his use of *uideo* and the insistent emphasis in the *DRN* on the role of sight in perception see Catrein 2003: 51–8.   **claranda:** an uncommon word, first attested in L. (*OLD* misleading: Enn. *Sc.* 326 V.², 274 Jocelyn exemplifies *clareo*). It picks up the opening image: as Epicurus had brought light into intellectual darkness, so his disciple L. will illuminate his often difficult doctrines by the clarity of his exposition: 1.933–4 (= 4.8–9) *obscura de re tam lucida pango | carmina* (Stokes 1975: 101–2). Cf. 87–93n. For the metre of line 35, with diaeresis and false verse-ending after the second foot, cf. e.g. 251, 353, 887, 1038. In this instance the effect is offset by the syntactical coherence of *res* with *hasce* preceding, enclosing

the phrase.   **foras praeceps ... agendus** 'bundled out neck and crop', a
vividly unceremonious turn of phrase. L.'s imagery is consistently physical
(Catrein 2003: *passim*), as in the personification of *religio* as a monster lowering over mankind at 1.62–79 (West 1969/1994: 57–63); cf. e.g. in this
book 38–40, 359–62, 525 and nn.

38–40 Fear of death disturbs human life and corrupts its pleasures. The
point is expressed in a remarkable image. Death is conventionally 'black'
(Ferber 1999: 23 s.v.); L. figures it as a noxious cloud of mud stirred
up from a well or spring of clear water, making it undrinkable. Cf. West
1969/1994: 3).   **liquidam puramque:** the same collocation at Cic. *Caec.*
78 *ita probata fides ut quicquid inde haurias purum te liquidumque haurire
sentias*; cf. *Fin.* 1.58, citing Epicurus: *quo minus* [sc. than a society at odds
with itself] *animus a se ipse dissidens secumque discordans gustare partem ullam
liquidae uoluptatis et liberae potest*. For *liquidus* = 'clear' of liquids and also
'pure', 'untroubled' of qualities and feelings see *OLD* 5a, 9, 10. Epicurus
taught that without an understanding of nature unalloyed enjoyment was
impossible: οὐκ ἦν ἄνευ φυσιολογίας ἀκεραίους [*liquidam puramque*] τὰς ἡδονὰς
ἀπολαμβάνειν (Κ. Δ. 12, 74 Usener).

41–7 Some deny that they fear death, appealing to 'common-sense' theories of the nature of the *animus*, but they deceive themselves. Here and
at 91–3 L. insists on the fundamental tenet that salvation was only to be
found within the faith (Introd. 1).

41–5 quod 'although', literally 'as to the fact that'; *quod* takes its semantic colouring from its apodosis, which begins grammatically at line 46 but
the sense of which is signalled by *idem* in line 48 (n.).   **ferunt** 'declare'
(*OLD* 33), more pompous than *dicunt* or *aiunt* would be, reflecting their
(false) confidence.   **Tartara leti** 'Death's infernal regions'.   **animi:**
probably used inclusively for the whole soul, *animus + anima* (94–7n.).
Wakefield commented 'i.e. *animae*', which he installed in the text, forestalling Lachmann, who however took it as dative. There is no compelling
argument either way; but Empedocles, fr. 105.2 περικάρδιον ... νόημα, 'the
blood around men's hearts' (Kirk, Raven and Schofield 1983: 311), tilts
the balance towards *animi*.   **sanguinis ... uenti:** genitives of material.
si fert ita forte uoluntas 'if that is where their fancy carries them'; though
such theories were seriously maintained by other schools, L.'s target is the
casually held views of those who prided themselves on their independence.
He insists that only a complete (Epicurean) comprehension of the workings of the material world can offer peace of mind (41–7n.). The wordplay in *fert ... forte* underscores the superficial character of their beliefs
(cf. 980–3n.). *si forte* is L.'s usual way of scornfully introducing a counterargument; cf. e.g. 533, 690, 722, 781, *al.*   **nec prorsum quicquam** 'nor

in any way whatsoever'; *quicquam* is adverbial accusative (*OLD quisquam* 5).
L. uses forms of *quisquam* with a negative (*OLD* 1a) 15x in this book. He
prefers the archaic *prorsum* (11x) to the much commoner *prorsus*.

46–7 hinc licet aduertas animum (= 181) 'from this one can perceive'
(*OLD animaduerto* 3c), here ironical following *animi natura*: if they *used*
their minds properly they would understand their nature. *hinc* here looks
forward = 'from what follows', *aduertas* is generalizing 2nd person present
subjunctive, as at e.g. 213 *cernas*, 370 *possis*, 854 *respicias, al.* (*NLS* 119).
Here, where the verb is in a subordinate clause, *licet* being effectively
a conjunction (*OLD* 1c), the subjunctive has to do double duty. The
reader is not directly addressed until line 135 *tu cetera percipe dicta* (n.).
laudis...causa '(merely) to show off', *laudis* emphasized by the enjambment.   **iactari** 'are bragged about' (*OLD* 11a); this is mere bravado on
their part, put on to conceal their fear of coming to terms with the facts.
probetur: subjunctive in a subordinate clause in indirect speech (G–L 650,
NLS 272).

48–86 L. appeals to contemporary experience. Rather than being sur-
prised by the 'vehemence and strangeness' of L.'s language (Bailey 1947:
993–4) we should remember that he lived at a time when the Roman
Republic was in its death-throes, and that exile, disgrace and judicial
and extra-judicial murder were part of the common experience of him
and his peers (Introd. 7). It is precisely the fact that his vivid imagination had these experiences to work on that transforms what might have
been no more than a string of philosophical commonplaces into lofty
and impassioned poetry. He would have been aware that Epicurus himself had endured exile: 'Nul n'a souffert plus que lui des bouleversements
politiques de l'époque' (Festugière 1968: 63); and, ironically, Memmius
himself was to go into exile in 52 BC to escape prosecution for electoral corruption (Fowler and Fowler 1997: x). The argument of the passage is firmly based on Epicurean doctrine (Fowler 1989: 135–40 and
n. 68/2007: 414–19 and n. 67).

48–50 These lines describe the *infamis uita* to which, according to their
protestations, they ought to prefer death.   **idem** 'but these are the
same men who...'; the word functions both as pronoun and, taking its
colour from the context, here practically = 'however' (K–S I 627–8). Cf.
OLD idem 10a, 121–2n.   **extorres...patria** 'banished from their native
land'; *extorris* + ablative of separation first attested here.   **conspectu ex
hominum:** for the placing of the preposition after its noun (anastrophe)
in phrases of this type cf. e.g. 140 *media regione in pectoris*, 463 *morbis in
corporis*, 1068 *tempore de mortis*, Catull. 69.6 *ualle sub alarum, al.* In such
phrases the genitive is syntactically equivalent to the attributive adjective

in e.g. 24 *tempore in ullo*, 114 *tempore in illo*, etc. (K–S 1 587–8). See also 66–7n. *portas... ante*, 374–7n. *quibus e*.   **denique** 'in the end', 'yet when all is said'; in spite of everything they cling to life.   **uiuunt** 'they go on living'; after the accumulation of words describing their woes, a surprise effect (what the grammarians called παρὰ προσδοκίαν, 'contrary to expectation'), emphasizing their perversity in not choosing the easy way out (Giancotti 1989: 423).

51–4 At the very time when, according to their professed principles, they should embrace extinction, they turn to attempts, by propitiatory sacrifices to the gods of the Underworld, to mitigate the rigours of the afterlife. Alliteration and the climactic placing of *religionem* underscore L.'s contempt.   **tamen:** take with *parentant*; to whatever straits they are reduced, they still persist in sacrificing.   **parentant:** properly used of sacrifice to the *di manes*, the departed ancestors.   **nigras...pecudes:** the correct offering to the infernal deities; on the connotations of *nigras* cf. 38–40n. **manibu' diuis:** 'the deified dead', a metrical version of the phrase commonly found in sepulchral inscriptions, *dis manibus*. For the elision of the final -*s* of *manibus* cf. in this book lines 905, 1016, 1025, 1038 and Introd. 18, Bailey 1947: 123–5. *Manes* generally signified 'the beneficent and worshipful rather than the maleficent and dangerous spirits of the dead' (Frazer on Ov. *F.* 5.421), but they still needed to be appeased (N–H 1970: 70 on Hor. *C.* 1.4.16).   **religionem:** pointedly ambiguous and to be read in mental inverted commas. As understood by these deluded devotees, *religio* meant the pious observance of religious duties; L. at the beginning of the poem had depicted it as a monster towering over (*superstans*) oppressed mankind, *horribili super aspectu mortalibus instans* (1.65); see West 1969/1994: 58–9; Kenney 1974a: 21. The point is driven home by the insistent alliteration of *a*. The 'long' (heavy) scansion of the first syllable is not arbitrary but testifies to an original prefix *red-* (Ernout–Meillet s.v.), reflected in the spelling *rell-*, attested, but generally avoided by editors. Cf. 642–56n. *relicuo*.

55–6 This has a proverbial ring; cf. Cato, quoted at Gell. 6.3.14 *aduorsae res edomant et docent quid opus siet facto*, Eur. fr. 237 Kannicht ἀλλ' οἱ πόνοι τίκτουσι τὴν εὐανδρίαν, 'it is trouble that makes it possible to achieve manliness'. It is allied to the commonplace that the true test of friendship is a friend's misfortune: Eur. *Hec.* 1226–7 ἐν τοῖς κακοῖς γὰρ ἀγαθοὶ σαφέστατοι | φίλοι, 'for it is in adversity that the good are most clearly revealed as friends', Enn. *Sc.* 210 V.², 351 Jocelyn *amicus certus in re incerta cernitur*, Ov. *Tr.* 1.5.25–6, 4.3.79–80, 5.5.49–50. See further N–H 1970: 397–8 on Hor. *C.* 1.35.26; Otto 1890: 21 s.v. *amicus* (6), 170 s.v. *ignis* (2); Sutphen at Haussler 1968: 131; Szelinski ibid. 232.   **in dubiis...periclis** 'in time of trouble and trial': *periculum* retains much of its original sense of 'test',

'trial', 'proof', as in the common phrase *periculum facere* (*OLD* 1).   **qui**
'what sort of man' (*OLD qui*[1] 2a).

57–8 Possibly suggested by Catull. 64.198 *quae* (sc. *querellae*) *quoniam uerae*
nascuntur pectore ab imo: cf. the list of 'apparent imitations' from the *Peleus*
and Thetis in Munro's note ad loc. Norden however suggested a common
source in Ennius (1934: 139 on Virg. *Aen.* 6.55 *funditque preces rex pec-*
tore ab imo).   **eliciuntur:** Gifanius' *eiciuntur*, adopted by Lachmann and
Munro, may seem to receive support from *nascuntur* in Catullus, but in this
context *elicio* is the appropriate word: the 'true utterance' is brought out
by external pressures, not expelled by forces within. Cf. Cic. *Deiot.* 3 *in qua*
quaestione dolor elicere ueram uocem possit etiam ab inuito. Contrast 497, where
eicio is the right word (n.).   **persona** 'mask', rather than 'civic dignity'
or 'social position', as argued by Farrington 1955.   **manet res** 'there
remains the reality'. This early correction has, *faute de mieux*, become the
received text. It has been questioned because it does not complete the
image of the torn-off mask, as might have been expected, but none of the
other attempts at correction, for which see Butterfield 2009, has produced
anything like so telling and forceful a conclusion to the verse. It 'satisfies
metre, sense and syntax so well indeed that it puts the modern conjectures to shame' (Reeve 2007: 210). The misreading of MANET RES as
MANARE by an inattentive copyist is indeed easier to account for than a
good many evident corruptions elsewhere in the *DRN* and other ancient,
or indeed modern, texts: 'The process of compilation [of the *OLD*] has
already yielded ... a file of all the known types of copying error, as found in
ancient manuscripts. The sheer randomness of some suggests that many a
famous textual crux may be strictly insoluble without knowing what irrelevant or lubricious thoughts were passing through the scribe's mind at the
time' (C. Driver, *The Guardian*, 2 May 1968).

59–86 The idea that avarice and ambition, with all their attendant crimes,
are motivated by the fear of death seems to be L.'s extension of the Epicurean theory that it was a desire for security (ἀσφάλεια = *stabilis uita*
(66)) that drove men to seek fame and status (K. Δ. 7, 73 Us.; cf. Cic.
Fin. 1.59–61). See also 65–73n. What lends L.'s exposition its peculiarly
urgent flavour is its contemporary reference: Heinze quotes a particularly
apposite passage from Sallust's *De coniuratione Catilinae*, published after 42
BC: 10.3–5 *igitur primo pecuniae, deinde imperi cupido creuit: ea quasi materies*
omnium malorum fuere, namque auaritia fidem probitatem ceterasque artis bonas
subuortit; pro his superbiam, crudelitatem, deos neglegere, omnia uenalia habere
edocuit. ambitio multos mortalis falsos fieri subegit, aliud clausum in pectore, aliud
in lingua promptum habere, amicitias inimicitiasque non ex re sed ex commodo aes-
tumare, magisque uoltum quam ingenium bonum habere. Whatever its historical
accuracy, this picture of a general moral decline in the late Republic, which

we meet also in Virgil and Horace, clearly reflects a widespread and pervasive perception and provides essential background to the understanding
of the *DRN* as a tract for the times. See Schiesaro 2007 on the Epicurean
implications of L.'s attack on 'the follies of a political system predicated
on the pursuit of honour, wealth and power' (49) here and at 2.9–16,
5.1123–35. 'All these [passages] identify the root cause of perverse social
pursuits in a misguided understanding of what is needed to attain a happy,
natural life' (49). See too Fowler 1989/2007: 414–21, arguing that 'the
role assigned [in this passage] to the fear of death is perfectly in harmony
with the Epicurean analysis of human motivation' (414).

59 auarities: avarice, traditionally one of the Seven Deadly Sins, has
tended in modern times to be generalized in terms such as 'the acquisitive
society'; ancient moralists, especially the Stoics, took it more personally. A
century and a half after L. Juvenal leads in to his denunciation of the vices
of contemporary Rome with *auaritia* (1.87). That it played a prominent
part in current thinking on what was tearing the fabric of Roman society
apart can be seen from the passage of Sallust quoted in the preceding
note; for its role in philosophy and satire see Rudd 1966: 314 s.v. Greed.

61–4 socios scelerum atque ministros 'as companions and accomplices in
crime', predicative. Unelided *atque*, generally avoided by later poets and
almost totally by the elegists, is used by L. 'freely as a metrical expedient,
one most convenient for the difficult task of transmuting Epicurean philosophical prose into Latin hexameters' (Butterfield 2008a: 392); of the
instances in the *DRN* 65 per cent (291/389) are in the fifth foot, serving to furnish the orthodox hexameter ending (ibid. 391). However, it
should be remarked that generally in these cases *atque* is used to link a pair
of nouns, adjectives or verbs (so in this book at 195, 804, 873, 891, 910,
1036, 1046, 1067; 179 the exception). This kind of phrasing can, as here,
impart weight and emphasis, a possibility to which Virgil was alive, as can be
seen in such a line as *Aen.* 6.622 *fixit leges pretio atque refixit.*   **noctes atque
dies** [= 2.12]: here too this usage is expressive, as Virgil recognized by
appropriating the phrase in the Sibyl's address to Aeneas, *noctes atque dies
patet atri ianua Ditis* (*Aen.* 6.127 and Austin ad loc.).   **uulnera** 'sores'; cf.
5.1196–7, where the word is similarly used of the irrational fears that nag
at men's minds because they misinterpret natural phenomena.   **non
minimam partem** 'in no small measure', emphatic litotes (327–30n.). For
the adverbial accusative 'of the part affected' (G–L 134; Roby 1102) cf.
6.1249 *bonam partem,* 1259 *nec minimam partem.*

65–73 The real *dulcis stabilisque uita* is the life of contented obscurity recommended in the famous precept Λάθε βιώσας, 'live so that no one will
ever know that you have lived' (Us. 551). To this truth, says L., men are

generally (*OLD fere* 3a) blind, seeing the lack of wealth and fame as next door to death. Their reluctance to face the idea of dying, 'as it were lingering before death's door', contrasts with the ability of the Epicurean to face it with serene equanimity. They cannot bear the thought of having to quit this life before they have attained what they see falsely as the security and enjoyment that wealth and fame, however acquired, bring with them. Their frame of mind is thus analogous to that of the hedonists pilloried at 955–62 (nn.); see Brown ad loc.

66–7 semota … uidentur: Lambinus' correction regularizes both sense and syntax, making *semota* neuter plural qualifying two nouns of different gender (136–9n.). The transmitted text, generally kept by modern editors, makes *uidetur*, for no good reason, qualify *egestas* grammatically but refer in sense also to *contemptus*.   **uidentur:** here = 'seem'; cf. 35–7n. **leti portas:** the image goes back to Homer (*Il.* 5.646, 9.312, 23.71), but L. could also have met it in a quotation from Theognis in Epicurus' letter to Menoeceus (D.L. 10.126). It was to be memorably developed by Virgil, who populates the anteroom to Hades with Grief, Cares, Sickness, Old Age, Fear, Hunger, Poverty and other fearful apparitions (*Aen.* 6.273–81). **portas … ante:** the postponement (anastrophe) of disyllabic and polysyllabic prepositions to follow their nouns (more usually in juxtaposition) is not uncommon in both prose and poetry (K–S I 586–7). See also 48–50n. **cunctarier:** the archaic form of the present infinitive, used freely (48x) by L. for metrical convenience (Bailey 1947: 84); in this book at 263 *secernier*, 443 *cohiberier*.

68–9 se … effugisse … remosse: it is the idea of escape from death rather than from oneself (1068–9n.) that is relevant here; *se* does double grammatical duty, functioning both as the subject of the two infinitives and as the object of *remosse*. This type of construction, styled ἀπὸ κοινοῦ ('in common'), is a form of ellipse, in which the sense of a word or phrase is felt as applying to more than one part of a compound expression (see H–S 834–6; Leo 1960: I 71–122; Kenney 1958: 55; Mayer 1994: 25–8). Other instances at 102–5, 264, 267, 288, 424, 633 (nn.). The ancient grammarians did not distinguish this usage from what was termed 'amphibole' (*OLD amphibolia* 'double meaning, ambiguity'; Bell 1923: 293–303), and in practice the distinction is not always easy to make. Accordingly in this edition relevant passages are listed in the index without discrimination. For the construction of *uolo* with accusative and infinitive in place of the usual prolative infinitive cf. 5.1120 *claros homines uoluerunt se atque potentes*, sc. *esse*; and see K–S I 714–15.   **longe longeque:** the words refer respectively to *effugisse* and *remosse*; for the chiastic structure cf. 2.106 *dissiliunt longe longeque recursant*, 6.690–1, and with other adverbs 3.286 *seorsum seorsumque*, 457 *pariter pariterque*. For intensive *longe longeque*, 'very far', cf. e.g. Cic. *Fin.* 2.68, Hor. *Sat.* 1.6.18, Ov. *Met.* 4.325, *al.* (*TLL longus* 1651.64–70).

70–1 sanguine ciuili 'by the blood of fellow citizens'. L. had lived through the Sullan proscriptions of 82–81 BC, in which some 500 of his political enemies were arbitrarily put to death; cf. Sellar 1889: 290.   **conflant** 'rake together' (*OLD* 7a); they are none too scrupulous about how their wealth is acquired.   **conduplicant … accumulantes:** the weighty words framing the line equate the amassing of wealth with the amassing of murders: misguided ambition is the way to death.

72–3 'C'est du Salluste en vers' (Martha 1867: 188). Writers moralizing on these troubled times repeatedly lament their effects on the ties of family and kinship. It is a favourite theme of Horace's (N–H 1970: 399 on *C.* 1.35.34), and a century later was to obsess Lucan. Virgil clearly had this passage in mind when he wrote:

> hic petit excidiis urbem miserosque penatis,
> ut gemma bibat et Sarrano dormiat ostro;
> condit opes alius defossoque incubat auro;
> hic stupet attonitus rostris, hunc plausus hiantem
> per cuneos geminatus enim plebisque patrumque
> corripuit; gaudent perfusi sanguine fratrum,
> exilioque domos et dulcia limina mutant
> atque alio patriam quaerunt sub sole iacentem.
>   (*G.* 2.505–12)

However, the conviction that ever since the Golden Age the human race had been in perpetual moral decline was a poetical commonplace going back to Homer and Hesiod: see Fordyce on Catull. 64.384–407. **fratris:** Macrobius' citation is 'non–specific', i.e. it is not this word that he is concerned to illustrate (cf. 94–7n. *quam*); the distinction, not always sufficiently appreciated by critics, is drawn by Housman (*CP*801). *fratris*, however, gives obviously more pointed sense than *fratres*, and is supported by Virgil's adaptation of the passage; *fratris* became *fratres* after *crudeles* preceding by 'perseveration' (cf. Reynolds and Wilson 2014: 232–3); cf. 14–15n. *ad fin.*   **consanguineum:** for *consanguineorum*, intractable even in Lucretian hexameters; the old form of the genitive plural survives in *diuum* (23x in the *DRN*), *deum* (22), *uirum* (10).   **mensas odere timentque:** *sc.* for fear of poison, but the words also recall a famous passage from Accius' tragedy *Atreus, oderint | dum metuant* (202–3 R.³, *ROL* II 168), uttered by Atreus, who murdered the children of his brother Thyestes and served them up at dinner (Fowler and Fowler 1997: 273 ad loc.). Seneca later commented *Sullano scias saeculo scriptum* (*De ira* 1.20.4).

74–7 ab 'as a result of' (*OLD* 15).   **macerat … illum esse potentem, |
illum aspectari:** *macerat inuidia* is syntactically equivalent to 'they are envi-
ous that'; for the construction and the sentiment cf. Plaut. *Bacch.* 543 *nullus est quoi non inuideant rem secundam optingere, Truc.* 745 *nam inuidere alii
bene esse, tibi male esse, miseria est.* Lachmann, followed by Munro, punctuated after *inuidia*, making all the indirect statements dependent on
queruntur in line 77; but L. wrote for readers of an unpunctuated text,
who would be expected to puctuate by ear as they read, and in the
absence of guidance in the phrasing would not pause after *inuidia* in the
expectation of a change of construction. On the 'linearity' of L.'s writing see Introd. 20–1.   **illum … illum:** not 'this man … that man', ἄλλον
μέν … ἄλλον δέ, but anaphora conveying the ambitious man's obsession
with his rival's success: '*he … he …* not I'.   **aspectari** 'is respected' (*OLD*
2a).   **ipsi:** Winckelmann's *ipsos* adds emphasis and deserves consideration; when used in this way the word usually follows *se* or *suus*, but here
the responsion with *illum* would demand that it begin the verse.   **in
tenebris … caenoque** 'in the obscurity of the gutter', 'in squalid obscurity',
hendiadys. For *caenum* used metaphorically see *OLD* 3, Otto 1890 s.v. (2).

78 intereunt partim 'some die' (*OLD partim* 1a), *sc.* on the battlefield in
quest of fame, or murdered in their quest of it by a potential rival.   **statuarum et nominis ergo:** L.'s almost Juvenalian formulation condenses
Enn. *Ann.* 404–5 Sk. *reges per regnum statuasque sepulcraque quaerunt, | aedifi-
cant nomen*; the archaic preposition *ergo* (= *causa*) lends additional weight
and dignity. According to a scholiast on K. Δ. 29 (77–8 Us.), Epicurus cited
crowns and statues as unnecessary and unnatural objects of desire; but
scorn of such trappings is not specifically Epicurean.

79–84 The paradox that men will kill themseles through fear goes back
to Democritus, who observed that in attempting to avoid death men pur-
sued it, ἄνθρωποι θάνατον φεύγοντες διώκουσιν (fr. 68 B 203 D–K). Seneca
ascribes the sentiment to Epicurus: *dicit 'quid tam ridiculum quam appetere
mortem, cum uitam inquietam tibi feceris metu mortis?'* (*Ep.* 24.23). The fear
of death is not a rational motive for seeking it: *stultitia est terrore mortis mori*
(*Ep.* 70.8). To quit life because life has become insupportable is a different
matter (940–9, 940–3nn.).

80 humanos = *homines*, as at 817, an exclusively Lucretian usage: Ov. *F.*
2.503 *pulcher et humano maior* is not strictly parallel.

82–4 These lines as transmitted, if *suadet* (84) be ignored, can be read as
a syntactical whole, with the anaphoric *hunc … hunc … hunc* functioning
both connectively and emphatically. The reader interpreting his text by ear
(74–7n.) will thus take all the infinitives *esse … uexare … rumpere … euertere*
as parallel, with the last limb of the utterance as a climactic summary.
Hence *suadet* cannot be taken as governing *euertere* and must be corrupt.

None of the suggested corrections carries overwhelming conviction, and Lambinus' *fundo*, 'utterly' (*OLD fundus* 1d), is adopted *exempli gratia*. Bailey's *summa... sede*, though subsequently withdrawn by its author, deserves consideration. The alternative approach, adopted by Munro and followed by Brown, is to keep *suadet* and posit a lacuna after 82; see critical note. The middle course of keeping *suadet* and punctuating strongly after 82, adopted by Bailey and Smith, gets the worst of both worlds: conventions of punctuation unknown to Roman writers and readers cannot be invoked to override basic grammatical and stylistic principles. No more convincing is the expedient adopted by Giancotti of keeping *suadet* and treating what follows *rumpere* in line 84 as an anacoluthon, leaving *suadet* without a subject to govern it (Giancotti 1989: 278 n. 28, 429).

83-4 Love of friends, family and country was a notable feature of Epicurus' character (D.L. 10.10); for a Roman these were primary loyalties. The catalogue of sinners in Virgil's Hell culminates in the traitors and the incestuous (*Aen.* 6.621-4). These are the lengths to which men may be driven by the fear of death.   **hunc...amicitiai:** apart from the weak caesura in the second foot, a non-caesural line, since the final syllable of *pudorem*, though elided, is nevertheless felt in reading (Soubiran 1966: 528-33); cf. 380, 395, 432, 770, 801, 836, and see further 102, 174, 186, 773, 976 and nn.   **uexare pudorem** 'to betray his honour' (Brown); cf. *OLD uexo* 6, *pudor* 2a, 3).   **amicitiai:** the archaic form of the genitive, freely used by L. (166x), both for metrical convenience and rhetorical effect (Bailey 1947: 75-7).

84-6 in summa: here, and here only in L. = 'in short', *denique* (*OLD summa* 7a). The first attested instance of this sense; elsewhere in the *DRN* = 'in the universe' (2.91, 1077). The alternative wording of the phrase, *ad summam*, found several times in L.'s contemporary Cicero, was ruled out here by the ambiguity which would arise from the juxtaposition with *pietatem*. **fundo:** first attested here = *funditus* (if indeed it is what L. wrote); cf. Virg. *Aen.* 10.88-9 *nosne tibi fluxas Phrygiae res uertere fundo* | *conamur?* **prodiderunt:** cf. 134 *transtulerunt*, 1028 *occiderunt*: the original quantity; the more familiar scansion in *-ērunt* probably represents a contamination between *-ēre* and *-ĕrunt* (Palmer 1954: 275).   **uitare...petentes** 'while they seek to avoid', the first attested occurrence of *peto* + infinitive (*OLD* 7c).   **Acherusia templa:** 25-7n.

87-93 A transitional passage, repeated in whole or part several times in the poem (see critical note); here it carries a particular emphasis from picking up the recurrent image of light dispelling darkness that informs the Proem (Stokes 1975: 102). The repetition of *nam* in line 87 so soon after *nam* in 85 may suggest that the verses have been inserted here *en bloc* without adaptation to their new context; cf. Bailey 1947: 1554 on

6.35–41. Such repetitions are not to be ascribed to poverty of invention. The essence of poetry, more especially of didactic poetry, is that it is memorable: the mother of the Muses is Mnemosyne. These identical or near-identical repetitions reflect L.'s desire to hammer home his message. The Founder had insisted on the need for his disciples continually to return to and memorize the central tenets of the faith (D.L. 10.35–6); and long before him Democritus had remarked that 'it is good to say twice what is necessary' (fr. 25 D–K). Cf. Gale 1994: 116–17; Kenney 2007: 94 and n. 13.

88–90 in tenebris...in luce: that such fears are childish was a commonplace, to which L. imparts a new twist by the emphasis on the opposition between darkness and light. Our bodies may be in daylight, but our minds remain in the dark. Diogenes of Oenoanda imparts a fresh twist to the cliché with his comparison of death to a 'mask that frightens small children' (Hammerstaedt and Smith 2011: 103–4).   **finguntque futura:** sc. *esse*, 'and imagine will happen' (*OLD fingo* 8b).

91–3 igitur: L. habitually rounds off an argumentative sequence with a summary conclusion introduced by an assertive conjunction: cf. 128 *igitur*, 175 *ergo*, 203 *nunc igitur*, 228 *quare* (n.), 323 *igitur*, 521 *ergo*, 830 *igitur* (830–69n.).   **animi:** to be construed ἀπὸ κοινοῦ with both *terrorem* and *tenebras*.   **lucida tela diei** 'the bright shafts of day'; the image provides a transition to the idea that these errors must be *attacked* with the weapons provided by Epicurean philosophy, as Epicurus had attacked the monster Superstition and returned from the campaign victorious (1.62–79). Metaphorical darkness will be assailed with the metaphorical weapons of reason.   **naturae species ratioque** 'nature's outward appearnce and its explanation' (Brown): *species* = the phenomena, *ratio* the workings of the atomic system which produces them (*OLD ratio* 12a). The two words span the process by which the enquirer must arrive at enlightenment. Throughout the poem L. can be seen implicitly or explicitly urging his readers to observe the world about them and to draw the appropriate conclusions. On the range of meanings of *ratio* in the *DRN* see Bailey 1947: 645–6 on 1.51.

II. ARGUMENT

A. THE SOUL IS MATERIAL

94–135

The *anima* is physically part of the body, not something abstract, a harmonious relationship of its parts, as argued by Simmias and denied by Socrates in Plato's *Phaedo* (85e–86d, 91c–95a). That this theory still had enough life in it to be worth refuting is suggested by the fact that Cicero found room for a brief discussion of it in the *Tusculans* (1.19–21). L. no doubt saw it as affording him a good target for his sarcastic rhetoric.

94–7 Primum 'in the first place' = *principio*.   **animum:** 'mind' may be used for convenience to render *animus*, but no single English term is wholly satisfactory. L. distinguishes *animus*, the rational part of the soul, from *anima*, the irrational part (117–20n.). In this he follows Epicurus, who considered the common distinction in Greek between 'mind' (νοῦς) and 'soul' (ψυχή) unsatisfactory, preferring to distinguish between two parts of the ψυχή, the rational (τὸ λογικὸν μέρος) and the irrational (τὸ ἄλογον μέρος). This is the distinction intended to be conveyed by L.'s use of *animus* and *anima*, corresponding to the two Epicurean 'parts'; the two are conjoined in 'one Nature' (136–7) to form the whole soul. That, however, leaves him with no one word for that whole corresponding with ψυχή. Thus he is forced either to couple the two or for the sake of brevity to use one or the other for the whole, as at 43 (n.), 143, 150, 275 (*anima*) and 169, 175, 237, 708 (*animus*). It is not until lines 421–4 (n.) that the point is made explicitly. It is not difficult to guess why he resorted to this expedient: a faithful Latin rendering of the Epicurean terms which would fit economically into hexameters would not be easy to devise. Cf. 228–30n. and see below on *saepe*.   **mentem quam saepe uocamus:** L. treats *animus* and *mens* as interchangeable, though in common usage *animus* embraced the emotions as well as intellect; cf. 139 (n.), 142, 398, 402.   **quam:** Charisius' citation is 'non-specific' (72–3n.), since what he is illustrating is the adverbial use of *primum*; however, L. regularly allows the attraction of the relative pronoun to the gender of its predicate, and the correction of MS *quem* to *quam* was made independently by humanist scholars on that ground; cf. 99–100, 1.834, 4.132.   **saepe** 'commonly', but strictly speaking inaccurately, since *animus* (= θυμός) embraces the emotions, whereas *mens* is properly the intellect. L. seems to acknowledge the point implicitly in such phrases as *mens animi* (4.758) or *animi ... mens consiliumque* (3.615) or *mens animusque* (3.130, 142, 398, 402); occasionally he uses *mens* alone = *animus* (3.101, 152, 228).   **consilium uitae regimenque** 'the rational and controlling power of life' (Brown), rendering the Greek terms τὸ λογικόν and τὸ ἡγεμονικόν.   **ac:** here for the more usual *quam* (*OLD atque* 15); cf. 1087–94n. *et.*   **manus ... oculi:** the fundamental doctrine is reinforced by L.'s insistent emphasis on the physical, what can be experienced, as fundamental to our understanding of the world: hands, feet, eyes can all be seen and felt, and the *animus*, though it cannot be seen, is every bit as corporeal as they are.   **animantis** picks up *animus* to underline through the etymological connexion the fact that the *animus* is an integral part of the living creature.   **exstant:** here, as commonly in L. (but cf. 193–4n. *exstat*), *exstare* is equivalent to *esse* (*OLD* 4).

After this verse one or more lines have fallen out; the sense must have been 'but there are some who hold that...'.

98–101 sensum animi 'the mind's power to feel'.   **certa** 'defined', 'particular' (*OLD* 3a); cf. 104.   **habitum quendam uitalem corporis** 'a sort of life-giving state of the body' (Brown). *uitalem* is glossed in what follows, *quod faciat nos | uiuere cum sensu*.   **harmoniam:** there are only two exceptions to the rule that L. avoided transliterating Greek technical terms: *harmonia* in this passage and in the otherwise unattested sense of sexual coupling at 4.1248; and *homoeomeria* at 1.830, 834 (Sedley 1999: 237–8). In both cases he is refuting a Greek theory, and the emphasis on its Greekness might well appeal to contemporary prejudice. However, whereas *homoeomeria* is otherwise unattested in classical Latin and is 'glaringly not at home in the Latin language' (Sedley 1999: 237) and embodied a theory which needed careful unpacking for L.'s readers, *harmonia* was a seminaturalized and relatively familiar musical term, also used by Cicero in his discussion of this theory (*Tusc.* 1.41; cf. *TLL* s.v. 2337.1–21) and offered a concept which it was relatively easy to grasp. L.'s rebuttal is to dismiss the term back to where it belongs, in musical not philosophical theory. The *patrii sermonis egestas* is here no more than marginally relevant (258–61n.). On the position that L. was attacking, most familiar from Plato's *Phaedo* (85ff.), see Bailey 1947: 1004–5, Ernout–Robin ad loc.   **Grai quam dicunt** 'as the Greeks call it'; on the attraction of the relative pronoun to the gender of *harmonia* see 94–7n. *quam*.   **quod faciat nos** 'which is supposed to make us...'; the subjunctive indicates that this is part of the indirect statement. **uiuere cum sensu** 'to live and feel'. For *facio* + accusative and infinitive = 'cause to' cf. 301; elsewhere in the poets Enn. *Ann.* 439 Sk., Lucil. 1270 M. (*ROL* III 1224), Virg. *Aen.* 2.538–9, Ov. *Met.* 7.691 and Börner ad loc., *al.* (*TLL facio* 115.37–116.69, K–S I 694). It is not uncommon in prose and was not avoided by Cicero (*Brut.* 142).   **nulla...in parte** 'in no defined part'; cf. 98, 104.   **cum** 'although' (*OLD cum²* 7b); cf. 106–11n. *cum.* **siet:** archaic for *sit*; also at 2.962, 1079.

102–3 Since the theory of *harmonia* was not empirically verifiable, recourse was had to analogy, here to that of health, more commonly to the musical analogy to be scornfully dismissed at 131–2. On L.'s employment of analogy as an argumentative tool see Schrijvers 2007. Scientists seeking to translate mathematical concepts into physical terms still resort to analogy: a famous example (subsequently overtaken by his General Theory of Relativity) is Einstein's depiction of space–time as an elastic sheet.

102 For the rhythm of the verse, with weak caesura in the second foot and strong caesura only in the fourth, cf. 122, 317, 525 (nn.), also 83–4n. *hunc...amicitiai.*   **bona...ualetudo:** *ualetudo* is most commonly used in the neutral sense = 'condition' (*OLD* 2) and so requires qualification to avoid ambiguity.

102–5 L. unceremoniously dismisses the analogy with health: good health is said to be 'of' the body in the sense that it belongs to and is inseparable from it, but it is not physically part of it.   **sic** appears to do double duty, picking up both the immediately preceding *ut* at line 102 and also the argument of lines 98–103, 'so on the basis of this belief…', a variant of the ἀπὸ κοινοῦ construction.   **mi** = *mihi*, in L. only here and at 1.924; cf. Austin on Virg. *Aen.* 6.104.   **magno opere** 'very greatly' (3x elsewhere); cf. 688 *tanto opere* (n.), *OLD* s.vv.   **diuersi** 'in all directions'; they are completely at sea.

106–11 As different parts of the body feel pain and pleasure independently of each other, so also do the body and mind (therefore the mind is part of the body). The argument is in the form of a syllogism, with the premisses presented in reverse order and the conclusion left to be inferred by the reader.   **in promptu quod cernitur:** echoing a fundamental Epicurean tenet, that the evidence of our senses is the only reliable guide to the truth: cf. 1.422–5, 699–70 *quid nobis certius ipsis | sensibus esse potest, qui uera ac falsa notemus?*, 4.478–521, D.L. 10.32, 52. Epicurus had specifically invoked this principle in discussion of the corporeal nature of the soul: it is what we can see and feel, τὰς αἰσθήσεις καὶ τὰ πάθη, that offers the only solid ground for belief, ἡ βεβαιοτάτη πίστις (D.L. 10.63).   **itaque** 'and so' (*OLD* 1).   **aegret:** *aegreo* is attested only here and at 824, where it is an easy correction of MS *aegrit*: the common word is *aegroto*. Here the grammarian's citation is specific. MS *aegrum* is in itself unobjectionable but would require the addition of *est* to make sense.   **cum** 'although', here with the indicative (*OLD cum²* 7c), as not uncommonly in L.; cf. in this book 146, 150, 645, 653. This usage is archaic (Lindsay 1907: 69–71, Bennett 1910, 1914: I 141–2). Cf. also 106–11n. *cum*, 359–64n. *praesertim cum*, 847–51n. *si*.   **parte latenti:** i.e. in the *animus*, contrasted with the visible parts of the body, those *in promptu*.   **retro…contra…uicissim** 'in turn the exact converse' (Brown), a striking and expressive tautology to focus on a crucial flaw in his opponents' case.   **ex animo** 'in the mind', as against 914, where it means 'in the heart', the more usual sense of the phrase (*OLD animus* 8b).   **in nullo…dolore:** the phrase *in dolore esse* seems to be unique in surviving literary Latin.

112–16 In sleep the mind is active though the body is not. The full explanation of the mechanism of sleep that is to follow at 4.907–1036 is here taken for granted.   **praeterea:** much favoured by L. (94x, 13 in this book) to emphasize or add an argument.   **onustum** 'heavy', weighed down by sleep; cf. 4.956 *sopor ille grauissimus*.   **aliud:** sc. the *animus*.

curas cordis: for the alliteration cf. e.g. 994, 6.645 *cernentes pauidi complebant pectora cura*. The use of *cor* possibly carries the implication, to be stated explicitly at 140 (n.), that the mind is situated in the chest.

117–20 The *anima* too is corporeal, consisting of particles of air and heat. **animam** 'vital principle'; translators resort for convenience to 'soul' or 'spirit', but see 94–7n. The distinction between *animus* and *anima* is now explicitly drawn.   **quoque … in membris** 'also in the body' (*OLD membrum* 2); unlike the *animus* it is diffused throughout it, *per totum dissita corpus* (143). It has a distinct physical existence; it is not a condition or relationship.   **neque harmonia** 'and not because of any "harmony"'. **sentire:** Wakefield's correction of MS *interire* turns out to have been anticipated by the humanist Francesco Bernardino Cipelli (?1481–1542): see Deufert 1996, and cf. 244, 321, 969 and nn.   **detracto corpore multo** 'even when much of the body is lost': *tamen* in line 120 shows that the participle has concessive force; cf. 171, 402–5, 441–2, 1036–8n. *quorum unus Homerus sceptra potitus*.

121–2 eadem rursum 'again on the other hand', *rursum* reinforcing *eadem* (sc. *uita*), which itself has an adversative colouring (48–50n.).   **corpora pauca** 'those few atoms', sc. which comprise the *anima*; they are called *corpora* again at 125, *semina* at 127; cf. 31–4n., 179–80n. *corporibus*. These atoms of heat and air are few in comparison with those of the visible body, but their presence is a condition of life.   **caloris | … aer** 'heat … air', varied at 126 as *uapor* and *uentus*. Greek *aer* was fully naturalized by the time of Cicero; contrast Enn. *Ann.* 131 Sk. *uento quem perhibent Graium genus aera lingua*. When L. comes to discuss these phenomena more scientifically he distinguishes between *uentus* and *aer* (232–6n.).   **per os:** L. is not here speaking scientifically: it was (and in some cultures still is) a popular belief that the soul leaves the body through the mouth. The Epicurean position is spelled out at lines 254–5.

122 For the rhythm of the verse, here with a strong caesura only in the fourth foot, cf. 102, 795, 893, 1082 (nn.).

123 A vivid and picturesque description of the departure of life from the body; cf. 1.810–11 *uita quoque omnis | omnibus e neruis atque ossibus exsoluatur*.

124–5 If the *anima* were a *harmonia* its existence would depend equally on all parts of the body, which has been shown not to be the case. **ex aequo** 'equally' (*OLD aequum* 2c); on the use of *ex* to form adverbial phrases cf. K–S I 506–7; H–S 266; McKeown on Ov. *Am.* 1.10.33. **salutem** 'life', 'existence' (*OLD* 2).

126–9 L. writes as if he has demonstrated that the *anima* consists of atoms of heat and air, whereas all that has been provided is a description of a man's dying moments; the notion of soul-atoms was insinuated into the argument via the phrase *corpora pauca*, and their make-up is now taken as read. Thus *igitur* at line 128 takes as proved a position which will only be established in the full discussion that follows at 231–57. Footnotes had yet to be invented, and it is understandable that L. did not want to impede the flow of the argument by constant cross-referencing.

128–9 est...in ipso | corpore 'there *exists, there* in the body'; for this emphatic use of *ipse* cf. 459, 483, 506, 575, 590 and see the other examples of the idiom collected by Munro in his note on 4.736. The effect here is enhanced by the enjambment.

130–5 It was Aristoxenus, a pupil of Aristotle's, who had explained the soul as a harmony in musical terms (Cic. *Tusc.* 1.19), and Plato used the same analogy in the *Phaedo* (86b). The musicians, says L., may have 'harmony' back; philosophy has no use for it.   **quapropter quoniam:** an effective use of essentially prosaic words to enforce and dignify the argument. Propertius similarly used *quandocumque igitur*, both times referring to the inevitable approach of death (2.1.71, 2.13.17).   **animi natura...atque animae** = ψυχή: cf. 161 *natura animi atque animae* and n. Periphrases of this kind with *natura* are common in the *DRN*, but they are not purely formal; rather they serve as reminders that L. means the *animus* and the *anima* as those instructed in Epicurean doctrine know them actually to be.   **quasi** 'almost', 'as it were'; after the emphatic assertion of 94–7 the qualification is unexpected, but L. has a curious habit of occasionally apologizing in this way; cf. 280, 504, 707 and nn.   **harmoniai:** in grafting the archaic Latin termination in -*ai* (83–4n. *amicitiai*) on to a Greek word L. may well have intended a slightly grotesque effect in keeping with the sarcastic and dismissive tone of the passage; see next nn.   **organicos** 'musicians'. The word is rare in Latin, attested outside the *DRN* only in technical literature; elsewhere in the poem (2.412, 5.334) it is used in association with other Greek words, here with a quadrisyllabic Greek proper name ending the verse and finally dismissing this incursion from alien territory with another sarcastic quip. Harmonia in Greek myth was a child of the Muses (Eur. *Med.* 834) or of Aphrodite (Eur. *Phoen.* 7). L. tells the musicians that, however lofty her origins may be, she should be kept where she belongs. Cicero is similarly scornful of the theory and the term, which he likewise restores to its proper place in music (*Tusc.* 1.41; Boyancé 1963: 151 n. 1).   **Heliconi** is ablative (cf. 611 *parti*), introducing a lingustic incongruity like that of *harmoniai* at 131 by tacking another archaic Latin termination on to a Greek word.

133–4 '...(whether they received it straight from Helicon) or appropriated it from some other source as being in want of a term for the thing'.

siue picks up an unexpressed *siue* from the preceding verse: on this idiom see Vahlen 1907: 327–9, Housman on Lucan 1.234. The afterthought is not gratuitous satire: Epicurus insisted that words should be used in their primary sense (τὸ πρῶτον ἐννόημα, D.L. 10.32; cf. Cic. *Fin.* 2.6). L. implies that the use of second-hand metaphor (*transferre* = μεταφέρειν) does not advance understanding.   **aliunde:** from medicine (102–3) or perhaps from the workshop (*OLD organicus* 1) – Duff suggests carpentry.   **porro** 'in turn' (*OLD* 4).   **illam:** sc. *rem*, anticipating the relative clause (Bailey 1947: 105).   **transtulērunt:** 84–6n.

135 quidquid id est 'be that as it may', 'however that may be'.   **habeant** 'they can keep it'; the more usual form of the idiom is *sibi habere* (*OLD habeo* 1b). In contrast with the mock-elevated tone of line 132 the diction is abrupt and dismissive.   **tu:** that Memmius is formally the addressee of the poem we are reminded at 417–24 (n.), but it is aimed through him at the general reader, who is sometimes addressed brusquely (Kenney 2007: 92).

136–160

The relationship of the *animus* and *anima*. Though they are intimately linked (next n.), the *animus* is the dominant partner.

136–9 coniuncta teneri | inter se: enjambment, alliteration and the central position of *unam naturam* in line 137 emphasize their inseparability; cf. 333–6 (n.).   **coniuncta:** neuter plural, referring to nouns of different gender. The construction, rare in Cicero, is common in post-Augustan prose, frequent in L.: in this book at 283, 287, 332, 349, 412, 421, 458, 506, 552, 559, 601, 705, 920. Cf. 66–7n.   **unam naturam:** the ψυχή, the whole soul (94–7n.).   **caput . . . quasi** 'what we may call the head', the dominant partner, almost personified (*OLD caput* 13, 14a). Here the qualification is necessary, since L. is just about to affirm that it is the chest and *not* the head which is the seat of reason.   **quasi et:** cf. 174n.   **animum mentemque:** since L. uses the terms interchangeably (94–7n.), *-que* should be read as disjunctive = 'or' (147–51n.), 'whichever we want to call it'. Cf. 142, 398, 402.

140–2 situm . . . haeret 'is lodged in and does not move from . . .', in contrast to the *anima*, which is distributed throughout the body (143); cf. 548–50, 615–17. In situating the *animus* in the chest, L. was following both traditional belief and the consensus of ancient writers, Plato however being one of the dissident minority. It was a natural enough assumption in view of the behaviour of the heart in moments of emotional stress

as described here: cf. the interpolated scholium at D.L. 10.66, 'the rational part (τὸ...λογικόν) [is located] in the chest, as is evident from our
fears and joys'. However, to advance that as the reason, rather than the
rational activity of the mind, for locating it in the chest (and it is that
rational activity which he immediately goes on to insist on at line 145
(n.)) may seem illogical, even if it was established Epicurean doctrine.
This objection is met by Sanders (2008), arguing that for the Epicureans 'emotions are inseparable from value judgments' (364); and it is true
that the fears of a sane man, apart perhaps from phobias such as a horror of spiders, generally have a rational basis. See Ernout–Robin ad loc.
In the *DRN* it is the fear of death for which L. offers what Sanders terms
an Epicurean 'form of cognitive therapy' (365). Nevertheless, it remains
the case that L.'s treatment of the question might well puzzle an attentive
reader unversed in the finer points of Epicurean doctrine by taking such
a technical point for granted: his *ergo* is almost impatient = 'so it is self-
evident that...'   **hic...haec...hic:** the anaphora lends emphasis, as at
82–3 *hunc...hunc...hunc*, and the impetus it imparts to the expression is
calculated to hurry on the reader who might otherwise pause to dwell on
the logic of the argument.   **exsultat** 'leaps up'; the metaphor is as old
as Homer: *Il.* 10.94–5 κραδίη δέ μοι ἔξω | στήθεων ἐκθρώσκει, 'the heart leaps
up from my chest'.   **circum:** on the relatively common postponement
of disyllabic prepositions to follow their nouns see 66–7n. *portas...ante*; on
monosyllabic words see 374–7n. *quibus e*, and on L.'s usage Bailey 1947:
107.   **laetitiae** 'feelings of pleasure', 'moments of joy'; cf. Catull. 76.22
expulit ex omni pectore laetitias. On this type of plural 'concretizing' abstract
nouns cf. G–L 204 n. 2; Löfstedt 1942: 34–5; H–S 18; and cf. 154 *sudoresque*
(n.).

143–4 animae = ψυχή, the whole soul (94–7n). Here the terminologi-
cal slippage is perhaps slightly awkward, but there is no danger of misunderstanding L.'s meaning.   **paret** 'is obedient' (*OLD* 1c), sc. to the
animus.   **ad numen mentis momenque mouetur** 'is moved at the direction and impulse of the mind'. L. is translating the Greek terms νεῦσις and
ῥοπή, but the combination of assonance, alliteration and *figura etymologica* (H–S 790–3) lends a characteristic Lucretian emphasis; cf. 188 and
n. *momen* is first attested in the *DRN* (6x), very sparsely thereafter. As
is sometimes the case in Latin, 'only' has to be added in translation to
bring out the full sense (cf. 145 *solum*): see Shackleton Bailey 1947: 91;
Nipperdey–Andresen (6th edn 1908) on Tac. *Ann.* 13.3. See further
350–3n. *animam*, 588–91n. *dispertitam*.

145–6 idque picks up *idque* at 140, the intervening verses being parenthetical to the main argument. Emphasis is imparted by alliteration
and anaphora, the latter accompanied by variation of vowel quantity and

metrical ictus: *idque sibĭ* . . . *id sibī*; on such prosodic variation cf. 425–8n.
sapit: emphasized by *solum*, but somewhat surprisingly the only reference
to the rational activity of the *animus*, otherwise here and at 141–2 (n.)
described in terms of the emotions.   **cum** 'although' (106–11n. *cum*).
res…ulla 'anything whatever'; cf. 184. Modern editors retain MS *una*,
construing it as adverbial ablative, 'together', 'simultaneously', sc. with the
animus. This interpretation raises difficulties which seem to be underrated.
(1) It involves taking *res* as 'the impression' (Munro) or 'stimulus' (Smith
2001) or 'process' (Brown), senses not warranted by Lucretian usage or
indeed seemingly paralleled anywhere at all. The parallels adduced by
Wellesley (1974–5: 31–2 n. 2) do not stand up. Bailey's 'a little awkward'
greatly understates the case against it, and his translation 'when no single
thing stirs either soul or body' seems to sell the pass, being a rendering
of *res… ulla*; similarly Latham 1951/1994, 'when nothing moves either
the body or the spirit'. *neque res* cannot be read as equivalent to *nihil*; *neque*
must modify *animam*. (2) A point that has it seems been totally overlooked
is that it is surely unrealistic to postulate a reader confronted with a text
lacking such modern conventions as diacriticals who can be expected, with
res preceding, to take the last word in the line as adverbial *una*; *res* cries
out for its complement. The corruption of *ulla* to *una* in either a majus-
cule or a minuscule script is not difficult to account for. (3) The notion of
simultaneity imparted by *una* is irrelevant to the point that L. is making:
that nothing whatever experienced by body or spirit can affect the mind.
(4) The sense yielded by *una* is in any case ambiguous: it can equally well
mean either that body and soul are affected together or that the *res* does
not move them simultaneously, not quite the same thing.

147–51 quasi 'just as', 'so for example' (*OLD* 7).   **concruciamur:**
attested only here and probably coined by L., perhaps on the model
of Greek συμπάσχειν, 'experience/suffer together with'. The alliteration
with *corpore*, accentuated by enjambment, helps to underline the point
that the whole body is not affected; cf. 152–3n.   **-que** 'or'; for this disjunctive usage (*OLD* 7) cf. 193, 284, 466, 797, 841; similarly *ac* (164,
442), *atque* (333) and *et* (654, 694); see Fordyce on Catull. 45. 6.   **cum**
'although'.   **cetera pars animai** 'the rest of the soul' (94–7n.), as at 143.
per membra atque artus 'throughout the whole of the body', tautologously
expressed to drive home the point: like *membra* (117 and n.) *artus* can =
'the body' (*OLD* 4a). The same collocation at 703, 4.888, 1114.   **nulla**
nouitate 'by no new sensation', 'new' in the sense of 'untoward', 'incon-
gruous': cf. 2.970 *motus nouitate laborent*, '[so as to be] troubled by any
strangeness in their emotions' (Smith). See Ernout–Robin ad loc.

152 uerum 'however' (*OLD* 2). In lines 147–51 L. has enlarged on the
point made in line 145, underscored by *solum*, the capacity of the *animus* to

act and be acted upon independently of the *anima*. He now returns to the fundamental point from which the argument started (136–7), that the two are nevertheless intimately connected, as is shown by what happens when a sufficiently strong stimulus is applied. Alliteration and the positioning of *mens* add emphasis.   **uementi:** the contracted forms of *uehemens* and *uehementia* 'were the only forms known to Lucr. and all writers of the best ages' (Munro on 2.1024, citing Lachmann ad loc.).   **magis:** take with *uementi*.

153–8 consentire 'is equally affected by', a straight translation of συμπάσχειν (cf. 148 *concruciamur* and n.); so Cic. *ND* 3.28 *consensus, quam* συμπάθειαν *Graeci uocant*.   **uidemus ... uidemus ... facile ut quiuis ... noscere possit:** the recurrent Epicurean and Lucretian emphasis on the evidence of our senses, from which even the man in the street (*quiuis*) can, if properly instructed, draw the correct conclusions. Cf. 165 *uidemus* and see 35–7n. *uidetur.*   **sudoresque ... artus:** this catalogue of symptoms inevitably recalls Sappho's celebrated poem on the emotions felt by a lover on witnessing a meeting between the beloved and another (31 L–P) and Catullus' equally celebrated adaptation (51). It seems unlikely, in view of L.'s satirical and dismissive attitude towards Hellenistic and contemporary Roman love-poetry (Kenney 1970b/2007: 314–26), that he could have intended any apparent indebtedness to Sappho as a compliment, but he could hardly have failed to be impressed by the power and particularity of her poem. In comparison with both Sappho and Catullus his treatment is clinical, as in his description of drunkenness and epilepsy at 476–505. The one specific borrowing is *infringi linguam* (155), 'the voice dies away' (*OLD infringo* 2c), closely resembling Sappho's γλῶσσα ἔαγε; that her text as we have it may be corrupt does not affect the point, if the corrupt version 'was already established in the text in [L.'s] day' (Page 1955: 24).

154 If, as argued by Soubiran (1966: 151–9), elision of -*que* was total, so not affecting the metre, the verse has strong caesuras in the second and fourth feet and none in the third.   **sudoresque** 'and sweats', fits of sweating, plural of repeated events (Löfstedt 1942: 34–5); cf. 140 *laetitiae* (n.).

156 sonere: the archaic form of *sonare*, also at 873. L. uses such variant forms freely for metrical convenience (Bailey 1947: 85–6). One of the hallmarks of Augustan classicism is increased discretion in the use of such devices (Introd. 18). Cf. 184–5n. *perciet.*

159–60 The sequence of action is *animus* > *anima* > *corpus.*   **c(um) animo:** the only instance according to Soubiran (1966: 404) of the elision of prepositional *cum* in the entire corpus of epic from Cicero to Silius;

cf. 852–3n. *d(e) illis*. Elision of the conjunction as in *c(um) animi* immediately following is relatively frequent (Soubiran 1966: 405), but it is curious
that L. should elide the same monosyllable – and that one is a preposition
and the other a conjunction almost seems calculated to draw attention to
what he has done – twice in the same verse.   **percussast:** Nonius' citation is to illustrate *icit* and lends only indirect support to *perculsa est*. Elsewhere L. uses *percutio* 6x, *percello* 4x, with little if any difference of sense,
though *percello, pace* Bailey, is in general the stronger word (*OLD* 1–3; L.
inadequately illustrated). Other things thus being equal, the direct is to be
preferred here to the indirect tradition.   **exim** 'immediately', a common form of *exinde* (*OLD*, headn.), always in the poets before a consonant
(*TLL exinde* 1506.60–2).   **propellit et icit** 'strikes and drives forward';
an example of the figure dubbed by grammarians 'hysteron proteron', the
latter thing first, inverting the normal prose order (Bell 1923: 270–1; H–S
698–9). In such word-groups Latin does not always concern itself with the
'logical' order: Tibullus' *uir mulierque* (2.2.2) no more implies male dom-
ination than Ovid's *femina uirque* (*Am.* 1.10.36, *al.*) implies the converse;
and *itque reditque* (*Tr.* 5.7.14), *it redit* (*F.* 1.126) and *redit itque* (*AA* 1.93, *Met.*
2.409) all mean exactly the same thing. On the need to shake off 'the lineal
habit of mind' when reading Latin poetry see Postgate 1907–8: 167. Cf. in
this book 787 *crescat et insit* (contrast 795 *esse et crescere*), 797 *durare genique*.
icit: L. uses the simple verb only here and at 4.1050 *icimur*. In classical Latin forms other than the perfect participle *ictus* are rare except in
the archaic technical expression *foedus icere*, 'make a treaty'. Cf. 319–22n.
firmare.

                              161–176

The *animus* and the *anima* are corporeal. The argument had been succinctly summarized by Epicurus: if the soul were not corporeal it could
neither act nor be acted upon (D.L. 10.67). L. now explicitly demonstrates
what has hitherto been taken for granted.

161–8 Haec eadem ratio 'The same argument', underlined by *propellere*
following and picking up *propellit* from line 160.   **naturam animi atque
animai** = ψυχή, the periphrasis here a reminder of this fundamental point;
cf. 130–5n. *animi natura . . . atque animai*.   **corripere** 'arouse' (*OLD* 4d),
as at 925, 4.999.   **mutareque:** L. is less reluctant than Cicero or Augustan poets to attach *-que* to a short *e*, but his usage can hardly be called
'frequent' (Bailey 1947: 129), with 25 instances out of 1,288 occurrences
of the word in the poem (Paulson 1926: 126).   **regere ac uersare**
'cause to move in a straight line or change direction'; for *ac* disjunctive
(*OLD atque* 13) cf. 147–51n. *-que*. These are nautical terms: *rego* = 'steer'

(*OLD* 4a), *uerso* = 'change course' (*OLD* 6a); at 4.896–904 L. exploits the metaphor more elaborately to illustrate the way in which the mind sets the body in motion.   **uidetur…uidemus:** cf. 35, 153–6 and nn.   **sine tactu…sine corpore:** a fundamental premiss of the system: the Epicurean universe consists only of atoms and void, the solid and the vacant: only a material soul can act on other matter. Cf. 1.304 *tangere enim et tangi nisi corpus nulla potest res*; 1.434–44, esp. 443 *at facere et fungi sine corpore nulla potest res*; 2.434–5 *tactus enim, tactus, pro diuum numina sancta, | corporis est sensus.*   **nonne fatendumst…animamque?** 'must we not admit that the soul consists of matter?'; *corporea natura* = 'body'.   **fungi** 'is acted upon' (*OLD* 2a) = πάσχειν.

170–4 si minus offendit 'if it fails to strike': *si minus* = *si non*; *minus*, originally a colloquial and slightly milder variant for *non*, is standard Latin in the phrases *si minus* and *quo minus* (H–S 454–5).   **ossibus…adacta** 'by being driven in and laying bare the bones and sinews': *adacta* is causal, taking its colour from the context (119, 440–4n. *conquassatum…rarefactum*). The aspect of the perfect participle is often, as here, felt as contemporaneous rather than past; indeed it may originally have been a verbal adjective without any implication of past time (Laughton 1964: 2–3; K–S I 758). **languor terraeque petitus | …exsurgendi incerta uoluntas:** respectively the effects of the swoon on the *anima* and the *animus*.   **suauis:** the idea that a fainting-fit may be 'pleasant' has troubled critcs, but emendation is not called for, as well-documented experiences over the centuries attest: Sen. *Ep.* 77. 9 on the death of Marcellus, *paulatim defecit, ut aiebat, non sine quadam uoluptate, quam adferre solet lenis dissolutio non inexperta nobis, quos aliquando liquit animus*; Montaigne, *Essais* II 6 on fainting after falling off a horse; Wakefield ad loc. on being hit on the head with a stone when a boy; Pusey on 'the experience of becoming insensible' on nearly drowning when a boy as 'very delightful' (Liddon 1893–7: I 15); Coulton on being nearly suffocated by a school fellow, 'Then I felt a rather pleasant sensation, as the blood gathered in my head; almost a sort of alcoholic exaggeration' (Coulton 1943: 34) – this is the experience apparently sought by a number of young people which sometimes goes tragically wrong; and from a friend, 'As an old hand at fainting I can bear Lucretius out on *suauis terrae petitus*: it's a feeling as if a wave of healing balm and ease quietly sweeps over one.' Lucretius, as we have seen (153–8n.), is clinically precise in such descriptions.

174 The uneven rhythm of the verse seems to reflect the spasmodic attempts of the injured man to rise. The main caesura is a 'quasi-caesura', arising from elision (here, as it happens, of *quasi*). Generally elision of the first *longum* of the third foot of the hexameter is found only before a monosyllable, usually a conjunction or a preposition; in such cases what is

in question is aphaeresis or prodelision rather than elision, e.g. at 138 we
should hear *quasi (e)t* rather than *quas(i) et* (Soubiran 1966: 181, 527–8).
The principle may be extended to cover monsyllables deemed to be ety-
mologically separable from the word of which they form part, as at e.g. 612
quods(i) im | mortalis nostra foret mens, 715, 958, 1043, 1061, 2.1059 *sponte
sua fort(e) of | fensando semina rerum*; and Prop. 2.17.11 (two instances in
one line) *quem modo felic(em) in | uidi(a) ad | mirante ferebant (maerente* Hein-
sius, rec. Heyworth). Commentators repeat the opinion of Platnauer 1951:
8 that the verse has no caesura. Cf. 258n., 624–30n. *introduxerunt*; Bailey
1947: 112, 967 on 2.1059 with further Lucretian examples. On genuinely
non-caesural lines see 83–4n. *hunc... amicitiai.*

175–6 ergo: since the agents of damage to the *animus* (here = ψυχή:
94–7n.) are corporeal, it follows that so is the *animus*: only body can be
touched by body (161–7n. *sine tactu... sine corpore*).   **laborat** 'is in trouble', 'suffers' (*OLD* 3).

177–230

The structure of the *animus* and the *anima*: (*a*) the soul-particles. The soul
is composed of groups of atoms (179–80n.) which are extremely small,
smooth and light.

177–8 animus: as at 169, 175, 'the soul', though down to line 207 at
all events L. seems to be thinking of the *animus* proper, the mind.
quali... corpore 'from what sort of body': ablative of material (G–L 396;
NLS 41 (3) n. 1), not infrequent in L. (K–S I 394); cf. e.g. 179–80, 279–80,
302.   **constiterit** 'is made of' (*OLD consto* 36) = *constet*, as at 180 *constare.*
pergam... reddere 'I shall go on to explain', but similar periphrases elsewhere are often no more than a metrically convenient equivalent for the
future simple; cf. 420, 422, *al.*

179–80 persubtilem... minutis | perquam: for *perquam minutis*, ruled out
by metre; cf. 187. L. is fond of compounds with emphatic *per-* = 'very'
(*OLD per-*); cf. 181, 187, 204, 216, 249, 473, They seem to have been
generally regarded as too colloquial for literary use: Cicero is the only
writer of artistic prose who makes much use of them, and outside L. they
are rare in the 'higher' genres of poetry (Axelson 1945: 37–8; H–S 164).
The phrase translates the Epicurean term λεπτομερές, 'fine-particled' (D.L.
10.63); cf. the interpolated scholion ibid. 66, ἐξ ἀτόμων... λειοτάτων καὶ
στρογγυλωτάτων, '(constituted of) the smoothest and roundest of atoms'.
corporibus: L.'s description of them makes it clear that it is atoms that
he means, not the 'particles' formed by the different kinds of atom, as
apparently postulated at 231–57. At 1.483–4 he had warned his readers

that he would be obliged to resort to ambiguous terminology in referring to the two things: *corpora sunt porro partim primordia rerum,* | *partim concilio quae constant principiorum.* Accordingly we find *corpora, semina* (187), *figurae* (190), *elementa* (374) and *primordia* (392), all properly denoting atoms, used of the groupings of different atoms making up the *animus.*   **factum constare** 'made and consisting of'; the pleonasm serves to underline the point that the soul is a physical entity; cf. *OLD con-* 5 'expressing intensity of action (e.g. *contueor, consto, conitor*)'.

181–3 hinc 'from what follows', as at 46 (n.).   **aduertas animum:** the mind is invited to understand thoroughly (*pernoscere*) its own make-up and operation, picturing to itself (*proponit*) what is happening and then of its own volition (*incohat ipsa*) instantly starting to react to it. The stages of this process are reserved for full description at 4.877–906.   **adeo ... celeri ratione:** an adverbial periphrasis for *tam celeriter.* The speed of thought was proverbial from Homer onwards.   **quam:** sc. *quam quod,* understood from *nil* in line 182. This type of ellipse of *ut, cum, si, quid,* etc. after *quam* is common and seems to be colloquial: 'it is as old as the language itself' (Löfstedt 1936: 26). Cf. e.g. Catull. 10.32 *utor tam bene quam* [sc. *si*] *mihi pararim* and Fordyce ad loc.; H–S 594–5, 826.

184–5 perciet: L. chooses between 2nd conjugation *percieo* (4.563) and 4th conjugation *percio* (3.303) to suit the metre. Cf. 156n.   **quorum ... natura uidetur** 'which we see'; the periphrasis with *natura* is here quite colourless. For the treatment of *res* as if it were neuter cf. 1.56–60 *res ... eadem ... resoluat,* | *quae ... genitalia corpora ... et semina rerum* | *appellare suemus,* 449–50 *nam quaecumque cluent, aut his coniuncta duabus* | *rebus ea inuenies aut horum euenta uidebis*; Munro compares *inter alia* Sall. *Jug.* 41.1 *abundant earum rerum quae prima mortales ducunt.* See H–S 431–2.

186 Verses such as this, with the second foot consisting of a dactylic word, are not uncommon in L. (16x in this book), whether as here with a spondee in the first foot or as at line 206 a dactyl. The verse has only one real caesura, in the fourth foot (83n. *hunc ... amicitiai*).   **rutundis:** this is the usual spelling in L.'s MSS, a reminder that the orthography now in general use was normalized in the fourth century and cannot always be taken to represent the usage of the ancient writers faithfully. Where the consensus of the MS tradition offers such old spellings it is customary editorial practice to adopt them: cf. Housman 1938: xxi n. 1. However, given the long interval between L.'s autograph and the earliest extant MSS and the vagaries of copying practice in Carolingian scriptoria, there may be a case for normalizing in some instances, particularly that of prepositional prefixes, as has been done in this edition; cf. Kenney 2004: 369. See however 196–9n. on *conlectum.*

187–90 debet 'must', 'is logically bound to' (*OLD* 6b); cf. 758, 2.451–2 *illa quidem debent e leuibus atque rutundis | esse magis, fluuido quae corpore liquida constant.*   **momine ... moueri ... mouetur ... momine:** picking up *mobile* from line 186 and pressing the argument home by the combined effects of *figura etymologica* (143–4n.), enclosing word-order, chiasmus and alliteration *m...p...p...*[*im*]*p*[*ulsa*: 174n.]*...m...m...m.*   **tantillo momine:** take with both verbs (ἀπὸ κοινοῦ: 68–9n.). L. nowhere else uses *tantillus*, but *pauxillus* occurs at 229 and elsewhere (3x). Diminutives were generally avoided by Augustan poets as colloquial (Gow 1932: 150–7); even the elegists were selective in their use (Maltby 1999: 387–8); Catullus used them freely for emotional effect, but not in his epigrams (Fordyce on 3.18, Ross 1969: 225). See in general Coleman 1999: 59–60. Cf. 914 *homullis* (n.).   **flutat:** for *fluitat*; the contracted form also restored by conjecture at 4.77. Only in these two instances in the *DRN*; elsewhere L. uses the full form (6x), as at 1052. The analogous cases of *probet* for *prohibet* at 864 (also a conjectural restoration) and (apparently) *torrat* for *torreat* at 917 (n.) reflect L.'s readiness to manipulate the language freely (Introd. 18–19, Kenney 2007: 96–7); see Bailey 1947: 72–108 on his position 'midway between the early Latin of the comedies and tragedies, of Ennius and Lucilius ... and the fully developed language of the Augustan poets and, in prose, of his own contemporary, Cicero' (72).   **quippe ... creata** 'as being composed of' (*OLD quippe* 3).   **figuris** 'shapes', here meaning particles (179–80n. *corporibus*).

190–2 at contra ... natura: the rhythm of the verse, with only one dactyl and that not in the fifth foot, is graphically descriptive. The spondaic fifth foot was a hallmark of the Grecizing style: Catullus has 30 instances in the 408 verses of the *Peleus and Thetis* (see Fordyce on 64.2), not all of which are obviously onomatopoeic or descriptive. L. is more sparing: in this book also at 198, 249, 253, 417, 545, 907, 963 (= 8/1094).   **constantior** 'more closely composed'; L. exploits the primary sense of *consto* 'stand together' (*OLD* 1a, b; *TLL* s.v. 527–42 'una stare'). For the comparative form of a participle used adjectivally cf. e.g. 387 *dominantior*.   **actus** 'movement' (*OLD* 5a).

193–4 inter coheres closely with *se*, so does not produce a false verse-ending at the beginning of the verse; cf. 263, 283, 783, 803 and contrast 262–5n. *sub fin.*   **nimirum** 'obviously'; used frequently (34x) by L. to underline his argument.   **exstat** must here = *constat*; the construction with the ablative appears to be otherwise unexampled (but cf. 241–5n. *est elementis*). Heinze's correction *leuibu' constat* deserves attention as an example of a tendency of critics to eliminate, sometimes drastically as here, what they perceive as unacceptable anomalies of usage. The usually unspoken premiss of such attempts is often that an author may not do anything unless he does it at least twice. On '[t]he rage for conjectural emendation on analogical principles' see Kenney 1974b: 123–5 (= 1995: 160–2).

196–9 papaueris…aceruus…lapidum…spicarumque | noenu potest: the key words in the sentence are positioned so as bring out the emphasis, accentuated by the enjambment of 198–9, 'of *poppy-seeds*…a tall heap…but of *stones* or *wheatears* that is not at all the case'.   **papaueris:** for a word scanning ∪–∪∪ (second Paeon) in second place in the verse cf. 582–8n. *foramina,* 719.   **suspensa** 'checked', i.e. very light; cf. 5.1069 *suspensis…dentibus,* 'not closing the teeth', and the phrase *suspenso gradu* 'on tiptoe' (*OLD suspendo* 6b).   **tibi** 'as you can see for yourself', the so-called 'ethic' dative (G–L 351, *NLS* 66), signifying 'this concerns you'.   **diffluat** 'is dispersed'.   **conlectum** 'a heap'; Muretus' correction of MS *coniectum* is necessary: *coniectus* means the act of throwing, not its result. Cf. 4.414 *conlectus aquae* (corr. Lambinus: *coniectus* MSS). Whatever L. originally wrote, it is clear that the unassimilated spelling (not *coll-*) was the reading of the archetype of our MSS (cf. 186n. *rutundis*).   **spicarumque:** the emphatically descriptive rhythm of the verse, with a single dactyl in the second foot, is unique in L., and more than one editor from Lachmann onwards has found it unacceptable; but as their attempts to emend *spicarumque* away (see critical note) demonstrate, they can at best be regarded as offered *exempli gratia* and belong in the *apparatus criticus*. **-que** 'or' (147–51n. *-que*); stones and the ears of wheat are chosen as exemplifying weight and spikiness respectively, both characteristics contrasting with those of poppy-seeds and the particles of the *animus*; cf. 201–2 *pondere magno | asperaque* and *at contra* there picking up *at contra* from 198. **noenu potest:** sc. *aura. noenu* is emphatic for *non* (also at 4.712), formed from *ne,* the ancient Latin negative, and *oinos,* the ancient form of *unus*: hence properly *noenu'.* On the anomalous use of the elided masculine form rather than neuter *noenum* (thought to be the original form of *non*) see Skutsch on Enn. *Ann.* 435. The motive was no doubt metrical convenience.   **paruissima:** also at 1.615, 621, Varro, *Sat. Men.* 375; Festus p. 442 L. s.v. *spara*; unattested in classical Latin but not infrequent in later writers (N–W II 208). L. appears to distinguish between *paruissimus,* 'very small', and *minimus,* 'the least possible'. It is used effectively here, paired with *leuissima* in the next verse.   **proquam** 'according as' = *prout,* peculiar to L.; also at 2.1137, 6.11.

200 Verses with a word scanning – – ∪ ∪ (Ionicus a maiore), placed so as to produce a diaeresis after the second foot, occur 10x in this book; here the effect is more apparent than real, since *sunt* coheres closely with what precedes it, as *ita* does with what follows.   **mobilitate fruuntur** 'are able to move', have the power of moving (*OLD fruor* 2b); cf. 6.856 *tanto feruore fruatur* 'is so exceedingly hot'.

201–5 magis¹: take with both *magno* and *aspera*.   **eo...magis²** 'by so much the more stable', as if *quo magis* had preceded.   **mobilis egregie** 'exceedingly mobile' (*OLD egregie* 2).   **perquam** 'very', qualifying the adjectives in the next verse.

206–7 The admonitory tone and the insistence on the need to bear in mind what has just been expounded are both characteristically Epicurean: 'It is indeed useful to keep this elementary fact in mind too', χρήσιμον δὴ καὶ τοῦτο κατασχεῖν τὸ στοιχεῖον (D.L. 10.47; cf. ibid. 52).   **res...rebus:** cf. 1.330–1 *est in rebus inane,* | *quod tibi cognosse in multis erit utile rebus.* The word-play accentuates the point that grasping this one fact will help to make much else clear.   **o bone** 'my dear fellow', 'my good sir', like Greek ὦγαθέ; but its use by Horace (*Sat.* 2.3.32, 2.6.51) and Persius (6.43), who offer the only other examples of the phrase, suggests that it may have been felt as satirical and patronizing. Its occurrence here is not a reason for questioning the authenticity of lines 206–7 (Deufert 1996: 243–4; cf. Reinhardt 2010: 225). Clearly it is not Memmius who is addressed, and though later in the book he as clearly is (417–24), he is named only in Books I, II and V. On the implications of this for the order of composition of the poem see Townend 1978.   **cluebit** = *erit*, as at e.g. 1.449 *quaecumque cluent*, 'whatever exists' (*OLD clueo* 2b); cf. Greek καλοῦμαι = εἰμί.

208–9 An example of the 'proleptic' type of indirect question, familiar from the 'I know thee who thou art', οἶδά σε τίς εἶ, of the Gospels (Mark 1:24, Luke 4:34). In Latin it is predominantly a colloquial idiom (H–S 471–2, Bennett 1910, 1914: II 222–4).   **haec...eius** 'Another thing too makes clear its nature'; *haec* looking forward to *quod* at line 211 (46–7n.).   **quoque...etiam:** for the emphatic pleonasm cf. 292, 5.153, *al.* (Reinhardt 2010: 220).   **dedicat** = *declarat*, its primary sense (*OLD* 1), *de-* intensive. L. believes in letting the facts speak for themselves; cf. in this book 517, 641; and at 933–49 it is the personified sum of all things, Nature, who speaks.   **eius:** referring back to the *animus*, but it is the soul, the *anima*, that L. now proceeds to discuss. The transition is signalled explicitly at line 216.

210–14 contineat...conglomerari: the framing verbs with identical prefixes emphasize the point; cf. 253 *permanare...perturbentur* (n.). *conglomero* is otherwise attested only in Republican drama (Pacuv. 20ᵃ R.³ = *ROL* II 14, Enn. *Sc.* 302 J.) and technical writers.   **quod** 'namely the fact that', picking up *haec...res* from 208.   **secura quies** anticipates the comparison of death with sleep that is to be developed at 919–30.   **cernas** 'one can see' (46–7n.).   **ad** 'as regards', 'in respect of' (*OLD* 37).   **praestat** 'keeps safe', *praesto* = 'guarantee', 'undertake', 'execute', 'show', 'prove', etc. (Berger 1953: s.v.) is to be distinguished from its other sense, 'excel'.

Death, so to say, keeps faith; the commercial/legal metaphor is characteristically Roman. Cf. 332, 971 (nn.).

216–17 'It follows that the whole soul consists of a series of minute particles throughout the veins, flesh and sinews' (cf. 565–7, 691). It is unnecessary to punctuate after *seminibus* as most editors do (Flores an exception). The reader of an unpunctuated text would have no warning from
the structure of the sentence that he should pause there (whereas at e.g.
230 *quoniam* is a clear signpost) and should have no difficulty, reading the
two verses as a single connected utterance, in understanding the ablative
as expressing the ideas both of composition and connexion – which was no
doubt L.'s intention. It is often the use of syntactical as opposed to rhetorical punctuation that creates problems where an ancient reader would have
found none.   **animam totam:** the first unambiguous indication that it is
now the *anima* rather than the *animus* that L. has in mind.   **perparuis:**
on intensive *per-* 179–80n.   **uiscera** 'flesh' (*OLD* 1a), as always in L.

218–20 quatenus 'since' (*OLD* 8), its invariable sense in L. and first
attested in him; in the Augustan poets only in Horace and Ovid.
extima = *extrema*; cf. *intimus, infimus.*   **circumcaesura** 'outline', formed
on the model of Greek περικοπή, and found only here and at 4.647; Cicero
uses *circumscriptio.* So far from 'illustrating the poet's complaints of the
dearth of Latin technical vocabulary' (Brown ad loc.), this shows Latin
rising successfully to the challenge.   **praestat:** 210–14n.   **nec defit
ponderis hilum** 'and there is not the slightest loss of weight': *ponderis*
partitive/defining genitive, 'nothing in respect of weight' (*NLS* 72 (5)).
Cf. 230 *nil ponderis. hilum* is a word of uncertain origin and sense, used
like *floccus, naucus,* etc. to mean something very small. In L. and at Lucil.
1021 M. (but see Marx ad loc.) it is usually adverbial after a negative or
virtual negative, as at 514 (n.), 4.515 *si ex parti claudicat hilum.* It functions
as a more emphatic variation of the usual *nec... quicquam* (see e.g. 225).
Of the twelve occurrences of the word in L. eight are in this book (220,
514, 518, 783, 813, 830, 867, 1087). For this type of compound negative
expression one may compare Fr. *ne...pas, ne...point,* etc. (H–S 84*); cf.
on the etymology of *non* 196–9n. *noenu potest.*

221–3 quod genus est...cum 'as is the case when...'; cf. 597; elsewhere
quod genus functions as a conjunction in its own right = 'just as' (226, 276,
327, 431). A Lucretian formula (12x in *DRN*).   **Bacchi...flos** 'the bou-
quet of wine', an echo of Republican drama (Plaut. *Cas.* 639–40, *Cist.* 127,
Curc. 96, Pacuv. 291 R.³ = *ROL* II 314), but in all probability the expression in common use? At 2.656 *Bacchi nomine abuti* the sense of *abuti* is
rather 'turn to account' (*OLD* 2b) than 'misuse' (4). L. avails himself of

metonymy as one of the repertory of conventional poetic devices without evident embarrassment.   **spiritus** 'scent'; the first attested use of the word in this sense and only here in poetry (*OLD* 10).   **aliquo** 'any other'.   **sucus** 'flavour' (*OLD* 1c); cf. 226-7, 2.845-6.

224-7 nil...minor 'no smaller'. L. regularly uses the ablative of *nihil* with comparatives (e.g. 89, 96), and Heinsius' *nilo*, which supposes the loss of one letter from haplography in *nilooculis* in *scriptura continua*, is an easy normalization. However, L. nowhere else elides *nilo*, and *nil = non* is normal Latin, though verging on the colloquial (H-S 454).   **nimirum** 'obviously' (193-4n.).   **multa:** L. argues, and ends by stressing the point (229 *pauxillis*), that it is because the soul-particles are exceedingly small and light that there is no apparent diminution in the weight of the body when the *anima* leaves it. It is also implied by 209-10, though not actually stated until line 278, that they are also few in number (cf. 376 *numero...concedunt*). *multa* therefore introduces an apparant inconsistency, fastened on by Creech. The easy correction to *pauca* was made by Housman in his marginalia (see 513-16n. *aliquid prorsum...hilum*); on the corruption of words into their opposites in MSS see his note at Manil. 5.463 and Oakley on Livy 7.26.9; and cf. 819-20n. *uitalibus ab rebus munita*. However, here it may have been the consideration that these particles 'are numerous enough to diffuse the odour consistently and over a wide area' (Brown ad loc.) that dictated the expression. Alternatively, as suggested by Heinze, *multa* may be due to mere inadvertence on L.'s part, triggered by his penchant for alliteration; cf. 2.116 *multa minuta modis multis*, the recurring *multa modis multis* (12x) and other variations such as 507 *miserisque modis*. This is one of the apparent anomalies that might have been eliminated if the poem had received its final revision.   **rerum** 'these things', i.e. those mentioned at 221-3 and their like.

228-30 These verses return us to the point of departure at 177-8; cf. 28-30n. *manifesta patens...retecta*.   **quare etiam atque etiam** 'Therefore without a shadow of doubt', a favourite formula (13x), in this book also at 567, 686.   **mentis...animaeque:** another variation on the compound *animus* + *anima* formulation.   **pauxillis** 'tiny'; otherwise attested only at 1.835, 836 and in Republican drama.   **nil ponderis** 'no weight', partitive/defining genitive = 'nothing in respect of weight' (*NLS* 72 (5)).

231-257

The structure of the *animus* and *anima*: (*b*) the soul-elements. So far as the main argument is concerned, this section and the next are parenthetical, and a reader who is anxious not to lose the thread might do well to turn straight to line 323. For some of what is said here L. is our only authority, and it may be that he is drawing on a source distinct from his main sources (Bailey 1947: 1025). See, however, Brown ad loc.: 'The passage, however sketchy, is of great importance, since the explanation of consciousness in material terms is one of Lucretius' most serious problems [as indeed it still is in modern discussions of the subject], if his account of the soul's nature in III and its processes in IV is to carry conviction, while the account of consciousness presented here carries vital implications for the all-important conclusion that it must cease at death.'

232–6 The soul consists of *aura, uapor* and *aer. aura* 'wind' and *uapor* 'heat' we have already met at 126–9 as *uentus* and *calor. aer*, which at 122 was merely a variant for *uentus*, now figures as a soul-element in its own right, 'air' as distinct from 'wind' (*OLD* 1). It appears that this distinction was Epicurean, but L.'s brief explanation is not very enlightening: that all heat must have some air mixed with it because of the nature of heat. Any connexion with the idea that wind is air in motion (6.685 *uentus...fit, ubi est agitando percitus aer*), if intended, is obscure (Boyancé 1963: 155). **tenuis...quaedam...aura** 'a sort of fine breath'; the vague *quaedam*, leaving the precise nature of this 'breath' undefined, recurs at line 241, where it refers to the *quarta natura* (241–5n.). This may betoken an awareness on L.'s part that his argument here is negotiating thin ice.   **tenuis:** scanned as a disyllable, the *u* being treated as a consonant, as at 243, 383, 448; contrast 327–30n. *dissoluantur.*   **uapore...cui:** *misceo* can be construed indifferently with *cum* + ablative, ablative alone, or dative (*OLD* 1, K–S I 317–18), but L. nowhere else uses it with the dative, and there is no obvious motive for the variation here, since *quo* would scan equally well. **quisquam** 'any at all', here adjectival = *ullus*.   **et** 'as well', 'also' (*OLD* 5a).   **enim:** for its position cf. 560, 790, 876.   **constat** = *est*; here with the nuance that this is its invariable condition (*OLD* 5a, b).

237–8 animi 'the soul' (94–7n.).   **sat:** the only certain example in L., though restored by conjecture at 5.881, against a dozen of *satis*.   **cuncta** 'all together', the proper sense of the word according to the ancient etymologists (Festus p. 44 L. *cuncti significat quidem omnes, sed coniuncti et congregati*; Maltby 1991 s.v. *cunctus*).

239–40 '...since the mind does not admit that any of these things can bring about the motions which cause sensation and the thoughts which it turns over'. The intended sense is clear, but the text requires emendation to yield it. The repetition of *mens* in line 240 is eliminated by Bernays's *res*, 'the facts of the case', but the rest of the verse calls for more drastic treatment. Of the two solutions recorded here that of Saunders (1975) is preferred to that of Frerichs as eliminating the repetition while elegantly preserving the point: that the mind itself rejects an explanation that does

not satisfactorily account for its own operation; but there can be no cer-
tainty that this is what L. wrote.   **recipit** 'accepts', 'admits' (*OLD* 7b);
cf. 1.377 *scilicet id falsa totum ratione receptum est.*

241–5 This hypothesis of a 'fourth nature' which had no other name
earned the Epicureans a certain amount of ridicule; there is a similar
vagueness in L.'s discussion of the nature of the gods (never in the end
fully explained as promised) at 5.148–54, *tenuis* like the *quarta natura.* An
even more fundamental application of this type of reasoning, in which
recourse is had to some apparently arbitrary postulate to explain observed
fact, is the invocation of the *clinamen*, the atomic 'swerve', without which
nil umquam natura creat (2.224), there would have been no universe. On
the possibility that L. was influenced by Aristotle see Rist 1972: 78–9. In the
history of modern science analogies for this type of argument are offered
by phlogiston and ether (Leonard ad loc.); and more recently by the
description of a property of certain elementary particles as 'charm', and
the elusive 'Higgs boson' now (2013) proved to exist.   **quarta . . . natura**
'a fourth category of being' (*OLD natura* 14a); cf. 1.432 *tertia . . . natura*,
there however of something that does not exist, something other than
atoms and void.   **quaedam** as at 232 (n.) signals inability to offer a precise definition.   **nominis expers:** since Epicurus had not attempted to
name it, L. could hardly venture to do so.   **tenuius:** scanned here as
a dactyl; cf. 232–6n. *tenuis.*   **exstat** 'exists'; see next n.   **est elementis:** Cipelli's conjecture, made independently by Wakefield (cf. 117–20n.
sentire), eliminates two difficulties: (i) the altogether pointless repetition
e . . . ex, which is not paralleled by 6.353–4 *e paruis quia facta minute | cor-
poribus uis est et leuibus ex elementis*, where the repetition is not syntactically
otiose, as it is here, and which (*pace* Smith and Brown ad loc.) is irrelevant;
(ii) the necessity of understanding *exstat* in 243 as equivalent to *constat*
(cf. 193–4n. *exstat*). For a true parallel cf. 6.330 *adde quod e paruis et leuibus
est elementis.*   **didit prima** 'initiates and distributes'.

246 perfecta 'as being formed'; the context imparts a causal colouring to
the participle (170–4n. *ossibus . . . adacta*).   **figuris** 'atoms'; contrast 190
(n.).

247–51 The *sensiferi motus* are transmitted through a chain of substances
growing less and less rarefied and culminating in the core (*medulla*) of
the most massive bodily structures, the bones.   **motus:** accusative plural, picking up *motus* from 245.   **mobilitantur** 'are set in motion'; the
word is otherwise attested only in the Republican dramatists.   **uiscera**
'flesh' (216–17n.).   **persentiscunt | omnia** 'begin to feel throughout'.
The weighty compound (179–80n.), the spondaic fifth foot (190–1n.),
and the enjambment combine to expressive effect.   **postremis** 'last of

all', the adjective used adverbially, as often in expressions of direction or sequence, whether spatial or, as here, temporal (*NLS* 88, H–S 171–2). **datur ... ardor** 'there is communicated the resulting emotion, be it pleasure or its opposite'; for *ardor* of the emotions see *OLD* 4a.   **medullis:** generally used in the plural: each bone has its own *medulla.*

251 For the metre cf. 357n., 884–7n. *stansque iacentem.*

252–5 nec temere ... perturbentur 'But (*OLD neque* 5) pain or any other cause of harm (*OLD malum* 7a, b) cannot penetrate so far without incurring catastrophic consequences'; *temere = impune* (*OLD* 1b). L. envisages an extreme case, as 256–7 acknowledge.   **huc ... usque:** on into the bones and marrow.   **permanare ... perturbentur:** the completeness of the upset corresponds to that of the penetration: the point is emphatically underlined by the now familiar devices of the placing of the weighty compound verbs and the spondaic verse-ending.   **partes:** the particles of the *anima*, distributed throughout the body (216–17, 691); cf. 399 *pars ... animai.*   **per caulas corporis omnis** [= 702]: *caulae* are 'pores', Greek πόροι, 'passages'. L. uses the word 8x in this sense; elsewhere it = 'railing', 'lattice' (*OLD* 1). For its use of internal passages in the body see 702–8n. *dispertitus.* What is now described is the scientific, as opposed to the popular, account of the process of dying (121–2n. *per os*).

256 quasi 'almost', qualifying *summo*; such disturbances usually halt at the threshold of the body.

258–322

The structure of the *animus* and *anima*: (*c*) the interrelation of the soul-elements and their effects on behaviour. Cf. 231–57 headn.

258–61 Any shortcomings in the following exposition of these questions are to be put down to the lack of the requisite technical vocabulary in Latin. The words *patrii sermonis egestas* are repeated from 1.832, and at the outset L. had pleaded the 'poverty' of Latin, *egestatem linguae* (1.139), as an excuse for deficiencies in his exposition. These apologies should not be taken entirely at face value: they also carry an implicit invitation to readers to notice that in fact the challenge has on the whole been successfully met without compromising the poetic standards that L. had set himself (Farrell 2001: 40–3) – a claim made somewhat more explicitly in the first reference to the 'poverty' of Latin at 1.136–45 – or the clarity of his message, the σαφήνεια demanded by Epicurus (D.L. 10.13). In his exposition of processes such as those now described, the interaction and intermingling of the soul-atoms (262–5n.), he demonstrates how masterfully he has risen to the challenge. It must, however, be acknowledged that the linguistic resources available to Latin poets were inevitably narrower than what Greek poets could exploit. Already in L.'s time they could draw on a longer literary tradition with a profusion of literary dialects, a larger morphological range, and a flexibility exemplified, for instance, in the ease of forming compounds (cf. Kenney 2007: 96–7). The language of Latin poetry had yet to undergo the magisterial discipline of the great Augustans. Cf. 273–5n.   **summatim:** L. shares with other early writers a fondness for adverbs of this form (Bailey 1947: 136); in this book 307 *grauatim*, 527 *membratim*, 530 *tractim* (also 6.118), 542, 566 *mixtim*. Cf. 776–80n. *praeproperanter.*   **tangam** = *attingam*, as at Catull. 89.5 *qui ut nihil nisi quod fas tangere non est.* A compound verb is not infrequently followed in both Greek and Latin by its simple form, with the force of the compound persisting: cf. 1.941 *deceptaque non capiatur*, 2.566 *et res progigni et genitas procrescere posse*, and see Bell 1923: 338–9. The usage in Latin is as old as the Twelve Tables: 8.12 *si im* [= *eum*] *occisit, iure caesus esto*; it may have been Indo–European (Watkins 1966: 115–19, with list of previous discussions). For additional Greek examples see Renehan 1969: 78–85; 1976:11–27, and for Latin Housman on Manil. 3.328. Cf. in this book 287, 382, 432, 437, 662–3, 1005–7 and nn.

258 On the metre of this verse cf. 174n. Here and at 6.1067 *quae memorare que(am) in|ter se singulariter apta* L. treats *inter* as divisible for metrical purposes, just as Virgil does at *Aen.* 1.180 *Aeneas scopul(um) in|terea conscendit*; cf. Müller 1894: 461–2; Norden 1934: 429–31. Strictly speaking, there is no true caesura in the fourth foot, since *inter sese* cohere very closely, but the combination of anomalies is not such as to invite suspicion. The compound *intermisceo* is first attested in Augustan writers.

262–5 The atoms of the soul-elements are so thoroughly intermingled that neither they nor their properties can be assigned to particular parts of the body.   **inter ... cursant:** the type of separation technically styled 'tmesis', Greek 'cutting'; cf. 339–43n. *conque putrescunt*, 484, 824–7n. *praeter ... quam quod*, 860. It was a Greek licence, exploited freely by Ennius, sparingly by Virgil. L. employs it artfully here and at 343, 860, as elsewhere in the poem (1.452, 651; 5.287, 299) to enhance the sense: 'it is usually compounds of *inter* that he so divided' (Bailey 1947: 123). Contrast 484, where metrical convenience was evidently the primary motive.   **principiorum** = in effect *suis*, the motion proper to atoms. On L.'s readiness to use whatever synonym or equivalent for 'atom' is metrically convenient see Kenney 2007: 95–6.   **secernier:** 66–7n. *cunctarier.*   **unum** 'so as to stand on its own', predicative. The reference is to the soul-elements, not to the individual atoms, as is shown by the next verse.   **nec ... potestas** 'and their individual function cannot be separated so as to stand on its own', expanding the point made by *unum*, *spatio* ἀπὸ κοινοῦ modifying both *secernier* and *fieri*. What follows expresses the point positively.   **fieri diuisa:** a periphrasis for the unmetrical *diuidi*.   **sed...exstant:** i.e. the *animus* is a single entity (*OLD corpus* 11b) with diverse properties. *quasi* suggests that L. is aware that here his terminology is not entirely adequate: the reader needs to be cautioned against taking *corpus* = the human body. The rhythm of the verse, with a spondaic word occupying the second foot and producing a false ending there (cf. 193, 374 and nn.), is imposed by the antithetical phrasing: *multae uis*) (*unius*; *uis* = *uires* (N–W I 744)).

266–72 quod genus: 221–3n.   **uiscere** 'flesh'; the singular also at 719, 1.837 rather than the more usual plural (14x in the poem, of which 8 in this book).   **uulgo** 'as we commonly see' (*OLD* 3), the recurrent appeal to everyday experience.   **quidam** 'distinct', 'peculiar to it', qualifying all three nouns ἀπὸ κοινοῦ; the same contrast as at 264.   **color:** Lambinus' correction is supported by the same list of properties at 2.680–1 *denique multa uides quibus et color et sapor una | reddita sunt cum odore. calor* would 'itself exemplify the soul-elements rather than providing an analogy for them' (Brown ad loc.).   **et tamen...augmen** 'and yet from all these things [sc. together] there is, completed, a single mass of body'; *augmen*, 'the result of increase', is not attested in classical Latin outside L. (8x in the *DRN*) and was no doubt coined by him. Ovid similarly favoured forms in *-men*, used interchangeably with second- and fourth-declension forms (Kenney 1973: 127 nn. 88–90/2002: 69 nn. 250–2).   **mobilis illa | uis:** the *quarta natura*.   **initum motus...motus:** re-emphasizing what was described at 245–6 and rounding off the period.   **ab se** 'starting from itself'.   **diuidit** 'distributes' (*OLD* 6) ~ 245 *didit*.   **ollis** = *illis*, the other three elements. This old form of *ille* is transmitted 11x in the MSS of the *DRN* (always in the dative or ablative plural), as against 20 instances of *illis*. Virgil uses it 23x as a conscious archaism (see Horsfall on *Aen.* 7.458), and Quintilian comments on the judicious use of archaic words as imparting *uetustatis inimitabilem... auctoritatem* (*IO* 8.3.25). However, the earliest MSS of Virgil are much nearer to his autograph than L.'s to his, and are that much more likely to reflect his actual usage. Here the variation may have been dictated by the presence of *illa* ending the previous verse.   **motus²:** 'that motion', 'it'; L. does not shrink from such repetitions in the interests of clarity. Cf. 262–5n. *principiorum*.

273–5 penitus...latet...subestque |...infra: the reference is not to the distance of the *quarta natura* from the surface of the body, but to its 'remoteness from perception by the senses' (Bailey 1947: 1039); cf. 2.312–13 *omnis enim longe nostris ab sensibus infra | primorum natura iacet*, 4.111–12 *primordia tantum | sunt infra nostros sensus*. L. is constrained by the *patrii sermonis egestas* to use the language of spatial relationships here, but the reader with 262–5 fresh in mind who attends to what follows should be in no danger of misunderstanding him. As Bailey points out, 'if the *quarta natura* were always locally "beneath" the other elements, they would no longer be fully mingled with one another and be moving in and out of one another' (Bailey 1947: 1038). Cf. 282–7n. *atque...emineatque.* **anima...animae** 'the "soul" of the soul' (cf. 94–7n.), a metaphor for which he goes on to apologize with *quasi* at 280. The *quarta natura* is to the *anima* as the *anima* is to the body, initiating the sensation in the *anima* which is in turn communicated to the body. A striking parallel to the phrase is found in Philo, *De opificio numinis* 21.66, describing the mind of man (νοῦς) as 'as it were the soul of the soul, like the eyeball of the eye', ψυχῆς τινὰ ψυχὴν κάθαπερ κόρην ἐν ὀφθαλμῶι. See Jacobson 2004, arguing for a common Epicurean source.   **proporro** 'in turn', as at 281; the word is peculiar to L. (6x).

276–81 quod genus 'just as' (221–3n.).   **membris et corpore toto** 'throughout all the limbs and the whole body'; *toto* qualifies both nouns ἀπὸ κοινοῦ. The tautologous expression (*membra = corpus: OLD membrum* 2) emphasizes the completeness of the process: every part is pervaded by the power of the *anima*; cf. 375, 682–3, 737 for similar expressions. **et** can be read as explicative, reflecting the process of distribution, 'and so through the whole body'; see 344–9n. *maternis...membris aluoque.* **latens...est** = *latet*; cf. 273–5n. This type of periphrastic expression is characteristic of comedy and prose, rare in poetry (Blase 1903: 256–7; Kenney on Ov. *Her.* 16.57–8).   **animi uis...animaeque potestas** 'the force and power of the soul' (94–7n.).   **paucisque:** it was implied by 209–10, and might have been assumed, that the soul-atoms were few in number, but only now is it explicitly stated (cf. 224–7n. *multa*); the point is argued at 376.   **tibi** 'I assure you', 'believe me' (196–9n. *tibi*).   **nominis haec expers uis:** the *quarta natura.*   **minutis | corporibus** ~179–80 and n. **animae...anima** ~ 275, but now apologetically qualified by *quasi*. The apology is neatly eliminated by Lambinus' *animai*, but see 131, 707 and nn.   **dominatur corpore toto** ~138, amplifying what was said there. Cf. 709 *in nostro dominatur corpore*, there of the power of the *animus.*

282–7 commixta: see 136–9n. *coniuncta*, but here all the nouns are of the same gender.   **atque...emineatque** 'and one is higher or lower than another'. L. again uses, *faute de mieux*, the language of spatial relationships, as at 273–4. The three elements differ from each other, according to the size of their constituent atoms, in 'perceptibility'.   **emineatque** 'or stands higher' (147–51n. *-que*). The implications of this point are developed at 288–306.   **ut:** best taken as restrictive = *ita tamen ut* (*NLS* 167; K–S ii 250–1; H–S 641), qualifying what has been said: 'only to the extent that there is still seen to be a single whole composed of all these things';

quiddam... unum picks up 265 *unius corporis*, 270 *unam naturam*. The different elements form a single entity so as to give the *anima* its characteristic properties.   **ni:** for *nei*, the ancient form of *ne*, only here in L. in this sense 'or else' (but cf. 2.734 *niue* = *neue*), elsewhere = *nisi* (*OLD ni*[1]). To say 'lest so-and-so happen' is equivalent to saying 'otherwise it will happen'. **seorsum seorsumque:** the repetition imparts emphasis to the idea of separation in general; it does not imply the separation of the *aer* from the other two elements. Here and at 334, 564 OQ give the full spelling *seorsum*; at 631, 632, 637, 660, 796 *sorsum*. The trisyllabic scansion is required by metre only at 500 and 551 and nowhere else in the poem. In their text of the *DRN* overall the full spelling predominates (13x: 7), and is more likely to reflect L.'s practice, given *inter alia* the propensity of copyists to normalize the unfamiliar or seemingly anomalous. In the text of this edition the full form is therefore preferred throughout. (Information supplied by Dr D. J. Butterfield *per litt.*) Cf. 499–501n.   **diductaque soluant:** for the gender of *diducta* see 136–9n. *coniuncta*; the result would be the *diuisa potestas* (264) which the balance of the soul-elements ensures cannot happen, *soluant* = *dissoluant* after *diducta* (258–61n. *tangam*).

288–93 The three elements and the emotions. The thesis that emotions and behaviour are motivated by the admixture of bodily constituents (familiar in the theory of the four 'humours') was ancient; the idea that the decisive factor was the temperament of the mind appears to be due to Epicurus. In fact L. is our only source for this doctrine, but he can only have got it from Epicurean teaching, and it can be seen as a logical development of what has just been said about the temporary predominance of this or that soul-element – though introducing it with *etiam* does not assist the connexion of thought. That is neatly supplied by Faber's *etenim*, 'that is to say' (*OLD* d), 'you see' (Brown), though apart from the formulaic *quippe etenim* (21x), the word figures second in the sentence otherwise only at 6.912 *quinque etenim*; elsewhere (3x) it comes first. The whole passage from v. 286 is carefully articulated round the key words: *calor* (2vv.) + *uentus* (2) + *aer* (2) ~ *leones* (3) + *cerui* (3) + *boues* (4) + *cerui et leones* (1).   **ille** 'that we know', 'the familiar' (*OLD* 4a, 14), as at e.g. 308.   **quem sumit in ira** 'which it takes on when it is angry'. To punctuate after *sumit*, construing *in ira* with *feruescit* in the next verse, as some editors do, is to ignore the natural movement of the verse and the fact that L. wrote for readers who punctuated as they read, by ear. **feruescit:** sc. the *animus*.   **acribus:** Lambinus' easy correction is supported by Virgil's imitation at *Aen.* 12.102 *oculis micat acribus ignis* and by the sense: *acrius* can only mean 'more fiercely than usual', which is not to the point.   **frigida...aura:** i.e. *uentus*; cf. 299 *uentosa...frigida*. **ciet...concitat:** tautologous, since *ciet* may be read as = *conciet*, of which

concito is the frequentative form. The sense of *concitat* 'makes to shiver'
is unexceptionable, but *congelat* (Housman's marginalia) deserves consideration, though the word properly denotes stagnation rather than agi-
tation (cf. 299–300).   **etiam quoque:** emphatic pleonasm (208–9n.
quoque...etiam).   **pacati** = *placidi*; cf. 302 *placido...aere*. Air is, by definition, at rest (232–6n.).   **pectore tranquillo ...uultuque sereno** 'when
the heart is at peace and the expression serene', a picture of the Epicurean
ἀταραξία which L. has set out to help his readers to achieve. This sort
of ablative, in origin instrumental, is variously described as 'comitative',
'sociative', 'descriptive', 'of attendant circumstances', *et al.*; see *NLS* 43
(5); H–S 114–19; Palmer 1954: 300–3. Cf. 302 *placido...aere*.

294–5 calidi plus 'more heat', partitive genitive; that is, when heat is predominant over the other elements.   **efferuescit** qualifies both *corda* and
mens, but agrees, as usual in Latin, with the nearer subject; cf. 434–9n.
discedit.   **iram:** Bentley's conjecture, unmentioned or rejected without
argument by editors, gives appropriate sense. *iracunda*, 'prone to anger'
(*OLD* 1), shows that the point being made is the ease with which this temperament breaks out *into* (displays of) anger; the point is emphasized by
the framing of the verse by *iracunda...iram*. For L.'s propensity to drive
home points in this way cf. Index s.v. word-order, enclosing or framing,
and for the etymological nuance cf. 359–64n. *lumina...luminibus*. With
ira the verse can only mean 'the mind that is prone to anger is angry when
it is angry'. The MS reading here is not supported by *ira* at 288, which
is indeed the source of the corruption. Cf. Reynolds and Wilson 2014:
232–3.

296–318 A similar analogy between human and animal behaviour is
found in the pseudo-Aristotelian treatise *On Physiognomy* (Jacobson 2005:
31–2).

296–8 A particularly striking example of L.'s descriptive technique: the
roaring of lions is vividly conveyed by the sequence of intervocalic *r*s
(which should be rolled: Allen 1965/1978: 32) and the exactly descriptive *gementes* 'groaning', imitated by Virgil, *Aen.* 7.15 *gemitus iraeque leonum*;
discreet alliteration of *p* contributes to the effect.   **quo genere in primis**
[= 5.59] 'First in which category'.   **uis ...uiolenta** 'the mighty violence';
for the periphrasis cf. 6–8n. *fortis equi uis*.   **capere** 'have room for', 'contain' (*OLD capio* 25a).   **irarum fluctus** 'their swelling rage', suggesting
the image of water boiling over; cf. 295 *efferuescit in iram*.

299–301 For the sequence of events described cf. 246–51.   **mens**
'heart', rather than 'mind', since the Epicureans deemed the lower animals incapable of reason, ἄλογα, still the word in modern Greek for
'horse' or more generally 'animal'.   **et...auras:** the dactylic rhythm

of the verse suggests the precipitate flight of a frightened stag.   **faciunt...existere:** see 98–101n. *uiuere cum sensu.*

302 placido magis aere uiuit 'has more of calm air in its composition'; *uiuit* is colourless = *est* or *constat. aere* is ablative of material.

303–5 Powerful imagery imparts concreteness to and almost personalizes the forces acting on the *animus: subdita* is *vox propria* of deliberately starting a fire (*OLD subdo* 1b), and *telis perfixa* suggests a volley of (poisoned?) arrows. The abrupt shift from hot to cold emphasizes the two emotional extremes of anger and fear; the effect, as usual, is enhanced by alliteration. **nec nimis...percit** 'does not much [*OLD nimis* 2] excite'; for the form of *percit* cf. 184–5n.   **suffundens caecae caliginis umbra** 'clouding it [sc. *naturam*] with a shadow of murky gloom'. *umbra*, with *naturam* understood as the object of *suffundens*, should be preferred to *umbram* as giving a more focussed and concrete sense to the imagery, conveying 'the idea of anger clouding the judgment of its victim' (Brown ad loc.).

306 interutrasque 'in between'. Though formally an adverb and so used elsewhere in the *DRN* (5x), here apparently acting as a preposition governing the following accusatives. The word is peculiar to L. and its employment here syntactically unique, but he is an adventurous writer, and Avancius' easy correction to *inter utrosque* would represent a banalization.

307–9 doctrina: i.e. conventional, philosophically uncommitted teaching, as distinct from Epicurean *ratio* (321), which is the only avenue to real mastery of the passions.   **politos | ...pariter:** on the surface they may seem alike, but their underlying fundamental differences persist. **illa...uestigia prima** 'those original traces' of character which have just been discussed (*OLD ille* 2a).

311–22 These 'traces' cannot be altogether eliminated, rooted out (310 *radicitus euelli*) of the soul, but they can be reduced to a point where they no longer pose an obstacle to the attainment of happiness (320–2). Epicurus rejected the notion of other philosophical schools, that man could be perfected by philosophy: 'the just man [is he who] enjoys the greatest peace of mind', ὁ δίκαιος ἀταρακτότατος (K. Δ. 17, D.L. 10.144).

311–13 The analogy between men and animals cannot be pressed too closely, as indeed is to be implicitly acknowledged at lines 314–18; human behaviour is considerably more complex than that of animals. Anger, properly controlled, might on occasion be accounted a virtue: cf. Cic. *De Leg.* 1.21 *solent enim* [sc. the Epicureans], *id quod bonorum uirorum est, admodum* [an important qualification] *irasci.* Conversely, forbearance might be regarded in some instances as a vice: pagan ethics generally did not subscribe to the idea of turning the other cheek.   **quin**

'so as to prevent' = consecutive *ut... non* (*OLD* 4). **procliuius ... citius paulo ... clementius aequo** 'too readily ... a little too hastily ... too mildly'. **hic:** scanned *hicc*; the vowel is short. Cf. 912–15n. *breuis hic est fructus,* 854–8n. *hoc.*   **decurrat:** usually in L. of motion in a straight line (*OLD* 6) rather than downwards, and so probably to be read here, in spite of *procliuius,* the root sense of the word being 'downhill', as at 2.455. The point here is the speed and directness of such a man's arousal to anger rather than any suggestion of moral degradation, an irrelevant idea in this context.

314–18 So far L. has limited the discussion to three basic types of character, representing the three simple predominances. Once combinations are taken into consideration, many possible variations arise. These, however, he has now no time to explore: *quorum ego nunc nequeo caecas exponere causas.* Presumably his source, whatever it was (231–57n.), had gone into the question, but to follow suit would have unnecessarily extended what is in any case essentially a digression in a book whose purpose was primarily protreptic. At 4.1170 he similarly cuts short his list of lovers' hypocorisms with the brusque *cetera de genere hoc longum est si dicere coner.* Such formulas belong to a type of *recusatio* common in poetry from Homer onwards; L.'s use of it betokens an awareness of the long literary tradition to which he was heir, and also hints with *nunc* that he is fully capable of doing the subject full justice if called upon; cf. Virgil's *praeteritio* at *G.* 4.147–8 *uerum haec ipse equidem spatiis exclusus iniquis | praetereo atque aliis post me memoranda relinquo.* Cf. e.g. Hom. *Il.* 2.488–90, Aratus, *Phaen.* 456–61, Enn. *Ann.* 469–70 Sk., and closer than any of these Cic. *Arat.* 234 *quarum ego nunc nequeo tortos euoluere cursus.* L. borrowed freely from Cicero's translations of Aratus' *Phaenomena* and *Prognostica,* both youthful works (Bailey 1947: 30; Soubiran 1972: 74–6; Kenney 2007: 95).   **naturas ... sequaces** 'the various temperaments of men, and their consequent behaviour' (Brown); *sequaces,* sc. *qui naturas sequuntur.*   **nec ... principiis** 'nor to find a name for every possible combination of atoms', i.e. *tot nomina figurarum quot habent principia figuras.* For the metre of line 317 cf. 102n.   **unde** = *ex quibus,* sc. *figuris.*   **uariantia:** only here and at 1.653, for the unmetrical *uarietas.* Cf. 675 *retinentia,* 851 *repetentia* and nn.   **rerum** 'what we see'; not things in general, but those under discussion here, human temperaments.

319–22 L. continues the transition back to the main argument: he cannot now pursue the matter into all such details, but one great principle he *can* affirm securely, that in no man is the imbalance of elements and their consequent charactistics so severe that it cannot be corrected by Epicurean *ratio.* This authoritative claim effectively rounds off the preceding discussion and facilitates the transition to the next topic.   **illud in his rebus**

'this fact', a formulation peculiar to and favoured by L. (15x).   **uideo firmare potesse** 'I am clear that I can assert', sc. *me*, omitted in a form of ellipse not uncommon in later writers, particularly Ovid (H–S 362); in L. also at 4.457, 5.390.   **uideo** 'perceive' (*OLD* 14); cf. Catrein 2003: 46–70).   **firmare** = *affirmare* or *confirmare* (*OLD firmo* 10), also at 6.940. On the use of simple in place of compound verbs, often if not primarily for metrical convenience (Pearce 1966: 318), there is a substantial literature: in addition to H–S 298–300 see for a convenient summary Maurach 1995: 112–14, and for a more broadly based discussion, covering also the point commented on at 258–61n. *tangam*, Bell 1923: 330–9. Other instances in L. at 160 *icit* (n.), 1.448, 6.1235 *apisci* for *adipisci*.   **potesse:** the archaic form of *posse*, *possum* having originated as a compound of the indeclinable adjective *potis/pote* (463–9n. *potis est*) + *sum*. For other such variants see *OLD possum* headn., and cf. 1010, 1079 and nn.   **usque ... nobis** 'that those remaining traces of different natures that reason is powerless to expel are so trivial that ... ', i.e. [*ea*] *naturarum uestigia quae ratio nobis depellere nequeat usque adeo paruula linqui, paruula* predicative as its position at the beginning of the verse signals. A little remains that *ratio* cannot dislodge, but it can be discounted.   **nobis:** Cipelli's conjecture, made independently by Lachmann (117–20n. *sentire*).   **dignam dis degere uitam:** alliterative emphasis imparts emphasis and rounds off the argument authoritatively. The Epicurean gods lived in serene detachment (18–22n.), the supreme example of ἀταραξία, and though they did not intervene in human affairs, they nevertheless passively influenced men's behaviour through the influence of the images of themselves (εἴδωλα, *simulacra*) which they constantly and involuntarily gave off. By contemplating these images, perceived in dreams, men could help themselves to attain the same state of security, freedom from disturbance, and become like them (5.1169–81, 6.68–79). Epicurus had promised a disciple that he would live like a god among men (D.L. 10.135), and according to Diogenes of Oenoanda (52 IV 2–3 Chilton) wrote of influences 'that make our dispositions godlike'. Cf. Introd. 1–2.

323–349

The relationship of body and soul: (*a*) they are indissolubly linked, and life can continue only while they remain linked. L. here states rather than demonstrates (Boyancé 1963: 159).

For a stylistic analysis of this section see Introd. 21–2.

323–6 The relationship is one of mutual protection: 'The soul encompasses the whole body, and being bound to it binds it in its turn', τὸν ὅλον ἄνθρωπον διέζωσεν οὕτως καὶ ἀντέδησε δεσμουμένη (Diog. Oen., Chilton

37 1 8–10; 1971: 16).   **haec ... natura:** the soul, picking up *mentis naturam animaeque* from line 228.   **tenetur** 'is protected', echoing Epicurean terms such as στεγάζειν 'shelter', συνέχειν 'hold together', περι-
έχειν 'enclose', of the body as protector of the soul.   **corpore ab omni:**
because, as we have seen (216–17), the *anima* is distributed throughout
the whole body. For the grammatically superfluous *ab* with the instrumental ablative cf. e.g. 429, 522, 567, 819–20n. *uitalibus ab rebus munita*; not
uncommon in the poets as a metrical expedient, and not unknown in
prose writers (*OLD* 21; H–S 122).   **est custos** 'is the guardian'; for the
image cf. 396 *uitai claustra coercens*.   **salutis** 'life' (cf. 124–5n.).   **communibus inter se radicibus** 'by their shared interlocking roots': their inter-
dependence is strikingly figured in the image of roots, not merely intertwined, but shared. For *radix* connoting stability (*OLD* 2) cf. 2.103 *ualidas
saxi radices*, 'enduring bases of stone' (Munro).   **nec ... posse uidentur**
'and clearly cannot', as at 333 below.

327–30 turis: this, not *th-*, is the spelling in Virgil's capital MSS, which
antedate L.'s by some five centuries.   **haud facile** [= 330] 'impossible';
see Munro ad loc. on 'that common rhetorical device of bringing your
meaning out more strongly by understating it', what the grammarians call
litotes or meiosis (H–S 777–8). Cf. e.g. Catull. 11.16 *non bona dicta*, 'my
maledictions'.   **quin intereat natura quoque eius:** i.e. without its also
ceasing to be frankincense.   **dissoluantur:** the *u* is treated as a vowel
to give a dactyl in the fifth foot, as at 706, 815. Where the word occurs
elsewhere in the verse, as at 455, 815, *al.*, it should probably be read in
the same way even though the metre does not positively require it.

331–2 These verses resume (*ita*) the argument so far and should be pre-
ceded and followed by full stops.   **implexis ... principiis ... | inter se:**
the enjambment and the causal ablative underscore the point, '*because*
they are so intertwined' (170–4n. *ossibus ... adacta*).   **ab origine prima**
[= 5.678]: that this is the case will be discussed at 445–58 (n.).   **consorti ... uita:** the scientific explanation is illustrated by a legal metaphor:
'they are coheirs or copartners of a life, which is a *sors*, a patrimony or
capital, which cannot be divided but must be used by them in common'
(Munro ad loc.). On *consortium* see Berger 1953 s.v. Legal metaphors are
a good deal commoner in Roman poetry than in Greek. Cf. 210–14n.
praestat, 970–1n. *uitaque ... usu*.   **praedita** is predicative with explana-
tory/consecutive force = 'so that they are endowed'.

333–6 L. enlarges on the pregnant formulation of line 332.
nec ... potestas 'neither power of either body or mind [*atque* disjunctive: 147–51n. *-que*] can feel separately without the power of the other':
uis and *potestas* mean exactly the same, an example of L.'s indifference

to stylistic elegance where clarity of exposition is paramount. Strict usage would demand *utra* here rather than *quaeque*, properly signifying one of three or more, but *sibi* has an affinity for *quisque* (*OLD quisque* 2), and Latin writers often express themselves more informally than the standard grammar books allow to appear.   **eas:** the correction is necessary: MS *eos* would have to refer to *corporis atque animi*, in which case L.'s usage would require a neuter.   **conflatur ... accensus** 'is kindled and blown into flame'; the same image, there in a simile, at 4.925–8. For *accendere* of initiating sensation cf. 2.943, 959; here, however, L. is not dealing with the genesis of sensation, which was shown at 246–51 to originate with the *quarta natura*, but emphasizing that it depends for its existence on the existence of the body. Every word in line 335 is pressed into service to drive the point home.

337–43 Common experience shows that the soul cannot exist apart from the body. The point is developed more fully at 445–525.

337–8 praeterea 'moreover' (*OLD* 2), introducing the appeal to common-sense.   **nec ... durare uidetur** 'can be clearly seen not to last'. Whereas the processes in the body giving rise to death may not be directly percep-tible to an observer, what happens to the body after death, as described in line 343, is something that can be seen and smelt. *uidetur* is certainly not, as suggested by Ernout–Robin ad loc., a metrical eke to round off the verse.

339–43 enim: for the elision cf. 904. Elision of the final syllable of a cretic sequence (– ⏑ –) is comparatively rare in Latin poetry (Soubiran 1966: 207–38). L. never elides a long vowel or diphthong in this position, only syllables in –*m* (ibid. 219).   **umor aquae** = *aqua*, a Lucretian periphra-sis; cf. 427 *umor aquai*.   **dimittit ... | qui datus est:** the heat is not a prop-erty of the water as scent is of frankincense (327–8) but something added from outside without changing its 'nature'. In contrast the *anima* is vital to the existence of the body.   **neque ... conuellitur** 'though it is not torn apart because of that' (*OLD neque* 5, 147–51n. -*que*).   **animai | disci-dium** 'the rending apart of the soul', an ambiguous phrase, applicable to both the dissolution of the *anima* as it leaves the body and its separation from it as an entity, but the ambiguity is pointed; the two things are part and parcel of the same process and happen simultaneously. The conclu-sion is enforced by the following emphatic alliteration: dissolution is total. **conque putrescunt:** the tmesis, besides, as at 484, serving to introduce a word otherwise excluded by metre, also enhances the sense, as at 262 (n.).

344–9 ex ineunte aeuo ~ 331 *ab origine prima* (n.); a Lucretian cliché (6x; also at 745).   **mutua ... motus** 'their shared contacts learn the motions of life'; formally a 'Golden' line, with two epithet–noun phrases framing a central verb. Here the effect serves to reflect the balanced mutuality of the body–soul contacts, but this is not a characteristically Lucretian device; it is Virgil and Ovid who make the most conspicuous use of it (Winbolt 1903: 219–23; Wilkinson 1963: 215–17; Bömer on Ov. *Met.* 2.163). There is a slight awkwardness in making *contagia* the grammatical subject of the sentence, but the sense is clear and expressively conveyed.   **contagia:** the word is not attested before L., and was probably coined by him for the metrically intractable *contagio*, preferred by prose writers. He also uses *contages* twice (734, 4.336), but not *contactus*.   **maternis...membris aluoque** 'in the body and womb of the mother'; *aluo* particularizes *membris*; cf. 1.348 *in saxis ac speluncis* 'in caves among the rocks', Cic. *Pro Sulla* 82 *his temporibus et periculis* 'in these dangerous times'. Some grammarians class this type of phrase as an example of the 'explicative' use of conjunctions, *ac, et, -que* = 'that is' (*OLD atque* 8, *et* 11, *-que* 6). Alternatively it can be seen as a special case of hendiadys, 'the resolution of a complex expression into its parts' (Moore 1891: 273; Bell 1923: 258–61; cf. Serv. on Virg. *Aen.* 1.61). On the difficulty of classifying this usage see H–S 782–3. Cf. 554–7n. *sine corpore et ipso* | ... *homine*, 790–3n. *atque.*   **reposta** = *reposita*: the word agrees grammatically with *contagia* but refers in sense to *corpus atque anima.* For the contracted form cf. 851 *posta*, 871 *posto.*   **sine peste maloque** 'without doom and disaster' (Brown), = *sine mala peste*, a phrase found in imprecations (*OLD pestis* 1 *sub fin.*).   **causa salutis** ∼ 324, ring-composition formally rounding off the section.   **eorum:** sc. the body and soul.

350–369

The relationship of body and soul: (*b*) refutation of two fallacies: (i) that the body itself does not feel; (ii) that the eyes do not see, but the *animus* through them. Various philosophical schools held these or similar views; some scholars have thought that L. has the Stoics principally in mind (cf. Kenney 2006: 361–2). The section is parenthetic to the main argument. For a full discussion see Rist 1972: 81–2.

350–3 Quod superest [= 905] 'next', 'again', a Lucretian cliché (22x), not necessarily marking the last in a series of arguments.   **refutat:** as at 5.727, the word must here mean 'attempt to disprove', apparently an isolated early instance of the 'conative' or 'inceptive' use of the present tense, otherwise not reliably attested in Latin before the Augustan period (Bennett 1910, 1914: I 26; Blase 1903: 112 (the Ciceronian examples irrelevant), H–S 316). Lambinus' *renutat* 'denies' is thus a plausible correction; a copyist might well have been puzzled by *renutat*, otherwise attested only at 4.600. In either case the construction with accusative and infinitive is on the analogy of *negare.*   **animam** 'only the spirit', sc. *solam* (143–4n. *sub*

fin.).   **nominitamus:** for the unmetrical *nominamus*, but the frequentative is pointed: this is what we commonly refer to as 'sensation'. Apart from
inscriptions, the word is attested only in L. (5x) and was probably coined
by him.   **uel manifestas** 'quite clear' (*OLD uel* 5c). For the metre of this
verse cf. 35 (n.). Here the word-order, with the emphatic preposition *contra* central in the verse, throws the two mutually supporting adjectives into
relief.

354-5 'for who will ever tell us what bodily sensation is if not the actual
sights and lessons of experience?' Only the senses can tell us about sensation.   **corpus sentire** is equivalent to a substantival phrase = *corporis
sensus* (see Bailey 1947: 102 for other Lucretian examples). Greek, pos-
sessing a definite article, makes a much freer use of this construction.
adferet 'will bring us the news' (*OLD* 14b).   **palam ... dedit** 'has made
plain', literally 'has placed in public': the news is already there in the public domain, *do* here = 'place', 'make', rather than 'give'. On the conflation of what were originally two distinct roots see Ernout–Robin on 1.228,
Ernout–Meillet s.v. *do.* Cf. 603–6n. *prodita.*

356-8 at, as commonly, introduces an objection put into the mouth of
an objector (*OLD* 4).   **enim** 'yes, for ...', 'admittedly, but ...' (*OLD* 5a,
b); γάρ is similarly used in Greek. What the body loses when the spirit
leaves it is something that is not *proprium*, does not belong to it; sensation
is inherent in the *anima*, not in the body, to which it is communicated
by the *anima.* The point was stated somewhat more explicitly by Epicurus:
the body when alive does not possess sensation 'itself in its own right', αὐτὸ
ἐν ἑαυτῶι (D.L. 10.64).   **multaque** 'and many other characteristics', sc.
such as heat (215), motion, etc. Sensation, that is, is not the only bodily attribute that is not *proprium.*   **perdit cum expellitur aeuo:** this early
correction gives good sense and is close to the transmitted text. Munro's
conjecture *perdit quam expellitur ante* accounts ingeniously for the presence
of *quam* in the MSS, and the order *quam ... ante* is paralleled at 973, but
the sense is less appropriate: the idea that the body loses some attributes,
such as strength or beauty, before death is less relevant to the point made
in line 357.

359-64 L. has just argued that the *animus* cannot experience sensation
divorced from the body. He now argues similarly that it cannot perceive
on its own. The view that he rejects is stated very clearly by Cicero, who
attributes it to the Stoics (*Tusc.* 1.46). He selects one sense, eyesight, as representative, and evidently expects the reader to accept that his demonstration applies with equal force to the organs of hearing and smell.   **posse:**
it is not to be believed that the eyes cannot see on their own, but function only as 'doors' through which images pass. The point is sharpened

if *posse* is emended to *per se*, contrasting with *per eos* following and playing elegantly on the literal and transferred senses of *per* (*OLD* 1, 15b), as
suggested by Butterfield (2009: 311–12), noting that *per se* concludes the
verse 3x elsewhere (1.445, 2.241, 1050).   **foribus:** *fores* are the valves of
a door, the parts that open; L. evidently found θυρίδες in the Greek source.
Cicero uses *fenestrae*, properly window-openings, which blurs the image.
desiperest: that this, as conjectured by Lambinus, and not the transmitted
difficilest, is what L. wrote is conclusively demonstrated by Buglass (forthcoming).   **contra…trahit** [sc. *nos*] **…ad ipsas** 'seeing that our eyesight
leads us in the opposite direction, for it pulls and pushes us to the eyes
themselves'. There is no appeal from the evidence of the senses: what
we experience when we see shows conclusively that seeing is done *with*
and *by*, not through, the eyes. For *trahit…detrudit* cf. Plaut. *Capt.* 750 *et
trahi et trudi simul.* The image of the facts of the matter physically compelling acceptance of the correct doctrine is characteristic; cf. 2.868–9 *in
promptu cognita quae sunt* | *…ipsa manu ducunt et credere cogunt.*   **praeser-
tim cum:** to cite an especially obvious case. For causal *cum* + indicative
see *OLD cum²* 6a and cf. 441 *cum…nequit.*   **cernere** 'distinguish': the
original sense of the word is 'sift' (*OLD* 1). For the agricultural origins
of much Latin metaphor see Marouzeau 1949: 7–25, Weise 1909: 18–20.
lumina luminibus 'our eyes…the light'. Ancient readers were responsive
to this type of verbal play, here underlining a paradox. It goes back to a
state of mind in which words and the things represented by them were
thought of as intimately connected. Thus etymology, true or false, was a
serious poetical device (cf. Fraenkel on Aesch. *Ag.* 687). Remarks by commentators on 'puns' and 'false antitheses' are largely beside the point. See
in this book 295, 378–80, 414–15, 449–52 (nn.).

365–6 We ourselves (*ipsi*; cf. 863 *ipse*) are to an actual door, on the theory
rejected here, as the *animus* is to the eyes; but a door, however bright the
light that comes through it, is not dazzled, whereas our eyes are: therefore our eyes are not analogous to a door: QED. The syllogistic argument
depends on a rigid application of the door analogy, which L. then goes
on to ridicule with a characteristic *reductio ad absurdum* to round off the
argument.   **qua** 'through which', sc. *uia* 'by what way' (*OLD* 3).   **suscipiunt** 'receive', 'undergo' (*OLD* 3b).   **reclusa** 'by being opened'. The
scansion *rē*- before mute and liquid tended to be avoided by Augustan
poets. L. varies his usage freely, particularly with *repleo* (*rĕ*- and *rē*- 6x each).
Cf. 360 *rĕclusa.*

367–9 This reasoning, which was to excite the scorn of Lactantius (*ineptis-
simum, De Opif. Dei* 8.12), is characteristic of L., who delights in rounding
off a passage by imparting a flippant or sarcastic twist to the argument.
So, in a famous example, at the end of his polemic against the theory

of *homoeomeria*, the atoms are imagined as crying with laughter at this explanation of their actions (1.919–20).   **iam** 'in that case' (*TLL* s.v. 129.19–36), as at 676, 5.679, Manil. 3.296.   **debere uidetur** 'obviously must'.   **postibus ipsis** 'the doors, posts and all', literally 'even the posts', so necessarily the doors too. L. was perhaps influenced by the Greek use of αὐτός in phrases like αὐτῆισιν ῥίζηισι 'roots and all' (Hom. *Il.* 9.542) and αὐτοῖς ἀνδράσιν of ships taken 'with their crews'. The idiom seems not to have gained any further foothold in Latin.

370–395

The relationship of soul and body: (*c*) refutation of the teaching of Democritus about the arrangement of the soul- and body-particles. Like its predecessor, this section is only loosely connected with the main argument. 'Lucretius deals with the matter somewhat cavalierly' (Rist 1972: 80).

370–1 Illud in his rebus 'this', emphatic; here as elsewhere introducing a rebuttal.   **nequaquam ... possis** 'one may not' (46–7n.).   **Democriti ... ponit** [= 5.622] 'which the great Democritus [*uiri* honorific: Housman, *CP* 906] laid down'. What he actually said has to be deduced from references in later writers.   **sancta:** transferred epithet (enallage: Bell 1923: 315–29, H–S 159–60), referring to Democritus himself but also conferring sanctity on his opnions. L.'s phrasing was perhaps influenced by Lucil. 1316 M. *Valeri sententia dia*, imitated also by Horace, *Sat.* 1.2.32 *sententia dia Catonis*.

372–3 'that the atoms of body and soul are arranged separately, one by one, and so bind the body together'. This alternation, in an *abab* sequence, is attested only here. All that our other source, Alexander of Aphrodisias (third century AD), tells us is that the atoms were described as juxtaposed, τῆι παρ' ἄλληλα θέσει (Bailey 1947: 1056 and n. 1).   **priuis:** sc. *principiis*, for the unmetrical *singulis*.   **alternis** 'alternately', adverbial (*OLD* s.v.), also at 1.524 of the arrangement of atoms and void; cf. Virg. *Ecl.* 3.59 *alternis dicetis*: *amant alterna Camenae*, where however *alternis* is registered by *OLD* s.v. *alternus* 1b 'neut. pl. as sub.'   **uariare:** here intransitive.

374 Metrically a doubly anomalous verse: (i) it begins with two spondees followed by a diaeresis; (ii) it includes one of the only two hiatuses, as distinct from 'prosodic hiatus' (1082–4n. *sed dum abest*), in the *DRN*; the other at 6.755 *loci opus*. The early poets seem to have avoided eliding the -*ae* of the genitive, which was felt as a true diphthong (Leo 1912: 334–60); at 1.139 *linguae* (*e*)*t* is a case of aphaeresis or prodelision rather than elision proper (Soubiran 1966: 181–2). Virgil does not elide -*ae* (genitive or dative) in the *Eclogues* but admits it in hiatus: 7.53 *castaneae hirsutae*;

cf. *G.* 2.144 *oleae armentaque laeta.* Lachmann's easy correction *elementa minora animai* appears therefore tempting at first sight, but it seems hardly likely that such an obvious metrical anomaly should have been introduced by a copyist or interpolator.

374–7 cum...tum 'as...so', i.e. 'both...and' (*OLD cum²* 14a), like Greek μέν...δέ.   **quibus e** [= 839, 858]: the postponement of monosyllabic prepositions is rarer than that of disyllables (140–2n. *circum*); Ennius had given a lead (*Ann.* 482 Sk. *contempsit fontes quibus ex erugit aquae uis*), and L.'s example was followed by later poets (Housman on Manil. 1.244). Cf. 67, 463, 824 (nn.).   **numero...concedunt** 'are few in number', *numero* ablative of respect (G–L 397; *NLS* 55). This statement is supported by Diogenes of Oenoanda (37 1 2–5 Chilton).   **rara** 'at wide intervals', adverbial.   **dumtaxat...possis** 'to the extent that one may guarantee the following...', *dumtaxat* 'at least' (*OLD* 3) qualifies *ut*; the reservation defines the hitherto unspecified degree of *raritas.*

378–80 'The intervals between the particles of soul in our bodies are as great as [i.e. cannot be smaller than] the smallest objects which cause sensation when they touch us.' We do not feel the touch of very small things because they impinge on us between the widely spaced soul-particles from which sensation arises. The interval between such particles must be larger than the largest objects of which we cannot feel the touch. The usual illustrations from common experience follow.   **prima...corpora:** the first as we go up the scale of size, the smallest. At 1.61 L. had so entitled the atoms themselves, an apparent inconsistency in his technical terminology which led Munro to speak of 'his usual indifference to ambiguity'; but the echo of the phrase in *exordia prima* at line 380 and the word-play *corpora...in corpore* in line 379, as Brown points out, indicate that he is making a point: 'the intervals between the *prima exordia* (or *prima corpora*) of the soul match the size of the *prima corpora* to which we are sensitive'. The sentence is carefully constructed, with the words in the correlative clauses positioned so as to exploit the word-play: *quantula prima...| corpora...corpore, tanta | ...prima.*   **exordia prima** = 5.677, there picked up by *ab origine prima* in the next verse and as here exploiting the word-play to make the point.

381–2 adhaesum | corpore 'its adhesion to the body'; for the ablative cf. 382 *membris...[in]sidere.* This type of construction, with a verbal noun governing a direct or indirect object, is colloquial; cf. e.g. Plaut. *Amph.* 519 *quid tibi hanc curatio est rem?* = *cur hanc rem curas?* (Bennett 1910, 1914: II 252), otherwise seemingly only attested in Cicero's letters in phrases of the type *quid mihi auctor es?*, 'what do you advise?' (*Att.* 13.40(343 SB).27). Cf. H–S 34. The usual construction of *adhaereo* or *adhaeresco* is with the dative or a preposition, as at 6.897 *in taedai corpore adhaerent*. The word *adhaesus* is peculiar to L. (4x), who affects such fourth-declension abstract nouns (Bailey 1947: 135).   **incussam sidere =** *incussam insidere* (258–61n. *tangam*).   **cretam:** 'd'où provient cette craie?' ask Ernout–Robin. Whereas encountering a dust-cloud, especially in a hot dry country, might be a not uncommon experience, having chalk 'shaken on to' one (an apparently unique sense of *incutio* (*OLD* 2a)), seems to imply a deliberate act rather than accident. Of the various explanations offered, the most plausible is that the reference is to the use, well attested, of chalk as a cosmetic; but one wonders how relevant such an illustration would be to L.'s evidently intended readers, Memmius and his peers.

383–7 aranei͡: scanned as a trisyllable by 'synizesis', collapsing of vowels into a diphthong; cf. 877 e͡icit, 919 re͡i.   **tenuia:** scanned as a dactyl (232–6n. *tenuis*).   **obretimur** 'we are enmeshed as we go', for the more usual *irretimur*; the word is attested only here, and was clearly coined by L. to describe the not uncommon experience of walking into a spider's web. **supera =** *supra*; if his MSS may be trusted, L. uses both spellings indifferently (14:18x).   **uietam | uestem:** the spider's moulted skin; see on arachnid ecdysis Wellesley 1974–5: 32. Commentators unfamiliar with this phenomenon have read the phrase as a second reference to the spider's web, citing Q. Serenus, *Liber medicalis* (*PLM* III 21) 957 *ex oleo necti uestis debebit arachnes*; but such a pointless tautology is unlikely for L. For *uestis* of the sloughed skin of a snake cf. 614, 4.61. However, as compared with walking into a cobweb, having spiders' moults falling on one's head must always have been an unusual experience. This illustration and that of chalk are perhaps best explained as examples of the lightest objects known to L. – and as a keen observer of the natural world, he may well have been familiar with the life-cycle of spiders.   **papposque** 'thistledown'; cf. Nicander, *Alex.* 126–7 'like the freshly-scattered thistledown which roams the air and is fluttered by every breeze' (Hollis 1998: 178).   **qui … grauatim** 'which as a rule are hard put to it to fall owing to their excessive lightness', the expression playing on the literal and extended senses of *grauatim*, 'heavy' and 'with difficulty'. The word, for the usual *grauiter*, is otherwise attested in classical writers at Livy 1.2.3; cf. on adverbs of this type 258–61n. *summatim*. At this point L., without acknowledging that fact, passes to considering the part played by weight in the process of touch. The crucial factor would appear to be the difference in size between the two classes of objects, those which are both light and very small such as particles of dust and chalk, and those which are light but larger such as the threads of a web or a feather. The latter can span the intervals between the soul-particles but are too light to excite a response from them. Why this should

be so is not explained, and the explanations offered by the commentators
(see e.g. Bailey, Smith and Brown ad loc.) can only be speculative.

388–90 itum 'comings and goings'. The uncompounded form of the verbal noun (only here in L.) is rare; when Cicero uses it in a letter, it is
in a play on words, *Att.* 15.5(383 SB).3 *quis porro noster itus, reditus, uultus, incessus inter istos?*   **cuiusuiscumque** 'each and every', an emphatic
conflation of *quiuis* and *quicumque*, otherwise attested only at Mart. 14.2.1
quouiscumque loco 'at each and every place you choose'.   **priua** = *singula*,
as at 372 (n.). These insects are very light and their feet are very close
together, so that they may steer clear of the soul-atoms or touch them too
lightly to trigger a response: a further case in point.   **et cetera:** L. may
have felt that a more explicit identification of body-vermin, a favourite
source of jokes in comedy and epigram, was inconsistent with the dignity
of *epos*; as it is, apart from the pseudo-Virgilian epyllion so titled, this is the
only appearance of the word *culex* outside comedy, satire, epigram and
technical writing.

391–5 'So many atoms spread throughout our bodies must first be started
into motion before the soul-atoms are shaken into sensation and, jostling
in the wide spaces between them, can clash and leap apart again.' Marullus' transposition of lines 392 and 393 allows a straightforward construction of L.'s Latin; in the text as transmitted *multa* 'many things' is unvcharac-
teristically vague, and it is only when the passage is reread that it becomes
clear that *semina*, not *primordia*, is the subject of *sentiscant*. No competent
Latin poet set syntactical traps of that kind. An alternative solution which
keeps the transmitted order of the verses is Müller's ingenious transposition of *in nobis* and *primordia*. This has the additional merit that it obviates
the need to impart to *semina* at 393 the special sense of 'soul-atoms'. However, the change is hard to account for as accidental, and the motive of an
interpolator unclear.   **multa ciendum:** the construction of the gerund
with a direct object is chiefly archaic and post-classical (*NLS* 206 Note ii);
L. not infrequently prefers it to the usual construction with the gerundive
(Bailey 1947: 103–4).   **semina ... primordia:** soul-atoms (cf. 143, 217,
276–7), but in the case of the latter now perhaps thought of as grouped in
particles. They are so far apart that many must be moved from their places
before they can begin to interact and set off sensation.   **sentiscant concussa** 'are shaken and so begin to feel'; *sentisco* here used absolutely: cf.
249 *persentiscunt*.   **tantis interuallis** 'in spite of the size of the intervals',
which are normally too great to allow contact, ablative of 'attendant circumstances'. A new detail in the account of sensation: the *sensiferi motus*
entail that the soul-atoms cease to maintain their usual intervals through
contact with each other. Wakefield's correction of *quantis* gives easy sense;
the intervals between the soul-atoms are 'so great' as compared with those

of the body-atoms. Cf. 276–81n. *paucisque*, 374–7n. *numero... concedunt.*
Lachmann's *quam in his*, introducing prosodic hiatus (1082–4n. *sed dum
abest*), is neat, but *his* requiring the reader to look back to line 380 is awkward. Turnebus' *quam sis* 'over their intervals', i.e. those assigned to them,
gives good sense, with anaphora of *quam* in place of a connective, but *sis*
= *suis* is found elsewhere in L. only in a quotation from Ennius (1025).
tuditantia 'repeatedly striking'; the rare frequentative form of *tundo*, also
at 2.1142, reflects the speed of their motion, once imparted.

396–416

The relationship of soul and body: (*d*) the dominant role of the *animus* in
sustaining life. Cf. 136–60, where it was shown that in sensation the *animus*
regulates the *anima*.

396–7 magis... coercens = *coercentior*, with adjectival force, as in *dominantior* following.   **uitai claustra** [= 1.415]: 'the bars of life'. For the
metaphor cf. 323–6n. *est custos*; here the image is that of a door preventing
the soul from escaping (*OLD claustrum* 1a).   **dominantior** ~ 138 *dominari.*

398–401 Though it is true that so long as a man retains consciousness he must be alive (402), the converse, which L. now asserts, does
not necessarily follow. Even before the invention of modern techniques
of prolonging life, a man with concussion or a stroke might lie in a
coma, alive but without any sign of mental or emotional activity. What
is maintained here is not supported by any extant Epicurean source. As
Brown points out, the emphatic denial in lines 398–9 is implicitly con-
tradicted at 713–40, where it is argued at some length that some soul-
atoms remain in the body long enough to breed maggots.   **mente
animoque** ~ 402 *mens animusque* (94–7n., 136–9n. *animum mentemque*).
temporis... partem pars... animai: the chiasmus and the word-play accentuate the point; cf. 402 *manet* [= *remanet*: 258–61n. *tangam*]... *remansit.*
comes insequitur 'follows in its train', 'comme l'esclave accompagne son
maître' (Ernout–Robin), sustaining the image of *dominantior.*   **gelidos... linquit** 'leaves cold', *gelidos* predicative.

403–5 quamuis est: the construction of *quamuis* with the indicative rather
than the subjunctive, as at e.g. 307–8, 874, is characteristic of verse from
L. onwards and of post-Augustan prose (H–S 603–4); cf. 705–6 *quamuis... eunt.*   **caesis** 'cut off' (*OLD* 8a).   **truncus** 'the trunk'; the
enjambment imparts emphasis; read as = 'mutilated' the word is otiose
after *caesis.*   **adempta... remota** 'despite the loss of vital spirit released
from the limbs' (Latham); for the concessive force of the participle

cf. 117–20n. *detracto corpore multo. membris* must be read ἀπὸ κοινοῦ with both participles. The limbs, containing only *anima*, die almost instantly; the trunk, the seat of the *animus*, can survive. The anaphora of *circum* identifies the simultaneity of the loss of limbs and *anima*. Here the sense 'limbs' is more appropriate than 'body'; the old correction *remotis* removes any possible ambiguity, but spoils the point brought out by *circum...circum*.

aetherias uitalis: not properly a breach of the 'rule' proscribing the use of two attributive adjectives with one noun, since *aetherias...auras* is in effect an ornamental paraphrase for 'air', syntactically equivalent to a noun, *aetherias* being 'epitheton ornans'; see Munro on 1.258, with examples from Catullus, Virgil and Propertius, and cf. H–S 160–1. *aetherius* is properly used of the upper air, *aether*, as at 1044, rather than the air we breathe, *aer*; but the distinction is not strictly observed by the poets (Lunelli 1969: 11–47), and L., if his MSS may be trusted, uses *aerius* and *aetherius* indifferently, with a preference for *aetherius* (13:8x).

406–12 omnimodis 'altogether' = *omnino*; among writers of the classical period only in L., frequent in later writers.   **ut, lacerato oculo...potestas:** for the implied comparison of the eyeball to 'the soul of the soul' cf. 273–5n. *anima...animae.*   **cernundi:** the original spelling of the gerund and gerundive of 3rd and 4th conjugation verbs; cf. 626 *faciundum.* In the normalized spelling of modern editions it occurs principally in *eo* and its compounds and in legal phraseology such as in the *quaestio de pecuniis repetundis*; but a good many instances are preserved in MSS of classical authors, including L.'s (N–W III 331–40). That L. employed them for special effect seems improbable; their sporadic attestation is more likely to be due to haphazard scribal normalization. This is one of the cases where the editor follows the MSS in a spirit of resignation. Cf. 513–16n. **uiuata potestas** [= 558, 680]: *uiuatus* 'lively' is otherwise attested only by Festus, pp. 516–17 L. *uiuatus et uiuidus a poetis dicuntur a ui magna*; the word is overlooked by *OLD.*   **et...relinquas** 'and so long as you do not leave...'; the force of *ne* is continued in the *et*-clause; cf. Housman on Manil. 4.909; H–S 536, and 730–4n. *neque cur...quareue.* Some of the tissue surrounding the eyeball (*orbis = oculus: OLD orbis* 8b) must be left; the pupil (*acies = pupula: OLD* 4a) cannot function in complete isolation. **id quoque...eorum:** a condensed way of saying 'Just as the *animus* cannot be completely separated from the body without death ensuing, so the complete separation of eyeball and pupil will entail the destruction of both, and so of the eyesight.'   **eorum:** neuter plural, sc. *orbis et pupulae* (136–9n. *coniuncta*).

413–16 tantula pars...media illa 'that middle part, small as it is'; cf. 5.593 *tantulus ille queat tantum sol mittere lumen.* The language conjures up a picture of the setting sun.   **incolumis quamuis alioqui** 'though

otherwise unharmed'. The ellipse of *est* with *quamuis* is normal syntax
(*OLD quamuis* 4c), and Kannengiesser's *alioquist*, besides being unnecessary, engenders an unwieldy clash of consonant groups, -*st spl-*.   **uincti:**
normal Lucretian usage would require *uincta* (136–9n. *coniuncta*); here
the masculine may be due to the proximity of *animus*, but metrical expe-
diency may also have played a part. There is an apparent analogy at Livy
21.50.11 *rex regiaque classis una profecti*, perhaps to be explained by reading
classis = 'the crews', *classiarii* (K–S I 52). For similar variations of concord
see H–S 435.

B. THE SOUL IS MORTAL

417–424

These lines usher in the central portion of the book (417–829) and its
message: that death is not to be feared. What has preceded has cleared
the ground for the demonstration that now follows; and the concluding
section (830–1094) will celebrate and illustrate the implications of the
great truth now established. To signal the importance of what he is about
to say, L. dignifies it with a second prooemium addressed to Memmius.

417–20 Nunc age 'Come now' (*OLD ago* 24), a Lucretian formula (15x)
taken over from Greek didactic: cf. e.g. Nic. *Ther.* 359 νῦν δ' ἄγε, *al.* It signals a new and important theme, as in Virgil's use of it in the prooemium
to the second, 'Iliadic', half of the *Aeneid* (7.37).   **natiuos ... mortalis:**
the soul does not exist either before birth or after death, the framing of
the line by these words (*nunc age* standing outside the syntactical structure)
underlining the point, further reinforced by the weighty spondaic ending.
leuis 'light', being composed of very small and smooth particles (203–5).
dulcique reperta labore: cf. 2.730–1 *nunc age dicta meo dulci quaesita labore* |
percipe. A literary topos: cf. Pind. *Ol.* 1.19 γλυκυτάταις ... φροντίσιν, 'sweetest
cares', Asclep. *AP* 7.11.1 (*HE* 942) γλυκὺς Ἠρίννας οὗτος πόνος, 'this sweet
labour of Erinna'. L. is the first Roman poet to use *labor* of his poetry
(Kenney 1977b/1995: 12–13 and n. 34); cf. 1.24–5 *uersibus ...* | *quos ego*
de rerum natura pangere conor, and Cowper, aptly quoted by Smith ad loc.,
'There is a pleasure in poetic pains, | Which only poets know' (*The Task*
2.285–6) – though it is perhaps ironic that earlier in the same book of the
poem in a passage recalling the familiar words of his hymn, 'He plants his
footsteps on the sea, | And rides upon the storm', he proclaims that it is
God who creates and controls the tempests (2.130–2), phenomena that L.
goes to great lengths to demonstrate are due to natural causes, not divine
caprice (6.96–422 *passim*; cf. Kenney 2007: 99–101).   **digna tua ... uita**
'that shall be worthy of your way of life', *digna* predicative. For *uita* in this
sense = βίος (*OLD* 6a, 7a) cf. Virg. *Aen.* 6.433 (Minos) *uitas et crimina discit,*

Laus Pisonis 5–6 *hinc tua me uirtus rapit et miranda per omnes* | *uita modos*;
and for the virtues attributed to Memmius by L. cf. 1.26–7 *Memmiadae
nostro, quem tu, dea, tempore in omni* | *omnibus ornatum uoluisti excellere rebus*,
140 *tua … uirtus*. The message of L.'s poem and the doctrines pressed so
forcefully on Memmius are those appropriate to his character and way of
life. The interplay of endings in long and short *a* imparts solemnity to the
message, as at 13 *aurea, perpetua semper dignissima uita* (n.). This interpretation gives good and pointed sense, but since Creech first voiced suspicion of the transmitted text ('haec intellegi non possunt') *uita* has been
under critical fire, and various corrections have been proposed (Butterfield 2008b). Of these the best are *mente* (Müller) and *cultu* (Butterfield),
the latter better as giving a metrically and rhetorically more effective conclusion to the verse. Lachmann's *cura* is ruled out by the fact that elsewhere
in the *DRN* the word always means 'anxiety', 'worry' (*OLD* 1), never mental application (3).   **pergam disponere** 'I shall proceed to set out'; cf.
421 *dicere pergam* and see 177–8n. *pergam … reddere*.

421–4 tu … eorum 'See that you join each of them under a single name.'
The emphatic *tu*, after the similar use of σύ by Greek poets, and the
periphrastic imperative *fac … subiungas* are in the high didactic style: Memmius is to pay special attention to what follows. The ellipse of *ut* is common with *fac, facito, malo, uolo, nolo, et sim.* L. has now used *anima* and *animus* indifferently for the whole soul, ψυχή, some eight times (94–7n.); that
only now is he explicit on the point in this emphatic manner is because, as
noted by Brown ad loc., whereas one of the ensuing proofs concerns only
one part of the soul, nevertheless the death of that part must necessarily
occasion the death of the other and thus of the whole soul; cf. 136–7. In
fact the distinction between *animus* and *anima*, important in the preceding Section A, becomes for the most part immaterial in what follows; but
see 445–8n. *mentem.*   **subiungas:** so the older editors and Lachmann
(who however emended to *uni subiungas nomen*); Munro and later editors
read *sub iungas*. The separation of prepositional prefixes from their nouns
is not uncommon in L., but none of the other examples cited by Munro
at 1.841 can be construed ambiguously; in that respect this case would be
unique. There is in fact no substantive distinction of sense between the two
readings, and the distinction between *subiungas* and *sub iungas* would not
have been perceived by an ancient reader, who, whether he was reading
silently or aloud, nevertheless punctuated by ear. Writing without division
of words (*scriptura continua*) on the Greek model in Latin MSS (1068–9n.
fugit … effugere) was not generally adopted until well after L.'s time, and
his early copies may have had interpuncts between the words, as in the
Gallus papyrus. In any case, the inevitable imposition of modern conventions of punctuation on texts written to be read by ear cannot be allowed

to dictate interpretation.   **uerbi causa** 'for example' (*OLD uerbum* 13).
quatenus 'since' (218–20n.).   **est...est** 'the two are so conjoined as
to constitute a single object' (Latham). The verb, as not infrequently, is
attracted into the number of the predicate; cf. e.g. Ter. *And.* 555 *aman-
tium irae amoris integratiost,* Ov. *Met* 1.292 *omnia pontus erat,* 15.529 *unumque
erat omnia uulnus* (K–S I 40–1). The variation *unum...res,* the interlacing
expression with *inter se* to be read ἀπὸ κοινοῦ, and the framing of the line
by *est...est* are designed to drive home the point, admirably brought out
by Latham's adroit paraphrase. L. is perhaps rebutting the view held by
some authorities that the soul had both a mortal and an immortal part
(Boyancé 1963: 160).

425–829

L. now proceeds to set forth the proofs, here presented according to the
numeration of Bailey (but cf. Boyancé 1963: 161 n. 1), of the mortal
nature of the soul. This is the major premiss of the conclusion to which
the book looks forward: that death is not to be feared.

(I) THE SOUL DOES NOT SURVIVE THE DEATH OF THE BODY

425–444

(**Proof 1**) The soul is made of far smaller particles than water, mist or
smoke: but when a vessel containing water is broken the water runs away,
and mist and smoke can be seen to disperse: therefore when the body,
which is the vessel of the soul, is irreparably damaged, the soul must be
dissolved into its atoms. The argument, relying heavily on analogy and
interrupted by the amplifying parenthesis at 428–33, is couched in the
form of a syllogism.

425–7 tenuem constare minutis | corporibus 'it [sc. the *anima,* not expli-
citly mentioned until line 437] is finely composed of tiny particles', *tenuem*
predicative.   **docui:** at 177–230.   **quam liquidus umor aquai:** sc. *est,*
as at 456 with *cum* and 614 with *ut.* Contrast 2.456–7 *omnia postremo quae
puncto tempore cernis | diffugere, ut fumum nebulas flammasque,* but that, which
Bailey (1947: 89) calls the 'normal' construction, is in fact a secondary
development (*NLS* 256–7; K–S II 465). L. varies the prosody of *liquidus*
according to the incidence of the verse ictus; cf. 145–6n. *idque,* 4.1259 *cras-
saque conueniant līquidis et līquida crassis* and Munro ad loc., N–H 1970: 364
on Hor. *C.* 1.32.11.

428–33 L. interpolates a proof of what he has just asserted since, though
it follows by implication from what was said at 179–230, it was not explicitly demonstrated there. The passage is loosely constructed and has the

air of an afterthought, but that is not a sufficient reason for expelling
lines 430–3 (Deufert 1996: 247–9). The *anima* is more easily dispersed
than water, mist or smoke, and must therefore be more finely constituted.
a: 323–6n. *corpore ab omni.*   **tenui…magis:** take together.   **quippe
ubi** 'seeing that', a common argumentative formula in L. (11x).   **imaginibus** 'images' (*imagines, simulacra* = εἴδωλα), the films which according
to Epicurean theory were constantly given off from the surface of all bodies; impinging on the eyes, or in sleep directly on the *animus*, they cause
vision. The atoms of the soul are so fine that it is moved even in sleep
by those given off in the 'images' of smoke or cloud, fine as they are.
alte | …altaria: the word-play appears to reflect popular etymology, which
derived *altare* from *altus* (Fest. p. 27.1–2 L.; Maltby 1991 s.v. *altare*).
uaporem…fumum 'hot smoke', hendiadys; *uapor* in L. always = 'heat'.
ferreque = *efferreque* after *exhalare.*   **procul…dubio** 'without doubt',
more commonly in L. *dubio procul* (8:5x); *procul* not uncommonly functions as a preposition. These *simulacra*, now mentioned for the first time –
full discussion is reserved for later (4.45–521, 722–857) – do indeed come
from outside and are not produced by the mind itself. Since this part of
his argument depends on doctrine not yet expounded, L. interpolates a
further parenthetical explanation.   **feruntur:** given that the phrase *simulacra feruntur/-antur* is found 8x elsewhere in the poem, Creech's correction may be thought to impose itself, picking up as it does *ferreque*
from the previous verse. MS *geruntur* is easier to account for if L. in fact
wrote *genuntur* 'are begotten', as conjectured by Lambinus and correctly
restored by him elsewhere (4.143, 159), but that does not give appropriate
sense.

434–9 The appeal to the evidence of the senses and what by analogy we
deduce from it must be equally valid in the case of processes which we
cannot directly perceive.   **nunc igitur quoniam** appears at first sight to
pick up *quoniam* from line 425 and introduce the conclusion, but in fact
it resumes after the parenthesis to enunciate the minor premiss of the
syllogism. For the anacoluthic effect cf. 554–7n. *sic.*   **undique** qualifies *diffluere…discedere* in the next verse, not *quassatis.*   **uasis:** for the
image cf. 440, 555, 793. The conceit that was touched on earlier (323–6)
of the body as protector of the soul is now developed through a slightly
different metaphor, the body as a vessel containing and holding the soul
together. The comparison was a commonplace; cf. e.g. Cic. *Tusc.* 1.52 *corpus quidem quasi uas est aut aliquod animi receptaculum.* For a history of the
image see Görler 1997. 'Strictly speaking, Lucretius' body–vessel analogy
is not a metaphor or a simile as it is in Plato and the Stoics, but a piece of
physical doctrine: for an Epicurean the body is in fact a "vessel" in a quite
literal sense' (207).   **diffluere umorem et laticem discedere:** elegant

variation with chiasmus and repetition of prefix. **discedit** agrees with
its nearer subject (294–5n. *efferuescit*). **perire** = *disperire* with *diffundi*
preceding and *dissolui* following. The proliferation of words connoting dispersal underlines the point, further emphasized by *ocius et citius* following: the dissolution of the soul is swifter than that of water, mist or smoke
because it is so much finer.

440–4 quippe etenim [= 800] 'For in fact', a favourite phrase of L.'s
(21x). **cum** 'as soon as', but also with a causal nuance (359–64n. *praesertim cum*); this follows *because* it has lost its protective 'vessel'. **conquassatum ... rarefactum** 'if it should be shaken or rarefied' (119, 170–4n.
ossibus ... adacta); *rarefacio* is attested only in L. (4x). **ac** 'or', as at 164
(cf. 147–51n. *-que*). The body does not need to be completely shattered
for death to occur; if enough blood is lost it may lose coherence to an
extent that allows the *anima* to escape through its interstices (*foramina*,
πόροι); cf. 458 *fatisci*. The analogy with the *uas* also holds in such instances.
qui ... ullo 'how can we possibly believe that it can be held in by any
air?', i.e. by any kind of air that might be imagined. The rhetorical question is equivalent to a statement = *nec ullo*. In early and colloquial Latin
nullus may serve as a more emphatic form of the simple negative *non*: cf.
e.g. Plaut. *Bacch.* 90 *tu nullus adfueris, si non libet*, 'you needn't put in an
appearance at all if you don't want to', Cic. *De Leg.* 2.15 *Zeleucum istum
negat ullum fuisse*, 'he says that this Zeleucus never existed at all'. See H–S
205; Hofmann 1951: 80; Fordyce on Catull. 17.20. **cohiberier:** 66–7n.
†incohibescit†: if this is what L. wrote, the sense must be 'which (though)
rarer than the body, (yet) strives to hold it in'. However, (i) the inceptive/
conative sense is not wanted; (ii) even if that force is 'hardly felt' (Smith
ad loc., comparing 890 *torrescere*; cf. H–S 298), L. is asking how the air
could possibly 'contain' the soul, not suggesting that it tries and fails; (iii)
the word is otherwise unattested, though in an inventive writer like L.
that is not a decisive objection. The same objection can be made against
Bergk's *incohibensque est*, 'which is rarer than the body and more incapable
of retaining (the soul)' = *c. q. n. magis rarus est magisque incohibens*. That
entails taking the prefix *in-* in its negative sense, as in *incohibilis* 'hard to
hold together', a word otherwise attested only in Aulus Gellius and Ausonius. The expression is too awkward and un-Lucretian to pass muster. The
same objections apply to Woltjer's *incohibens sit*. Of other corrections the
best is Lachmann's *is cohibessit* (= *cohibuerit*: N–W III 510), an improvement on Lambinus' *am cohibessit*, 'how can that air which is rarer than our
body hold it in?' (Munro). This gives good sense and picks up *cohiberier*
neatly from the preceding verse; for the perfect subjunctive in rhetorical
questions see *NLS* 119; K–S I 178. It requires line 444 to be punctuated
as a separate question, with the ellipse of *est* in consequence thrown into

greater relief. In the light of all these uncertainties the obelus is the safest resort.

445-458

(**Proof 2**) The growth and development of the soul is parallel to that of the body. The idea was a commonplace, predating Epicurus and apparently accepted by him without discussion (Bailey 1947: 1072-3 ad loc.). L.'s previous references to it (331-2, 344-9) are almost casual; evidently he took it for granted.

446-8 sentimus ... senescere ... tenero ... sententia tenuis: the word-play reinforces the logic. For the Epicurean exploitation of this technique see Friedländer 1941/1969 *passim*. **sentimus:** the appeal to the evidence of the senses is not, strictly speaking, valid for the process of begetting (*gigni*). **mentem:** it is the *animus* that L. has in mind here; cf. *animi ... sententia*, 450 *consilium*, 453 *ingenium*; but at 455 he applies the argument to the *anima* (421-4n. *tu ... eorum*). **infirmo ... teneroque ... | corpore:** for the descriptive ablatives cf. 288-93n. *sub fin.* **uagantur** 'walk unsteadily', 'totter'. **sequitur** 'accompanies', 'matches' (*OLD* 14); cf. 724. The mind moves uncertainly, like the body. **tenuis:** here scanned as a disyllable by synizesis.

449-54 uiribus ... uis | ... uiribus: L. plays on the senses of the word: physical strength, mental power, and the metaphorical power of time. **quassatum ... obtusis:** cf. 434, 441; but the image now is of the body shaken by physical forces like the strokes of a battering-ram, 'the frame is shattered, its powers blunted'. *obtusis* does double duty: the faculties are dulled (*OLD obtundo* 3b) as the body succumbs to the 'blows' dealt by the process of ageing. L. habitually expresses the power of time in physical terms: 5.314 *ualidas aeui uires*, 379 *immensi ualidas aeui ... uires.* **claudicat ... delirat ... labat:** the language of this succinct depiction of the effects of old age is beautifully devised, *claudicat* 'limps' sustains the idea of the physical decay which the mind shares with the body, as well as describing slowness of perception and hesitation in speech (*OLD* 1); *delirat* 'wanders' (with an eye on the original literal sense 'stray from the furrow' in ploughing (*OLD* 1; cf. 359-64n. *cernere*)), inability to keep to the point: the tongue is *animi interpres* (6.1149); *labat* (Lachmann's almost certain supplement) 'totters', figuring indecision and inaction. For *labo* of the failing of the faculties cf. Cels. 2.7.21 *mens labat, OLD* 4a. **deficiunt ... desunt:** picking up *diffluere ... discedere* from 435 before making the comparison explicit in the following lines. **uno tempore** 'at the same moment' (*OLD tempus* 1).

455–8 dissolui: probably, as elsewhere, though the metre does not enforce it here, as it does at 330 (n.), to be scanned as a quadrisyllable.   **quoque:** sc. along with the body; cf. 445–6, 457 *pariter.*   **conuenit** 'it follows', is consonant with what has been established (*OLD* 6a); but cf. 459–62n. **ceu fumus:** Epicurus is said to have said that at death souls were 'scattered like smoke', καπνοῦ δίκην σκίδνανται (227 Us.), but the image was old, both literary, as when the apparition of Patroclus disappears 'like smoke', ἠΰτε καπνός (Hom. *Il.* 23.100), and popular, as when men fear (falsely) that at death the soul scatters 'like a breath or smoke', ὥσπερ πνεῦμα ἢ καπνός (Plato, *Phaedo* 70a).   **in altas aeris oras:** the stately epic language invests the possibly depressing image of dissolution and oblivion with dignity. For the construction with *fumus* nominative cf. 427n.   **fessa fatisci** [= 5.308] 'worn out and (so) falling apart', *fessa* predicative; the sense reinforced by the *figura etymologica*, since both words come from the same root. L. uses the deponent *fatisci* for the more usual active probably for metrical convenience; otherwise it is found only in Republican dramatists, Varro, and later archaizing writers.

459–462

(Proof 3) Just as the body suffers disease and pain, so the mind suffers grief and fear; (but the body is mortal): therefore the mind is mortal. This argument is also attributed by Cicero to Panaetius, a Stoic philosopher of the second century BC (*Tusc.* 1.79). This proof, which is syllogistic in form (but cf. next n.), still concerns the parallel experiences of body and soul; it paves the way to their shared experiences.

459–62 Huc accedit uti 'Furthermore', a regular Lucretian formula (9x) to introduce a new argument.   **corpus ut ipsum** 'just like the body' (128–9n.).   **suscipere** 'undergo', as at 366 (n.), sc. *uidemus* supplied from preceding *uideamus.*   **quare … conuenit** 'therefore it follows', which strictly speaking is untrue. The 'pains' suffered by the mind are so called by analogy with physical pains, assisted by the ambiguity of *acris* in line 461 (*OLD acer* 11b, c); that the dissolution of the *animus* entails that of the whole soul is now taken for granted. The argument from derangement that follows is rather more cogent. Cf. 484–6n.

463–473

(Proof 4) In disease the mind can be seen to share in the derangement of the body.

463–9 quin etiam 'Moreover', introducing an even more compelling example, a Lucretian formula (12x); in this book at 487, 540, 592, 657. **morbis in corporis:** for the postponement of the preposition cf. 374–7n. *quibus e*; but in such phrases the genitive is regularly treated as if it were an adjective agreeing with the noun, and the preposition is sandwiched between them. Cf. Kenney on Ov. *Her.* 17.87, K–S 1 587–8, Bömer on Ov. *Met.* 5.336. Here the postponement is dictated by the metre.   **auius errat** 'wanders lost'; cf. 453 *delirat* (n.), Enn. *Sc.* 241 V.², 202 J. *incerte errat animus,* there of infirmity of purpose.   **dementit...deliraque:** continuing the image of straying. *dementio* is attested only here and in a handful of places in later writers, but that the notion of the mind's being astray was inherent in *demens* is evident from Enn. *Ann.*199–200 Sk. *quo uobis mentes, rectae quae stare solebant,* | *dementes sese flexere uia* [*uiai* edd.]?   **interdumque** 'or sometimes'.   **lethargo** 'coma'; L. uses the Greek technical term, perhaps thinking the Latin equivalent *ueternus* insufficiently precise. His description may indeed draw on clinical observation; cf. Ernout–Robin ad loc., pointing to Celsus' distinction between madness, *morbus phreneticus,* and coma, *lethargus* (3.20). He may have been thinking of a form of malaria (Jones 1909: 68). But see 824–7n. *lethargo.*   **aeternumque soporem** 'and unbroken sleep', here describing coma, not death, as at 921: 'characteristically loaded and tendentious, as it anticipates Lucretius' conclusion while he is still stating the argument' (Brown ad loc.). Certainly the behaviour of the bystanders that he goes on to describe is indistinguishable from that of mourners at a deathbed. For *aeternus = perpetuus* 'unchanging', 'enduring' (*OLD* 1b) cf. 907, 1.34 *aeterno deuictus uulnere amoris.*   **oculis nutuque cadenti** 'with drooping eyes and head'; *cadenti* does double duty ἀπὸ κοινοῦ. For *cado =* 'droop' (*OLD* 7) cf. 4.952 *bracchia palpebraeque cadunt. cadenti* agrees as usual with the nearer noun. **ad uitam...reuocantes:** then as now attempts would be made to awaken a patient from a coma by such stimuli as calling his name; cf. Celsus 3.20.3 *si...continens* [~ *aeternum*] *ei somnus est, utique excitandus est*; and one of the signs of the approach of death, *signa letalia,* listed by Pliny is *a somno mouentium neglectus* (*NH* 7.171). What L. describes, however, evokes a picture of the week-long mourning ritual of the *conclamatio* (Serv. on Virg. *Aen.* 6.218, Σ Ter. p.59.10–13 Schlee); only when this had been faithfully performed was the deceased deemed to be definitively dead.   **potis est** *= potest*; also at 1069, a metrically useful variant (11x in L.), only rarely resorted to by post-Republican writers. Cf. 319–22n. *potesse.*   **lacrimis rorantes ora genasque:** the description of these 'mourners' is more scornful than sympathetic, echoing as it does that twice attributed by L. to the atoms, reduced to helpless merriment by the absurd positions to which opponents of his arguments are reduced: 1.920 *lacrimis salsis umectant ora genasque,* 2.977 *lacrimis spargunt rorantibus ora genasque.*

470–1 fateare necessest: a recurrent formula (12x; also 1.974 *fatearis... necesse est*), in this book also at 543, 578, 677. On L.'s tendency to hector his readers cf. Kenney 2007: 82.   **penetrant...contagia morbi** 'the disease enters and affects the mind'; for *contagia =* 'contacts' cf. 343. Here the sense of 'infection', as in the description of the plague at 6.1236, is also felt.

472-3 The minor premiss of the syllogism, though appended rather with the air of an afterthought: bodily disease affects the mind; but pain and disease in the body lead, as we know from common experience, to death: therefore the mind must perish as the body perishes.   **fabricator:** a striking metaphor, as Heinze remarks, since disease is generally thought of as a destroyer. For the paradox one might compare Macaulay's description of Voltaire as 'the very Vitruvius of ruin'.   **perdocti** 'thoroughly instructed'.

474-5 That these verses have no conceivable relevance to the context hardly needs demonstration, and Naugerius' and Lambinus' deletion has been generally accepted without question. This is classified by Deufert as belonging to the intervention of a 'philosophically motivated reader', but how such an interpolator could have imagined that he was underpinning L.'s argument (Deufert 1996: 310–11, 310n.) is not easy to see.

476–486

(Proof 5) The effects of drunkenness. Whereas disease attacks the body, which then communicates its effects to the mind, drunkenness attacks the *anima* directly (483); the argument of the preceding section is reversed. Drunkenness was a topic of interest to philosophers in antiquity, including Epicurus (476–7n.).

476-83 An eight-line period building up to a rhetorical question to which there can only be one answer is framed by two responding couplets in which alliteration reinforces the intervening description of the power of alcohol to invade the body and derange the mind.

476-7 Food and drink were thought to be distributed through the body by the veins (2.1125, 1136, 4.955); as the *anima* is *per totum dissita corpus* (143), it follows that wine first affects the *anima*, which in turn affects the body.   **discessit diditus:** the repeated prefixes emphasize the completeness of the distribution.   **ardor:** according to Plutarch Epicurus thought that wine might be either heating or cooling (*Against Colotes* 6 = *Moralia* 1109–10, 58–60 Us.); L. follows the common view.

478-81 This catalogue of symptoms reflects common observation, but is vividly expressed in L.'s best manner (cf. 154–6). It is artfully arranged to lead to a climax: the phrases decrease in length, to culminate in a series of single words *clamor singultus iurgia*, conveying a picture of progressive loss of self-control, summed up in the expressive *gliscunt* (n.).   **grauitas:** the *anima* can no longer hold the body up; cf. 5.556–7 *nonne uides etiam quam magno pondere nobis* | *sustineat corpus tenuissima uis animai ... ?*   **tardescit:**

attested only here and evidently coined by L.   **madet:** commonly used
of drunkenness (*OLD* 3), here to convey how the atoms of the *anima* and
animus are permeated by those of the wine; cf. 485 *insinuarit.*   **nant** 'are
awash', an expressive metaphor first found in L.; used by Virgil of sleep
(*G.* 4.496, *Aen.* 5.856 *natantia lumina*) and by Ovid of death (*Met.* 5.71
oculis… natantibus) as well as of drunkenness.   **gliscunt** 'grow', an old
word, originally it seems of agricultural application (cf. 359–64n. *cernere*);
Columella uses it = 'thrive' of livestock, *paleis… etiam gliscit*, sc. *asellus*
(7.1.1). As a poetic and expressive synonym of *cresco* it is a favourite of Tacitus'.   **cetera de genere hoc** [= 744] 'etc.', a Lucretian formula (11x; *c.
d. g. horum* 3x). The dry and summary character of the verse, unreflect-
ingly termed 'weak' by some commentators, perhaps suggests that details
here were felt by L. to be inappropriate to the dignity of *epos*; cf. 388–90n.
et cetera. Clinical descriptions, as of epilepsy (487–91n.) or the Athenian
plague (6.1145–55), were another matter.

482–3 The question, with forceful alliteration of *c* and *u*, and insistent
repetition of *cur*, reprising 476–7, rounds off and encloses the paragraph.
corpore in ipso [= 493, 506, 590] 'there in the body' (128–9n.). The unexpressed corollary is that if this can happen while the *anima* has a solid container in the shape of the body, it must *a fortiori* be in even worse case after
death, when its only container is air (cf. 440–4). The point is explicitly
made later, at 506–9, 603–6.

484–6 This is the argument on which the whole demonstration from
463 to 525 is based, though L. appends it to the section on drunkenness.
He reasons from probability: the behaviour of the soul in delirium, drunkenness, etc. does not prove conclusively that it dies with the body, but if
it can be so grievously afflicted in such states then it is fair to conclude
that the consequences must extend finally to dissolution.   **quaecumque**
'anything which', referring to the *anima.*   **inque pediri:** for the metrically intractable *impediri*, by tmesis.   **insinuarit** 'has found its way in',
i.e. into the atomic structure. L. uses the word both intransitively, as here,
and transitively; cf. 502, 671, 1061 (nn.).   **causa** 'disease' = αἴτιον in
the medical sense, and so equivalent to *morbus.*   **aeuo** 'life', as at 344,
357.

487–509

(Proof 6) The effects of epilepsy. This disease was much discussed by medical writers, as was intoxication by philosophers (Bailey 1947: 1077–8): see
Segal 1970, suggesting that L.'s description may be indebted to the Hippocratic treatise *On Breaths* (Περὶ Φυσῶν). The style of that work, that of 'a
rhetorical sophist' (Jones 1923: 221) 'may have interested Lucretius the
poet' (Segal 1970: 184). L. no doubt knew that Julius Caesar was a sufferer

(Suet. *Iul.* 45). Along with dementia, epilepsy was indeed one of the most striking instances of the disturbance of the *anima* in disease available to him.

487–91 quin etiam 'moreover'.   **subito … ut fulminis ictu:** the sudden and instantaneous onset of the attack is vividly conveyed by the structure of the sentence, with the image of the thunderbolt picking up and reifying *subito*, and the expressive enjambment of *concidit*. The simile may, as suggested by Brown ad loc., carry a polemical implication. L. would have been well aware of the fact that epilepsy was commonly called 'the sacred disease' (ἡ ἱερὴ νόσος, *morbus sacer*), and of the belief, vigorously refuted at some length by Hippocrates (Περὶ Ἱερῆς Νόσου 1–5), that it was of divine origin. Thus the comparison with the thunderbolt may have been meant to make the point that epilepsy, like all other phenomena, was to be ascribed to natural causes. His readers would in due course come to a long and careful explanation of how thunderbolts are caused (6.379–422).   **ante oculos … nostros:** again the appeal to the evidence of the senses.   **concidit et spumas agit** 'falls down and foams at the mouth': the symptoms which identify the disease; cf. 6.793 *concidere et spumas qui morbo mittere sueuit*, Celsus 3.23.1 *homo subito concidit, ex ore spumae mouentur*.   **artus:** accusative of respect, of what is referred to (*NLS* 19 (ii); G–L 338); cf. Virgil's imitation, *G.* 3.84 *micat auribus et tremit artus*.   **desipit** ~ 464 *dementit*; the *anima* is deranged by what is happening to the body, vividly illustrated by the simile following at 493–4.   **extentat neruos** 'his muscles become rigid', literally 'he tightens his muscles'. Latin not infrequently says 'do' for 'allow to be done', 'to have happen to one'; cf. 877, 1029–33, 1090 (nn.). This idiom is widely attested in Latin poetry from Virgil onwards; see e.g. Housman on Manil. 1.487, Lucan 1.103, *CP* 41, 613, Fraenkel 1957: 215 n. 2, Goodyear on *Aetna* 119.   **inconstanter** 'irregularly' (*OLD* 1).

492–4 'Obviously because the spirit, torn apart by the violence of the disease, is in commotion, whipping up foam, as in the ocean' eqs. To produce a satisfactory text of this dramatic description some corrections of what the MSS offer are necessary.   **ui** (Brieger), picking up *ui morbi* from 487, was corrupted to *uis* to agree with *distracta*, an example of the propensity of copyists to attend only to the immediate context: it is the soul, not the disease, that is torn apart (cf. 501, 507, 590, 799).   **turbat agens anima spumas** 'the soul is in turmoil, driving foam before it': *turbat* (here intransitive, as commonly in L.) is *vox propria* of the behaviour of a disorderly mob (*OLD* 1a, c); the soul-atoms are figured as milling about at sixes and sevens; *agens*, suggesting spindrift scudding before a gale (*OLD* 4b), neatly introduces the following simile. Tohte's correction of the transmitted *animam spumans*, engendered by the preceding *agens*, gives straightforward sense, but entails accepting a metrical anomaly, that the *-a* of *anima* must be treated as metrically 'long' or 'heavy' before *sp-* following. This licence is unparalleled in L., but is several times attested in his contemporary Catullus; cf. 64.176 *nulla spes*, 17.24, 44.18, 53.63. L. not infrequently allows a vowel to be read as metrically 'short' or 'light' in such a position, as at 1.372 *cedere squamigeris* (see Bailey ad loc.); and there seems to be no compelling reason for denying him the reverse licence. Its uniqueness should not count against it: 'it makes no sense that a poet shall never do anything unless he does it at least twice' (Kenney 1999: 400).   **ut in aequore salso | uentorum ualidis feruescunt uiribus undae:** cf. Enn. *Ann.* 453 Sk. *in mare salsum* and Skutsch ad loc. Epic diction and the fourfold alliteration of *u* graphically represent the violence of the dispersion of the soulatoms.

496–8 omnino 'generally' (*OLD* 4), identifying the primary cause; the role of pain is secondary.   **semina uocis:** L. assumes, what he will demonstrate later, that sounds are composed of atoms: 4.443–4 *haud igitur dubiumst quin uoces uerbaque constent | corporeis e principiis, ut laedere possint.* **eiciuntur** 'are forced out'. Lambinus' correction is demanded by the sense; cf. 495 *exprimitur. eliciuntur* 'are enticed out' is far too mild a term, whereas at line 58 it is the *mot juste* and correction there is uncalled for (57–8n.). **glomerata** 'in heaps', pell-mell; the sounds are inarticulate, not properly formed by the tongue (4.549–52).   **qua** 'where', sc. *uia* (*OLD* qua 3). The origin of this usage (see Ernout–Meillet s.v.) is implicitly glossed at 736 *qua possint uia nulla uidetur.*   **consuerunt:** for *consueuerunt*; cf. 650 *abstraxe* (n.), 6.83 *cresse.*   **et sunt munita uiai** 'and (where) there is a paved road for them', a curious metaphor. It is used at 5.102–3, more aptly, of the evidence of the senses as 'the highway of belief, the nearest way into the precincts of the mind of man', *uia qua munita fidei | proxima fert humanum in pectus templaque mentis.* L. has a weakness for genitive phrases of the type of *strata uiai, saepta domorum, prima uirorum,* primarily it would seem for metrical convenience (Bailey 1947: 91–2). On analogous idioms in Greek see Headlam and Knox 1922: 49–50.

499–501 desipientia fit: because, as is then explained, the *animus* is involved with the *anima* in the dissolution. *desipientia*, attested only here in classical Latin, is coined from *desipio* on the model of *sapientia* from *sapio.* Its position here creates a diaeresis after the second foot, but *fit* coheres so closely in sense that the metrical anomaly is not felt.   **ut docui:** at 492–4.   **seorsum:** the trisyllabic form required by metre only here and 551 (282–7n.), *sorsum* (17x) and *sorsus* (3x) indifferently to suit the metre. See Introd. 18 n. 73, 282–7n.   **disiectatur … distracta** 'is dispersed and torn apart'; *disiecto* first attested in L. (3x) and only sparsely thereafter. As often, the repeated prefixes accentuate the point: dissolution is total. **eodem illo … ueneno** 'the very same [*OLD ille* 3] poison', sc. the *corrupti* *corporis umor* (503), the *uis morbi* (487). For *uenenum* = 'destructive agent' (*OLD* 3a) cf. 1.759–60 (the elements earth, air, fire and water in Empedoclean theory) *inimica modis multis sunt atque ueneno | ipsa inter se sibi.*

502-5 reflexit...reditque | in latebras 'has turned back and returned to its lair','comme un serpent uenimeux' (Ernout–Robin), playing on the literal sense of *uenenum.* The intransitive use of *flecto* and *reflecto* is rare (*OLD* s.vv. 3d, 2c), but L. freely uses normally transitive verbs intransitively; cf. 493 *turbat* and see Bailey 1947: 105. **reditque** = *rediitque*; cf. 1042 *obît.* **umor:** medical writers ascribed epilepsy to a temporary excess of one or other of the 'humours' (bile, serum, phlegm = χολή, ἰχώρ, φλέγμα; to be distinguished from the four of medieval and early modern medical theory). L. does not specify which he takes to be responsible, probably because the question was disputed, nor does he explain the process by which the overflowing of the *umor* sets in train the violent consequences. At 4.664 fever is ascribed to excess of bile. **quasi uaccillans primum consurgit** 'rises, as it were staggering at first'. On L.'s habit of apologizing for an expression where no apology seems to be needed see 130–5n. *quasi.* This spelling of *uacillo* is sporadically attested in MSS and is ascribed by Nonius Marcellus (p. 50 L.) to Cicero at *Phil.* 3.31, where it is in fact found in one MS. L. uses it with the normal spelling at 479 and 7x elsewhere; here the scansion assists the description of the man's clumsy attempts to get on his feet. For similar variations of quantity for metrical convenience cf. 648 *relicuo*, 994 *cuppedine* (nn.) **receptat** = *recipit*; as at 352 (n.), the frequentative form serves metrical convenience.

506-9 ~ 440–4, summing up this part of the argument by reiterating the point made there, implied at 483 (n.), and repeated at 603–6: if the soul can be so affected while it is in the body, it is unlikely to be able to survive outside it. As at 484–6 (n.) L. reasons from probability. **haec:** *animus* and *anima.* **tantis...morbis:** sc. coma and intoxication as well as epilepsy. **corpore in ipso** [= 483, 590] 'while actually in the body' (Brown), as opposed to being outside it (508). Cf. 128–9n. **iactentur...laborent:** for the causal subjunctive after *ubi* = 'when' (*OLD* 9a), here virtually = *cum*, cf. 4.195 *ubi tam uolucri leuitate ferantur*; the grammars appear to offer no other instances; *ubi* + indicative in a causal sense is also very sparsely attested (H–S 652). **miserisque modis:** cf. 1.123 *simulacra modis pallentia miris.* Such plural expressions with *modus* are common in the comic poets (Löfstedt 1942: 59–60) and clearly appealed for their rhetorical effect to Virgil, who repeats *DRN* 1.123 verbatim at *G*.1.477 and has the phrase *modis miris* five times elsewhere (cf. Löfstedt 1942: 62). **laborent** 'suffer'. **cum ualidis uentis:** the fragile soul could hardly expect to survive in this robust company; the ironical suggestion of personification is maintained in *aetatem degere* = 'live'; cf. 512 *mortalem uiuere mentem.*

510–525

(Proof 7) Medical treatment entails altering the atomic structure of the mind; but change implies death: therefore the mind, and hence the soul, is mortal. The minor premiss of the syllogism is a fundamental Epicurean axiom (517–20n.).

510–12 mentem: sc. when, as is the case with the body (*corpus ut aegrum*), it is sick.   **cernimus ... uidemus | ... praesagit:** the evidence of our senses (the point being reinforced by the pleonasm framing line 511) forewarns us that the *animus* is mortal.   **flecti** 'influenced', 'changed' (*OLD* 8a), as at 516, 522, 755; perhaps also glancing at the idea that the sick mind is astray (453, 464 (nn.)).   **mortalem uiuere** 'live under sentence of death', *mortalem* predicative: a pungent oxymoron.

513–16 Change of any kind entails addition, subtraction, or rearrangement of the atoms, *traiecere* = *traicere*, the old spelling (Lindsay 1922: 140). On the survival of such forms in the tradition cf. 406–12n. *cernundi*. **aequumst** 'it stands to reason'; cf. 5. 1089–90 *quanto mortalis magis aequumst tum potuisse | dissimilis alia atque alia res uoce notare!*, 3.455, 464 *conuenit. eum* must be understood as the antecedent of *quicumque* following. *aequum* here is given a section to itself by *OLD aequus* 9, but it is better understood as belonging to the general notion of what is equitable and reasonable (6).   **aliquid prorsum ... hilum** 'something, if only a very little', *hilum*, reading almost like an afterthought (cf. 518, where it qualifies preceding *quicquam*), is best taken epexegetically in apposition to *aliquid* rather than, as elsewhere, adverbially, in which case it regularly follows a negative. Here, *pace* Heinze, followed by Butterfield (2009: 312–13), it is difficult to take the expression as virtually negative. The solution apparently adopted by several translators, but ruled out by the resultant syntax, is to read *hilum* as a noun agreeing with *aliquid*: 'some little' (Munro, Smith), 'some small whit' (Bailey), 'quelque peu' (Ernout). The anomaly of such a reading was recognized by Housman, who in the marginalia in his copy of Munro's edition of 1873, now in the library of St John's College, Oxford, emended *aliquid* to *aliquod* (Butterfield 2009: 313). However, nowhere else in L. and very rarely, it would seem, elsewhere is *hilum* qualified by an adjective or pronoun; and Housman evidently did not have enough confidence in his suggestion to publish it. An alternative solution is to read *aliqui* or *aliqua* (Butterfield) 'somehow'; the latter word, otherwise attested only in Plautus (*CLE* 491.3, cit. *TLL* s.v. 1608.30–2, is clearly a stone-cutter's error), would then join other such instances in this book (248, 659, 963, 1012 (nn.)). However, the required sense here is 'something' rather than 'somehow'.   **adoritur et infit** 'attempts and begins'; the pleonasm, reinforced by *quaerit* following, perhaps suggests that however slight the intervention, the result, in terms of disturbance of the atomic structure, will be the same. **aliam quamuis naturam** 'anything else whatever'; the principle, fundamental to Epicurean theory, admits of no exceptions (see next n.).   **flectere** 'change'.

517–20 What is immortal cannot change, for change entails the death of what was there before. An Epicurean axiom: lines 519–20 are repeated several times in the poem (see critical notes). The atoms themselves are immortal; their combinations (the gods being a special case: 23–4n.) are subject to change, i.e. are mortal. Cf. 701, 715–16, 756, repeating the axiom in different words.   **transferri . . . tribui . . . defluere:** passive and intransitive variants of *traicere, addere, detrahere*. For *defluo* = 'depart', 'disappear' see *OLD* 4b; the only occurrence of the word in the poem, probably chosen by L. as a variant of the more usual *diffluo* to respond to *detrahere* – an example of L.'s close attention to the nuances of the language. **nec . . . uult** 'declines to allow'; *nolo* and *non uolo* often mean something a good deal stronger than 'be unwilling' (*OLD nolo* 1b). For the quasi-personification cf. 208–9n. *dedicat.*   **quicquam . . . hilum** 'anything whatever'.   **suis . . . finibus** 'outside its own boundaries': an important image, recalling the great celebration of Epicurus and his achievements at the beginning of the poem: *refert nobis uictor quid possit oriri, | quid nequeat, finita potestas denique cuique | quanam sit ratione atque alte terminus haerens* (1.75–7). The 'boundaries' and the 'boundary-stones' represent the fixed properties of the atomic combinations; any substance that 'quits its limits' thereby ceases to exist as such.   **continuo** 'immediately', but also, since the sequence of events is logically dictated, 'accordingly', 'thereby' (*OLD* 2).

521–2 ergo picks up *at* from line 517; formally these verses are part of the syllogism, but as with 484–6 and 506–9 (nn.), the summary is relevant and rounds off the whole sequence of argument from line 463. **mortalia signa | mittit:** the main clause is enclosed by the two subordinate clauses, so embodying textually the point on which L. goes on to insist, that all escape routes from the Epicurean position are logically blocked off.   **flectitur** 'is changed'.

523–5 The two arguments are portrayed as adversaries; the true argument cuts off the retreat of the false, brings it to bay, and hews it down in open combat. L.'s readers might be reminded of the debate between the Unjust and Just Reasons in Aristophanes' *Clouds* (see Dover 1960: lviii); and the title Καταβάλλοντες, *Throws*, by which one of Protagoras' works sometimes went (Guthrie 1969: 264), figured debate as essentially a combat between adversaries. The violent and aggressive tone imparted to the image here is characteristic of L.; cf. his description of Epicurus' battle with superstition: *quare religio pedibus subiecta uicissim | obteritur, nos exaequat uictoria caelo* (1.78–9); see Sykes Davies 1931–2: 34, Boyancé 1963: 306–7. L. wrote for victory: see below.   **eunti** = *abeunti* 'as it tries to escape', inceptive/ conative present (G–L 227 n. 2; K–S 1 120–1; H–S 316). Cf. 526–30n. *ire*.   **ancipitique refutatu** 'with two-edged refutation', referring to the dilemma posed at 521–2, but also exploiting the literal sense of *anceps*; cf. 6.168 *ancipiti . . . ferro* 'a double-edged axe'. *refutatus* is evidently a Lucretian coinage, like *adhaesus* at 381 (n.). For the rhythm of the verse cf. 102, 317; here it gives a picture of a mighty weapon descending once and no more, leaving Truth (probably the proper title of Protagoras' *Throws*) standing erect and triumphant over the prostrate corpse of Error.   **conuincere** = both 'defeat' and 'refute' (*OLD* 1, 3). From the outset of the poem L. figures himself as a fighter in a war of reason against error; cf. 5. 735 *difficile est ratione docere et uincere uerbis* (Kenney 2007: 92).

526–547

(Proof 8) Often a man is seen to be dying gradually; this proves that in the process of dying the soul is destroyed piecemeal. This section has no very close connexion with what has preceded or what follows; and 538 *ut diximus ante* seems most naturally to refer to 580–91 below. Hence on internal grounds Giussani's suggestion that it belongs after 669 has much to commend it.

526–30 If, as seems likely, L. expected his readers to recollect Plato's famous description of the death of Socrates (*Phaedo* 117e–118a; cf. 607–12n. *uidetur*), the allusion may, as suggested by Brown ad loc., carry a polemical implication: that this very graphic portrayal of the death of a believer in the immortality of the soul by another believer, if critically considered, in fact demonstrates that it *is* mortal.   **ire**[1] = *obire* 'die' (*OLD eo* 4b), a sense found twice elsewhere in the *DRN* (2.962, 6.1243) and occasionally in later writers. Cf. 524 *eunti*, 594 *ire*, 319 *firmare* (nn.).   **paulatim . . . membratim . . . tractim** 'gradually . . . limb by limb . . . draggingly', with *particulatim* following (542), 'piece by piece', strikingly exemplify L.'s predilection for adverbs in -*im* (258–61n. *summatim*), here lovingly exploited to enhance the picture of gradual dissolution as the slow departure of life is reflected in the heavy spondees and weightily anomalous rhythm of line 527 – 'the most effective instance of sound answering to sense that I know of in the whole range of Latin poetry' (Munro).   **post inde** 'next, from there . . .'; more commonly *post deinde*, a redundancy characteristic of early Latin (Skutsch 1985: 163 on Enn. *Ann.* 9).   **alios** '(all) the others' (*OLD* 6a), as at 550, 1038.   **gelidi uestigia leti:** for the personification of death cf. 1.852 *leti sub dentibus ipsis*.

531–2 The intended sense is clear: since the soul is torn apart in the process of dying, it must be mortal. The transmitted text is open to three objections: (i) L. nowhere else postpones *atque* (or indeed *at*: Norden 1934: 402–3); (ii) the reference must be to the *anima*, not the *animus*; (iii) *haec* is superfluous. None of the solutions proposed (see critical notes) is free from objection. *Pace* Heinze (1897: 130) and Clausen (1991: 546), none that entails retaining *haec* is satisfactory, and any that necessitate the elision of -*ae* must also be ruled out (see 374n.); 1.139 *linguae et*, cited by Clausen (1991: 545 n. 6) is a case of aphaeresis or prodelision, *linguae* (*e*)*t*. The postponement of *atqui* (Lambinus) is as unacceptable as that of *atque*, and in any case L. nowhere else uses the word (curious, in view of its evident utility in argument). Replacing *atque* with *itque* (Winckelmann, Munro) postulates a fairly simple process of corruption, and for *ire* = 'pass away' cf. 526 (n.); but even if the elision of -*ae* can then be swallowed, Munro's emendation of *haec* to *hoc* = *ergo* ignores the fact that when L. uses the word in this sense it regularly begins the sentence. Heinze's *ergo*, with the deletion of *haec*, and reading *animae*, cuts the Gordian knot (for the position of *ergo* + elision cf. 184, 969), but leaves the *ratio corruptelae* unexplained. All things considered, the obelus is the prudent recourse (so Müller).   **uno | tempore** [= 454] 'together'   **sincera exsistit** = *integra exit* 'leaves whole/intact'. For *exsisto* = 'emerge' cf. 2.796 *neque in lucem exsistunt primordia rerum*, 5.212 *liquidas exsistere in auras*. *sincerus* properly means 'unmixed', 'with nothing added'; for 'whole', 'with nothing subtracted' the usual word is *integer*. For the process by which the primary senses of *incolumis, integer* and *sincerus* became confused see Housman, *CP* 788, and cf. 717–21n.   **habendast** [= 819] 'must be taken to be' (*OLD* 24b); cf. 831 *habetur*.

533–9 The alternative theory which L. now proceeds to refute is otherwise unattested; he deploys the standard rhetorical technique of attributing a feeble argument to an imagined hostile interlocutor or sceptical reader. **quod si forte:** dismissive; cf. 45 *si fert ita forte uoluntas* (n.).   **ipsam** 'of its own accord' (*OLD* 7), attributing to it a reluctance to accept dispersion; or perhaps 'while remaining itself', 'without losing its integrity'.   **partis** sc. *suas*.   **in sensu debet maiore uideri** 'ought to be seen to have more sensation' (*OLD in* 37a); here *in* virtually = *cum* (580–1n.). The degree of sensation depends on the concentration of soul-atoms, but outside the body there is nowhere for the soul to cohere in and maintain its identity other than the circumambient air.   **ut diximus ante** is generally taken to refer to 531–2, but 443–4 seems more relevant. Cf. 526–47n.   **dispargitur:** L.'s MSS appear to offer this spelling and the commoner *disperg-* indifferently; but passages such as 2.1134–5 *in cunctas undique partis | plura modo dispargit* and 4.895 *et dispargitur ad partis*, where the original *a* of the stem is retained, exploiting a pseudo-etymological relationship of sound and sense, suggest that the spelling with *a* should probably be assumed everywhere. Here the assonance with *a* adds emphasis to the point. Cf. Friedländer 1941: 34/1969: 350. Cf. 661 *conspargere*, where the spelling contributes to the sonority of the verse.

540–1 quin etiam 'Moreover'.   **si iam libeat** 'even if one *were* disposed, for the sake of argument'; for this use of *iam* (*TLL* s.v. 128.1–38) cf. 766, 843.   **falsum** 'what is not true' (*OLD* 1).   **dare** 'allow', 'grant' (*OLD* 16b), as at 876.

543–5 Even if the soul were not dispersed after death, but contracted in on itself in the process of dying, it would still lose its identity as sensation ebbed away. Here, as elsewhere, L. anticipates a point to be developed presently. That dying entails that the soul starts to disintegrate before it quits the body is not explicitly demonstrated until lines 580–1.   **neces-sest:** this is the most usual form of the phrase (cf. Munro on 2.710), recurring, if the editorial consensus may be trusted, some ninety times in the poem, fifteen in this book. L. occasionally omits *est* where it can be easily understood (Bailey 1947: 103), but there is no obvious reason for its omission here. What MS authority, if any, earlier editors had for supplying it here is unclear, but the general silence is curious.   **dispersa per auras:** cf. 539 *foras dispargitur*, 4.569 (the voice) *perit frustra diffusa per auras*. **contracta suis e partibus** 'drawn together [sc. so as to make a whole] out of its different parts'.   **obbrutescat** 'becomes stupid'; the root sense of heaviness is felt (cf. 6.105 *bruto pondere pressae*), with the gradual numbing of sensation that marks the departure of life from the body suggested by the slow spondaic ending of the verse, and the inceptive force of the verb, which is otherwise attested only in a fragment of the Republican dramatist Afranius, fr. 418 R.[3] *non possum uerba facere: obbrutui.*

546–7 A summary paraphrase of lines 526–30, rounding off the argument. Rhythm and phrasing mirror the even and inevitable departure of life and sensation, with *magis et magis . . . minus et minus* imparting an almost soothing effect.   **totum:** later (713–40) L. envisages the possibility that some soul-atoms may in fact remain in the body after death.

548–557

(Proof 9) The mind is as much part of the body as the organs of sense and can no more exist outside it than they can. The premiss of this proof was argued at 94–7, 136–40, and is restated at 615–23, 784–97.

548–53 pars una 'an individual part' (*OLD unus* 6), further defined by the following relative clause.   **alii** 'all the others'.   **sensus** 'sense-organs' (*OLD* 2), as at 262, 630 and (probably) 562. Greek distinguished αἴσθησις

'sensation' and αἰσθητήριον 'sense-organ'.   **qui ... cumque:** for the separation (tmesis) of *quicumque* cf. 940, 1075. The word is often treated in this
way by the poets.   **atque ... -ue:** *-ue* is here connective, not disjunctive
(31–4n. *quoue*). For the similar use of *uel* in enumerations cf. 5.965 *glan-
des atque arbuta uel pira lecta*.   **secreta** 'if removed' (440–4n. *conquassatum ... rarefactum*). For the neuter plural cf. 136–9n. *coniuncta*.   **nequeunt sentire nec esse** 'can neither feel nor exist' = *nec sentire nec esse queunt*.
sed tamen 'but rather', 'but on the contrary'.   **tabe:** cf. for the scansion
1.806 *ut tabe nimborum arbusta uacillent*, 3.732 *fameque*, 734 *contage* (n.). In
Augustan verse *tabē* is usual (N–W I 734).

554–7 **sic** answers formally to *uelut ... ueluti* preceding, but syntactically
the lines are anacoluthic, since the *quoniam* clause that introduces the
period 548–57 lacks an apodosis. Logically they constitute the conclusion of a syllogism whose premisses are: (i) the mind is an organ of the
body like any other (548–50); (ii) the other organs cannot exist independently (551–3): *ergo*, neither can the mind. For a similar discrepancy
between logical and syntactical structure cf. 434–9n. *nunc igitur quoniam.*
In neither case is the argument seriously impaired.   **sine corpore et
ipso | ... homine** 'outside the body and the man himself, *et* epexegetic; the
mind, as L. goes on to emphasize, is an integral part of the whole man
(cf. 344–9n.), but here the explicatory phrase is syntactically parenthetic,
since the following *quod* can only refer to *corpus*.   **uas:** see 434–9n. *uasis*,
but for the point now made the vessel-image is inadequate, as indeed L.
acknowledges, since it does not illustrate the interconnexion at the atomic
level between body and soul, which is *nexam per uenas uiscera neruos* (217;
cf. 325, 331, *al.*) and must therefore share in the dissolution of the bodily structure.   **ei:** always a spondee in L. and always at the end of the
verse (9x). The comic poets use both *ēī* and *eı̂* (Lindsay 1922: 168); the
spondaic scansion is rare in all periods, but generally the oblique cases
of *is* were avoided by Augustan and later poets (N–W II 378–9; Axelson
1945: 70–3; Kenney on Ov. *Her.* 20.29).   **corpus adhaeret:** to say that
the body clings to the soul rather than, as might be expected, the soul to
the body, can be read as an example of the kind of idiom found in the use
of *compenso*: cf. Ov. *Her.* 3.51 *tot tamen amissis te compensauimus unum*, 'I have
gained you in recompense for the loss of so many', and Barchiesi ad loc.
(*OLD compenso* 3 inadequate). Similarly *muto* can be used both of giving
and receiving in exchange (*OLD* 1–3). The point here is of the mutuality
of the union, not which constituent adheres to which.

558–579

(Proof 10) The soul cannot function without the protection of the body:
the converse of what was argued at 323–49.

558–62 uiuata potestas = 409 (n.), 680.   **coniuncta** 'because they are
joined'. The periphrasis *corporis atque animi...potestas*, being plural in
sense = *corpus atque animus*, is treated as if it were indeed grammatically
plural, with the participle, following the usual rule, neuter plural. This
construction is essentially an extension of the usage normal with nouns
'of multitude' such as *pars* or *turba* (G–L 211; H–S 436–7); here the effect
is less obtrusive because a verse apiece is allotted to subject and predicate.   **edere** 'perform' (*OLD* 5); cf. 2.311 *proprio dat corpore motus* (*OLD
do* 24a).   **animi:** as explained at 159–60, it is the *animus* that initiates
these motions, though as emphasized at line 565 L. is concerned in this
section with the whole soul, *animus + anima* (cf. 445–8n. *mentem*).   **nec
autem** 'nor again', 'nor on the other hand' (*OLD autem* 1a).   **sensibus:**
the sense-organs (548–53n. *sensus*). They are still there in the dead body,
but without soul they cannot function.

563–5 radicibus: here probably 'roots' rather than 'anchorage' as at 325
(n.); cf. Hom. *Od.* 9.390 (the blinding of the Cyclops) σφαραγεῦντο δέ
οἱ πυρὶ ῥίζαι, 'its roots crackled in the fire', apparently the only other
place where the eye is credited with roots (Jacobson 2002–3: 132).
ipse 'on its own' (*OLD* 7).   **seorsum corpore** 'separately from the
body' ~ 554 *sine corpore*, for the usual *seorsum a*, seemingly a unique
instance; but no critic or editor has yet ventured the obvious correction.
uidetur 'it is evident'; singular because it is the whole soul that is in
point.

566–79 The choice of the eye to illustrate the general point to which
L. now returns, the intricate interconnexions of body and soul, perhaps
reflects his evident interest in the phenomena of light and vision (cf.
359–69).

566–72 mixtim: found only here and no doubt a Lucretian coinage; cf.
526–30n. *paulatim. mixta* (Q), which would give perfectly good sense (cf.
283 *commixta per artus*), is a well-meaning attempt to correct *mixti*, the reading of the archetype. This is an instance of a frequent source of corruption
in classical texts, replacement of the remains of the original reading by
a superficial repair of the damage – superficial, but sometimes, as here,
plausible: for it is a fair guess that if OV had not survived, *mixta* would
stand unchallenged in our texts. One can only guess at the number of such
cases which still, in default of better MS evidence or exceptional editorial
diuinatio, lurk undetected. Cf. Ov. *Am.* 1.10.30, where the correct reading
licenda only surfaced in 1965 from an eleventh-century MS, previously mis-
dated and neglected by editors (Munari 1965: 62 n. 1; cf. Kenney 1966:
269), to displace 'the vacuous *locanda*' (McKeown ad loc.).   **tenentur**
'are protected' (323–6n. *tenetur*).   **magnis interuallis** 'with wide spaces

between', descriptive ablative (288–93n. *pectore tranquillo*).   **mouentur | ...motus** 'make motions': this kind of 'internal' or 'cognate' accusative is found from Plautus onwards in such phrases as *pugnam pugnare, uitam uiuere, somnium somniare* (G–L 333.2, *NLS* 1.1, 13; Müller 1908: 4–55, H–S 38–40). It is even commoner in Greek.   **in auras:** take with *eiecta* in the next verse.   **tenentur:** sc. *ab aere.*

573–5 'For (in that case) air will be body and, what is more (*OLD atque* 2), a living thing [*OLD animans*² 1a], if it is going to be able to contain the soul within itself and confine it to those motions which it used to make within the sinews and inside [*ipso*: 128–9, 482–3nn.] the body.' Some alteration of the transmitted text is necessary if the point is to emerge: *aer* must be the subject and the soul the object of the verbs *cohibere* and *concludere* (cf. 569 *conclusa*, sc. *corpore*), and Wakefield's correction achieves this economically. If the soul could stay together in the air after leaving the body, that could only happen because the air was acting as a solid object, like the body, and holding it together, in which case, like the body, it would receive life from the soul – which is absurd. Giussani's objection to this interpretation, supported by Bailey, that 'no believer in the immortality of the soul would say that the air holds it together', misses the point: that this is the position, whether they would admit to it or not, to which holders of that belief are driven by the logic of scientific fact. The *reductio ad absurdum* is characteristic: 367–9, 624–33nn.

576–9 quare etiam atque etiam: the emphatic formula hammers home the inescapable conclusion of the chain of proofs begun at line 425.   **resoluto corporis omni | tegmine:** a translation of a phrase from Epicurus' discussion of the question, τοῦ στεγάζοντος λυθέντος, 'when the protecting agent is dissolved' (D.L. 10.65); cf. 323–6n.   **uitalibus auris** 'the breath of life'; cf. 405 *uitalis... auras.* The recurrence of *aura* in this quite different sense so soon after *auras* at 570 may be purely inadvertent and without significance, but may, as suggested by Brown ad loc., be intended to convey the picture of the expiring breath mingling with the air into which it escapes.   **sensus animi** 'the mind's power to feel'; cf. 98 *sensum animi.* **coniunctast causa duobus** 'what kept them alive is linked to both'; cf. 559 *inter se coniuncta ualent uitaque fruuntur. causa,* sc. *salutis*; cf. 348 *coniuncta est causa salutis.*

580–591

(Proof 11) The manner in which the dead body decays shows that in death both body and soul are broken up; the point touched on at 337–43 is now developed.

581 discidium 'the tearing apart', both of the soul from the body and
the constituent atoms of the soul from each other (339–43n. *animai discidium*).   **in taetro … odore** 'with a foul smell'; for *in = cum* cf. 533–9n.
in sensu debet maiore uideri. The perceptible evidence of the dissolution of
the body points by analogy to a corresponding dissolution of the soul.

582–8 The soul-atoms, as they disengage themselves from their atomic
interconnexions and escape through the pores of the decaying body, are
imaged as a panic-stricken mob of refugees fleeing pell-mell through
the winding streets of a city in an earthquake collapsing in ruins about
them: a dramatization of what was described at 2.944–51.   **uti fumus:**
cf. 455–8n. *ceu fumus* and L.'s description at 4.90–4 of the dispersal of
smells, smoke and heat from their host bodies.   **putre** 'in ruins', predicative.   **anima emanante:** Wakefield's correction, though 'a more
considerable change' of the MS text than Lachmann's (Smith ad loc.),
has the merit of picking up *emanarit* from line 503; and in fact 'the transposition of adjacent nouns is a feature of the textual tradition of Lucretius'
(Clausen 1991: 545). Moreover, Lachmann's *usque* is not only 'gratuitous'
(Bailey) but inappropriate in sense.   **uiarum omnis flexus** 'all the winding paths'. The effect of the diaeresis after *uiarum*, imparting a false hexameter ending to the verse (35–7n.), is offset by the elision.   **foramina**
'pores', but the word can also refer to the exit from a building (*TLL* s.v.
1032.79–1033.17). For the metre with a diaeresis following two dactyls cf.
196, 719; here the abrupt effect of the sense-pause adds to the force of
the rhetorical question. There is one caesura only, in the fourth foot.

589–91 dispertitam '(only) after being scattered into its parts'.   **sibi
distractam** 'torn apart from itself', *sibi* dative of disadvantage, an extension of its common use with verbs of taking away (G–L 345 Remarks 1;
K–S I 313–14; H–S 92–3).   **corpore in ipso** 'while actually in the body'.
prolapsa … enaret 'before it could begin to slip away and float out', inceptive imperfect (G–L 233; Roby 1470; *NLS* 200 (ii)). In such phrases with
priusquam the sense with the subjunctive is not always 'purely temporal'
(K–S II 370–1; H–S 601), but has a potential nuance, as here and in other
Lucretian examples (4.841–2, 845, 5. 1379–81, where n. b. *possent*). For
eno of motion through the air (*OLD* 1b) cf. 4.177–8 *mobilitas ollis* [sc. the
'images'] *tranantibus auras | reddita*, Enn. *Ann.* 18 Sk. *transnauit* [Venus?]
cita per teneras caliginis auras and Skutsch ad loc., Cic. *Arat.* 588–9 *at parte
ex alia claris cum lucibus enat | Orion*; this last passage is probably what sug-
gested L.'s use of *eno* here.

592–606

(Proof 12) In a fainting-fit the soul is clearly so greatly shaken that dissolution cannot be far off. The illustration resembles that of drunkenness at
476–87.

592–6 quin etiam 'What is more': even in life the soul can be severely shaken; *a fortiori* in death it must obviously perish.   **finis . . . intra:** for the anastrophe of the preposition cf. 140–2n. *circum.* The 'boundaries of life' are the surfaces of the confining body; cf. 256 *fit in summo quasi corpore finis.*   **dum** 'even while': *tamen* following imparts a concessive nuance. **uertitur** 'moves about' (*OLD* 3a), sc. the *anima* (594), for the more usual *uersatur* (*OLD* 10a).   **ire** 'depart' = *exire* (*OLD eo*¹ 4a, b); cf. 526–30n. *ire.*   **toto . . . de corpore:** the soul, already shaken and partially detached from its anchorage, is on the point (next n.) of casting adrift completely. **uelle** 'is ready to', 'is about to' (*OLD uolo*¹ 5a); the process by which in the descendants of Latin the inflected future tense came to be replaced by the use of modal auxiliaries can be seen beginning already (H–S 314). Lachmann's correction of what has strayed into this position from line 596 gives good sense and is in effect glossed by *quasi supremo . . . tempore* following. L.'s description does not have to be read, as assumed by Butterfield (2008a: 360–1), from the point of view of the fainting man; his own suggestion *partim*, on the other hand, offers a superfluous qualification and provides a rhetorically limp conclusion to the verse.   **quasi supremo . . . tempore** 'as if its last hour had come'.   **uultus** 'expression', 'looks' (*OLD* 1a).   **molliaque exsangui cadere omnia corpore membra** 'and the limbs collapse limply and the body is drained of blood', *mollia* and *exsangui* predicative. The early correction of the MS text adopted here gives good sense and produces a 'Golden' line (344–9n. *mutua . . . motus*). Bailey's objection, that the reading of OQV in line 594 presupposes *omnia membra* here (see critical note) is no obstacle to acceptance: the corruptions in lines 596 and 594 took place, in that order, at two different stages of copying. However, Winckelmann's *cadere omnia membra colore*, strongly supported by Butterfield (2008a: 360), also deserves consideration; it too produces a 'Golden' line, and the oxymoronic *exsangui . . . colore*, 'bloodless colour', is a conceit worthy of L. The loss of a word at the end of a verse is easier to account for than its disappearance from the middle, as postulated by Lachmann's supplement.

597–602 quod genus est . . . cum 'as happens when', 'just as when' (221–3n.).   **cum perhibetur** 'when, as we say' (*OLD perhibeo* 2b). L. uses both the common types of expression for 'faint'; cf. Plaut. *Mil.* 1331–2 *animo male* | *factum est huic miserae*, 1347 *animus hanc modo hic reliquerat*, Cels. 2.10.18 *ante finis faciendus est* [sc. of bloodletting] *quam anima deficiat.*   **trepidatur** 'there is general alarm'; their behaviour unwittingly mimics what L.'s instructed readers know is actually going on in the body of the sufferer. The impersonal passive is common with intransitive verbs (*NLS* 60, G–L 208.2).   **extremum . . . uitae reprehendere uinclum** 'hold on to the last link with life'; for the transferred sense of *uinculum* see *OLD* 5; here the image suggested is that of a boat held by a single

remaining mooring (*OLD* 2a).   **conquassatur ... cum corpore collabefiunt:** the repeated prefix and the concluding alliteration of *c* emphasize the
interconnexion of mind and spirit and the simultaneity of their dissolution
along with the body. Both *conquasso* and *collabefio* are first attested in L. (3x
and 2x respectively).   **haec** 'these things', neuter plural, even though
here all the nouns are feminine.

603-6 The fourth repetition of this crucial point; cf. 440-4, 506-9n.
tandem strikes, as often, a note of impatience: 'how can you possibly
doubt?'   **prodita** 'thrust out' (*OLD* *prodo* 1), sc. the *anima*; cf. 591 *prolapsa*. For *do* = 'place' cf. 354-5n. *palam... dedit*.   **foras, in aperto,
tegmine dempto:** the structure of the verse, with the three adverbial
phrases in asyndeton and increasing in length, exemplifies a common
rhetorical device, heightening the picture of the soul's helpless plight in
this alien and hostile environment.   **tegmine dempto** ~ 576-7 *resoluto
corporis omni | tegmine* (n.).   **aeuom:** masculine, as shown by *omnem*; cf.
2.561 *aeuom... per omnem*, Plaut. *Poen.* 1187 *uitalem aeuom*. For similar variations of gender see N-W I 789-808.   **minimum quoduis ... tempus** 'for
however short a time'.

607-614

(Proof 12A) The soul is felt by the dying man to depart gradually, not to
leave the body as a whole at one place. Editors have puzzled themselves to
discover a connexion with what has preceded, but none of the alternative
places suggested for the passage is a clear improvement. In fact a logical
connexion can be shown to exist, and there is no good reason to deny
the passage the status of a separate proof. L. has argued at 580-91 and
again at 593-606 from outward and visible signs; he now argues from the
personal experience of the dying, something evidently assumed to be common knowledge. The connexion with what has preceded is signposted by
incolumem de corpore toto at line 608, picking up 594 *toto... de corpore*.

607-11 uidetur 'it is clear': L. appeals to common experience, but how
many deathbeds had he attended? If challenged, he might have appealed
to the analogous phenomena of fainting-fits or epileptic seizures, the experience of which the sufferers can communicate afterwards; or he may
be generalizing from the famous case of Socrates as described by Plato
(*Phaedo* 118a); cf. 526-30n.   **ad iugulum et ... fauces:** sc. as was pop-
ularly supposed (121-2n. *per os*).   **superas:** the adjective, also attested
at 6.855 *supera de... parte*, was clearly what Virgil read in his text of the
DRN, reproducing the phrase *superas... ad auras* four times (*G.* 4.486, *Aen.*
5.427, 6.128, 7.768). It gives a more straightforward construction than
supera, whether read as an adverb (so most editors), or as a preposition

(Wellesley 1974–5: 38–9). Wellesley's objection to the first alternative is well taken, but a second preposition after *ad* is superfluous. The corruption is easily explained by haplography of *s* before *succedere*; *supera* is found elsewhere in the *DRN* 12x. *superas* was in fact the vulgate before it was arbitrarily deposed by Lachmann; of subsequent editors only Bockemüller and Brieger have retained it.   **in certa regione locatam** 'in the particular region where it is located' (Smith), its fixed place (*OLD certus* 1a, b). The dying man feels in each part of his body the dulling of sensation that betokens the piecemeal dissolution of the *anima*.   **sensus alios in parti quemque sua** 'each sense in its own place': the construction is a conflation of *sensus alios in alia parte* (*OLD alius*¹ 2) and *sensum in parte quemque sua*; cf. for a similar conflation of constructions 333–6 (n.). This is preferable to interpreting the phrase as a Grecism = 'the senses as well', sc. as the *anima*; the other instance of this usage adduced by Munro, 1.116, is not truly parallel, and the senses do not undergo dissolution 'as well' as the *anima*, but as part and parcel of the process of dissolution. Alternatively Winckelmann's *uarios* neatly disposes of the grammatical difficulty and deserves serious consideration; cf. 6.984 *uarii sensus animalibus insunt*. **parti:** archaic ablative (N–W 1 364–5), for metrical convenience (Bailey 1947: 73); cf. 132 *Heliconi* (n.).

612–14 As he likes to do, L. rounds off the sequence of argument with a sarcastic *reductio ad absurdum*.   **quod si immortalis:** for the 'quasi-caesura' cf. 174, 258 (nn.).   **sed magis:** for the expected *quam potius* after *tam*. The phrasing promotes expectation of another verb opposed in sense to *conquereretur*, such as *gauderet*; cf. 2.508–9 *cedere item retro possent in deteriores | omnia sic partis, ut diximus in meliores*, sc. *progredi* (Bailey ad loc.). That would reflect the view of believers in the immortality of the soul who despised the body and considered the soul well rid of it; cf. the Greek saying that the body is a tomb, σῶμα σῆμα. If the text is sound, this would appear to be an example of the type of ellipse styled zeugma, in which one part of an expression must be supplied from the other part, which may be, as here, opposed in sense. Heinze compared a particularly striking example at Livy 45.20.9 *his auditis prostrauerunt se omnes humi consulesque et cunctos qui aderant orantes, ne noua falsaque crimina plus obesse Rhodiis aequum censerent quam antiqua merita, quorum ipsi testes essent*, sc. *prodesse*. Cf. also Virg. *G.* 1.92–3 *ne tenues pluuiae rapidiue potentia solis | acrior aut Boreas penetrabile frigus adurat*, where some such verb as *diluant* must be understood with *pluuiae* (Bell 1923: 312); *Aen.* 2.780 *longa tibi exilia et uastum maris aequor arandum*, where Servius noted 'subaudiendum *obeunda*' (but see Austin ad loc.); 5.340–1 and Williams ad loc. On zeugma in general in Latin poetry see Bell 1923: 304–14; Getty 1955: lxii–lxiii; H–S 831–4. This last authority, however, obscures the distinction between true zeugma and Ovid's favourite figure of syllepsis, neatly illustrated by Fowler: 'See Pan with flocks, with fruits Pomona crowned' is zeugma, whereas the departure of Miss Bolo 'in a flood of tears and a sedan chair' is syllepsis. See Tissol 1997: 219–22 for a full discussion.   **ire foras:** sc. *incolumem.* **uestemque:** for *uestis* of a discarded body cf. 386, and of a snake's sloughed skin 4.61. The image of the body as the garment of the soul is Platonic (*Phaedo* 87b–e, 91d).

<h2 style="text-align:center">615–623</h2>

(Proof 13) The mind, like everything else in the universe, has its fixed place in the scheme of things: *ergo* it cannot exist outside the place appointed for it. L. enlarges on the point at 784–99, where it forms part of the case against the pre-existence of the soul; here he is arguing against its survival after death.

615–21 animi ... mens consiliumque: the periphrasis perhaps suggests the absurdity of supposing that the rational faculty could be migratory within the body.   **unis | sedibus et certis regionibus** 'in a single, a fixed place', previously defined as the chest (140), *et* epexegetic, adding emphasis. The unusual use of *unus* in the plural (also at 2.919, 5.897) is dictated by metrical convenience.   **omnibus** 'for all men'; the juxtaposition with *regionibus* produces a 'somewhat harsh' expression (Munro), which like the awkward construction at 620–1 (see below) might have been elim-inated in revision.   **reddita** 'duly allotted' (*OLD reddo* 10a).   **quic-quid** 'each thing', 'any particular thing' (*OLD quisquis* 7b), for the more usual *quicque* (cf. 618 *cuique*), 'an archaism not uncommon in Lucret.' (Munro on 2.289); cf. 787 *quicquid* (n.).   **ita ... ordo** 'and accordingly [*OLD ita* 6a] where it can exist, though with its parts diversely arranged, yet in such a way that the order of its members is never reversed'. The early correction *partitis*, made independently by several later scholars, is closer to the MS text than Lachmann's *perfectis*. *Pace* Brown ad loc. the word can denote arrangement, which is indeed its primary sense (*OLD partio* 1).   **multimodis:** sc. diversely in different species, but with the proviso indicated in the following restrictive *ita....ut* clause = 'provided that' (282–7n. *ut*), that within each species the arrangement is uniform. The argument is severely compressed, and the transition from the idea that each thing has its fixed place in the scheme of things (618–19) to the corollary that within each thing each of its parts similarly has its fixed place is left to be understood. Munro suggested a lacuna after line 619 in which specific reference was made to the human body. The passage may be one of those that lacked a final revision.

622–3 L. rounds off this proof by invoking the argument from impossi-bility widely exploited by the poets, the *adynaton*, Greek ἀδύνατον, 'the

impossible'; other examples in this book at 748–53, 784–6 (nn.), elsewhere at 1.159–66, 881–92. See Gow on Theoc. 1.132–6; Canter 1930;
Dutoit 1936: 31–4; Shackleton Bailey 1956: 277; Rowe 1965.   **res rem:**
sc. things of the same kind.   **fluminibus:** probably best read as ablative
of origin after *creari* (*OLD* 1b); alternatively taken by Munro as an instance
of the ἀπὸ κοινοῦ construction, with *in* to be supplied from *in igni* follow-
ing, as at 4.147–8 *ubi aspera saxa | aut in materiam ligni peruenit*, 6.1116–17
Atthide temptantur gressus oculique in Achaeis | finibus. Cf. 4.1024, with *propter*.
See Clausen on Pers. 1.131, and for instances in Greek Pfeiffer on Callim.
fr.714.3.   **in:** for the more usual *ex*, *metri gratia*.   **igni gignier algor:**
the assonances *gn- g- gn- g-* lend emphasis and perhaps impart a flavour
of contempt for the view attributed to L.'s adversaries. *algor* is one of a
number of abstract nouns in *-or* affected by L.: *amaror* 'bitterness', *aegror*
'sickness', *leuor* 'smoothness', *luror* 'yellowness', *stringor* 'touch' (693(n.)).
Such formations were evidently considered strange and archaic; in later
writers they occur sparsely, usually with a consciously archaic flavour.

624–633

(Proof 14) In order to continue to exist independently of the body,
the soul would need to be equipped with sense-organs, which is ridiculous. A characteristic Lucretian *reductio ad absurdum*, syllogistic in form
(631–3 *at…igitur*). The belief that he is refuting is ascribed by Cicero to
lack of imagination: *Tusc.* 1.37 *nihil…animo uidere poterant, ad oculos omnia
referebant.* Once it is accepted that the soul is material, this argument falls
to the ground.

624–30 sentire: and thus to live; cf. 633 *sentire…esse.*   **quinque, ut
opinor** 'with all five, I take it'; the qualification is sarcastic.   **faciundum est** 'we must hold it to be', *esse* understood; for this sense of *facio* cf.
878, *al.* (*OLD* 2ob). For the form of the gerundive cf. 406–12n. *cernundi*.
sensibus auctam 'furnished with sense-organs' (548–53n. *sensus*). *augeo* =
'enlarge', 'equip with' (*OLD* 6a). Cf. Catull. 65. 165 *nullis sensibus auc-
tae* (sc. *aurae*).   **nosmet…nobis:** the repetition and the emphasis
imparted by the suffix *-met* (*OLD* headn.) underline the absurdity of what
we should be obliged to believe.   **infernas animas Acherunte uagari:** L.
sardonically pictures these souls imagined by believers in their immortality
as wandering about aimlessly in the Hell which he is presently to argue is a
figment of minds enslaved by superstition (978–1023).   **uagari:** there
is no case for accepting Q's *uagare* as an archaism deliberately affected
by L., as some editors do. Though the active form of the verb is attested
(*OLD uagor* headn., N–W III 99), elsewhere L.'s MSS consistently (15x)
transmit the normal deponent.   **pictores…et scriptorum saecla priora** 'the painters and poets of old'. L. may have had in mind the ghosts

encountered by Odysseus in his descent to the Underworld in Book 11 of the *Odyssey*, who, if Achilles' famous outburst (488–503) is anything to go by, do not find life in Hades particularly enjoyable. There was at Delphi a famous painting by Polygnotus (*c.* 475–445 BC) of the conversation of Odysseus with Tiresias.   **introduxerunt** 'have brought on to the scene' (*OLD* 1c). Generally printed by earlier editors as two words, but treated as a fully compounded verb by writers from Ennius onwards (fr. 9 dub. Sk.). In any case, a caesura would be felt after *intro-* (174n.).

631–3 ipsa 'by itself, 'on its own' (*OLD* 7), to be understood ἀπὸ κοινοῦ with all the preceding nouns.   **animae:** possessive dative.   **per se** 'acting on their own', sc. apart from the soul.   **possunt:** sc. *animae*, understood from line 630.

634–669

(Proof 15) When the body is divided, the soul is divided too. A point already touched on at 526–47 and 580–614 is now discussed from a slightly different angle, with appeal now lying to the experience of sudden and violent mutilation. Wounds and death in battle would no doubt have been familiar to not a few of L.'s readers, but his chief illustration is second-hand (642–56n.).

634–9 toto…corpore…totum 'in the whole body in its entirety' (*OLD totum* 1a); the repetition underscores the point.   **animale** 'alive', because completely pervaded by the *anima*.   **subito…celeri:** sc. so ruling out the hypothesis of a gradual withdrawal of soul from one part to another while maintaining its identity (cf. 533–9). In such cases there is no time for that to happen.   **medium** 'in two', predicative, as commonly with verbs like *diuidere* (*OLD* 2).   **uis aliqua…uis animai:** for the periphrasis cf. 583, but the repetition of *uis* perhaps makes a point: the force that holds the spirit together is not proof against a force that delivers a death-blow to the body.   **dispertita…discissa…dissicietur:** the threefold repetition of the prefix emphasizes the point at issue. Plato, in arguing for the immortality of the soul, had insisted that it is not torn apart by the dissolution of the body, and had similarly thrice repeated verbs compounded with διά (*Phaedo* 84b6–7). L.'s corresponding repetition of *dis-* slyly hints that Plato got it wrong.   **dissicietur:** the invariable spelling *metri gratia* for the formally correct *disicio*, which suggests the scansion *dĭsic-*; cf. *di(s) iungo* and its forms (*OLD* s.vv.).

640–1 A paraphrase of the fundamental axiom enunciated at 517–20 (n.).   **discedit** 'is divided' (*OLD* 2b), virtually = *scinditur*.   **ullas** 'any at all'; *ullus* is generally used with a negative or conditional implication (G–L 317, Roby 2278–80; K–S I 637–42); here *quod* is felt as equivalent to *si quid.*   **scilicet** 'obviously'; the point hardly needs making.   **abnuit** 'denies'; the word is found only here in the poem. For the personification cf. 208–9n. *dedicat.*

642–56 Gruesome descriptions of death in battle were a feature of epic from Homer onwards, but L.'s vivid portrayal of the carnage inflicted by scythed chariots, a *tour de force* of rapid narration, with momentum imparted by enjambment, is based on literary sources. Scythed chariots had figured as early as 331 BC in the battle of Arbela (Quint. Curt. 4.9.5, 15.7, Diod. 17.58.5; Friedrich 1948), but it is thcir usc by Antiochus III at the battle of Magnesia in 189 BC, celebrated by Ennius in the *Annales* and later by Livy (37.41), that is evoked in this passage. L. was evidently drawing on Ennius (Skutsch 1985: 644–6); see below on 654–6. At 5.1301 *falciferos...currus* they figure again in his account of the escalation of weaponry over the centuries.   **falciferos:** the word is first attested here, a calque of the word used by Greek historians to describe these vehicles, δρεπανηφόρος, 'sickle-bearing'. The usual word is *falcatus*, but L. is partial to compounds in *-fer*: 11 *floriferis*, 240 *al. sensiferos*, 1012 *horriferos*, etc.   **de subito:** a variant for *subito*, archaic and colloquial; classical Latin writers prefer to form such adverbial phrases with *ex* (124–5n. *ex aequo*).   **permixta caede calentis** = 5.1313, used there of lions maddened by slaughter; the scythes are hot with the blood of their victims (cf. *OLD caleo* 4b).   **tremere ... uideatur:** proving that part of the *anima* remains in the severed member.   **cum ... tamen** 'although ... yet' (106–11n. *cum*).   **mens ... atque hominis uis** 'the man's mind', hendiadys. For *hominis uis* = 'warrior' cf. 6–8n. *fortis equi uis.*   **mobilitate mali:** cf. Quint. Curt. 4.15.17 *quia calidis adhuc uulneribus aberat dolor, trunci quoque et debiles arma non omittebant donec multo sanguine effuso exanimati procumberent.*   **et simul...quod** ~ *cum... non quit* preceding: for this use of *et simul* to give an additional reason for the man's unawareness of what has happened to him cf. 4.1276 *et simul ipsa uiris Venus ut concinnior esset.* Earlier editors, followed by Lachmann and Munro, punctuated after line 646; the less abrupt punctuation after 647 now generally adopted gives a better connexion of sense, since what follows effectively constitutes the apodosis of a concessive clause: in spite of his mutilation the man presses on. **in...studio...dedita:** a rare variation of the usual construction with dative (*OLD deditus* 2b); otherwise only at 4.815 *in rebus deditus*, Catull. 61.97–8 *in mala | deditus uir adultera.*   **rēlicuo:** the invariable scansion in L. (4x); cf. 656 *rēliquias.* This 'weighting' of the first syllable has been ascribed, as with *religio* (51–4n. *religionem*), to an original prefix in *red-*, but this seems to be doubtful. The scansion evidently did not commend itself to the Augustans, who avoided the word altogether; trisyllabic *reliquus* is not found before Persius.   **petessit** 'tries to get to', sc. *homo*, understood from 645;

cf. 652 *alius.*   **nec tenet** 'and does not grasp' (*OLD teneo* 23), exactly as
in English.   **laeuam** 'his left arm'; the absolute sense only here, but supported by *dextram* at 651.   **abstraxe** = *abstraxisse*; cf. 1.223 *consumpse*,
5.1159 *protraxe.* Later poets on the whole avoided such contracted forms
of consonant-stem verbs, in contrast with vowel-stem verbs; cf. 498 *consuerunt* (n.), 683 *cresse, al.*   **rotas falcesque rapaces** 'the wheels with
their snatching scythes', hendiadys.   **cum scandit et instat** 'while he per-
severes in climbing', sc. on to the chariot to get at the driver, another condensed expression in hendiadys form (Bell 1923: 261-2).

652-6 This graphic description is clearly based on lines from Ennius' no
less graphic treatment of the battle of Magnesia: Enn. *Ann.* 483-4 Sk. *os-
citat in campis caput a ceruice reuolsum | semianimesque micant oculi lucemque
requirunt.* It was further exploited by Virgil, *Aen.* 10.394-6 *nam tibi, Thym-
bre, caput Euandrius abstulit ensis; | te decisa suum, Laride, dextera quaerit |
seminanimesque micant digiti ferrumque retractant.* Servius, our authority for
the Ennius fragment, tells us that Varro Atacinus borrowed the first verse
as it stood; Ennius' description was evidently a celebrated *tour de force.*
Virgil's transformation of the blinking eyes of the original into twisting
fingers was probably suggested by L.'s line 653. The metre of line 652,
with a weak caesura in the third foot followed by a bacchiac word ($\smile$ $-$ $-$),
reflects the awkward efforts of the wounded man to rise.   **cum**
'although'.   **propter** 'nearby', but in his blind fury he does not see it.
et 'or' (147-51n. *-que*); cf. 694, 1068-9 (nn.).   **uiuenteque:** 161-7n.
mutareque.   **uultum uitalem** 'the expression of life'.   **reliquias:** see
above on 647 *relicuo.*

657-61 'or if you should choose to hack into a number of pieces on this
side and that [sc. of its middle] a snake with its flickering tongue, its threat-
ening tail, and its long body . . . '. The early correction *serpentem . . . utrimque*
offers the simplest solution of the problems posed by the MS text, providing an object for *discidere* and allowing the three descriptive ablati-
val phrases to qualify the snake itself. *serpentis . . . utrumque* cannot possibly mean 'both parts of a snake'; and L. could not reasonably expect a
reader who had not reached line 668 to understand it to mean 'the body
and soul of a snake' (Nicoll 1970, following Diels). Of other suggested
solutions the best, though difficult to justify palaeographically, is Müller's
toruum (reading *serpentem*). L.'s threefold characterization of the snake,
centring on head, body and tail, is echoed by Virgil, *G.* 3.422-4 *iamque
fuga timidum caput abdidit alte, | cum medii nexus extremaeque agmina caudae
| soluuntur, tardosque trahit sinus ultimus orbis*; it contrasts its normally men-
acing and collected appearance with the frenzy of self-inflicted activity following its mutilation. *minanti*, however, of the snake's tail, is odd (except
in the case of rattle-snakes, unknown to the ancients); it is the front end

with which menace is associated: Virg. *G.* 3.421 *tollentemque minas et sibila colla tumentem*, *Aen.* 2.206–11, *Culex* 170–3. Lachmann's *micanti* substitutes a word which merely duplicates *uibrante* and is elsewhere used of the snake's tongue (Virg. *G.* 3.439, *Aen.* 2.475).   **quin etiam** 'moreover'. **sit libitum … cernes** '(if) you should take it into your head … you will see'. The combination of subjunctive protasis and indicative apodosis is normal Latinity from Plautus onwards (Bennett 1910, 1914: II 274–6); there is no necessary suggestion of vividness (Kenney 1958: 63 n. 2, 1959: 246–7; Leo 1960: 237).   **discidere** 'cut apart', a rare word, otherwise attested only at 669, Ter. *Ad.* 559, Suet. *Cal.* 33.1.   **ancisa** 'hacked', literally 'cut around', from *am(bi)* + *caedo*, an even rarer compound of *caedo*, found only here in literary Latin. For its formation cf. *amputo, anquiro.* **tortari** 'writhe in torment'; the word otherwise attested only at Pompon. fr. 40 R.³ *tortor* ('pro *torqueor*', Non. p. 267 L.).   **conspargere:** cf. 539 *dispargitur* (n.).   **tabo** 'gore', a word almost peculiar to epic poetry.

662–3 'and the first part you will see attack itself behind with its mouth in order to bite (itself), smitten with the burning pain of the wound'; *retro* does double duty, qualifying *petere* and taken with *ipsam se* virtually = 'its own hinder part'.   **ipsam seque** for the usual *seque ipsam*, imparting additional emphasis and making a more dactylic and faster-moving line. On *-que* attached to the second word of a phrase as standard prose usage see K–S I 583, and cf. 939, 962 *aequo animoque*.   **petere:** felt as *repetere* after *retro*. L. likes to play on *retro* and *re-*; cf. 1.785, 1059, 2.130, 283, 4.310, *al.*   **morsu premat** 'bite', not 'assuage'. The various corrections suggested betoken unease on the part of some editors as to awkwardness in the phrasing, but L. may have intended the word-order to reflect the snake's broken writhing.

664–6 A *reductio ad absurdum* rounds off the argument.   **dicemus … ?** 'shall we say?'; the indicative seems to pose the question more sharply than would a deliberative subjunctive.   **particulis** picks up *partis* from 659; this is the only occurrence of the word in L. in the non-technical sense of 'small part'. Elsewhere (4x), as at 708 (n.), it is used of atoms or groupings of atoms.   **unam:** *animans* 'living creature' is always feminine in L. (N–W I 916).

667–9 una: sc. the *anima.*   **simul cum | corpore:** the strong enjambment reinforces the emphasis on the intimate interconnexion of soul and body.   **quapropter … mortale … putandum est:** the conclusion invokes once again the fundamental axiom asserted at 517–20 and 640–1. **utrumque:** both soul and body.   **disciditur:** cf. 657–61n. *discidere.*

(II) THE SOUL DID NOT EXIST BEFORE THE BODY

670–678

(Proof 16) The soul does not remember any previous experience.

670–3 Praeterea: at 417–18 L. had announced that he would demonstrate that minds and souls are *natiuos et mortalis* (n.). Having shown that the soul cannot survive the death of the body, he now turns to prove that it cannot have existed before the body to which it belongs. This is not announced as a new topic, since the idea that the soul was immortal necessarily entailed its pre-existence, as was assumed by philosophers such as Pythagoras and Plato who held that view.   **nascentibus insinuatur** 'winds its way in … at birth' (Brown), sc. as an existing entity; cf. 1.113 *an … nascentibus insi-nuetur* and *extrinsecus insinuatas* at 689, 698. L. uses *insinuo* both transitively (either, as here, passive or as reflexive + *se*) and intransitively, as at 485 (n.), in all 13x. The word is chosen to underline the implausibility of the idea that the soul, intimately connected as it is with all the internal windings (*sinus*) of the body, could be introduced into it as an entity.   **super** 'as well', adverbial = *insuper* (*OLD super*[2] 3), sc. in addition to the events of this present life.   **anteactam aetatem** 'our past life', when on the rejected theory the soul was occupying another body, not when it was 'between bodies' and not leading an active existence; cf. 673 *uestigia gestarum rerum*, 675 *actarum … rerum*. With verbs of remembering the accusative is commoner than the genitive in early Latin (Bennett 1910, 1914: II 88, 213; K–S I 471–2). Plato did in fact hold that there was some 'recollection', ἀνάμνησις, though it probably did not extend to the memory of specific events (Bluck 1981: 30–61). See next n.

674–6 If the soul cannot remember anything that it has actually done or experienced in a previous existence, it cannot be the soul that it supposedly was then, which must therefore have perished: change = destruction of what was there before, an implicit appeal to a now familiar axiom. **retinentia** 'grasp', i.e. memory, picking up *tenemus* from 673, for the metrically impossible *memoria*. The word is attested only here, but *retineo*, with or without *memoria*, = 'remember' is not uncommon from Cicero onwards (*OLD* 12). Cf. 314–18n. *uariantia*.   **non … id ab leto iam longiter errat** 'that state of affairs in that case [*iam*: 367–9n.] is not far astray from death'; *longiter* (not registered in *OLD*) is otherwise unattested, but L. has no aversion from adverbs in *-iter*, which tended to be avoided by classical poets (Axelson 1945: 62–3), though not by L.'s admirer Ovid. The grammarians who have preserved this reading, whose text is transmitted in MSS as old as or older than those of L., are unlikely to have invented the form. *longius* '(not) very far' = 789 (n.), 5.123, though in itself perfectly good and idiomatic Latin (788–9n.), must be accounted a banalization.

The case for *longiter* presented by Timpanaro (1970/1978) is conclusive. **ut opinor:** sc. whatever anybody else may choose to believe.   **quae fuit ante** 'which previously existed', sc. as 'they' maintain; the words have to be read in mental inverted commas. 'It' was in fact quite a different soul, which perished with its owner. L. recurs to the theory of metempsychosis at 741–7 (n.).

677–8 The essential point that souls are both *natiuae* and *mortales*, repeated with variations at 686–7 and 711–12.   **nunc … nunc** 'now … just now'; L. plays on two senses of the word (*OLD* 1, 4). *Pace* Butterfield (2009: 314–15), this is linguistically defensible, charateristically Lucretian, and rhetorically more effective than his suggested *nunc … inde*. The evidence of Apuleius, who uses *nunc* = 'just now', both absolutely and glossed by *nuper* (*Met.* 7.21.4, 9.16.3; see Hijmans, *al.* ad locc.), suggests that this sense was in current use long after Plautus.

679–697

(Proof 17) The soul is far too intimately connected with the body for it to have been introduced as an entity: a point already made allusively by *insinuatur* at line 671 (n.).

679–85 iam perfecto 'when it was already complete': *iam* qualifies *perfecto* (cf. 540 (n.)). This was the Pythagorean doctrine expressed by Ennius in lines with which L. would have been familiar, *Ann.* 8–10 Sk. *oua parire solet genus pennis condecoratum, | non animam. [et] post inde uenit diuinitus pullis | ipsa anima.*   **animi:** in spite of the caveat at 422–3 (n.), it is a little odd that L. uses *animus* here, especially as he unobtrusively changes to the feminine at 684 and thereafter refers to the *anima*. Brieger's *animae* has been generally ignored by editors, but with 558 *animi uiuata potestas* and 674 *animi mutata potestas* in his mind an inattentive – or perhaps excessively conscientious – copyist might well have written *animi*. On this type of error by 'perseveration' see Willis 1972: 92–5, Reynolds and Wilson 2014: 232–3. Cf. Müller ad loc. See however 702–10n. *animi.*   **uiuata potestas** = 409 (n.).   **gignimur** 'are born' (*OLD* 3), as indicated by *nascentibus* at 671, not 'conceived'.   **uitae … limen:** *limen* only here of the entrance to life, elsewhere of death: 2.960 *leti … limine ab ipso*, 6.1157, 1208; cf. 3.67 *leti portas*, 5.373 *leti … ianua.*   **haud … conueniebat** 'it would be inconsistent' (*OLD conuenio* 6), sc. *uiuere* (cf. 684), so as to be seen growing along with the body. The imperfect indicative is idiomatic, an extension of the regular usage with verbs connoting potentiality, as in *poterat, potuit* = 'could have', or obligation, as in *debebat, debuit* = 'ought to have', etc. In Augustan and post-Augustan Latin a further extension takes place; cf. the common *tempus erat* = 'it is (high) time'. That there is no difference in sense is shown here by the present tense-sequence with *uideatur* and

conuenit following. See Blase 1903: 149–51; H–S 327–8.   **in ipso sanguine:** the idea of a close connexion between the blood and the soul was
seemingly hinted at in line 442 (n.), though the notion that the soul con-
sisted of blood had been summarily rejected earlier (41–5n.).   **cresse =**
creuisse, here equivalent in sense to *crescere.* For this timeless use of the perfect infinitive in a manner akin to the Greek aorist see Bennett 1910, 1914:
I 427–8. In Augustan elegy it becomes something of a mannerism, being
especially convenient for fitting in to the second half of the pentameter.
uelut in cauea per se sibi uiuere solam 'to live all on its very very own in a
cage', the expression accentuating the absurdity of the idea. It figures in
Seneca's dismissive catalogue of the many questions that have been can-
vassed about the soul (*Ep.* 88.34), which looks very much as if Seneca had
L. in mind when writing it. *cauea* glances contemptuously at the labelling
by the Pythagoreans and others of the body as a tomb or prison of the
soul (Plato, *Gorg.* 493a, *al.*). On *per se sibi* cf. 145 (n.).   **ut ... tamen** 'but
only on condition that', *ut* stipulative (Bennett 1910, 1914: I 263–7; H–S
641), a further comment on the absurdity of the idea of an imprisoned
soul. At 445–6 L. had been at pains to stress that the simultaneous development of body and soul is something that we can perceive for ourselves.
affluat 'abounds in' (*OLD* 2), underlining the absurdity of supposing that
the soul could survive in such conditions.

686–7 ~ 677–8 (n.).

688–97 The soul cannot pre-exist the body, being too closely connected
with it for that to be possible; nor for the same reason can it survive
the death of the body. There is some awkwardness of construction, since
lines 690–4, which illustrate by examples the intimate interconnexion of
the two, form a substantial parenthesis in the sequence of argument and
obscure the correspondence of *nec* at 695 with *neque* at 688. Lachmann's
transposition of 690–4 to follow 685 disposes neatly of that difficulty, but
somewhat impairs the sequence of thought, making it necessary to refer
the *quod*-clause of 690 back to 684 rather than to what has immediately
preceded it. This has led some editors, including Munro, to expel line
685, which however seems too Lucretian to lose. Moreover, it is by no
means clear, *pace* Brown ad loc., how the displacement of 690–4 could
have come about. This may be one of the passages which L. might have
tidied up if he had lived long enough to put the finishing touches to
the *DRN*, and it seems safest to leave the transmitted text as it stands.
tanto opere adnecti 'so very closely connected'; cf. 105 *magno opere* (n.).
adnecti 'fastened on', 'annexed', not, as has been shown to be the case,
truly *connected* (691 *conexa,* 695 *contextae*); the word only here in L. and
chosen to make the point.   **insinuatas** 'if they had wormed themselves
in'.   **quod fieri totum contra manifesta docet res** 'that the whole thing

happens in the opposite way is shown by the clear facts of the case'; cf.
4.1088 *quod fieri totum natura repugnat.* L. goes on to argue in what follows
that just as the soul cannot extricate itself from the body in one piece,
so it could not survive if introduced as an entity from outside.   **conexa
est:** sc. the *anima*; cf. 217 *nexam per uenas uiscera neruos.* The unmetrical
transposition in OQ (see critical notes) is a reminder of the flagrancy of
some errors when a copyist is not attending to his task.   **dentes quoque**
'even the teeth', classified as bones.   **sensu:** for the construction with
the ablative cf. Plaut. *Mil.* 262-3 *non potuit quin sermone suo aliquem fami-
liarium | participauerit de amica eri,* Apul. *Met.* 9.33.3 *statim meum dominum
comis hospes opipari prandio participat.*   **morbus** 'toothache', for the more
usual *dolor dentium.*   **stringor** 'twinge', literally 'touch' (cf. *OLD stringo*
6a), attested only here; on words of this type in L. see 622-3n. *igni gignier algor.*   **et lapis oppressus subito sub frugibus asper** 'or a rough
stone lurking under the bread suddenly bitten on'; *subito* reflects common experience and the word-play with *sub* sharpens the point. MacKay's
subito sub (MacKay 1950) is further from the transmitted text than *subsit si* (Clark 1911: 74) or *subiit si e* (Bernays, introducing a very harsh
elision), but this is one of those cases where the demands of effective
sense should be paramount. 'How can this verse be deprived of *subi-
tus* in some form, its chief point?' (Romanes 1935: 34).   **oppressus**
'when bitten on'; cf. 663 *premat.*   **frugibus** 'bread' (*OLD frux* 3b); cf.
4.1093 *laticum frugumque cupido.*   **nec ... uidentur ... posse** 'and equally
clearly they cannot', *nec* picking up *neque* from 688 after the parenthesis,   **saluas exsoluere sese** 'free themselves unharmed', *saluas* predicative; the word-play with *exsoluere* accentuates the point.   **exire ... sese:**
theme and variation, alliteration and word-play ('*saluas* ex*soluere*') underline the point.   **neruis ... ossibus ... articulisque:** the expressive tri-
colon crescendo emphasizes the complexity of the bodily structure from
which the soul would have to disengage itself while still preserving its
identity.

698-712

(Proof 18) If the soul cannot exist separately, *in cauea*, it would have to pervade the whole body at once if introduced from outside; but it could not
do this without losing its identity. No known Epicurean doctrine appears
directly to underlie this passage, but the point follows on logically from
that of the previous section. The argument relies heavily on the perhaps
dubiously appropriate analogy of food.

698-700 quod si forte picks up *si* from line 679; *forte,* as often, is scornful.
insinuatam 'after it has wound its way in'.   **permanare ... solere** 'to be
in the habit of oozing in': *soleo* generally connotes volition or custom; its

occurrence here seems to convey a sarcastic suggestion that a pre-existent and sentient soul might choose what to do in the process of entering its new host.   **tanto quique magis** [= 5.343] 'all the more'; *quique* is attested only at these two places; *qui* is evidently the old form of the ablative of the pronoun (*OLD qui²*), but the precise syntactical function of *quique* in this phrase is uncertain, though the sense is clear (*OLD quique* headn.); cf. 738 *utqui* (n.).   **fusa** 'by being combined'.

701 A last crisp restatement of the axiom first enunciated at 517–20 (n.). Its brevity seems to reflect L.'s conviction that his readers will by now be seised of the point.

702–8 dispertitus 'by being spread about'; Lachmann's correction, together with those previously made to the unmetrical readings in OQ at lines 702 and 705 (see critical notes), restores good sense and a satisfactory structure to the paragraph. The only objection that might be made to it is that there is no mention anywhere else of food being distributed *per caulas*, only *in membra atque artus* (703) and *in uenas* (2.1125, 1136, 4.955, 6.946). L.'s argument, however, seems to entail that he envisaged two processes at work in the absorption of food by the body: (i) its distribution through the veins to different parts of the body; (ii) its further dispersion on arrival at its various destinations through 'pores' at what in modern terminology might be called the intercellular level. The *caulae* referred to in lines 702 and 707 are not as elsewhere 'pores' on the surface of the body but minute spaces within it. Athenaeus (3.102) quotes a passage from a comedy in which a cook professing Epicurean learning and airing it with a display of technical vocabulary speaks of 'juice' or 'flavour' being distributed evenly 'into the passages', εἰς τοὺς πόρους. This interpretation is supported by the responsion between *per caulas…in membra atque artus* (702–3) and *per caulas…in artus* (707). **dispertitus…diditur…disperit:** the point is underlined, as so often, by the repeated prefixes.   **disperit** 'loses its identity'.   **aliam naturam** 'a different substance' (*OLD natura* 8a). The analogy between the change of food into blood, flesh and bones, etc., and the rearrangement of the atoms of the original *anima* to form a different one, is the point on which the argument turns.   **anima atque animus…animi natura:** 'the soul…the soul'; notwithstanding *dominatur* following (709), which seems to echo what was said of the dominant role of the mind at 138–9 (n.), the concluding reference to the *anima* at line 712 indicates that this must be the sense here also.   **quamuis integra recens in | corpus eunt** 'though [sc. as proponents of the rejected theory contend] they enter whole into their new body', *integra* predicative, neuter plural following the usual rule. The indicative with *quamuis* is normal syntax (402–5n.), but the sense dictated here by the argument is that of a contrary-to-fact concessive/conditional clause: this is what *would* happen if a pre-existing soul, postulated for the sake of argument, were to attempt to take up residence in a new body. The crisp expression, accentuated by the striking enjambment created by Marullus' neat correction, hints that however quickly and neatly such a hypothetical transfer was carried out, the soul could not survive it. **recens** 'new-born'; cf. Varro, *RR* 2.8.2 *pullum asininum a partu recentem.* **quasi** 'as it might be', implicitly deriding the notion that the introduced soul could survive intact the same process of absorption as that undergone by food. **particulae** 'soul-particles': here and at 2.833, 4.261 meaning the grouping of atoms into larger combinations. Cf. 179–80n. *corporibus.*

709–10 The argument is rounded off by a characteristic *reductio ad absurdum*: the logical consequence of the theory that L. is refuting would be that the soul which governs all our actions could somehow have pieced itself together again after being dispersed in the process of entering the body. **nunc...tunc** underlines the absurdity of the idea. *tunc* was emended to *tum* by an early editor in accordance with L.'s marked general preference for *tum* (103x: *tunc* 9x; see Gaertner 2007: 216 n. 24). Here however the responson with *nunc* and the rhetoric clearly demand the more emphatic form of the word, 'at the very moment when' (*OLD tunc* headn.).

711–12 This final variation on the theme of lines 417–18 is pointedly anthropomorphic: the soul has a 'birthday' and a 'funeral' (the original sense of *funus*: *OLD* 1) – those of its equally mortal host, the body.

713–740

(Proof 19) The appearance of maggots in the decaying body proves that the soul-atoms which animate them have been dispersed in the process of dying. L.'s introductory question refers specifically to the issue of survival rather than pre-existence, but the one necessarily implies the other. (670–3n. *Praeterea*). He proceeds by posing a series of dilemmas.

713–14 The question clearly expects the answer 'yes' and gets it, though after what was said at 398–401 (cf. 425–44) it seemingly expects 'no'. However, as appears from what follows, L. assumes, though he does not say so explicitly, that some soul-atoms remain in the body long enough to find new hosts. The mechanics of the process are not explained. **necne:** very rarely found in direct questions rather than *anne*: *OLD* 1 quotes only three examples, all from Cicero (so H–S 465).

715–16 Another variation of the fundamental axiom. **haud erit ut...possit** 'in no way will it be possible', an emphatic periphrasis for *haud poterit.* **merito immortalis:** for the 'quasi-caesura' cf. 174, 258 (nn.).

717–21 ita sinceris membris 'with its limbs so intact': *sincerus* here = *integer*, as at 532 (n.). The phrase answers *partibus amissis*; but L. uses *membrum* in the sense 'constituent part' (*OLD* 3a) only twice elsewhere, in both cases of parts of the universe (5.381, 445), as against 111 in the usual sense of 'limb'. A little anthropomorphic joke (cf. 711–12n.)? For those reluctant to credit him with a sense of humour Faber's *sincera ex membris*, conjectured independently by Winckelmann (reading *e)* and approved by Müller (1974: 760), offers a more straightforwardly prosaic interpretation.   **unde … uermīs:** for the metre of the verse cf. 196, 588 (nn.). **rancenti:** for the unmetrical *rancido*. The word recurs only in the *Liber medicinalis* (969) of L.'s third-century imitator Q. Serenus. Cf. below on *exos*.   **uiscere** 'flesh'.   **exspirant … animantum:** L. asks 'How can the dead body breed creatures endowed with soul?', sc. except by their acquiring their *animae* from the *anima* of the corpse; but instead of answering explicitly, he conveys the answer by a play on words, *anima* is 'breath' as well as 'life' and 'soul', and the airy nature of the soul has been previously established at 232–6 (n.). The dying body 'breathes out' parts of the soul and so imparts animation to – maggots (Read 1940: 38–40). Wakefield had seen the point: '*Exspiravit*, quasi *animas* scilicet, *animatos vermes*', neatly accentuated by the assonance *exspirant … animantum … tanta.* **exos … exsanguis … perfluctuat:** a vivid and repellent picture of the wriggling mass of white maggots. *exos* is a rare word, recurring, like *rancenti*, in Q. Serenus (670), as is *perfluctuo*, attested only here.   **tumidos** 'swollen', 'bloated', reflecting clinical fact, rather than 'heaving' (Munro, Bailey).

722–9 L. sarcastically imagines some of the absurd explanations to which those unwilling to accept the obvious answer to the preceding question might be driven. In particular the picture at lines 727–8 of souls hunting for maggot-particles with which to construct themselves new domiciles seems at first sight too ludicrous not to be a product of his own invention; and it is indeed a favourite tactic of his, as Heinze remarks ad loc., to attack an opposing position by rebutting an absurd special case of his own devising. However, this especially outré example may, as argued by Jacobson (1999), have been suggested to him by an equally bizarre description by Empedocles of how individual body-parts wandered about in search of others to join up with (Kirk, Raven and Schofield 1983: 302–3).   **quod si forte** 'But if by any chance', *forte* dismissive.   **priuas:** i.e. one soul per maggot.   **nec reputas** 'but [*OLD neque* 5] you don't stop to consider'.   **hoc tamen … agendum** 'there is still, it seems, this question to be debated and brought to a decision'; the pompous periphrasis, with its legal flavour, suggests arrival at a judicial verdict (*OLD discrimen* 1b) and paves the way for the heavy irony that follows.   **utrum tandem** 'whether

in fact', 'whether really' (*OLD tandem* 1a).   **semina quaeque** 'the several
seeds' (*OLD quisque* 1b), those appropriate for forming maggots.   **uermiculorum:** *uermium* would not scan, but the diminutive is the proper word
for a maggot.   **ipsaeque** 'of their own accord', picked up by *ipsae* at line
730; why should they go to so much trouble when they would be far better
off staying as they are?   **ubi sint** 'a place to live', final subjunctive (*OLD
ubi* 7b).   **quasi** 'as it were', implicitly querying the plausibility of this
process, as at 707 (n.).

730–4 neque cur…quareue = *neque cur…neque cur*; see *OLD neque* 7f,
8a; and cf. Reinhardt 2010: 206, 406–12n. *et…relinquas.*   **laborent** 'put
themselves out' (*OLD* 2).   **neque…dicere suppeditat** 'no explanation
is forthcoming', literally 'provides a saying', an apparently unique usage,
with the substantival infinitive as the direct object of the verb (*OLD suppedd-
ito* 1c *sub fin.*).   **alguque:** a rare and archaic word, found almost always
in the ablative singular, here and at 5.747 a metrically convenient synonym
for *algor*; otherwise attested almost exclusively in Republican drama and
L.'s contemporary Varro.   **magis his uitiis affine laborat** 'suffers more
from these afflictions because more liable to them': *magis* does double duty
with both *affine* and *laborat. affinis*, properly 'in contact with' (cf. 734 *contage*), here and at Cic. *Inv.* 2.33 *aliis affinem uitiis* has the rare sense of
'inclined to', 'given to' (*OLD* 4b).   **contage:** for the unmetrical *conta-
gio*. The word does not occur in classical Latin outside the *DRN* and was
no doubt coined by L. With *contagē* here contrast *contagĕ* at 4.336; consis-
tency is imposed by Wakefield's tentative *contage e/ ex*; for postponement of
the preposition cf. 374–7n. *quibus e.* However, if L. invented the word, he
may have scanned it to suit himself; cf. 533 *tabē* (n.).   **fungitur** 'suffers',
'experiences'; cf. 168 *fungi* (n.). In old Latin *fungor* commonly takes the
accusative, as at 940, 956, 1028; here it is felt as passive in sense.

735–6 quamuis…utile 'as useful as you like', sc. to envisage.   **cui
subeant** 'for them to enter by', final. At 6.1246 *subeo* is used with the
accusative, reflecting the general practice of writers in construing *subeo* =
both 'enter' and 'come up to' (*OLD* 6, 10) indifferently with accusative or
dative.

738–40 The second of the two alternatives posed at 727–8 is dismissed
by a summary restatement of what was argued at 688–97.   **utqui** 'that
in any way whatever', an emphatic form of *ut* found also in Plautus and
probably colloquial; cf. *atqui. qui*, the old ablative of the pronoun, normally = 'how', as at 443, is used as an enclitic like Greek πως 'somehow'.
**neque enim poterunt subtiliter esse | conexae neque consensus contagia
fient** 'nor will they be able to be firmly entwined [sc. as has been shown to

be the case], nor will the interconnexions that belong to [i.e. are essential to] common sensation occur'. The repeated prefixes as usual underline the point. For *consensus* = συμπάθεια cf. 153–8n. *consentire*. Lachmann's correction is called for by the sense: the interconnexions are not brought about by *consensus*, but cause it; the genitive is that of definition. Cf. 331 *implexis...principiis*, 'it is *because* the atoms are so closely interlaced' (n.).

741–775

L. now turns to demolish the theory of the transmigration of souls, metempsychosis, associated particularly with the Pythagoreans. He had touched on it in passing at 670–8 (nn.), and earlier in his criticism of Ennius in the Proem to Book 1 (Kenney 1970b: 373–80/2007: 307–14), and it has been implicitly glanced at in the preceding sequence of proofs. His method of refutation by anticipation (754–9, 760–4, 765–8nn.) shows that this was territory for which he was well prepared. It is interesting to note that Ovid, who clearly admired him greatly (*Am.* 1.15.23–4, *Tr.* 2.425–6), in the grand monologue of Pythagoras at *Met.* 15.75–478 expresses his distinctively unLucretian conviction of the immortality of the soul in equally distinctive Lucretian didactic mode (Kenney 2009a: 151–2).

741–747

(**Proof 20**). The first of two proofs that, since mental as well as physical characteristics remain constant in a species, and do not pass into other species, soul and body must grow together. Cf. 784–6n. This argument had already been deployed at 445–58 (n.) to prove that they also perish together.

741–3 triste...seminium 'the grim breed'; *seminium* seemingly a technical term used by breeders: cf. Varro, *RR* 2.1.14 *tertia pars est quo sit seminio quaerendum*, 2.6.1 *e quo seminio ego hic procreaui pullos.* **sequitur** 'goes with'; cf. 448 (n.). **a patribus datur** 'comes from their sires'. This emphasis on the transmission of characteristics through the male line recalls the idea that the female was no more than a receptacle for the male seed and was not truly related to her offspring: Aesch. *Eumen.* 657–66, Diod. 1.80.4 (ascribing it to the Egyptians); cf. Needham 1959: 43–6. The point is a red herring in any case; and it is not possible to evade the question by taking *patribus* as = 'parents' and *patrius* as = 'inherited'; there is no reliable instance of *patres* = 'father and mother' in literary Latin before the age of Ausonius and Claudian (Austin on Virg. *Aen.* 2.579). It is tempting to see this as an interpolation to provide an immediate answer to the preceding question (Müller 1975: 372–5, Deufert 1996: 251). Straightforward sense and syntax are restored by following Lambinus' learned friend in deleting the verse, which obviates the need to emend *ceruos* in line 742 to *ceruis*.

744–8 et...cetera de genere hoc [= 481 (n.)] 'and all other such characteristics'.   **iam...| ex ineunte aeuo** 'from the very beginning of life' (Munro).   **membris |...ingenioque:** emphasizing the common development of body and soul from the moment of generation (next n.). **generascunt** 'come into being', a unique Lucretian coinage for *gignuntur*, the inceptive form underlining the point.   **certa** 'fixed' (*OLD* 1). **semine seminioque** 'in virtue of its seed and breed', causal ablative: the seed characteristic of its parentage, -*que* epexegetic.   **crescit cum corpore quoque** 'with each individual body', making the point that this happens in each individual in each and every species; cf. 769 *quoque* (n.). The alliteration *c- c- c- qu- -qu-* adds further emphasis, assisted by the ending of three successive verses by -*oque*. That has been felt as excessive by some editors, who avoid it by reading *toto* for *quoque* with Q. This however produces a cliché (8x in this book, 7x elsewhere), inducing the critic to invoke the maxim 'utrum in alterum abiturum fuit?', i.e. in which direction is an accidental change more likely to have occurred? (Reynolds and Wilson 2014: 222).

748–753

(**Proof 21**) Characteristics do not pass from one species to another. On the argument from the impossible (*adynaton*) see 622–3n.

748–53 mutare...| corpora 'pass from one body to another' ∼ 755, where the point implicitly glanced at here, that change = death, is explictly enunciated. For this sense of *muto* see *OLD* 6a and cf. Greek ἀμείβω.   **Hyrcano de semine:** to contrast with the proverbially timid stag (see below) and underline the absurdity of the theory he is attacking L. names a breed of dogs renowned for its ferocity. The Hyrcani lived by the Caspian Sea and their dogs were popularly supposed to interbreed with tigers and other wild animals (Grattius, *Cyn.* 161–6); the tradition of such unions was at least as old as Aristotle (*HA* 8.706a).   **saepe** 'as one might commonly see', sc. if this absurd theory were true.   **cornigeri incursum cerui:** the only occasion on which a stag's antlers would normally be used as a weapon is in the rutting season; for their timidity in general cf. Virg. *G.* 3.539 *timidi dammae ceruique fugaces.*   **tremeretque...fugiens** 'would flee in alarm'. **ueniente columba** 'when a dove came at it to attack'; cf. 821 *ueniunt aliena salutis*, 833 *uenientibus...Poenis*; similarly in English 'come on'.   **fera saecla ferarum** 'the wild breeds [*OLD saeculum* 2] of wild beasts'; the *figura etymologica* brings out the point: the beasts have remained as nature has made them, man has evolved from his primitive beginnings to develop speech and reason, a topic to which L. addresses himself in Book v.

754–759

(**Proof 22**) (Anticipation of a counter-argument.) To say that the soul changes when it enters a new body is to admit that it is mortal.

754–5 illud ... quod aiunt 'They are wrong who say that ...'   **immortalem** 'while still remaining immortal', predicative: the word is placed so as to complement *flecti* (= *mutari*, 511n.) at the end of the verse and so to emphasize the contradiction.   **mutato corpore flecti** 'changed by changing bodies'.

756 ~ 701 (n.). The last reprise of the great axiom. L. has faithfully followed the Master's precepts (87–93n.).

757–9 The application of the axiom to the particular case is developed explicitly. Once it is conceded that the parts of the soul can be transposed it follows that they can or must – for the *ut*-clause can be read as either final or consecutive – be dissolved throughout the body and perish with it. **traiciuntur ... ordine migrant** ~ 513.   **debent posse** 'it follows that they can'.   **denique** 'in the end', the word, as often in L., signalling the logical outcome of events and processes.

760–764

(**Proof 23**) (Anticipation of a counter-argument.) If the theory is amended to allow that souls remain constant to a particular species, this takes no account of the fact that the mind of a child or young animal is obviously undeveloped. Thus the soul that enters a new abode must either have changed or be changed in the process, therefore cannot be immortal. The point is further developed in the next proof.

760–4 hominum ... humana: sc. and the same is true of animals.   **prudens** 'discreet', able to judge the consequences of its actions, *prouidens* (*OLD prudens* headn.).   **puer** 'child': in this sense generally found only in the plural (*OLD* 4a).   **doctus** 'well trained'.   **fortis equi uis** = 8 (n.).

765–768

(**Proof 24**) (Anticipation of a counter-argument.) Nor will it do to say that the mind becomes young again when it enters a new body, since change connotes death.

765–8 scilicet ... | confugient 'I dare say *they* will take refuge (in the position) that ...': *confugio* is used like a verb of saying with *oratio obliqua*, as at Cic. *Verr.* 2.3.191 *an quoniam hoc non audes dicere, illuc confugies, uecturae difficultate adductus ternos denarios dare maluisse?*; cf. the analogous use of *refuto* (350–3n.) and *discrepat* = 'is inconsistent with the fact that ...' at

1.582.   **in tenero tenerascere:** as at 753, the *figura etymologica* sarcastically emphasizes that the point made by these imagined opponents is precisely what disables their argument.   **tenerascere** 'becomes young': the
word, attested later only in technical prose (*OLD* s.v.), was probably coined
by L., like *generasco* at 745 (n.), to underline the implausibility of the theory
that he is refuting.   **si iam** [= 540 (n.)] 'even if'.   **mutata per artus** ~
758 *dissolui... per artus. mutata* causal, 'by being changed'.   **tanto opere**
'so completely' (*OLD opus* 5b).   **amittit uitam** ~ 759 *intereant.*

769-771

If body and soul grow to maturity together, they must have originated
together. A subsidiary argument, picking up what was said at 741-7, 760-4
(qq.v.); not arising from the preceding train of thought, but serving to
round it off. Cf. 772-5n.

769 quoque: any individual body whose fate it shares. In echoing the point
previously made at line 747 L. discreetly varies the alliterative pattern.

770 On the metre see 83-4n. *hunc... amicitiai,* and cf. 5.847 (of the
aborted growth of monstrous natural 'experiments') *nec potuere cupitum
aetatis tangere florem.*

772-775

If the soul were immortal it would have no reason to quit its habitation
when the body dies. This argument does not cohere closely with what has
preceded, but it provides a fine scornful flourish in L.'s best manner to
conclude the sequence of argument begun at line 741. Formally it is connected to the context by the responsion 769 *quoue... 772 quidue.*

772 quidue... sibi uult... exire? 'Or what does it mean by leaving?', literally 'What does its leaving mean?', *exire* being treated as a noun and subject of the sentence. *Pace* Bailey ad loc. and Butterfield (2009: 315) the
expression has its common idiomatic meaning 'have as its object' (*OLD
uolo¹* 16), and *sibi* calls for no special explanation, let alone emendation.
senectis 'aged', a rare adjective, sparsely attested after L., though the feminine singular *senecta,* a more metrically versatile alternative for *senectus,* is
common in poetry of all periods.

773-5 an metuit... manere... ne... | **obruat...?** 'Does it shrink from
remaining for fear that...?': *metuit* does double duty with *manere* and with
the *ne*-clause.   **an metuit... putri:** the verse has caesuras, strong and
weak respectively, only in the second and third feet, since the elided syllable of *manere* is felt (Soubiran 1966: 536-8); cf. 83, 625 (nn.).   **domus:**
a traditional image, allied to that of the body as a prison or tomb. It was
used by Bion (Introd. 14-16, and cf. 931-77nn.): 'Just as when we are

evicted from a house when the landlord removes the door or the roof or
blocks up the well, so when landlady Nature takes away the use of eyes or
ears or limbs, I am evicted from the body' (Hense 1909: 15–16). Cf. Cic.
De Sen. 84 *ex uita ita discedo tamquam ex hospitio, non tamquam domo: com-
morandi enim natura deuersorium nobis, non habitandi, dedit* and Powell ad
loc. For the idea that our possession of life is not a freehold cf. Eur. *Suppl.*
534–5 οὔτι γὰρ κεκτήμεθα | ἡμέτερον αὐτὸ πλὴν ἐνοικῆσαι βίον, 'for we pos-
sess nothing of our own except a tenancy of life'. L. goes on to invest the
image with a specifically Roman character (970–1n. *uitaque... usu*). On
death figured as emigration or change of abode (ἀποδημία, μετοίκησις) see
Harrison 1986: 505–6.   **obruat:** sc. *se*, as argued by Brown, referring to
the subject of the sentence, the soul (*NLS* 36 (ii); G–L 520). This gives
more pointed sense than taking it as intransitive, a usage nowhere else
attested for this common verb. The strong pause after the first dactyl and
the placing of the enjambed verb provides a descriptive effect which in
later epic becomes almost a cliché (Winbolt 1903: 13–16).   **immortali:**
anything, that is, which is really immortal.

776–783

(Proof 25) It is totally absurd to imagine souls struggling or waiting in
line for admission to the next available body. L. winds up the sequence
of arguments against pre-existence in characteristically sardonic fashion.
That the position which he attacks was not in this case an Aunt Sally of
his own devising seems to be shown by the neo-Platonic passages cited by
Heinze ad loc.

776–80 'Then again (*OLD denique* 2a), it is clearly quite ridiculous (to
imagine that) souls are there on the spot (*esse... praesto*) at (human) love-
making and the births of wild animals, that huge numbers of immortal
beings should be on the alert for mortal bodies, and that they should
be falling over each other in their haste to be first and foremost in the
struggle to insert themselves.' The second infinitive-clause amplifies the
first to accentuate the absurdity; the asyndeton – 'corrected' in the old
editions by reading *et spectare* – is only apparent. The slightly awkward
separation of *immortales* from *animas* arises from L.'s wish to focus on
the absurdity of what is envisaged by the juxtaposition *immortalis mortalia.*   **conubia... Veneris** = *concubitus*; the high-flown expression contrasting with the suggestion of voyeurism implied by the pictured scene.
The scansion of *conubia* has occasioned some debate; the case for *conūbia*
(– ◡ ◡ ◡) rather than *conūbja* (– – ◡) by synizesis was argued powerfully by
Munro (cf. Conway, Austin on Virg. *Aen.* 1.73).   **immortalis mortalia:**
for the word-play cf. 869 *mortalem... mors... immortalis* (n.).   **innumero
numero:** the same oxymoronic jingle at 2.1054, producing an effect of

which L. was evidently fond; cf. 2.1086 *numero...innumerali*, 6.485 *innumerabilem...numerum.* The same conceit is rather differently employed in the epitaph supposedly written for himself by Plautus, *et numeri innumeri simul omnes collacrimarunt* (*FLP* 47, 50).   **certareque:** cf. 163 *mutareque* (161–7n.).   **praeproperanter** 'in a tearing hurry', a Lucretian variant of the usual *praepropere.* Cf. 1063 *praecipitanter;* L. evidently had a weakness for adverbs of this type (Bailey 1947: 137). On his similar penchant for adverbs in *-im* see 258–61n. *summatim.*   **prima potissimaque:** a collocation which seems to have been a favourite of Livy's, perhaps, like our 'first and foremost', something of a cliché.

781–3 si non forte 'unless we are to suppose', ironical.   **uolans aduenerit:** as if from some sort of waiting-room in the ether. **neque...hilum** 'and not at all', adverbial accusative, as at 813, 830; see 218–20n. *nec defit ponderis hilum.*

(III) SOME GENERAL CONSIDERATIONS

784-799

(Proof 26) Everything in nature has its place, and that of the soul is within the body, without which it cannot exist (615–23n.). Most of this passage recurs in Book v (see critical notes), slightly adapted for its new context (Boyancé 1963: 217–18, Sedley 1998: 70–1). This is the first of a short series of general arguments against the immortality of the soul with which L. concludes his case; some have been touched on earlier.

784–6 L. now deploys the figure of the *adynaton* (622–3n.) to bring out the full absurdity of the belief that he is refuting. On this figure as belonging to 'the area of popular speech and beliefs' cf. Rowe 1965: 392–5, showing that the poets used it in full awareness of such associations. L. is tilting against what he would have regarded as typical superstitions. His first three impossibilities reprise and vary the similar catalogue at 1.161–2 (if nothing could be created from nothing, then) *e mare primum homines, e terra posset oriri | squamigerum genus et uolucres erumpere caelo,* eqs. The third also recalls the occasional reports in the scientific literature of fish being unearthed by the plough. One such case is recorded by Livy in a list of prodigies in the year 173 BC (42.2.5). These were evidently taken seriously at the time, something L. declines to do. Similarly, as suggested by Heinze, blood in wood and sap in stone may refer to bleeding or sweating statues, a type of portent familiar also in modern times. Such phenomena, however, also had a specifically Epicurean relevance, recalling L.'s rejection of the views of Anaxagoras at 1.875–920 (Piazzi 2005: 55–8); cf. 1.881–4 *conueniebat...fruges..., minaci | robore cum saxi franguntur, mittere*

signum | sanguinis aut . . . , cum lapidi in lapidem manare cruorem. What might
be termed the scattergun style of L.'s attack shows him already modulating
into the diatribe mode.   **in alto:** Lachmann emended to *salso* because
of the similarly worded verse at 5.128 *sicut in arbore non arbor, non aequore
salso,* in a similar list of *adynata,* but that verse was clearly retailored to suit
its new context, and the change weakens the alliterative sequence *ae- ar-
ae- al-.* Moreover *in alto* accentuates the postulated paradox.   **quicquid**
= *quicque* (615–21n. *quicquid*).   **crescat et insit** 'to exist and grow', technically *hysteron proteron*: see 159–60n. *propellit et icit.*

788–9 animi: here specifically the *animus,* as shown by what follows. See
794–9n.   **longius** 'at all far', an idiomatic nuance not noticed by *OLD*;
for this sense of the comparative cf. the common *saepius, citius* (H–S
168–9). Lambinus, who had read *longiter* at 676 (n.), proposed it here
in conformity, followed by Lachmann, who likewise emended *longius* at
5.133. However, there is no justification for seeking to impose a rigid con-
sistency of usage on L. in such a case.

790–7 If the *animus* could exist outside the body, it could, *a fortiori,* exist
anywhere within it; but it has been shown that it has a fixed place there:
therefore it cannot exist outside it. The argument is in syllogistic form with
the minor premiss unexpressed.

790–3 quod si . . . enim 'but if indeed . . .'. If this is what L. wrote, *enim*
cannot have its usual inferential sense, though that is the connexion that
the context might lead the reader to expect. It must be asseverative, as
in the colloquial *quod enim* and *quia enim* (H–S 508, 575), analogous to
the Virgilian *sed enim,* 'but in fact', an archaism favoured by him (4x) and
taken up by later poets (Quint. *IO* 9.3.14, Austin on *Aen.* 1.19). Lachmann termed the construction here with *quod si* a solecism, and indeed
the only parallel, and that hardly an exact one, is from a more colloquial
and less correct writer than L., Varro, *RR* 2.4.8 (sows when breeding are
driven into muddy places and pools) *ut uolutentur in luto, quae enim illorum requies, ut lauatio hominis.* There is an additional harshness in the asyndeton between *manere* in line 793 and the preceding infinitives (cf. below).
However, the verses recur without variation at 5.134–7 as part of a passage
evidently adapted by L. to its new context (784–99n.), and none of the
suggested remedies carry much conviction.   **prius** 'rather', 'more probably' = *potius* (*OLD* 2).   **animi uis** = *animus;* cf. 788 *animi natura* and on
periphrases with *uis* see 6–8n. *fortis equi uis.*   **tandem . . . manere** 'while
at all events (*tandem*) it remained in the same man, its container'. The asyn-
detic qualification has the air of an afterthought, making the point that
the soul would in any case be unlikely to choose to exist outside the body.

For *tandem* as equivalent in sense to *saltem* see Munro ad loc. Metrically the verse is an oddity, with four elisions and only quasi-caesuras (174n.) throughout.   **atque:** epexegetic = viz., identifying the man with his body; cf. 344–9n. *maternis… membris aluoque.* For the image cf. 434–9n. *uasis,* 505.

794–9 After reiterating the fundamental point established at 140–2 (n.) in lines 794–6, driving it home by emphatic alliteration, L. proceeds to broaden the argument, focussed hitherto on the *animus,* to embrace the *anima* as well, as he had previously done at 702–8 (n.); cf. below on 798–9. Though logically defensible (so Brown ad loc.), this perhaps verges on a type of argumentative sleight of hand of which these are not the only instances in the poem (Kenney 2007: 101–3, 106–7).

794–7 quod quoniam 'but since', like *quodsi* 'but if'. Only here in the *DRN,* but Ciceronian; on this type of *quod*-phrase see H–S 571–2.   **in nostro … corpore:** Lambinus' addition of *in* produces straightforward syntax and closer responsion with *extra corpus* at 797; after *quoniam, in* could have dropped out early through a well-attested type of corruption by haplography (Clausen 1949: 311, 1955: 52).   **quoque:** sc. as in the rest of the universe; cf. 787.   **dispositumque … possit:** a verse with weak caesuras in second and third feet and a quasi-caesura in the fourth.   **anima atque animus:** see 794–9n.   **totum … extra corpus** 'right outside the body'. The position of *totum* in the self-contained spondaic first foot reinforces the point, which is further driven home by the emphatically holospondaic verse. If even inside the body the mind and spirit can exist only in their assigned places, how much less likely is it that they could exist at all when completely separated from the body.   **durare genique** 'come into being and last'; for the word-order cf. 159–60n. *propellit et icit. geni = gigni: geno* is the original form, of which *gigno* is a reduplication, restored to L. elsewhere by conjecture (428–33n. *feruntur*).

798–9 A characteristically summary conclusion: the *anima,* here used inclusively to embrace the mind (cf. below), cannot come into being or exist outside the body, therefore it must perish with it at death.   **interiit, periisse:** an Augustan poet would have been unlikely to ignore the opportunity offered of emphatic anaphora by writing *periit, periisse.* That however entails scanning *ubi* as an iambus against L.'s overwhelming preference for pyrrhic *ubi*: of the six instances of this scansion in a total of 122 occurrences two are found in this book (619, 728), but perhaps he rejected *periit* as too obvious (Introd. 18–19).   **distractam in corpore toto:** cf. 588–91. Strictly speaking, this applies only to the *anima,* but the *animus* is inextricably bound up with it (136–7) and cannot exist independently.

800–805

(Proof 27) The union of the mortal (body) with the immortal (soul) is grossly improbable. Hitherto L. has argued from observed fact; he now changes to a more aprioristic form of reasoning which paves the way for his concluding arguments (806–29). A return to first principles provides an appropriate close to this main portion of the book.

800–1 A series of substantivized infinitives expresses the rejected view, given its comeuppance by the crisp *desiperest*, as at 361, 5.1041–3. L. makes effective use of this rhetorical ploy several times: cf. 359–61, and the really monumental example at 5.156–65.   **quippe etenim** 'for in fact' (440–4n.).   **iungere:** shorthand for 'to postulate that one can join'. **consentire** = συμπάσχειν, as at 153 (n.).   **fungi mutua** 'to act on each other', with both the active and passive senses of *fungor* felt (*OLD* 2a, 3). Cf. 168 *pariter fungi* (n.). *mutua* is adverbial accusative (*NLS* 13 (iii), K–S I 280–1); cf. 2.76 *inter se mortales mutua uiuunt*, 5.33 *acerba tuens*.

802–5 The sentence begins as if L. intended to ask 'What two things could be more different and incompatible than the mortal and the immortal?'; it ends as if the question had been 'What could be more unlikely than that the mortal and the immortal could co-exist?' Nevertheless it is clear that there is nothing haphazard or hand-to-mouth about the construction of the sentence: the emphatic *diuersius... disiunctum discrepitansque* does not merely restate the same point three times: there is a transition from the idea of difference via that of incongruity to that of inconsistency, exploiting the distinct but allied senses of *discrepito*. This was evidently a coinage of L.'s, attested only in the *DRN* (3x) and in the *Notae Tironianae*, a system of shorthand devised by Cicero's secretary Tiro. The transition is assisted by the deliberately ambiguous (not, *pace* Bailey, grammatically impossible) *inter se*, which refers both backwards, to the point that these two things are *res inter se diuersae et disiunctae*, and forwards to the point that the following hypothesis in lines 804–5 is *inter se disiunctum discrepitansque*, internally inconsistent, not self-consistent.   **concilio:** a technical term (for its metaphorical employment by L. see Sykes Davies 1931–2: 37), used in Books I and II, along with the verb *concilio* and the noun *conciliatus* (a Lucretian coinage) of combinations of atoms. Since the union of body and soul is at the atomic level, *concilium* is the proper word to describe it. The thought is compressed and the point is made by implication: if, as has been proved, body and soul are linked in a *concilium*, it is unthinkable that the soul should be immune from the physical shocks to which the body is exposed. In that case the familiar axiom entails that it is mortal. **saeuas...procellas:** a powerful metaphor for the stresses and strains of life,

which also glances at the reminder which follows of the continual battering from outside to which all atomic compounds are exposed.

806–818

(**Proof 28**) What is immortal must satisfy certain conditions, which are
met only by the atoms, the void, and the universe as a whole, the gods
constituting a special case (23–4n.). These verses recur in Book v (see
critical notes) as part of a proof that our world is not eternal. There the
corollary that the world does not satisfy these conditions is explicitly stated;
here, unless a lacuna is posited after line 818, the reader is left to deduce
that the same is true of the soul for himself. In its other setting the passage
is perfectly appropriate and belongs there, whereas here, unless there has
been damage to the text, it has been imperfectly assimilated to its context.
However, given the fact, as it must be accounted (Kenney 1998: 25–6), that
the poem lacked its final revision when the poet died, it seems more likely
that the passage was inserted by L. to fill out his parade of proofs rather
than by a later interpolator, as argued by Deufert (1996: 72–5), following
Lachmann and others.

806–10 L. sets out the three truly immortal things in turn. (1) *The atoms.*
solido cum corpore: with no void in them; cf. 1.510 *sunt igitur solida ac
sine inani corpora prima.*   **sibi** 'to their undoing', dative of disadvantage.   **artas . . . partis** 'their tightly packed parts', touching on the apparent paradox discussed at 1.559–634 and alluded to at 2.478–99, that the
atoms, though indissoluble, nevertheless consist of 'parts' which, 'though
they are physically inseparable from the atoms, can be distinguished in
thought' (Smith on 1.615; see D.L. 10.56–9, Rist 1972: 52–5). The jingle '*artas . . . partis*', enclosing the clause, neatly hints at the binding motif.
ante: at 1.503–50, especially 528–30 *haec neque dissolui plagis extrinsecus
icta | possunt nec porro penitus penetrata retexi | nec ratione queunt alia temptata
labare*, the point enforced by the heavy alliteration.

811–13 (2) *The void.*   **neque ab ictu fungitur hilum** 'and is not in the
smallest degree affected by blows', i.e. is intangible. As at 168 (n.) *fungitur*
is passive in sense, hence instrumental *ab.*

814–18 (3) *The universe.* The same point is previously expounded at
2.303–7 *nec rerum summam commutare ulla potest uis, | nam neque, quo possit
genus ullum materiai | effugere ex omni, quicquam est extra, neque in omne | unde
coorta queat noua uis irrumpere et omnem | naturam rerum mutare et uertere motus.*
fit 'is to be found' (*OLD fio* 1b), practically = *est*, as at 6.829 *magna mali fit
copia circum.* The correction of MS *sit*, which in fact antedates Lachmann,
is demanded by the sense, as it is at 5.359 *quia nulla loci fit copia circum,*
in yet another exposition of this same topic (*sit* MSS), where it was also

restored by Lachmann. For L. it is just as much a fact that there is no *loci copia* ouside the universe for things to dissolve into (see 1.951–1051) as that the atoms are impervious to blows from without and that the void is intangible. The indicative is required to match those preceding.   **quasi:** almost 'if they could'.   **dissoluique:** on the scansion see 327–30n. *dissoluantur.*   **sicuti...aeterna** 'as in the case of the universe, (which is) eternal' (*OLD sicut* 3). *sicuti* is here and at 2.536 the reading of OQ, at 5.361 *sicut*, which is the vulgate in all three places. See Skutsch 1985: 697–8 on Enn. *Ann.* 549, arguing powerfully for *sicuti* against Lachmann (q.v. on 2.536) and Housman (*CP* 671), notwithstanding the fact that *sicuti*, though restored sporadically by editors, is almost totally avoided by later poets (Skutsch 1985: 697 n. 34). Its occurrence, universally supported by the MSS at *Arat.* 131 by L.'s contemporary Cicero, suggests that this form of the word was still acceptable to the Roman ear in L.'s day. **summarum summast:** the whole sum of things, 'the universe regarded as an aggregate of individual worlds' (Bailey 1947: 640 on 1.235, q.v. on L.'s extremely flexible use of *summa*). The phrase is used by other writers with a wide range of meanings: 'the supreme command' (Plaut. *Truc.* 24–5), 'crowning achievement' (Pliny, *NH* 7.99), 'what it comes down to' (Sen. *Ep.* 40.14). Here the superlative nuance may be felt: 'the *summa par excellence*', 'the one and only *summa*'. In classical Latin this usage is rare and has a colloquial flavour (H–S 55–6).   **neque[1]** does double duty, picking up the *quia*-clause of lines 814–15 and looking forward to *neque* following. By L.'s standards the sentence is somewhat loosely constructed, but the sense is clear.   **quis** 'any', used after the negative for the more usual *ullus* or *quisquam* (*OLD quis[2]* 2b). Both *quis* and *qui* are used adjectivally (*OLD quis[2]* 4), but the variation between the forms here and at 5.362 (see critical notes) is more likely to be due to the accidents of transmission than to the poet. The variation between *diffugiant* here and *dissiliant* there on the other hand must surely be authorial.

819–829

(Proof 29) The soul enjoys no special protection from injury: it is afflicted not only by the ills of the flesh but by maladies peculiar to itself. Though it may be thought that *magis* at line 819 can be read as providing an implicit connexion with what has preceded (n.), one might have expected L. to go on to demonstrate formally that the soul does not satisfy any of the conditions for immortality just laid down. As Brown notes, this apparent lack of continuity in the sequence of argument is more likely to be due to the unrevised state of the poem at L.'s death than to textual damage, and it lends no support to Lachmann's deletion of the intervening section (806–18n.). The concluding verses of the passage (see especially 825–7) certainly assist the transition to the Conclusion of the book, for it is precisely these self-tormenting tendencies in men that provide L. with much of the material for his great peroration. The argument is loosely articulated by a string of conjunctions and anaphoras, *quod si . . . quod . . . quia . . . quia . . . praeter . . . quam quod . . . aduenit id quod . . . adde . . . adde quod*, perhaps suggesting that L. is impatient to clear out of the way points which seemed too obvious to need developing. Characteristically ironic is the suggestion that these fears, in which fear of the hereafter predominates, if rightly understood, prove that there is no hereafter.

819–20 magis: looking forward to *quod* rather than referring back, to suggest that this argument might seem even more convincing than those (mistakenly) accepted by believers in the immortality of the soul; but an implied antithesis with what has preceded may also be felt.   **habendast:** sc. the *anima*, last mentioned at 799. On the implications for the state of the text see 819–29n.   **uitalibus ab rebus munita** 'protected by vital forces', like the Epicurean gods (23–4n.), as noted by Giussani ad loc. If this is a deliberate allusion, is L. perhaps slyly suggesting that his opponents are reduced to stealing arguments from the enemy's armoury? For the expression cf. 2.575 *uitalia rerum*, glossed by Bailey ad loc. 'the forces which give life to things'. For *ab* with instrumental ablative see 323–6n. *corpore ab omni*. However, if that is the sense, this appears to be the only attested instance of *munitus ab* = 'protected by'; elsewhere it always = 'protected from'. To accept the usual meaning here entails that *uitalibus* must either be emended or explained as a euphemism for its opposite. However, in its euphemistic sense *uitalis* is attested only of things associated with funerals: *uitalis lectus* = 'bier', *uitalia*, sc. *uestimenta* = 'grave-clothes'. Lambinus' *letalibus* is not palaeographically implausible, since words are sometimes corrupted into their opposites (Housman on Manil. 5.463), but the word occurs nowhere else in the *DRN* and is first attested in Virgil. Too much should not be made of syntactical singularities that are not actual solecisms (Kenney 1999: 399–400 and nn. 2, 6), and L., writing when the language of Latin poetry was still in a formative stage, had an adventurous way with it.   **tenetur** 'is protected'.

821–3 aut quia. . . | aut quia: subordinate to the preceding *quod*-clause, offering alternative explanations of this untenable hypothesis. **non . . . omnino** 'not at all' (*OLD omnino* 3a).   **ueniunt** 'attack', as at 752, 833.   **aliena salutis** 'hostile to its survival' (Latham): see *OLD alienus* 11b. *alienus* is constructed indifferently with genitive, dative and ablative with and without *ab* (*OLD* headn.); here and at 6.69 *alienaque pacis*, 1065 *aliarum rerum aliena* with genitive, at 3.961 with ablative, elsewhere only in prose writers.   **quid noceant** 'what harm they do', *quid* virtually = *quantum*. After 823 a verse or verses have been lost containing the

main clause of the sentence and showing (or simply stating) that these conditions cannot apply to the soul. Any supplement can only be suggested
exempli gratia; see critical notes for proposals.

824–7 L. now develops the point made at 459–62 (n.): that the soul suffers grief and fear, so cannot be immortal. Its afflictions – anxiety, conscience, madness, dementia – are the symptoms of what is fundamentally
wrong with it: fear of death.   **praeter . . . quam quod** 'apart from the
fact that', leading to expectation of the usual *huc accedit ut/ uti/ item* (9x in
the poem); instead there is a switch to a personal construction *aduenit id
quod . . . macerat* 'there arrives [cf. 821–2 *ueniunt . . . ueniunt*] that which torments', that is the perceived susceptibility of the mind to anxiety and fear.
The separation of *praeterquam* into its component parts (tmesis: 262–5n.
inter . . . cursant) is less common than that of *ante-* and *priusquam* and occurs
only here in L.   **morbis cum:** on the postponement of monosyllabic
prepositions see 374–7n. *quibus e.* There is no metrical reason for it here,
and given the choice L. generally prefers a spondaic word in the fourth
foot (Bailey 1947: 113), unlike later poets, who generally conformed to
the so-called 'Lex Marxii' (Marx 1926: 198), preferring a lack of coinci-
dence of verse ictus and dynamic accent at this position in the verse: see
Austin on *Aen.* 1.1, Drexler 1967: 98–103. Possibly L. meant the juxtaposition of *cum* with *corporis* along with the alliteration, to suggest the tightly
knit connexion of body and soul.   **inque metu male habet** 'terrifies and
vexes it': *male habere* is a colloquial idiom, frequent in comedy (*OLD habeo*
22b), here combined with the quasi-instrumental *in metu.*   **praeteritisque . . . remordent** 'and even when its misdeeds are past, the memory of
them returns to torment it': an artfully constructed verse, articulated on
three perfect participles: *praeteritis* complements *futuris* in line 825, *male
admissis*, treated as a substantive, is varied by *peccata. remordeo*, first attested
in the *DRN*, is similarly used of the pangs of conscience at 4.1135 *cum con-
scius ipse animus se forte remordet*; after L. it occurs almost exclusively in the
poets, always of mental anguish.

828–9 proprium 'peculiar to it', as opposed to the diseases which it shares
with the body (824).   **lethargi:** 'this insistence upon mortality concludes with a dramatic plunge into the black waters of forgetfulness'
(Hadzsits 1935: 97). The words *lethargus, lethargicus, lethargia* from Greek
λήθαργος were used loosely by ancient medical writers to describe a number of conditions; but whereas at 465 it is a symptom of a disease shared
with the body (n.), here the image evoked by *nigras . . . undas* of the waters
of Lethe, which when drunk induced oblivion, together with the context,
points to the *obliuia rerum* described as a symptom of mortal illness. To
a twenty-first-century reader the picture may suggest the disabling loss of
memory associated with dementia in one of its several forms; in the ancient

world fewer people survived long enough for there to be such a general awareness of the condition as there is today. For *nigras* cf. Virgil's description of the waters of Styx at *Aen.* 9.105–6 *per pice torrentis atraque uoragine ripas | adnuit.*

III. CONCLUSION

830–869

Death then does not concern us: to be dead is the same as never to have been born. From all that has been said – *igitur* here is surely the most heavily loaded conjunction in all Latin literature – it follows that death is not a thing to be feared. In the rest of the book L. develops this theme in terms which are fundamentally Epicurean but which also owe much to the literary-philosophical *consolatio*: see Introd. 26–8, and for a historical survey of what was in effect a literary sub-genre see Scourfield 1993: 15–33.

830–1 This famous pronouncement follows closely the words of Epicurus himself, ὁ θάνατος οὐδὲν πρὸς ἡμᾶς, 'death is nothing to us' (K. Δ. 2.71 Us.; cf. D.L. 10.124, 125). Cicero condenses L.'s expression: *Fin.* 2.100 *scripsit* [sc. Epicurus] *mortem nihil ad nos pertinere.*   **ad nos** 'so far as we are concerned' (*OLD ad* 24c). Like other parts of the Epicurean message, the sentiment passed, in a debased form, into the common stock of popular wisdom, frequently appearing on tombstones (Lattimore 1962: 84–6). One example seems intended to recall L.'s line: *non fueram, non sum, nescio, non ad me pertinet* (*CLE* 1585.2).   **habetur** 'is proved to be' (531–2n. *habendast*).

832–42 We shall be concerned by what happens after we die no more than we were by what happened before we were born: an old Epicurean argument ([Plato], *Axiochus* 365d) exploited by Seneca and picked up by Montaigne (Summers on Sen. *Ep.* 55), here given a specifically Roman cast. L.'s transference of it to the Roman context of the Punic Wars was calculated to bring it home to contemporary readers. The vocabulary and phrasing of lines 833–7 parody the high epic style, and the irony is pointed: these events were at the time world-shaking and so presented themselves to the first great national poet – but what are they to us now? The Romans looked back to the Punic Wars as one of the great crises of their history: Livy describes what was seen to be at stake in language which seems reminiscent of L.: *in discrimine est nunc humanum omne genus, utrum uos an Carthaginienses principes orbis terrarum uideat* (29.17.6). The common model was Ennius, echoed also by [Virg.] *Cul.* 34, Lucan 1.304–6; and Hannibal continued to haunt the declamatory tradition for centuries to plague Roman schoolboys (Juv. 10.147–67), already for L. a subject for sardonic reflection.

832-3 anteacto: sc. before we were born.   **nil...aegri** 'no discomfort', genitive 'of the rubric', defining the class to which a thing belongs: 'nothing (in the sphere) of discomfort' (*NLS* 72 (5) Notes (ii)); cf. 1050 *quid...mali?*   **ad confligendum uenientibus** 'coming on to the attack' (748-53n. *ueniente columba*). The march-like rhythm, increasing in tempo and urgency, signals a transition to the high epic style.

834-7 L.'s language echoes with mocking effect that of Ennius, *Africa terribili tremit horrida terra tumultu* (Sk. 309), describing '[p]resumably the panic caused in Africa by the arrival of Scipio's fleet' (Skutsch ad loc.). Catullus appropriates and further inflates L.'s phraseology to describe Jupiter's ratifying nod, *quo motu tellus atque horrida contremuerunt | aequora concussitque micantia sidera mundus* (64.205-6).   **sub altis aetheris oris** 'under the lofty regions of ether', a stately paraphrase for 'here on earth'. Gifanius' correction of MS *auris/-as* is demanded by sense and Lucretian usage: the regular collocations are *aetheris orae* and *aeris aurae* (402-5n. *aetherias uitalis*).   **fuere:** sc. *omnia*, in view of the parallelism, accentuated by the rhyme *contremuere...fuere*, rather than *omnes humani*, extracted from the following indirect question, the reading supported by Housman (1937: I xli).   **utrorum ad regna cadendum | ...esset** 'which of the two it should be to whose dominions all mankind must fall'. *cadendum esset* = 'there was to be a falling'; for this impersonal use of the neuter of the gerundive see G-L 427 n. 2; *NLS* 204. The usual construction with *cado* = 'fall under the power of' is with *sub* or *in*; the use of *regna* rather than *regnum*, if not dictated purely by metrical convenience, suggests that it is territorial empire rather than 'rule' in the abstract that is in question, as at 5.1130 *regere imperio...et regna tenere*, making *ad* more appropriate here. On the possible ambiguity cf. Löfstedt 1942: 54 n. 1, noting that in Virgil singular and plural have become virtually interchangeable.   **humanis** = *hominibus* (80n.).   **terraque marique:** a cliché, but here pointed, looking forward to the dramatic concluding flourish of line 842.

839-42 discidium: the dissolution of the *concilium* referred to at line 805. From all that has been established in the first part of the book it follows that the separation of body and soul entails the end of sensation, which is for us the end of existence: so far as we are concerned the two are identical (841). The dictum of Epicurus quoted above (830-1n.) continues 'what has been separated cannot feel and what cannot feel has nothing to do with us': the dispersed atoms of body and soul no longer have anything to do with the *concilium* that was 'us'.   **quibus e** = 375 (n.).   **uniter apti** [= 846] 'fitted into a single being'; *uniter* is attested only in L. and a scholium on Juv. 3.297 (p. 50 Wessner); in L. always qualifying *aptus* (5x) and probably coined by him.   **sensumque mouere** 'or [147-51n. *-que*] affect our senses', the only valid test. Epicurus equated death with loss of sensation, στέρησις αἰσθήσεως (D.L. 10.124).   **non si terra mari miscebitur et mare caelo:** not even the final catastrophe in which the world itself will perish will concern us. This was an idea that men found hard to come to terms with (5.91–109), and L. will go on to prove its inevitability at considerable length (5.235–415). His language here, however, is calculated to make the reader think of the proverbial saying (Otto 1890: 345), the ancient ancestor of 'après moi le déluge', ἐμοῦ θανόντος γαῖα μιχθήτω πυρί, 'when I am dead, let the earth be mingled with fire', paraphrased by Cicero in a reference to those *qui negant se recusare quominus ipsis mortuis terrarum omnium deflagratio consequatur* (*Fin.* 3.64). What men speak of lightly is, whether they like the idea or not, going to happen. After *non si*, 'not even if', one might expect the subjunctive, as at e.g. 6.1076 *non si Neptuni fluctu renouare operam des,* Virg. *Aen.* 2.522 *non si ipse meus nunc adforet Hector,* 12.203–5; the future indicative *miscebitur* insists that this is not a possibility but a fact.   **terra mari ... mare caelo:** the Punic Wars were confined to earth and sea (837); in the final cosmic destruction the heavens too will perish. The point is reinforced by alliteration and chiasmus.

843–61 A parenthetic digression which however follows on naturally from what has preceded (*qui non erimus* at 840 picked up at 843–4) and is relevant to the thesis that *mors nil est ad nos,* but which is not provided with a neat transition back to the main line of argument at line 862.

843–6 si iam ... sentit 'even if the soul does continue to experience sensation'; on *si iam* see 540–2n. Siebelis's transposition of *nostro sentit,* independently proposed by Winckelmann, produces a more straightforward word-order, but the separation of adjective–noun phrases is so much a feature of developed Latin poetical style (Winbolt 1903: 216–18, Wilkinson 1963: 213–20) that this is an insufficient reason to emend the text. **distractast:** here of the separation of the soul from the body, not as elsewhere (501, 507, 590, 799) of its dissolution (*OLD* 1a, b); cf. 330 *extrahere.* **animi natura animaeque potestas** = *animus + anima*; for the periphrases cf. 277, here perhaps to emphasize the point that for the complete 'us' to continue to exist both constituents of the soul, with their respective properties and characteristics, must be present.   **comptu ... coniugioque | ... consistimus:** the repetition of the prefixes emphasizes that the true 'us' is a *concilium* and that any sensation which might conceivably be possessed independently by the soul after leaving the body is irrelevant. *comptus* as a substantive = 'union' is attested only here; elsewhere it = 'ornament' or 'hair-style', as at 1.87 of Iphigenia, *infula uirgineos circumdata comptus.* *coniugium* only here in L. and attested only here in this non-matrimonial sense (*OLD* 4).

847–51 Even if in the course of time our atoms were to recombine in the same configuration, that would still not be the old 'us'. This contingency is not, like its predecessor, admitted purely for the sake of argument; L. is prepared to accept it as a possibility (854–8n.). In its original, cyclic, guise, the idea was Stoic.   **si** = *etsi*, 'even though', as shown by *tamen* at line 850 (cf. 946–7 *si . . . tamen*); but even without such signposts *si* must often be read as concessive (G–L 604 Remarks 1; H–S 671).   **collegerit . . . redegerit . . . fuerint** 'if it/they should have . . .', perfect subjunctive.   **collegerit aetas:** time, as often in the poets, ancient and modern (Ferber 1999: s.v. Time), is figured as an active agent; so, in the famous speech of Sophocles' Ajax, 'All things the long unnumbered years bring out from obscurity and hide again', ἅπανθ' ὁ μακρὸς κἀναρίθμητος χρόνος | φύει τ' ἄδηλα καὶ φανέντα κρύπτεται (*Aj.* 646–7).   **ut sita nunc est** 'in its present arrangement'; cf. 857 *in eodem, ut nunc sunt, ordine posta*, apparently the only example of *situs* = 'placed', sc. as to its own constituents (*OLD* 3d). *ut* = 'as', as at 857, rather than 'where', as Munro apparently took it. The local sense of *ut* is rare, and there are no certain examples in L.; cf. Fordyce on Catull. 11.3.   **nobis . . . nos:** the reconstituted 'us' would not be the original 'us', the present *concilium*.   **lumina uitae:** i.e. life here on earth under the sun; cf. 1025 *lumina . . . reliquit*, 1033 *lumine adempto*, 1.170 *oras in luminis exit*.   **id quoque factum** 'even if that did happen' (*OLD quoque* 4).   **repetentia nostri** 'the recollection of ourselves', sc. as we were; *nostri* objective genitive, *repetentia* only here in classical Latin, but its use by L.'s imitator Arnobius (third century AD) at *Adv. Nat.* 2.26, 28 guarantees it (Munro ad loc.).

852–3 et nunc 'and as it is' (*OLD nunc* 11a), relegating the preceding speculations to their proper place as of no consequence to us here and now. Susemihl's *ut*, independently suggested by Heinze, gives a good logical connexion – 'we should not be concerned (in the hypothetical case), just as we are not (in the actual case)' – but it does not improve the sense or the argument.   **ad nos de nobis . . . | qui fuimus:** cf. 849–50 *nobis . . . nos* and n.   **neque:** whether Lachmann's metrically improved version of the humanist supplement *nec* should be preferred to Merrill's *nil*, transposed to follow *iam* by Garcia Calvo (Butterfield 2008c: 30 n. 44), turns on whether variation should be preferred to anaphora; and if anaphora is preferred, then *nunc nil* perhaps deserves consideration. Lucretian usage offers no decisive guidance.   **d(e) illis:** cf. Virg. *Aen.* 6.38 *grege de intacto*; according to Soubiran (1966: 404) the only instances of elided *de* in epic poetry from Cicero to Silius; cf. 159 *cum animo* (n.).   **illis:** any former selves that there may have been.

854–8 The possibility of such recombinations, though not it would seem an idea attributable to Epicurus himself, is consistent with the Epicurean 'principle of plenitude': 'given infinite time, every possibility is sooner or later realised' (Sedley 1998: 175 and n. 29). L.'s wording is suitably cautious.   **cum respicias...possis** 'when one looks back...one can'. **tum motus materiai | multimodis quam sint** 'also how variously the atoms move', the point, as often, emphasized by alliteration. For the structure of the indirect question cf. 208–9n.; but here the adverb *multimodis* is used as if he had written *materies moueatur*. Cf. Sall. *Hist.* fr. 2.42 L. *Octauius et C. Cotta consulatum ingressi, quorum Octauius languide et incuriose fuit, Cotta promptius.*   **hoc:** to be read as *hŏcc* and scanned as 'long' or heavy (not, as stated by Brown, lengthening the vowel); see Allen 1965/1978: 75–7). Similarly at 932, 1024 and *hic* at 914 (n.).   **adcredere:** only here in L. The word is rare and the force of the prefix uncertain, whether 'believe in addition' or 'come to believe'.   **posta** = *posita*: 344–9n. *reposta.*   **haec...fuisse:** the verse was restored to what is obviously its proper place by Lachmann; it is a striking demonstration of unreflecting editorial conservatism that it took so long for it to be realized that it made no sense where it stood in the MSS.   **quibus e** = 375 (n.).

859–61 reprehendere = *repetere*, an unusual extension of the sense of this word (*OLD* 2a).   **inter...iectast:** cf. 262 *inter...cursant*, where as here the tmesis graphically illustrates the point.   **uitai pausa** (= 930) 'a break in existence'. This derivative of Greek παύω is frequent down to L., after whom it disappears from classical Latin to resurface in the archaizing writers of the second century AD; see Skutsch on Enn. *Ann.* 595. **uageque | ...omnes** 'and the moving atoms have all strayed far and wide at large away from the senses', a condensed and emphatic way of saying that the atoms have quitted the controlled motions which produce sensation (cf. 272) to pursue new and random courses. *uage* 'in all directions' only here in L. and otherwise attested only in prose.   **deerrarunt:** scanned as a trisyllable.

862–9 The argument now resumes from where it broke off at line 842 (843–61n.), to which *enim* refers back, with *accidere* at 864 picking up *accidere* from 841. The intervening passage, though formally a digression, is relevant inasmuch as it helps to substantiate the conclusion referred to at 864 *id quoniam mors eximit.* The point that nothing can happen to anybody who is not there to have it happen to him recalls a similar formulation in the pseudo-Platonic *Axiochus* 365d 'you will not be for it (misfortune) to happen to you', σὺ γὰρ οὐκ ἔσηι περὶ ὂν ἔσται; and, possibly picking up from this passage, is echoed by one of the interlocutors at Cic. *Tusc.* 1.12 *sint enim oportet, si miseri sunt; tu autem modo negabas eos esse, qui mortui essent. si igitur non sunt, nihil possunt esse; ita ne miseri quidem sunt.* On Cicero's engagement with L. in his philosophical works see Hardie 2007: 113. So later Seneca, *Ep.* 36.9 *mors nullum habet incommodum: esse* *enim debet aliquid cuius sit incommodum.*   **misere si forte aegreque futu-rumst:** a heightened version of the common expression *male alicui esse*; *cui* to be understood.   **ipse … in eo tum tempore** 'the actual self at that actual moment of time': the pleonasm and the sandwiched position of *tum* reinforce the point.   **id:** the possibility that when dead one can be 'there'.   **esseque:** 161–7n. *mutareque.*   **probet** = *prohibet*; this contracted form, restored here by Lachmann, is elsewhere attested only at 1.977 *est aliquid quod probeat officiatque*, where it is transmitted by QG (see p. 29).   **illum … conciliari** 'the man on whom misfortunes may be conferred', *concilio* 'acquire' usually of desirable objects; L. perverts the normal sense for the sake of a play on words: if there is no *concilium* of atoms there can be no *concilium* of misfortunes.   **nec … natus:** it makes no difference whether a man (has been born at some time or) has never been born at all. Pontanus' correction of the reading of O, since *an* properly introduces a second question (*OLD* 2, 3, 4), entails postulating a type of ellipse in which what is not expressed is to be inferred from what follows. This figure is technically known as *e sequentibus praecedentia* (Getty 1955: lv); Heinze cited examples from Livy (36.7.10–11, 44.25.11).   **iam:** sc. once death has occurred, qualifying *differre* and looking forward to *cum* following.   **mors … immortalis:** the conceit that death is deathless had been used by Amphis, a comic poet of the fourth century BC, *ap.* Athen. 8.336c (fr. 8, II 216–17 K–A 'Death is deathless when once a man is dead', ὁ Θάνατος δ' ἀθάνατός ἐστιν, ἂν ἅπαξ τις ἀποθάνηι; but what in the Greek is a mere jingle is here not only sonorous and dignified but makes a fundamental point. L. is insisting on what for him was an essential and central scientific truth revealed by Epicurus, that the price of the survival of the whole is the destruction of its parts. 'Change is the law of nature for all things that man can know by observation, and change is death. But if the basic matter of the universe is eternal, so are the changes through which it passes, and therefore death is eternal' (Michels 1955: 165–6). Cf. 1087–94n.

870–893

Fear of what may happen to the body after death is therefore (*proinde*) irrational. This was an Epicurean commonplace. This is the point in the argument where the diatribe-satirist takes over: in contrast to the treatment of the same topic by the author of the pseudo-Platonic *Axiochus* (365c) L. pulls out all the rhetorical stops at his command (Kenney 2007: *passim*) to enlist the emotional sympathies of his readers. At line 888 the argument shifts to a different but related topic offering scope for more keen sarcasm on another popular delusion, the importance of a 'proper' funeral (888–93n.).

870–5 ubi...uideas 'when one sees'.   **se...indignarier ipsum | ...fore ut** 'treating it as a grievance that he...' (Latham): the construction belongs to the proleptic 'I know thee who thou art' category (208–9n.), here with a variation of the usual accusative + infinitive (as at 884), contrived to bring out the absurdity of the man's behaviour. Alliteration sharpens the point. The *se ipsum* on whose behalf he protests is not the real 'self' at all, and it will not be 'he himself' that is to undergo these imagined indignities. L. goes on to suggest that what he really fears, though he will not admit it, is that they will hurt. Irrational as they are by the standards of a materialist philosophy, such feelings are quintessentially human. 'Certainly one's own death wd. be a much pleasanter idea if one cd. be quite rid of the lingering idea that the corpse is alive' – the words of a hard-headed Protestant Ulsterman (Lewis 2004: I 938).   **putescat:** only here in L., but to be preferred to *putrescat*: (i) it is closer to *putes* in OQ; (ii) L.'s usage corresponds to what appears to be the original distinction between the two verbs, relating respectively to *puteo* and *putris; putesco =* 'rot', 'stink', *putresco =* 'crumble away', 'decay', as elsewhere in the *DRN*; (iii) *putescat ~* σηπόμενος 'rotting', in the corresponding passage in the *Axiochus* (365c).   **posto** = *posito* (344–9n. *reposta*), 'buried', for the usual *composito*.   **interfiat** = *interficiatur*, a usage otherwise attested only at Plaut. *Trin.* 532.   **malisue ferarum:** here and at 888–93 L. is reviewing actual funeral practices, and this reference and that at line 888 must be to the Persian custom, which has survived down to modern times in the Parsee 'Towers of Silence', of exposing the dead to wild beasts and birds before burial. The practice had been known to the Greeks at least since Herodotus (1.140), and Cicero includes it in a list of burial customs (*Tusc.* 1.108).   **non sincerum sonere** 'does not ring true', like a flawed pot, a common metaphor; cf. Enn. *Sc.* 106 V.² (108 J.) *nam neque irati neque blandi quicquam sincere sonant* and Jocelyn ad loc. *sincerum* is adverbial (internal/cognate) accusative (G–L 333; *NLS* 13 (iv)). For the form *sonere* cf. 156n.   **caecum...stimulum** 'a hidden prick', sc. of fear; hidden, that is to say, from himself, as he continues to deny what he is subconsciously (878 *inscius*) afraid of. Cf. 1019, *stimuli* as the pangs of a guilty conscience, 4.1082 as what drives lovers to hurt the beloved in the frenzy of consummation.

876–8 dat 'grants', 'allows the truth of' (*OLD* 16b), for the usual *concedo*. **quod promittit et unde** 'neither what he professes to grant [sc. that 'he' will not survive after death] nor what that profession arises from [*unde = ex quo*, sc. *promittit*]'. For *unde* cf. Hor. *Sat.* 2.2.31 *unde datum sentis?*, 'what is the premiss for your opinion?', Pers. 5.124 *unde datum hoc sumis?* In his heart of hearts the man will accept neither conclusion nor premiss. **nec...se tollit et eicit** 'he will not uproot and cast "himself" out'. For the

idiom cf. 487–91n. *extentat neruos*; here it is pointed: the man will not make
the effort of intellect and will that is required to rescue him from his fears.
eicit is scanned as a disyllable by synizesis.   **facit** 'supposes' (624–30n.
faciundum est).   **esse … super** = *superesse*, tmesis.   **sui … ipse:** *ipse* is
the man as he is now, *sui* as he sees himself in anticipation; cf. 881 *ipse
sui miseret*. He will not understand that his corpse will not be 'himself'
and that the man who now exists, *ipse*, will not be there after death to
feel pity; *ipse* sharpens the absurdity, and Bailey's terming it 'redundant' is
imperceptive.

880–3 uolucres … feraeque: the classic fate of the unburied corpse (882
proiecto) in literary allusions from Homer onwards. Premising that 'Birds
and dogs, not birds and beasts, are the classic eaters of corpses', Feeney
(1978) argues persuasively that L. had 'a private obsession [sc. with lac-
eration by birds and wild animals] which is by no means confined to the
specific context of burial' but 'has a far wider reference' (16). Cf. 'the
images of biting and rending, so prolific in descriptions of *ferae* and *uolucres*' at ibid. 992–4. It is however clear from the context that it is funeral
practices that L. has in mind here.   **miseret:** the active form of the verb
used personally is very rare; otherwise in classical writers only at Enn. *Ann.*
162 (see Skutsch ad loc.), *Sc.* 192 V.² (182 J.), Ter. *Hec.* 64, V.F. 2.92.
neque … se diuidit: he cannot distinguish his true self as it exists now, sc.
from his future corpse, but persists in participating in his 'own' suffering.   **illim** = *illinc*, i.e. from the corpse. Cf. 160 *exim*, but the two forms
are differently derived (*OLD* s.vv. headnn.).   **proiecto** 'cast out', almost
a technical term for unburied corpses (*OLD proicio* 7a); cf. 6.1155 *proiecta
cadauera*, of plague victims.   **illum | se fingit** 'identifies himself with it'
(Smith).   **sensuque suo contaminat adstans** 'and standing there [sc. in
imagination] he infects it with his own sensations', attributes to the inan-
imate corpse what the living man would feel. *contamino* only here in L.,
in what is close to its original meaning = *contingo*; but already the later
and familiar sense of 'change' or more specifically 'spoil', sc. by contact, is
felt.

884–7 hinc '*this* is why', looking back to 870, with *indignatur* picking up
indignarier there.   **in uera … morte** 'in death as it really is'.   **nullum … alium se:** there is only one self, which ceases to exist when the *con-
cilium* of body and soul is dissolved.   **uiuus … peremptum | … stansque
iacentem:** the oppositions bring out the paradoxical absurdities of the
position that L. is attacking, and round off the argument, highlighting
the absurdity of a living man's mourning for a 'self' bereaved of a 'self'
(*sibi* dative of disadvantage). Bailey's offhand 'the usual Lucretian redun-
dance' does him no credit.   **stansque iacentem:** for the metre cf. 35–6n.

hasce secundum res, 251, 1038, here dictated by the juxtaposition of the two words to bring out the absurdity of the man's behaviour.   **se** picks up *se* from the previous verse, the anaphora further rubbing the point in and supporting this early supplement against Orth's *ipsum* (*pace* Butterfield 2008c: 30 n. 44).   **uriue** reintroduces the subject of cremation, lost sight of since line 872; see next n.

888–93 Up to this point L. has been dealing with the fate of the body after death in general terms. He now proceeds to pour scorn on the belief that it is a misfortune not to have a proper funeral, whatever form that might take in a particular society. This seemingly always has been and still is the general belief of mankind, summed up in homely fashion by Mr Polly, the eponymous hero of H. G. Wells's novel – 'Got to put 'em away somehow, I suppose' – and was a favourite Aunt Sally of philosophers in antiquity: 'The wise man', said Epicurus, 'will not trouble himself about funeral rites', ταφῆς φροντίζειν (D.L. 10.118). L.'s contemptuous enumeration is characteristic: cf. Bion (Hense 31), Cic. *Tusc.* 1.103–8. The topic was not Epicurean property: Cicero quotes a well-known retort by the Cynic Diogenes on the subject (loc. cit. 104), and as authority for his catalogue of practices he cites the Stoic Chrysippus; and it was a Stoic, Lucan, who wrote of the dead of Pharsalus *caelo tegitur qui non habet urnam* (*B.C.* 7.819). Petronius exploits the theme in a burlesque declamation (115.17–18), from which it may be inferred that by the latter part of the 1st century AD it had become somewhat trite. L. develops it less because it was strictly relevant to his main argument, though on Epicurean premises the views that he attacks were certainly irrational, than because it offered a fine opportunity for a series of crushing sarcasms in his best vein. Though *uriue* in line 887 can be seen as paving the transition, it remains true, as remarked by Heinze, that the distinction between the two topics of the fate of the dead body and a decent burial is blurred.   **morte malumst malis morsuque:** the strong alliteration and word-play in *malumst malis* contribute to the tone of scornful irony that informs what follows.   **qui** 'how' (*OLD qui²* 1).   **torrescere ... suffocari ... rigere | ... cubat ... urgeriue ... obtritum:** the words are all such as attribute sensation to the corpse, underlining the irrationality of these fears. Conventional methods of disposal – cremation, embalming and entombment, inhumation – are just as unpleasant to a 'sentient' corpse as being devoured by wild beasts. *torresco* is attested only here in classical Latin.   **in melle situm:** honey was commonly used for embalming. In more recent times, before the invention of preservatives such as formaldehyde, bodies might be transported in a cask of rum or brandy. **atque** 'or' 548–53n. *atque...-ue.*   **rigere | ...saxi:** sc. by being laid in a rock-cut tomb after embalming. The chilly discomfort of this situation, in which the body, laid *summo... aequore,* has no covering, is ironically

contrasted with that of the buried body, which has too much.   **obtritum pondere terrae:** pressed down and crushed, ironically glancing at the
conventional pious wish, *sit tibi terra leuis*, a formula worked to death both
in literature and in actual use (Lattimore 1962: 65–72). The effect is reinforced by the ponderous rhythm of the verse, for which cf. 122, 785, 1082
(nn.), here with only a weak caesura in the second foot and a quasi-caesura
in the third.

894–911

Regrets for the loss of present happiness can have no meaning for the
dead. The opening verses of this passage have been so often quoted out
of context that there is a danger of overlooking the tone of irony, rising at
times to parody and overt mockery, that pervades the argument. L. attacks
these conventional ideas using the technique of the diatribe. There are
some effective strokes of satire, but he makes little allowance for ordinary
human nature (Introd. 27–8).

894–9 Conventional sentiments of mourning described by L. so that he
can demolish them. To put an argument to which you have a ready answer
into the mouth of a real or imagined adversary is a stock rhetorical device,
which was much in vogue in diatribe and satire for its dramatic and enliven-
ing potentialities. Though L. clearly rejects the sentiments that he purports to quote, the expression is not for the most part overtly sarcastic
until lines 904–8. The mourners' utterances are conventional (Lattimore
1962: 172–7); especially close is an epitaph from third-century Alexandria:
'No longer, Philoxenus, does your mother receive you and cast her arms
lingeringly about your lovely neck, nor do you go to the famous city with
the young men and rejoice in the shaded level of the gymnasium' (ibid.
176 and n. 25). Virgil paid L. the compliment of imitation in his idyllic
picture of country life, *dulces pendent circum oscula nati, | casta pudicitiam
seruat domus* (*G.* 2.523–4), and so in turn did Gray:

> For them no more the blazing hearth shall burn,
> Or busy housewife ply her evening care:
> No children run to lisp their sire's return,
> Or climb his knees the envied kiss to share.
> (*Elegy Written in a Country Church Yard* 21–4)

894–7 Iam iam non 'Now, now, no more', 'never again', an emphatic variant of *non iam*. The usual sense of *iam iam* to express 'the imminence of
a situation' (*OLD iam* 5, significantly not citing this passage) clearly will
not do here: the man is dead, not dying.   **non domus accipiet te laeta
neque uxor | optima** 'neither your happy home nor your best of wives
will welcome you': editors who continue to punctuate after *laeta* (most

recently Flores (2002)) do so in flat defiance of the sense: a Roman matron would not race her children to the door to greet her husband, and the formal *accipiet* contrasts with the scampering ahead of the children, *occurrent...praeripere*. Munro, though keeping the comma, noted that 'Virgil and Gray I fancy joined the *uxor* with the *domus*'; Virgil and Gray were in the right of it.   **optima...dulces:** conventional epithets of mourning. **praeripere:** infinitive of purpose, usually found after verbs of motion and fairly common in old and colloquial Latin but relatively rare in classical writers, who generally prefer the construction with the supine (*NLS* 20; Bennett 1910, 1914: I 418–19; H–S 334–5).   **tacita** 'heartfelt' (Duff). **factis florentibus:** best taken as dative depending, like *tuis*, on *praesidium*, 'you will no longer be able to protect your prosperous affairs or your dependants'. The alternative interpretation, taking *factis florentibus esse* as a periphrasis for *florere*, 'live in prosperity' (Smith), is unsatisfactory on several counts: (i) this use of the descriptive ablative is difficult to parallel; (ii) it relies on an artificial punctuation, in which *esse* does double duty against the run of the sentence; (iii) it shifts the emphasis from the man's anxiety about how his family will fare without him to preoccupation with his own welfare. *praesidium* is almost a technical term in the vocabulary of personal relationships; cf. Horace to Maecenas, *o et praesidium et dulce decus meum* (*C.* 1.1.2 and N–H ad loc.). L.'s implicit rejection of the natural concern of a man for what will happen to his family when he dies, though of a piece with his scornful rejection of all conventional mourning, denies a basic human need; this is a sentiment that, in the speech put into the mouth of Hector in the scene of his parting with Andromache, forms part of one of the most moving episodes in all literature (Hom. *Il.* 6.456–65). Even the austere Epicurean morality allowed that such concerns were legitimate: it must be accounted to the credit of Epicurus that he 'could not wholly reconcile his philosophy with his humanity' (Sikes 1936: 134), and his will included full provisions for the care of his dependants and the freeing of his slaves (D.L. 10.16–21). That these things will not trouble a man when he is dead is completely beside the point.

898–9 More scornful echoes of the clichés of mourning.   **misero misere:** cf. Cic. *Att.* 3.23(68 SB).5 *quem ego miserum misere perdidi* and Shackleton Bailey ad loc., noting that this was colloquial speech, common in Plautus.   **omnia...tot** 'all the many', an unusual collocation: Müller (1974: 763) could only cite Min. Fel. *Oct.* 5.4 *tot omnibus saeculis*; add Tert. *Apol.* 35.9 (*TLL omnis* 620.77–9, but overlooking L.).   **ademit | una dies:** cf. 5.1000 *una dies dabit exitio*, *CLE* 405.1 *abstulit una dies anima* [*sic*] *corpusque simitur*, 1307.7–8 *apstulit haec unus tot tantaq. munera nob(is)* | *perfidus infelix horrificusque dies*. A traditional motif, variously applied; cf. Soph. *Ant.* 14 (Eteocles and Polynices) 'slain in one day by each other's hands', μιᾷ

θανόντοῖν ἡμέραι διπλῆι χερί, Eur. *HF* 510, Men. *Dysc.* 187–8, *Karched.* 8 Sandbach. In the sense of a particular day, as opposed to a period, *dies* is masculine in old Latin and classical prose: so Enn. *Ann.* 258 Sk. *multa dies in
bello conficit unus,* where see Skutsch on '[t]he commonplace that one day
is sufficient to make an end of great good fortune'. L. might, it may be
suggested, have written *unu' dies,* but he employs this licence more sparingly than Ennius, and in only five of forty-nine instances is it found in the
nominative of a 2nd declension form (Bailey 1947: 124). In this case he
evidently preferred the variation of gender. On the whole question see the
magisterial discussion of Fraenkel (1917/1964).

900–1 illud in his rebus non addunt 'What they do not add is this fact'
(319–22n.).   **nec** 'yet ... not', adversative (339–43n. *neque conuellitur*).
super: usually taken = 'also', as at 672 (n.), but Bailey's tentative suggestion that it should be taken with *insidet* as equivalent in sense to *superesse,*
forming what is in effect a compound verb cohering in sense with *una* following, deserves consideration. Alternatively, rather than taking *insidet* =
'is present' (*OLD* 4, including this passage), it could be read = 'lies heavy
on' (*OLD* 5), imparting a more effective nuance.   **una** 'together', i.e.
'with you', but the reference may be to *earum ... rerum*: the yearning passes
along with its object.

902–3 The parodically elevated tone is brought down to earth with a
bump, as the dispassionate voice of reason and common sense asserts itself,
a favourite technique of L.'s (Kenney 1981: 20; 2007: 101, 106).   **dictisque sequantur** 'and speak accordingly', sc. with their conclusions (*OLD
sequor* 10a).   **dissoluant ... se** 'free themselves'; *dissoluo* only here in L.
in this sense (*OLD* 3b) for the usual *exsoluo* (7x); elsewhere (38x) it =
'break up', 'dissolve'. Cf. 696, 1.932 *religionum animum nodis exsoluere pergo.*

904–8 L. mocks the commonplaces of the formal *lamentatio* and the epitaph. Grief was recognized by Epicurus as natural (D.L. 10.119); what L.
attacks is not mourning in itself but its more extravagant manifestations.
He seizes on the conventional promise never to forget the dead person
with all the scorn that he habitually brings to bear on a false philosophical position. Such rigour, however, betokens the rhetorical satirist rather
than the philosopher: mourning, as Epicurus clearly realized (and modern social anthropologists would agree with him) meets a universal human
need for some sort of ritualized comfort in bereavement, a way of coming
to terms with what has been lost, of achieving 'closure' in contemporary
parlance. The reflection that the dead person's troubles are over may be
comforting up to a point, but it does not always do much to assuage the
sense of loss felt by friends and family. 'The fact that there is an end to one's
life compels one to take an interest in things that will continue to live after

one is dead.' So Paul Dirac (though the words are taken out of context) in a letter to a friend (Farmelo 2009: 221). **tu quidem:** as opposed to *nos* (906). For the elision cf. 339n. **aeui | quod superest** 'for all time to come', partitive genitive. **horrifico...busto** 'on the dreadful pyre'; *horrificus* possibly borrowed from Cic. *Arat.* 121–2 *Lepus...fugit ictus | horrificos metuens rostri tremebundus acuti*; see 314–18n. and cf. 1012 *horriferos* (n.). **cinefactum** 'turned to ashes', 'incinerated'; the word is attested only here; Nonius Marcellus' comment (p. 133 L.) suggests that L. may have coined it on the analogy of compounds such as *tepefactus* and *labefactus*. **prope** '(standing) nearby', adverbial. *bustum* is properly the burnt-out pyre, as explained by Servius on Virg. *Aen.* 11.185 '*pyro' est lignorum congeries, 'rogus' cum ardere coeperit dicitur, 'bustum' uero iam exustum uocatur,* and is so used by L. here; poets were not always so punctilious in observing these distinctions. **insatiabiliter defleuimus aeternumque:** the effect of this verse on the cultivated Roman ear cannot have been other than grotesque. Three metrical features combine to make it unique in serious Latin poetry: (i) the fact that it consists of three words only; such verses are extremely rare; (ii) its single caesura; (iii) its 'neoteric' spondaic quadrisyllable ending (190–1n.). 'Surely these pathetic rhetorical figures and astonishing rhythms are meant as sarcastic caricatures of the mawkish clichés used by such *stulti* and *baratri. Insatiabiliter* for instance is not necessarily an elevated word. Its only other use in Lucretius [6.978] is of swine rolling in filth' (West 1969/1994: 29). 'The word...is charged with emotion, exaggerated if not insincere...it was difficult to use [it] seriously' (Syme 1958: II 727 and n. 3). Compare Horace's use of the otherwise unattested *insolabiliter* of mourning (*Ep.* 1.14.8), in a passage with Lucretian echoes, which it is difficult, for one reader at least, to take seriously (Kenney 1977a: 230–7). L. may be deriding the often limping hexameters found on Roman gravestones: cf. e.g. *CLE* 526, especially 10–11 *hunc fleuit populus pius, hunc miseri ingemuere parentes | perculsi longo luctu tristitiaque perenni.* So might a modern satirist mock the verses in the 'In Memoriam' columns of local newspapers. L. clearly had a weakness for formations of the type of *insatiabiliter* (Bailey 1947: 137), which were popular with the older writers, but which are relatively rare in classical Latin, apart from a few exceptions such as *amabiliter.* They survived in colloquial usage (interesting examples in Pompeian graffiti) to resurface in some of the Church Fathers. Cf. 776–8on. *praeproperanter,* 1063 *praecipitanter.* **defleuimus:** *defleo* is virtually a technical term for the formal lament (*OLD* 1c). Until it was expelled by Lachmann, *deflebimus,* the reading of the old editions, stood in the text. That the MSS all read *defleuimus* is not in itself a compelling argument: confusion of *b* and *u* is one of the commonest of copyists' errors. Reading *deflebimus,* the words must be imagined as uttered before the funeral, at the *conclamatio,* the previous

ritual of mourning (Serv. on Virg. *Aen.* 6.218, Don. *Comm. Ter.* I 346 Wessner; cf. Virg. *Aen.* 11.59 *haec ubi defleuit,* referring to words uttered over
the body of Pallas), with the two futures *deflebimus...demet* reinforcing the
sense in an extended 'theme and variation' (Henry 1873: 745–54). Reading *defleuimus,* the words must be taken as uttered after the funeral: 'we
wept our fill [*de-* intensive; *OLD* s.v.] at the pyre, and (still) [allowing *-que*
a slight adversative nuance: *OLD* s.v. 8; cf. 147–51n.] our mourning will
never be done'. Whether the scene is more effective if the mourners are
described as bewailing the horror of what they have seen rather than what
they are going to see is perhaps a moot point. In the circumstances, this
seems to be one of those cases where the unanimous testimony of the MSS
must sway the balance, *faute de mieux* (cf. Housman 1938: xv).   **aeternumque...maerorem:** one of the commonest sentiments of all epitaphs,
ancient and modern (Lattimore 1962: 243–6). Greek epitaphs favoured
ἀείμνηστος, 'always remembered'.   **nulla dies:** see 898–9n. *ademit nulla
dies.*

909–11 hoc: the speaker.   **quid...amari** 'what bitterness', defining
genitive (832–3n.).   **somnum...atque quietem** ~ 904 *leto sopitus.*
Death as sleep was and is a popular consolatory image (Lattimore 1962:
82–3); for it as a standard element of the *consolatio* cf. Hor. *C.* 1.24.5–6 *ergo
Quintilium perpetuus sopor | urget* and N–H ad loc. L. as a good Epicurean
disdains this trite symbol and turns it back on the innocent speaker: 'If you
really believe that the dead are "at rest", where is the sense in perpetual
mourning?'   **si res redit** 'if what it all comes down to (in the end)', a
Terentian idiom (Foster 1971).   **cur quisquam** 'why (ever) anyone...';
the implicitly negative rhetorical question imparts emphasis to the pronoun (41–5n. *nec prorsum quicquam*). For *cur* after *quid est? et sim.* see *OLD*
s.v. 3.   **tabescere** 'waste away'; used sneeringly of the ravages of love at
4.1120.

912–1075

In response to critics who have found the concluding part of Book III struc-
turally unbalanced, Reinhardt has suggested that it provides 'a symbolic
katabasis', in which the object of Nature's scornful harangue is transported
from a banquet clouded by the fear of death into an Underworld, where
he is confronted with her in the role of prosecuting counsel in a trial and,
after a 'parade of heroes', is returned to the upper world and a survey of
'[p]atterns of misguided behaviour caused by fear of death, to be observed
in the world we live in' (Reinhardt 2004: 31–2 and n. 14, suggesting a possible precedent in Apollonius' *Argonautica,* where the voyage of the heroes

is similarly likened to a katabasis). Such an interpretation postulates expectation on L.'s part of a sophisticated readership, but it would be in keeping with his tactic of turning poetic myth to polemical account, as in his description of the birth of Epicurus (14–15n.).

912–930

There is no occasion to lament the loss of trivial bodily pleasures. L. passes to the superficial complaining of the hedonist, whose philosophy is that expressed by the comic poet Amphis *ap.* Athen. 336c (K–A) 'let us drink and be merry, man is mortal, our time on earth is short', πῖνε, παῖζε· θνητὸς ὁ βίος, ὀλίγος οὑπὶ γῆς χρόνος. On the prevalence of a trivialized Epicureanism in the Roman world see Rostovtzeff 1957: 56 and Pl. vii. L.'s choice of the dinner-table for this shallow moralising is apt, as is shown by the scene in Petronius' *Satyricon* in which Trimalchio displays to his guests a miniature silver skeleton and declaims:

> eheu nos miseros, quam totus homuncio nil est!
> sic erimus cuncti, postquam nos auferet Orcus.
> ergo uiuamus, dum licet esse bene   (34.10)

and by the solicitations of the tavern-keeper in the pseudo-Virgilian *Copa*:

> pone merum et talos; pereat qui crastina curat:
>   Mors aurem uellens 'uiuite' ait, 'uenio'.
>   (37–8)

The '*carpe diem*' motif is typical of sympotic poetry: see N–H 1970: 134–6; Schulz-Vanheyden 1969: 137. L. similarly satirizes the conventional poetic portrayal of love in the great diatribe of Book iv (Kenney 1970b/2007). The situation is piquant: the real Epicurean arraigns the false (Martha 1867: 143–4).

912–15 Hoc…ut dicant 'This is what men do [sc. bewail their lot] when they are at table, wine-cup in hand with garlanded brow, saying in heartfelt tones…': the *ut*-clause is consecutive, explaining their behaviour; it is the setting that inspires these maudlin reflections. The writing is informal but not 'clumsy' (Bailey) or 'gauche' (Ernout–Robin),   **discubuere** 'have taken their places at table' (*OLD discumbo* 2a; cf. *accubo* 1a, *accumbo* 1a). Roman men reclined to dine; women traditionally sat. **ora** 'their heads' (*OLD os* 7 'the face as implying the head').   **coronis:** the garland was indispensable wear for festive occasions.   **ex animo** 'sincerely', from their heart of hearts (OLD *animus* 8b): the wine brings out what is really preying on their minds, *in uino ueritas*; cf. e.g. Hor. *Sat.* 1.4.89 *uerax aperit praecordia Liber*, Otto 1890 s.v. *uinum* 2.   **breuis hic est fructus** 'short is this enjoyment': *hic* is the pronoun, scanned *hicc*

(311–13n. *hic*), not the adverb.   **homullis** 'poor mortals', the word also in Varro's *Menippean Satires* 92, 244 and Cic. *Pis.* 59; cf. Petronius' *homuncio* (912–30n.), Plaut. *Capt.* 51 *homunculi quanti* [of what little worth] *sunt, quom recogito!*   **fuerit** 'will be over and done with', future perfect.

916–18 tamquam … eorum 'as if [*OLD tamquam* 2] when they are dead this were the worst of their troubles', *mali* defining genitive with *hoc* (832–3n. *nil … aegri*).   **miseros** 'poor dears' heavily ironic.   **sitis … arida:** for the distribution of noun and adjective between the two verbs see Housman on Manil. 1.269–70 (but n.b. *Addenda*, withdrawing *DRN* 5.625–6 as not strictly parallel), McKeown on Ov. *Am.* 1.10.19. If this is the single instance in L. and is accounted an anomaly, it is worth noting that the anomaly would be removed by replacing the verb at the end of the line by a noun, as conjectured by Lachmann and Housman.   **torrat:** this reading has solid MS support, and the only objection of substance that can be made against it is that there is no other evidence for a form *torrēre* bearing the same relationship to *torrēre* as e.g. *feruĕre* to *feruēre, tuor* to *tueor*; perhaps not an overwhelmingly strong objection in the case of so innovative and original a writer as L. *tortet* (Romanes 1934: 25; West 1961) is palaeographically easy; at line 661 *tortari* passive = 'writhe', but = 'torture' it is attested in the Republican writer of *palliatae* Pomponius, fr. 40 R³. *et ubi insilui in coculeatum eculeum* [a kind of rack], *ibi tolutim tortor* ('*tortor pro torqueor*', Non. p. 267 L.). Lachmann's *torres* (= *torris*, but the form is attested only in glossaries), literally 'torch', rendered 'drought' by Munro, is perhaps not too daring a metaphor for L., but hardly to be introduced by conjecture. Housman's *aridu' torror* (*CP* 432) imports a word otherwise unattested in Latin writers, apart from Enn. *Ann.* 558 Sk., if Baehrens's 'probable' (Skutsch ad loc.) restoration of *torroribus* for *terroribus* is accepted. See also 898–9n. *sub fin.* on the rarity of this type of suppression of final *-s* by L. The MS testimony is equivocal: in favour of *torrat* rather than *tortet* cf. 5.902 *torrere atque urere.*   **aliae:** genitive singular, the form otherwise reliably attested only at Cic. *De Div.* 2.30.   **cuius** 'any', picking up *tamquam.*   **rei:** scanned as a monosyllable by synizesis (383–7n. *aranei*).

919–30 Even when we are only asleep we do not regret the loss of our daytime pleasures: *a fortiori* we shall not miss them when we are dead. L. recurs to the image of death as sleep to reinforce his point that it is absurd to anticipate a sense of loss that one will not be there to feel. The argument that such behaviour is illogical and inconsistent was not specifically Epicurean but belonged to the commonplaces of the philosophical *consolatio*: Cic. *Tusc.* 1.92 *habes somnum imaginem mortis eamque cotidie induis: et dubitas quin sensus in morte nullus sit, cum in eius simulacro uideas esse nullum sensum?*

The repetition of the keyword *desiderium* (918, 922) shows that these verses belong where the MSS transmit them and do not require to be transposed or bracketed, as has been suggested.

919–22 se uitamque 'his living self', hendiadys, picked up and varied by *desiderium nostri* at 922.   **requirit** 'misses', 'feels regret for' (*OLD* 5).   **sopita** 'at rest', sc. as you yourselves would have it, picked up from their '*sopitus*' at 904, neuter plural following the usual rule.   **nostri** 'our present selves'.

923–5 A brief anticipation of the full account of sleep at 4.907–61; cf. 916–18 *principio somnus fit ubi est distracta per artus | uis animae partimque foras eiecta recessit | et partim contrusa magis concessit in altum.* **haudquaquam ... | longe** 'at no great distance', as shown by the speed with which a man can wake up, graphically pictured in the next verse. In sleep the soul-atoms do not stray very far afield; in death they are dispersed beyond recall.   **cum ... ipse** 'when a man starts up from sleep and gathers himself together' – literally the soul-atoms are physically brought back. The repetition of the prefixes and the enclosing structure convey the rapidity of the process of awakening, *ipse* 'easily' = *sponte*, of his own accord; the 'sleep' of death cannot be shaken off.

926–30 si minus ... uidemus: heavily ironic.   **turba et:** Goebel's simple correction not only produces more straightforward grammar but also more Lucretian writing: commentators can offer no parallel for the combination of the double genitive and the awkward word-order in the transmitted *turbae disiectus materiai* = d. t. m. 'displacement of the disordered atoms'. For *turba* = 'disturbance' of the natural order cf. 2.127–8 *tales turbae motus quoque materiai | significant*; otherwise the word is very sparsely attested in this sense (*OLD* 1c).   **disiectus:** attested only here and probably a Lucretian coinage for the metrically intractable *disiunctio*.   **leto** 'in death'; cf. Virg. *Aen.* 9.433 *uoluitur Euryalus leto*. The easy correction to *letum* (Lindsay 1896: 13) ignores the fact that with the possible exception of 2.958 L. uses *letum* (33x) only of the state of being dead, not of the process of dying.   **exspergitus exstat** ~ 925 *correptus ... colligit.* **est ... secuta** 'has overtaken', picking up *consequitur* and rounding off the paragraph; but 'the stoppage of life' as a pursuer is a curious metaphor.

931–977

Nature herself is now figured as appearing in person to admonish the man who cannot bear the thought of dying. Personification, *prosopopeia*, is a device as old as the art of effective speaking. Aristophanes had dramatized the dispute between the proponents of the old and the new methods of education by bringing on stage the personified Reasons or Arguments (Λόγοι) on each side (cf. 523–5n.); Plato had made the Laws speak in a well-known passage of the *Crito* (50a); and Epicurus had personified Nature even if he did not put words into her mouth (469 Us.). This ploy particularly suited the diatribe-sermon: besides providing dramatic relief it allowed the speaker to upbraid and remonstrate with his audience in terms that might be resented if spoken *in propria persona* – an especially relevant consideration for L. Bion had made Poverty answer his imagined critics in person (Hense 1909: 7–8), and in satire Ennius had portrayed a disputation between Life and Death (Quint. *IO* 9.2.36 = *Sat.* 20 V.²). In L.'s great contemporary M. Terentius Varro we meet such personified abstractions as *Infamia, Veritas* and *Existimatio* (Norden 1966: 81–2). Cicero makes Rome upbraid Catiline and then, even more vehemently, Cicero himself (*Cat.* 1.18, 27–9 and Dyck ad locc.). The hectoring tone and alliterative vehemence of Nature's harangue are characteristic of the diatribe style, but L. has far transcended the diatribe. His Nature is no mere anthropomorphic figment: she exists in her own right as embodying the immutable and inexorable laws of the universe that form the subject of the poem.

'The reverence which other men felt in the presence of religion he feels in the presence of the majesty of Nature' (Sellar 1889: 301). In introducing this stupendous abstraction as interlocutrix in a dialogue with his readers L. has taken a leaf out of Bion's book, but the result eclipses the lowly origin of the device in the history of satire by the grandeur of its implication: it is not the arguments deployed by the poet or even the authority of Epicurus, but the very Sum of Things that stands there to convict the fool of his folly. What Nature is made to *say* does not mirror specific Epicurean doctrine at all closely, but what he wrote to Menoeceus (D.L. 10.125–7) bears a general resemblance.

For a thoughtful analysis of her speech, arguing that what L. is attacking is the irrational fear of imminent death, see Reinhardt 2002 and cf. 912–1075n.

931–2 si uocem... | **mittat:** almost a formula = εἰ φωνὴν λάβοι (Plato, *Prot.* 361a; cf. Hense 1909: 6; Norden 1966: 80–1). **hoc alicui nostrum...increpet** 'level the following reproach at one of us'; the construction of *increpo* with the dative, the usual case with *obicio* or *exprobro*, treating it as an ordinary verb of saying, is seemingly attested only here (*OLD increpo* 4, 6). On the scansion of *hoc* cf. 854–8n. *hoc.* **nostrum:** L. tactfully includes himself among the rebuked; on his evident wish not to give offence to Memmius and other distinguished readers see Smith 1992: 261 n. b ad loc.

933–4 quid tibi tanto operest ... quod ...? 'What is it that troubles you so much that you ...?', 'Why on earth are you so bothered?', an elaborate periphrasis for 'why?'. This type of expression is colloquial (Lindsay 1907: 79–80); cf. e.g. 715 *haud erit ut ... possit*, 1008–9 *hoc ... est ... quod*, Cic. *Verr.* 4.43 *quid erat quod confirmabat?*   **mortalis** 'mortal that you are': the vocative carries a predicative nuance, a reminder to the man of his condition. **nimis** qualifies *indulges* in the next verse.   **aegris | luctibus:** cf. Plaut. *Men.* 626 *quid tibi aegre est?*, *OLD aeger* 3, *aegre* 2, 4.

935–9 The first horn of the dilemma she proceeds to pose: if you have enjoyed life, why can you not leave it without repining? Implicit here and in what follows at 946–9 is the Epicurean tenet that pleasure is finite: 'complete pleasure can be attained in a limited time, and infinite time could not produce greater pleasure' (Bailey 1947: 1149–56, at 1150; see also Rist 1972: 111–13).   **si grata:** Naugerius' correction satisfies the demands of sense and form: *si* is needed to complement *sin* at line 940, and *grata* looks forward to 937 *ingrata*, 942 *ingratum*. The idea that one should be grateful for past pleasures is Epicurean: an old man should be a philosopher so that 'though growing old, he should renew his youth in benefits through thankfulness for the past' (D.L. 10.122); cf. Cic. *Fin.* 1.62 *sic enim ab Epicuro sapiens semper beatus inducitur: finitas habet cupiditates, neglegit mortem, de diis immortalibus sine ullo metu uera sentit, non dubitat si ita melius sit, migrare de uita. his rebus instructus semper est in uoluptate* eqs., Sen. *Ben.* 3.4.1 *assidue queritur* [Epicurus] *quod aduersus praeterita simus ingrati, quod quaecumque percipimus bona non reducamus nec inter uoluptates numeremus, cum certior nulla sit uoluptas quam quae eripi non potest*. So James Mill (father of J. S.) 'used to say that he had never known a happy old man, except those who were able to live again in the pleasures of the young' (Mill 1924: 41).   **pertusum ... in uas:** an adaptation of a traditional philosophical image of the mind as a flawed or tainted pot, developed at 6.17–23 (see Bailey ad loc.), suggested perhaps by the punishment of the Danaids, figured as a type of ingratitude (1008–9 and n.). Cf. 870–5n. *non sincerum sonere.*   **ingrata** 'unthanked', 'unappreciated' (*OLD* 2); cf. Plaut. *Amph.* 184 *bene quae in me fecerunt, ingrata ea habui atque irrita, Asin.* 136–7 *ingrata atque irrita esse omnia intellego | quae dedi et quod bene feci.* Ingratitude connotes insatiability, inability to be satisfied with what one has had: cf. Hor. *Sat.* 1.2.8 *praeclaram ingrata stringat malus ingluuie rem.* **cur non ... recedis?** as recommended by Bion (Hense 1909: 16) and after L. by Horace (*Sat.* 1.1.118–19, *Ep.* 2.2.214). The image of life as a visit or entertainment which a man should enjoy as long as he lives and leave contentedly when satisfied was a commonplace of popular wisdom exploited by the comic poets: cf. Men. fr. 416b Sandbach and Gomme and Sandbach 1973: 709, citing Alexis, fr. 219 K. (= 222 Arnott, q.v. ad loc.). So Cicero,

Fin. 1.49 *si* [*dolores*] *tolerabiles sint, feramus, si minus, animo aequo e uita, cum ea non placeat, tamquam e theatro exeamus.*   **aequo animoque** [= 962]: for the placing of *-que* cf. 662–3 n. *ipsam seque.*   **securam … quietem:** cf. 211 *leti secura quies*, the recurrent image of death as sleep (904, 910).   **stulte:** so St Paul, 1 Cor. 15: 35–6 'But some man will say, How are the dead raised up? and with what body do they come ? Thou fool [ἄφρων], that which thou sowest is not quickened, except it die' (an image with a Lucretian ring). For similarities between the diatribe and Christian homiletic cf. Norden 1958: 556–8. Cf. 1026 *improbe* (n.).

940–9 The second horn of Nature's dilemma: if you have not enjoyed your life, why do you want to prolong it? Better to make an end of it. Nature cannot be forever devising fresh diversions for you. As Seneca was to put it, '*malum est in necessitate uiuere, sed in necessitate uiuere necessitas nulla est'. quidni nulla sit? patent undique ad libertatem uiae multae, breues, faciles* eqs. (*Ep.* 12.10), a thought to which he recurs more than once (Summers 1926: 174 ad loc., 252–3 on *Ep.* 74), ascribing it to Epicurus. Seneca's suicide was in the high Stoic style (Tac. *Ann.* 15.64). Epicurus' actual words are not on record: Cicero appears to attribute to him the application to suicide of the Greek *lex quae in Graecorum conuiuiis obtinetur:* '*aut bibat … aut abeat*' (*Tusc.* 5.118), i.e. ἢ πῖθι ἢ ἄπιθι, pithily summing up the choice offered by Nature at 938–9. The Epicureans did not share the Stoic preoccupation with the ethics of suicide (Rist 1969: 233–55), simply allowing it as a last resort; and Epicurus himself did not take this way out when he was lying on his deathbed in the agonies of strangury and dysentery, describing the last day of his life as 'blissful', μακαρίαν (D.L. 10.22).

940–3 quae fructus cumque es = *quaecumque fructus es* 'whatever you have enjoyed', with the legal nuance of having had the use of, the usufruct (*OLD fructus* 1b; Berger 1953: 75 s.v. *usufructus*). For the tmesis cf. 550, 1075; and for the accusative with *fruor* cf. 4.1078 *nec constat quid primum … fruantur* and 730–4n. *fungitur;* but even in old Latin the usual construction of *fruor* is with the ablative.   **periere profusa** picks up the image of the leaking vessel from 936–7.   **in offensast** 'is hateful'; cf. Cic. *Att.* 9.2a (169 SB).2 *quin magna in offensa sim apud Pompeium.* The fact that *offensa,* noted as 'un-Ciceronian' by Shackleton Bailey ad loc., is nowhere else used by L. is not in itself a cogent argument against this easy correction. Lambinus' *offensust* is palaeographically plausible, but elsewhere in L. *offensus* is always literal = 'clash', 'collision'. The MS reading *offensost* can be defended on the analogy of expressions such as *in dubio esse* (H–S 153), but no parallel for such a usage is to be found in L.   **male** 'uselessly' (*OLD* 7a): *male* often reinforces *perdere* and *perire.*

944–5 Nature ends her tirade on a note of exasperation: 'I give up. There's no pleasing some people.'   **quod placeat** 'to please you', not parallel to the preceding *quod*-clause but dependent on it.   **eadem sunt omnia semper:** that life may in the end become too monotonous to be borne was a commonplace: Sen. *Ep.* 24.26 *quosdam subit eadem faciendi uidendique satietas et uitae non odium sed fastidium, in quod prolabimur ipsa impellente philosophia, dum dicimus quousque eadem?... 'nullius rei finis est, sed in orbem nexa sunt omnia... nihil noui facio, nihil noui uideo: fit aliquando et huius rei nausia'* – sentiments recalling the famous meditations of the Preacher (Ecclesiastes 1). As a consolation for the dying the idea is else-where ascribed by Seneca to a Stoic source (*Ep.* 77.6); but what follows here hints also at the Epicurean doctrine that pleasure does not increase with duration.

946–9 si...si = *etsi...etsi*, as signalled by *tamen.*   **non...iam** 'not yet': cf. e.g. Plaut. *Asin.* 233 *non omnino iam perii,* Cic. *Pro Quinct.* 40 *non adesa iam sed abundanti etiam pecunia, al.* (*OLD iam* 3d; *TLL iam* 93.35–8); more com-monly = 'no longer'.   **marcet** 'is withering away', the literal sense of the word rather than 'becomes enfeebled' (*OLD* 2), reflecting L.'s sharp eye for physical detail.   **omnia...saecla** 'all generations', sc. of living crea-tures, i.e. even the longest-lived; cf. 1090, 1.202 *multaque uiuendo uitalia uincere saecla.* Poets and rhetoricians made play with the thought that some creatures live longer than men. Cf. e.g. 5.1084 *cornicum...saecla uetusta* and Bailey ad loc., Otto 1890 s.v. *cornix* 1, citing also tigers, stags and rooks. **perges** 'though you shall': Lambinus' *pergas,* anticipated by Cipelli, 'nor-malizes' the syntax but weakens the sense of the last of Nature's sarcastic accumulation of absurdities.   **si numquam sis moriturus:** hugely ironi-cal. In Nature's scheme of things nothing is immortal except for the gods, the atoms, the void and the universe itself. Even managing somehow to set at naught my inexorable laws, she implies, would not in the end make you any happier.

950–1 quid respondemus? 'What do we say?' The indicative, answering the potentials *mittat...increpet* (932), though on the face of it dictated by metrical necessity, perhaps carries the implication that there is no answer to her indictment; Heinze compared Cic. *Att.* 16.7(415 SB).4 *nam si a Phaedro nostro esses, expedita excusatio esset; quid respondemus?* However, in colloquial Latin the indicative was commonly used in deliberative ques-tions: H–S 308; Bennett 1910, 1914: I 22–4, noting that the usage was confined to dialogue. For the phrase itself cf. Bion τί ἂν ἔχοις εἰπεῖν (Hense 1909: 8), Hor. *Sat.* 1.2.72 (in a passage of coarsely phrased dialogue) *quid responderet?*   **iustam...litem | ...ueram...causam:** the legal tone of these phrases looks forward to L.'s comments at 963, 971 (nn.), but both

intendere litem and *uera causa* and other such phrases occur in both technical and non-technical contexts, reflecting an important characteristic of
Roman society (Crook 1967: 7–8).

952–62 An old man who complains of having to die is rebuked even more
sharply. The man just addressed is in the prime of life, and one may well
feel that, logically indefensible as his attitude may be from an Epicurean
standpoint, there is some excuse for him. It is old men who cling to life
on whom Nature unleashes the full force of her contempt. The trait that
she attacks was proverbial: cf. e.g. Soph. fr. 66 Radt (63 N.², 66 Pearson)
'No one loves life like a man who is growing old', τοῦ ζῆν γὰρ οὐδεὶς ὡς ὁ
γηράσκων ἐρᾶι, Aristot. *Rhet.* 2.13.8 '[old men] are fond of life, especially
in their last days, because they want what they lack and cannot have'.

952–4 grandior…seniorque 'one getting on in years' (Stallings 2007),
her version implicitly acknowledging, what other translators gloss over by
varying the expression, that there is no real difference of sense.   **hic**
'hereupon', 'now' (*OLD hic²* 6), in this sense not infrequent in dialogue or
narrative.   **lamentetur:** emphasized by its position straddling the main
caesura. To use the word of mourning one's own death perverts its proper
function and evinces gross self-pity: cf. Pacuv. fr. 268 R³. *conqueri fortunam
aduersam, non lamentari decet.* It is for others to decide whether to mourn a
death.

955 abhinc 'hence', 'away' = *hinc*; this local sense is next attested in
Apuleius (*Fl.* 16), but it is clearly what the sense requires and suits the colloquial tone of Nature's harangue: cf. Plaut. *Poen.* 1035 *maledicta hinc aufer.*
baratre: for a judicious survey of the various explanations or corrections
of this word see Smith 2000. Two possible senses seem appropriate to the
context: Nature accuses the old man either of folly or, anticipating the
following image of life as a banquet, reprised from 938–9, of gluttony,
someone who is never satisfied, a bottomless pit: so e.g. Müller 1974: 763
'nimmersatt', comparing Hor. *Ep.* 1.15.31 *tempestas barathrumque macelli.*
However, neither this latter line of interpretation nor that which takes
the word as = 'one deserving to be thrown into a pit' is really convincing (Smith 2000: 35–6). Objections can also be raised against reading
barat(h)ro 'spendthrift', a word attested only by pseudo-Acro on Hor. *Sat.*
1.2.2. Alternatively for the sense 'fool' we have *balatro*, 'buffoon' (Varro,
RR 2.5.1, Hor. loc. cit.) or less aptly *blatero*, 'windbag' (Gell. 1.15.20). Better than either of these is *barde* or *baro*, 'blockhead' (Smith 2000: 38–40),
the metamorphosis of the first to *baratre* being easier to explain. However,
even the best of these suggestions fail to inspire anything like confidence,
and it seems best to retain the transmitted reading as possibly an otherwise unattested colloquial term of abuse, appropriate to the diatribe-style

of Nature's harangue. It is salutary to be reminded occasionally of how much Latin we do not know: a telling instance in the fragments of L.'s contemporary, the mime-writer Laberius, whose ninety-six surviving fragments yield forty-three *hapax legomena* (Panayotakis 2010: 63–4).

956–8 perfunctus 'enjoyed to the full' (179–80n.) For the construction with the accusative cf. 730–4n. *fungitur.*   **aues quod abest, praesentia temnis:** μεμψιμοιρία, discontent with one's lot, was a well-worn topic of popular discourse, familiar as the subject of Horace's first Satire; cf. Phaedr. 1.4, Sen. *Ep.* 74.12; Hense 1909: 38; Norden 1966: 42–3; also Aristot. *Rhet.* 2.13.8, cit. 952–62n. *sub fin.* L.'s expansion of the theme takes a proverbial form going back at least to Hesiod (Otto s.v. *certus* 1), recalling, no doubt with satirical undertones, its occurrence as a stock motif of Hellenistic love-poetry (Callim. *AP* 12.102 (= *HE* 1039–40, *Epigr.* 31.5–6 Pf.), Theoc. 6.17, 11.75). The idea behind the verse, that we should take no thought for the morrow, goes back through Epicurus to Democritus; debased and trivialized, it came to stand for Epicureanism in the eyes of the common man (912–30n.). The commonplace serves to make a point: the old man's behaviour is first described derisively in popular terms, its Epicurean implications then revealed in the next verse. L. returns to the point at the end of the book, echoing the words of line 957 (1076–84, 1082–3nn.).   **aues ... temnis:** on this type of asyndeton in a subordinate clause, in which the two verbs, as here, contrast in sense, see Leo 1912: 272 n. 4.   **imperfecta ... ingrataque:** *imperfecta* because he has never really begun to live: Sen. *Ep.* 23.9 (ascribing the sentiment to Epicurus) *molestum est semper uitam inchoare ... male uiuunt qui semper uiuere incipiunt*; *ingrata* because he has neglected or misused his opportunities. The thought behind the argument is that hinted at in lines 944–5 (n.), that true pleasure, defined as the absence of pain, must have a limit (5.1412–35). It is because the old man has failed to grasp this truth that he yearns for unattainable pleasures and so has missed the real pleasure that he might have enjoyed.   **elapsast:** positioned so as to blur the caesura (174n.), thus accelerating the verse and subtly assisting the sense: life has slipped by him all unawares.

959–60 The imagery is artfully ambiguous. The words *satur ac plenus* at line 960 look back to *imperfecta* at 958, but also to the idea of life as a banquet (938). The *lectus* on which the old man reclines is both dining-couch and bier, and the first has become the second before he is aware of what is happening to him.   **nec opinanti** 'unexpectedly': the old sense of *nec* = *non* (*OLD neque* 1) survives in this set phrase (H–S 448–9).   **caput:** he reclines in readiness, though he does not know it, for being laid out as a corpse.   **adstitit** 'has taken his stand'. Death comes for the old man suddenly and unawares, but he is always in the offing; see Hom. *Il.* 16.852–3

[= 24.131-2] (the dying Patroclus to Hector) 'you yourself have not long to live, but already Death stands by you', οὔ θην οὐδ᾽ αὐτὸς δηρὸν βέῃ, ἀλλά τοι ἤδη | ἄγχι παρέστηκεν θάνατος καὶ μοῖρα κραταιή; and see the many examples from Greek poets collected by Headlam and Knox on Herodas 1.16. **rerum:** the (good) things of life.

961-2 aliena tua ... aetate 'unbefitting your age'; on *alienus* + ablative see 821-3n. *aliena salutis.*   **annis agedum concede:** Romanes's neglected conjecture (Romanes 1935: 36) neatly restores pointed sense. The obvious objection that no plausible explanation of the postulated corruption of *annis* to the transmitted *magnis* suggests itself applies with equal force to all the solutions involving the necessary elimination of *magnis* – from which, *pace* Garton (1993), no satisfactory sense can be elicited. What Nature is saying to the old man is 'Be your age'; the alternative line of interpretation, that he is adjured to give way to the next generation (see Bailey ad loc., citing *inter al.* Epictetus 4.1.106 'give place to others', δὸς ἄλλοις τόπον), gives less pointed sense. It is the man's perverse failure to face his own situation squarely that earns Nature's scorn. The many solutions that have been proposed of this celebrated crux have been collected by Papanghelis (1979); the flow continues.   **agedum** 'come on now' (*OLD age* 24a) is found only here in L. (*nunc age* 15x), but the corruption is easily explained and the word suits Nature's impatient tone.

963 iure ... agat 'she would have a strong case' (950-1, 970-1nn.). **inciletque** 'and would reproach', reinforcing *increpet* and adding weight to Nature's rebuke by the retarding effect of the fifth-foot spondee (190-1n.). The word, of unknown etymology, is archaic, otherwise attested only in Lucilius and Republican drama.

964-77 Death is necessary so that life may go on. The physical doctrines on which the argument of this section is based have been touched on at 1.263-4, 2.71-9; cf. also 5.828-33. In incorporating this idea into his *consolatio* L. may have been breaking new ground; he was followed by Seneca (*Ep.* 36.11) and Plutarch (*Cons. ad Apoll.* 10.106c). To the man who can take a truly philosophical view of things this fundamental principle ought no doubt to be consoling, but it does little to reconcile the ordinary mortal to the prospect of his own extinction. See the two epigraphs to this edition.

964-9 rerum nouitate ... uetustas: abstractly phrased = *nouis rebus ... res uetustae.*   **extrusa** 'thrust out', a hint of the underlying cause of physical change, the ceaseless battering of the atoms against each other.   **ex aliis aliud** 'a new entity from other entities'.   **reparare necessest** 'it is necessary to renew'; the unexpressed agent and subject of the infinitive is Nature.   **nec quisquam ... deditur:** popular notions of death and the fate of the dead fly in the face of the fundamental laws of Nature.

The atoms that make up a human being do not run to waste into a
mythical abyss: they are needed for the birth of generations to come.
barathrum ... Tartara ... atra 'the black pit of Tartarus', hendiadys. For the
'terrible sound' of the verse Friedländer (1941: 26/1969: 345) compares
Enn. *Ann.* 451 Sk. *at tuba terribili sonitu taratantara dixit.*   **materies opus
est** 'matter is a need', 'there is a need'; for this construction with *opus*
(*OLD opus*[1] 13c) cf. 1.1051 *infinita opus est uis undique materiai*, 4.1268 *nec
molles opu' sit motus*, Plaut. *Capt.* 164 *maritumi omnes milites opu' sunt tibi*
and Lindsay ad loc. This is the usual construction with neuter pronouns
or adjectives, as at 2.20–1 *ergo corpoream ad naturam pauca uidemus | esse
opus*, but with substantives the construction with ablative is generally preferred in classical Latin (K–S I 388; H–S 123–4); and in the lines from
the *Captiui* preceding that quoted above that construction is repeated six
times (159–64).   **nec minus ... cadentque:** two ideas appear to be con-
flated: (i) *nec minus quam tu* (*cades*) *cecidere priora saecla*; (ii) *ergo omnia saecla cecidere cadentque*, rounding off the argument. The awkwardness of the
expression is compounded by the ambiguity of the transmitted *ante haec*: is
ante a preposition or an adverb? That difficulty at least is obviated by reading *antehac* with Cipelli (117–20n. *sentire*), independently conjectured by
Heinze. Cf. 2.299, where *post haec*, cited by Bailey in support of *ante haec*
here, was corrected to *posthac* by an early emendator (cf. Flores ad loc.).

970–1 alid = *aliud*, an archaic form used 6x by L. in this phrase. Catullus
uses *alid* (29.15), if Statius' correction of MS *alit* is accepted, and *alis* =
alius (66.28), otherwise these forms make no certain appearance in literary texts (N–W II 531–2).   **uitaque ... usu:** a commonplace sentiment,
expressed in a metaphor of the same type as that at 774 (n.). Bion had
said (Stob. *Flor.* 4.41.56) that the rich enjoy their possessions as a loan,
not a gift, from Fortune; and variations on the idea are cited by commentators both from philosophical and literary sources and also from grave-
stones. Lucilius had imparted a legal flavour to the idea, *cum sciam nihil
esse in uita proprium mortali datum* (fr. 701 M., *ROL* III 280, fr. 777); for
proprius connoting permanent legal possession cf. *OLD* 2a; Berger 1953:
s.v. L. uses specifically Roman terminology: *mancipium* and *usus* were both
terms of art (Berger 1953: s.vv.), and *mancipium* is a word that does not
belong in the poetic vocabulary, Ovid providing an isolated exception
(*Ex P.* 4.5.40; cf. Kenney 1969). Roman poets made more use than their
Greek predecessors of legal imagery and metaphor, particularly in love
poetry (Kenney 1969). L.'s message is designed to impress his readers the
more forcibly by being expressed in contemporary juridical terms (Sykes
Davies 1931–2: 53). Cf. further 950–1, 963 (nn.); Cic. *Tusc.* (*Natura*) *dedit
usuram uitae tamquam pecuniae nulla praestituta die*, *CLE* 183 *usuram uitae
sortem morti reddidit* (the syntax is opaque, but the image is clear); 1070–5n.

ambigitur status. Nature is speaking 'not as judge in a criminal court but
as one of the quarrelling parties to a trial' (Reinhardt 2004: 30, citing
Sen. *Cons. ad Polyb.* 10.4–5); the respondent is arraigned as a defaulting
debtor.   **mancipio...usu:** predicative datives. Some interpreters take
them as ablatives, but though *mancipio* = 'by *mancipium*' can be defended,
usu must mean 'for use'; cf. the analogy of *dono dare* (H–S 99). For *usu*
dative cf. 5.101 *oculorum subdere uisu*; naturally the form recommended
itself to poets for metrical reasons (N–W I 542; but their list is far from
complete).

972–3 respice does multiple duty = 'consider' (*OLD* 7) and 'look back',
both over past time and to the argument of 830–42, so signalling the
end of this section and preparing for a fresh topic. The rhetorical questions at 976–7 mark a climax and pause before the powerful denunciation of superstitious delusion that follows.   **quam nil ad nos...fuerit**
'how little the whole expanse of past time matters to us' ~ 830 *nil...est ad
nos*, underlining a fundamental point.   **anteacta...aeterni:** the adjectives are interchangeable (double enallage); cf. 1.558 *infinita aetas anteacti
temporis omnis.*   **quam nascimur ante** = *antequam nascimur.* The present
tense indicates that *nascimur* refers to all the successive generations of men,
not only this one.

974–8 hoc...nostram 'This then is the image that Nature shows us of
time to come after we finally die': *speculum* is 'reflection', not as translators
(Brown an exception) render it 'mirror', for which *exponere* 'display' (*OLD*
4a) is not the appropriate word. For this sense of *speculum* (*OLD* inade-
quate) cf. Plaut. *Men.* 1062–3 *quid uides? – speculum tuom. | quid negoti est?
tuast imago,* Cic. *Fin.* 2.32 *a paruis... aut etiam a bestiis, quae putat* [Epicurus]
esse specula naturae, Macrob. *Sat.* 5.2.13 *quid quod et omne opus Vergilianum
uelut de quodam Homerici operis speculo formatum est?* This reading allows *hoc,*
attracted as often into the number and gender of its noun (K–S I 334–5),
a clear reference = *anteacta uetustas temporis aeterni*: that is what Nature
shows us as the mirror-image of future time, and it is of course – a blank,
a reflection of, as far as we are concerned, nothing. 'The cradle rocks
above an abyss, and common sense tells us that our existence is but a
brief crack of light between two eternities of darkness...Nature expects
a full-grown man to accept the two black voids, fore and aft, as stolidly
as he accepts the extraordinary visions in between' (Nabokov 1967: 1–2).
numquid...quicquam...? naturally not, because there is nothing at all
there. Line 976 has two concealed caesuras by the elision of *ibi* and *horribile* (83–4n. *hunc...amicitiai*).   **omni somno securius** 'more carefree
than any sleep'; Latin can say either *omni securius* or *securius quam ullum,* but

the two constructions are not mixed.   **securius:** sc. what you see, which
is, paradoxically, nothing. Sleep produces dreams, which may be disturbing. There is a slight anacoluthon: *securius* must be referred to *speculum* or
futurum tempus, not to *numquid* or *quicquam*.

978–1023

Hell and its fabled punishments do not exist, except in men's deluded
imagination. This theme had already figured prominently in the Proem
(31–93); L. now returns to it to demonstrate that it is the sufferings of our
life on earth that are allegorized in these stories. The message is summed
up in the opening and closing lines of the section (978–9, 1018–23):
all this is to the address of the *stulti* (1023), who should welcome death
as a merciful release from their troubles rather than dread it. Denial of
the existence of Hell is appropriate to a *consolatio*, and we find Seneca
employing it in his *Consolatio ad Marciam*: *cogita . . . illa quae nobis inferos faciunt terribiles fabulas esse* eqs. (19.4), though elsewhere he dismisses it contemptuously as an Epicurean commonplace, 'that old Epicurean tune',
Epicuream cantilenam (*Ep.* 24.18). What notions of the afterlife may have
been entertained by the Roman man in the street is not really in point
here: the mythical underworld depicted by L. is that of Greek poets and
mythographers, familiar to a cultivated readership (Gale 1994: 88–90).
Memmius and his peers cannot have taken these legends seriously, and L.
is not primarily concerned to refute them, but to interpret them (Introd.
4–5; Gale 1994: 93–4). He had inherited a tradition of allegorical exegesis which originated with the Presocratics (Gale 1994: 21–6); for the
idea behind the present passage cf. Philo, *De Congr. Erud. Gr.* 57 (cit.
Boyancé 1963: 180 n. 4). The elaborate allegorical explanation of the
myths that follows, appropriate in the context of a *consolatio*, is perhaps
therefore unexpected, notwithstanding what is noted above, but the passage certainly belongs here: lines 976–7 and the words *horribile* and *triste*
there both round off their own section and assist with the transition to the
topic of Hades. No comparable transition, however, is provided at the end
of the section at line 1023. The subject of Hell also offers, as might be
expected, much opportunity for the display of sarcastic wit (985, 987–9,
989–91 (nn.)).

980–3 (1) *Tantalus*. L. refers to a form of the legend in which he was
punished for stealing the nectar and ambrosia of the gods by having a
large stone suspended over him, for fear of which he dared not eat or
drink (Pind. *Ol.* 1.55–64; cf. Virg. *Aen.* 6.602–3). Cicero explains the
story as symbolizing irrational fears in general: *omnibus enim quorum mens
abhorret a ratione semper aliqui talis terror impendet* (*Tusc.* 4.35; cf. *Fin.* 1.60).

cassa . . . inanis: Tantalus' fear of the stone is 'empty', baseless, because he does not exist; so is men's fear of the gods, who do not punish wrongdoing, but it is real enough, since it and they exist 'in life'. The image of the overhanging rock recalls that of *religio* at the beginning of Book 1 as a monster standing over (*super instans* ~ *superstitio*) grovelling mankind, *horribili super aspectu mortalibus instans* (1.65), and that is the point here too: *religio = superstitio = diuom metus* (West 1969/1994: 98). The better-known version of the legend found in the *Odyssey* (11.562–92) and frequently alluded to in later poetry has Tantalus standing in a pool of water which sank when he tried to drink from it and overhung by fruit-trees which withdrew their branches when he tried to eat (hence Eng. 'tantalize'). That version was allegorized by Teles (Hense 1909: 34–5) as figuring the avarice which cannot profit from its possessions; cf. Oltramare 1926: 54 n. 3; Hor. *Sat.* 1.1.68–9 *Tantalus a labris sitiens fugientia captat | flumina,* eqs.   **casumque** = both '(mis)chance', 'peril' (*OLD* 5, 8) and literally 'fall', alluding to the stone.   **ferat fors:** playing on the etymological connexion, real or fancied, between the two words; cf. 41–5n. *si fert ita forte uoluntas,* Enn. *Ann.* 185 Sk. *quidue ferat fors.*

984–94 (2) *Tityos.* He was a Giant, son of Earth, who for the attempted rape of Leto was condemned to have his liver perpetually devoured by vultures as he lay stretched out on the ground (Hom. *Od.* 11.576–81). To L. love, 'empty desire', κενὴ ἐπιθυμία, was the irrational desire *par excellence,* to be reserved for extended treatment later in the poem (4.1058–1191); cf. Hor. *C.* 3.4.77–8 *incontinentis nec Tityi iecur | reliquit ales* and N–R ad loc. He and Tantalus were held up to scorn as typical bugbears by Diogenes of Oenoanda, 'those Tityoses and Tantaluses', τοὺς Τιτύους καὶ τοὺς Ταντάλους (fr. 14.3.8 Chilton).

984–6 Tityon: classical Latin poets generally preferred the original spellings of Greek proper names rather than their Latinized forms: so 992 *Tityos.*   **uolucres:** traditionally vultures, but L.'s non-specific 'winged creatures' paves the way for his allegorical explanation (992–4n.). **nec quod . . . profecto** = *nec profecto quicquam sub magno pectore reperire possunt quod perpetuam aetatem scrutentur,* 'and they obviously cannot throughout all eternity be finding something to dig for in his vast breast': *quicquam* is antecedent of the *quod*-clause. The ironical implication of *magno,* 'great as it is', is explicitly developed in what follows.

987–9 quamlibet immani proiectu corporis exstet 'let his body as it lies outstretched be as huge as you like': for *proiectu* cf. 882 *proiecto corpore. quamlibet* qualifies *immani*; its normal use in classical Latin is as an adverb imparting concessive force to an adjective or participle, as here and at 5.1116 *quamlibet et fortes et pulchro corpore creti* (H–S 604); whereas *quamuis*, also originally an adverb, was freely used as a conjunction with the subjunctive on the analogy of *quamquam* (H–S 603–4). *quamlibet* therefore cannot be properly be said to 'take' the subjunctive (as it is construed here by Bailey); the concessive force of the clause resides in the jussive sense of *exstet*, 'let him be', as at 2.541–2 *quamlibet esto | unica res = esto res quamlibet unica*. Certain cases of *quamlibet* as a conjunction are late and rare: Quint. *IO* 1.1.18, cited by commentators, is not a true case in point; better examples at ibid. 12.1.24, Fronto, *Ep. ad M. Caesarem* 5.24, p. 73.7–8 van den Hout (Müller 1974: 763).   **qui...** | **obtineat** 'though he be such as to cover', *qui* generalizing (*OLD quis²* 3).   **nouem...iugera:** in Homer ἐννέα...πέλαθρα (*Od.* 11.577), but a *iugerum* is not strictly speaking a πέλαθρον, nor, as generally rendered, an acre. The point is the rhetorical exaggeration.   **dispessis** 'spread over', Turnebus' necessary correction of MS *dispersis* 'scattered', not the appropriate sense. Cf. the similar restoration of *dispessa* for *dispersa* by Munro at 2.1126; *sparsus* and *passus* and their compounds are commonly confused in MSS.

990–1 In conclusion the scientist takes over from the satirist: the story simply violates the laws of nature. Nothing is eternal but the atoms, the void, and the universe (and, by special dispensation, the gods).

992–4 The real meaning of the story is revealed. The real Tityos is the man torn by love and other irrational desires.   **hic:** probably the pronoun (scanned *hicc*: 311–13n.), 'Our Tityos is this man here, whom...'; cf. 4.1058 *haec Venus est nobis*; but the adverb *hic = in uita* (995) would be almost equally pointed. Cf. 1023 *hic* 'here on earth'. L. packs a great deal into these three verses, which are heavy with allusion.   **in amore iacentem** implies helplessness, the lover ensnared by his passion, the image elaborately developed in the great diatribe of Book IV (4.1146–8: Kenney 1970b: 385–8/2007: 321–4); it also suggests images of the lover as inactive (*Il. Lat.* 265 *dum iaceas in amore tuo, nos bella geremus, al.*: Fletcher 1968: 887), and tossing and turning on his lonely bed bemoaning the absence of the beloved or the hopelessness of his passion (Theoc. 2.6; Meleager, *AP* 5.166 (*HE* 4260–7), 215 (*HE* 4272–7); Ov. *Am.* 1.2, *al.*), or encamped on the beloved's doorstep (Meleager, *AP* 12.72 (*HE* 4990–5), Asclepiades, *AP* 5.189 (*HE* 1006–9)) – and most notably L. himself (4.1177–9) (Copley 1956: *passim*).   **uolucres** 'winged things', referring to the Erotes, Latin *Cupidines* 'loves', exploiting the ambiguity of the word for the allegory. Pius' comment 'curae et alati cupidines' shows that he had taken the point. 'The plurality of the Cupids is abundantly attested' (Pease on Cic. *ND* 3.60, citing many examples from Aeschylus onwards). In their prettified Hellenistic guise, equipped with all their conventional attributes

(Webster 1964: *passim*), they flit in and out of the love-epigrams of Meleager's *Garland*, where their function is that of tormenting the lover in various ways: Meleager, *AP* 5.262 (*HE* 4050–5), 139 (*HE* 4146–51), 12.126
(*HE* 4464–9), Asclepiades, *AP* 12.46 (*HE* 876–9), 166 (*HE* 888–93),
Posidippus, *AP* 12.45 (*HE* 3070–3), *al.* For close parallels with L.'s image
cf. Theoc. 13.71 'a cruel god was rending his heart [literally 'liver'] within
him', χαλεπὸς γὰρ ἔσω θεὸς ἧπαρ ἄμυσσεν; Moschus 1.16–17 'and Love like
a winged bird flies from one to another, man and woman, and perches on
their vitals', (Ἔρως) πτερόεις ὡς ὄρνις ἐφίπταται ἄλλον ἐπ' ἄλλωι, | ἀνέρας ἠδὲ
γυναῖκας, ἐπὶ σπλάγχνοις δὲ κάθηται; Phanocles, fr. 1.4–6 Powell 'his mind
was not at rest, but always unsleeping cares wore away his spirit', οὐδ' ἦν
οἱ θυμὸς ἐν ἡσυχίηι, | ἀλλ' αἰεί μιν ἄγρυπνοι ὑπὸ ψυχῆι μελεδῶναι | ἔτρυχον.
An anonymous epigram attributed to the Garland of Meleager by Gow
and Page suggests that an earlier poet might have had Tityos in mind in
describing the sufferings of the lover: *AP* 12.160.1–2 (*HE* 3776–7) 'Stoutly
shall I bear the harsh pain in my vitals and the bond of the cruel fetter',
θαρσαλέως τρηχεῖαν ὑπὸ σπλάγχνοισιν ἀνίην | οἴσω καὶ χαλεπῆς δεσμὸν ἀλυκ-
τοπέδης. L.'s lines must be read with an ironical inflexion imparted by mental quotation marks: 'The real Tityos is the man who "lies" (as the poets
tell us) lovelorn and tormented by those "winged creatures" (of poetic
fancy).' (For a full discussion see Kenney 1970a.)   **anxius angor | aut
alia quauis ... cuppedine curae** 'distressful anguish or cares through some
other desire'. L. proceeds to generalize the allegory, figuring Tityos' 'vultures' as typical of those cares which distract men from achieving *ataraxia*,
true Epicurean tranquillity of mind: cf. 5.43–6 *at nisi purgatumst pectus,
quae proelia nobis | atque pericula tunc ingratis insinuandum! | quantae tum
scindunt hominem cuppedinis acres | sollicitum curae quantique perinde timores!*
eqs. Petronius similarly allegorizes Prometheus' vultures as *liuor atque luxus*
(fr. 25 Ernout). Cf. also Cic. *Tusc.* 3.27 *aegritudo* [anxiety: *OLD* 2] ... *lacerat
exest animum planeque conficit*. As a metrically convenient variant form of
cupido = 'desire', *cuppedo* is attested only in the *DRN* (5x); elsewhere of a
market for delicacies, *forum cuppedinis* (*OLD* 1). Critics who are uneasy with
the foregoing interpretation find themselves hard put to it to suggest an
acceptable substitute for *uolucres*. *aerumnae* (Watt 1990: 122), as its author
allows, introduces an elision not otherwise attested in L.; and it is not easy
to explain how *uolucres* could have supplanted it. (It is easier to imagine
a reversed process by which *aerumnae*, originating as a gloss, might have
supplanted *uolucres*.) The weightiest objection to any such attempts is that
they feebly neutralize L.'s vivid and witty imagery.

995–1002 (3) *Sisyphus.* He was condemned to roll a huge stone up a hill
but never to reach the top (Hom. *Od.* 11.593–600). It is the nature of his
punishment rather than his crime (about which the ancient authorities

disagree) which led L. to include him, presenting him as a special type of *auaritia*, political ambition (cf. 59–64 (nn.)). Avoidance of politics and public life was an Epicurean tenet, dealt with by L. at 5.1120–35 and previously touched on in the Proem to Book II, where the Sisyphus allegory is foreshadowed by an image of struggle and ascent: 2.12–13 *noctes atque dies niti praestante labore* | *ad summas emergere opes rerumque potiri*. On the contemporary resonance of the passage see Fowler 1989: 139–41/2007: 419–21. L.'s treatment of the legend does not seem to be previously exemplified; cf. in later writers Phaedrus, *App.* 5.3–6; Macrob. *Comm.* 1.10.15.

995–7 in uita [= 979] ... **nobis ante oculos:** this is the most compelling of all L.'s interpretations: his poem is addressed to men such as Memmius, who knew all about what getting oneself elected to political office might involve.   **petere ...** | **imbibit** 'deeply thirsts to seek' (*OLD imbibo* 2b). *peto* and *recedo* are both technical terms of political language (West 1969/1994: 100–2). Cf. 1000–2n. *plani ... petit aequora campi*.   **saeuasque:** to be read ἀπὸ κοινοῦ, qualifying both nouns; a stock epithet but also reflecting historical fact: on the 'legal murders' of the proscriptions see Syme 1956: 197–201.

998–9 imperium quod inanest nec datur umquam: power over the *metus ... curaeque sequaces* (2.48) that bedevil mankind is conferred by reason alone: *quid dubitas quin omni' sit haec rationi' potestas?* (2.53).   **in eo** 'in doing so', sc. *in petendo*.   **durum sufferre laborem** [= 5.1272, 1359]: cf. Enn. *Ann.* 401 Sk. *post aetate pigret sufferre laborem*.

1000–2 Highly pictorial writing: the heavy spondees in line 1000 for his slow and toilsome ascent; the enjambed first-foot spondee in 1001 for the momentary pause at the top; and the predominantly dactylic 1001–2 for the headlong descent of the stone. Comparison with the famous Homeric prototype shows L. on the one hand treating the whole episode descriptively, whereas Homer makes no attempt to figure Sisyphus' laborious upward progress in the movement of the verse; and on the other hand exercising more restraint than Homer in describing the downward descent of the stone. Homer's line has the maximum number of dactyls and three weak or 'feminine' caesuras to give the headlong effect and imputes to the stone a malevolent enjoyment of the process: 'Once more down to the flat trundled the stone in its shamelessness', αὖτις ἔπειτα πέδονδε κυλίνδετο λᾶας ἀναιδής.   **aduerso ... monte** 'up the hill'.   **nixantem** 'with great effort'. This emphatic frequentative form of *nitor* is attested only in L. (also 4.506, 6.836) and was no doubt coined by him.   **plani ... petit aequora campi:** word-play spells out the point: 'in electoral terms the candidate goes down to the Campus Martius to stand for election again, *descendat in Campum petitor* [Hor. *C.* 3.1.11]' (West 1969/1994: 102).

1003–10 (4) *The Danaids.* For the murder of their husbands they were for ever condemned to draw water in leaking vessels or sieves. They do not figure in Homer's Underworld, but the story was famous: cf. e.g. Hor. *C.* 3.11.21–32, citing them along with Ixion and Tityos; Ov. *Her.* 14. In using them as a type of ingratitude L. harks back to Nature's reproach to the old man at 955–62; he also gives a twist to the argument. His first three examples argue that these legendary punishments are in reality no more than metaphors for the suffering that men inflict on themselves in this life: *diuum metus* (982), *curae* (994), *durus labor* (999). Inability to be satisfied, ἀπληστία, is a different matter, and the Danaids represent a type of behaviour rather than suffering. It is suggested by Heinze that this is why L. does not name them, but it is a curious fact that Plato does not name them in the *Gorgias*, where the allegory of the leaky jar first occurs (493d5–494a5). This metaphor is found nowhere else in Epicurean texts (cf. Reinhardt 2004: 38–46), suggesting that the whole concluding section of Book III can be read as 'a commentary on (certain aspects) of the *Gorgias*' (39). On the various versions and interpretations of the myth see N–R 149.

1003–7 animi ingratam naturam = *ingratum animum.* **explere...satiareque:** the words are synonymous and are both qualified by *numquam*, placed at the end of its verse to correspond with *semper* in the same position in line 1003. On *-que* appended to short *-e* see 161–7n. *mutareque.* **quod faciunt nobis annorum tempora circum | cum redeunt** 'as the seasons do for us [sc. *pascunt, explent, satiant*] when they come round...'. Much critical ink has been spilt on this passage, but it presents no special difficulty if read as an ancient reader unfettered by modern conventions of syntactical punctuation would have read it, with *annorum tempora* understood as subject of both the *quod-* and the *cum-*clauses. Lachmann was puzzled by *circum redeunt* – 'quid sit non intellego' – but return in this context implies cyclical motion. As Heinze remarked, the expression is bold, but can hardly be misunderstood. **ferunt** following *redeunt* = *referunt.* **umquam:** placed like *numquam* and *semper* preceding to emphasize the point of the obstinate ingratitude of such men.

1008–10 hoc, ut opinor, id est...| quod memorant 'this, I take it, is what is (really) meant by the story...' For the expression cf. 754, 933 (nn.), but this is rather more informal writing. **aeuo florente puellas:** the Seasons, Ὧραι, were represented as beautiful young women, here figured allegorically as discharging their bounty into the leaky vessels that are ungrateful men. The real Danaids, that is to say, ply their unrewarding task here on earth. **pertusum...in uas** [= 936]: L. seems to have in mind the passage in the *Gorgias* (493b) in which the part of the soul where the desires

are is compared to a jar with a hole in it, τετρημένος πίθος, figuring insatiabil-
ity, ἀπληστία, rather than wasted labour.   **potestur:** passive with *expleri*;
cf. 1.1045 *suppleri...queatur*; in classical Latin the construction is normal
with e.g. *coepi* (H–S 288). On the passive forms of *possum, queo* and *nequeo*
see N–W III 614, 626–7.

Servius' note on Virg. *Aen.* 6.596 refers to L.'s allegorical interpretations of Tityos, Tantalus and Sisyphus (in that order); he then adds *per
rotam autem ostendit negotiatores, qui semper tempestatibus turbinibusque uoluun-
tur.* From this it has been inferred that in the copy of L. used by Servius
or his source Ixion also figured and that there is a lacuna in our existing
text after line 1010 (so Munro): see Jocelyn 1986. Ixion naturally figured
in the standard list of notable sinners undergoing picturesque fates in the
Underworld; he is in Virgil's Hell (*Aen.* 6.601), and is listed by Seneca
along with Sisyphus and Tityos, though not Tantalus (*Ep.* 24.18). However, if L. had included Ixion, he is unlikely to have interpreted him as the
type of the *negotiator*, who would merely represent a particular case of the
curae personified in Tityos. As a type of ambition (Dio Chryst. 4.123) Ixion,
whose crime was the attempted rape of Hera, would duplicate Sisyphus; as
a type of those who act without *consilium, ratio* or *uirtus* (Macrob. *Comm.*
1.10.14), he lacks definition. Moreover, he does not figure in the *Odyssey*,
as L.'s three male sinners (though not the Danaids) do. The fact that Ixion
comes last, and is not actually named, in Servius' list, suggests that he has
strayed in from a note on *Aen.* 6.601 (itself difficult to interpret) and has
been tacked on to the Lucretian list by Servius or his source. In any case,
no hypothesis of a lacuna containing Ixion helps with the problem posed
by 1011–13 (n.). If L. had originally included him, his proper place would
have been after line 1002, before the Danaids.

1011–23 The terrors of Hell are really the pangs of conscience. This is a
general application of the principle enunciated at 978–9, to which we are
brought back, by the standard device of ring-composition with the words
Acherusia...uita at line 1023. The idea goes back at least to Democritus
(69 B 297 D–K).

1011–13 'As for Cerberus and the Furies and lightlessness, Tartarus belching horrific fumes from his throat – which do not and cannot exist anywhere...!' The apparently anacoluthic structure of the sentence, with a
relative clause following a nominal phrase without a verb, can be paralleled at 2.342–8, 4.123–6; here, as first suggested by Heinze (cf. Korenjak 2008), *iam uero* has exclamatory force, 'now, as for...!' (*OLD iam* 8a).
However, there are other anomalies: (i) the asyndeton between 1011 and
1012, surprising in such a short list; (ii) Lucretian usage requires *quae*
'things which' rather than *qui* in line 1013. (i) is neatly solved by the

early correction of *egestas* to *egenus*, but whereas other examples of asyndeton, albeit not in so short a list, are to be found elsewhere in L.,
the word *egenus* is not. (ii) can be met by postulating a lacuna after
1011 with Munro and allowing *qui* to refer specifically to *aestus*, but his
suggestion that it contained, *inter alia*, Ixion is improbable (1008–10n.).
That knot can be cut by reading *quae* or *haec* (Marullus); but in the
prevailing uncertainty it seems prudent, having registered misgivings, to
allow the lines to stand as transmitted. See further Jocelyn 1986.   **Tartarus…aestus:** the description would suit a volcano belching fire or a
cave exhaling noxious vapours; the ambiguity and the inflated epicizing
vocabulary (see below) may be designed to suggest the vagueness and con-
fusion of the Underworld topography and superstitious beliefs in general. Tartarus appears to be figured here as a monster, like Enceladus
buried under Aetna (Virg. *Aen.* 3.578–62).   **horriferos** 'awe-inspiring'
(28–30n. *diuina uoluptas…atque horror*); cf. Pacuv. fr. 82 R.³ (*ROL* ii 571)
horrifer | *Aquiloni' stridor.*   **neque súnt…nec póssunt esse profecto** 'obvi-
ously *do not* and *cannot* exist'.

1014–17 The guilty mind creates for itself images of punishments after
death like those seen and experienced in life. The word-order is contrived
to position *est* emphatically and to juxtapose *insignibus insignis*, with diaeresis after the second foot (186n.): 'But there does exist here on earth a fear
of punishment proportioned to a man's misdeeds, and there does exist
expiation of crime, in the shape of prisons' eqs. The gruesome inventory
of Roman inhumanity to man that follows also has its point: it is the fright-
ful particularity of what he witnesses that makes the guilty man imagine
corresponding torments in the hereafter, even though here and now he
may escape the consequences of his wrongdoing.   **poenarum** picking
up *Furiae* from 1011 and like the Ποιναῖ in Greek, personified in Latin
(*OLD poena* 1d); cf. Cic. *Pis.* 91 *o Poena et Furia sociorum*, and figuring them
as agents of Hell, *Clu.* 171 *a liberum Poenis actum…praecipitem in scelera-
torum sedem atque regionem.* These identifications make the point that the
mythical Poenae are all too real as they take physical shape here on earth
in the imagination of the guilty man.   **luella** 'expiation', hence 'punishment'; the word is attested only here. The spelling *luela* of the MSS was
corrected by Lachmann, but cf. *OLD* s.vv. *-ela, luela.*   **carcer:** perhaps
to be written *Carcer* as referring to the Tullianum, the condemned cell in
the State prison near the Forum; the list is specifically Roman.   **horribilis…iactu' deorsum** 'the dreadful hurling down'; Lambinus' conjecture is further from the transmitted reading than Cipelli's and Heinsius'
iactu' reorum, but gives a much more vivid sense. Mention of 'criminals'
is not wanted in connexion with any one punishment, and the word *reus*

occurs nowhere else in L. (*deorsum* 8x).   **saxo:** the Tarpeian Rock on the Capitol, from which criminals were thrown.   **robur:** probably 'cross', 'gibbet', though this sense is not otherwise attested before Silius Italicus; it would be odd if a list of Roman punishments omitted the most gruesomely conspicuous of all. 'Prison' (*OLD* 2c) would merely duplicate *carcer.* **pix lammina taedae:** pitch, metal plates, torches, indicating various forms of torture by fire.

1018–21 mens sibi conscia facti: echoed by Ovid, *Met.* 8.531–2 *mens sibi conscia facti | exegit poenas*; by Lucan 7.783–4 *hunc [Caesarem] infera monstra flagellant. | et quantum poenae misero mens conscia donat…!*; and most memorably by Juvenal 13.192–5 *cur tamen hos tu | euasisse putes, quos diri conscia facti | mens habet attonitos et surdo uerbere caedit | occultum quatiente animo tortore flagellum?*, where see Courtney ad loc., citing also Sen. *Ep.* 97.14–15, [Quint.] *Decl.* 314.17; and cf. further Cic. *Pro Rosc. Am.* 67, Hor. *Ep.* 1.1.60–1, Sen. *Ep.* 105.7–8. *facti* is certainly what L. wrote: the standard construction of *sibi conscius* is with the genitive, and modern editors who retain *factis* are unable to offer any parallel. The error was due to *factis* at 1014 by 'perseveration'.   **adhibet stimulos:** sc. *sibi*; *stimulos* further develops the image of torture; the primary sense of the word was 'goad', which was used as an instrument of torture (*OLD* 1a, b).   **torretque flagellis:** sc. *se*. For the lash as 'burning' cf. Hor. *Sat.* 2.7.58 *uri uirgis*, *Ep.* 1.16.47 *loris… ureris*, *Epod.* 4.3. *peruste funibus latus*. L.'s choice of *torreo* for the usual *uro* is rhetorically effective, with the assonance of terminations and the coincidence of ictus in *adhibet… torretque* binding the line together. Lachmann's emendation to *terretque* had been anticipated by John Wallis in his *Principles and Duties of Natural Religion* (1675), but since the book was published posthumously it remains uncertain whether this was a deliberate correction or the result of a misreading (personal communication from Dr D. J. Butterfield). In any case, the sense is inappropriate, since the mind is described as actually tormenting itself, not threatening to do so. Heinsius' *torquet* would have to be read as = 'torment' (*OLD* 5), but in the context it is the special sense of 'rack' that comes to mind (*OLD* 3a), which does not square with *flagellis* (contrast the passage of Juvenal cited above).   **nec uidet interea** 'and all the time it is unaware'.   **terminus … finis:** sc. death.

1023 hic … denique 'here on earth, in short' (*OLD denique* 3), clinching the argument.   **Acherusia … uita** 'a hell on earth' (Smith), echoing *Acherunte* at line 978 to drive home the point and round off the section. **stultorum:** the philosophically unqualified, Greek ἄφρονες, as opposed to the enlightened, *sapientes*, σοφοί. This terminology was in fact common to

Epicureans and Stoics alike (cf. e.g. Cic. *Paradoxa Stoicorum* 4); but when L. obliquely employs it at 1.641, calling the target of his polemic there *stolidi* without naming them, he evidently means the Stoics, who bulked largest among contemporary competing philosophical schools (Kenney 2006: 361–2, 364 n. 2).

1024–1052

Even the great and good have died. This is a rhetorical expansion of what was said at 946–9, returning us to the sequence of the *consolatio*. It takes the form of a harangue to be addressed to himself by the imaginary and typical individual at whom the argument is aimed. The thought is hackneyed, and precisely because of that effective: as Lattimore remarks, 'it is the consolation *par excellence* not only of classical but of modern times, representing as it does the ultimate if meagre solace which not even despair of immortality can take away' (1962: 250–1) – or to put it more prosaically, we are all in the same boat, the message summed up succinctly by Cicero, *non tibi hoc soli* (*Tusc.* 3.79; cf. Otto 1890: 328 s.v. *solus* (2)). The examples quoted by Lattimore range over a wide field of literary and epigraphical texts, demonstrating the popularity of the idea at all periods; see also Lavagnini 1947; N–H on Hor. *C.* 1.28.7. The use of historical and mythological *exempla* in this connexion was worked to death in the schools (Norden 1958: 276), but its power endured, as can be seen from the poem that especially invites comparison with this passage, the Tenth Satire of Juvenal. For a sensitive and wide-ranging analysis see Segal 1990: 171–86.

L.'s list, like Juvenal's, is carefully organized to exemplify particular attributes and to achieve a climax: Ancus = kingly virtue; Xerxes = absolute power; Scipio Africanus = military glory; Homer = literary genius; Democritus, ushering in Epicurus = wisdom. The key to the argument is the contrast between Epicurus – named only here in the poem – and the anonymous *tu* (1026, 1045). Cf. Schrijvers 1970: 231–4, and see the stylistic analysis of this section, Introd. 22–3. The lofty phrasing of the passage, reinforced by alliteration, assonance and the repetition of keywords (*multis, multi, magnis, magnum*) underlines the contrast between the deeds of these men and the insignificance of the complainant.

1025–6 L. quotes Ennius almost word for word, *Ann.* 137 Sk. *postquam lumina sis oculis bonus Ancu' reliquit.*   **sis** = *suis*; *pace* Festus (p. 387 L.). *sis oculis* should be read as instrumental ablative, not dative, 'has left the light with his eyes': Skutsch ad loc. compares *Ann.* 546 *corde relinquite somnum.* For the Romans Ancus was the archetypal 'good king', similarly invoked by Horace, *C.* 4.7.14–16, *Ep.* 1.6.7.   **improbe** 'in your shamelessness', predicative, the contrast with *bonus* underlining the man's

presumption in somehow expecting not to have to share the common lot
of all mankind, high or low. The phrasing and the sentiment are designed
to recall Achilles' words to Lycaon before killing him, 'even Patroclus is
dead, a better man by far than you', κάτθανε καὶ Πάτροκλος, ὅ περ σέο πολ-
λὸν ἀμείνων (Hom. *Il.* 21.107).

1027–8 inde 'since then'.   **occiderunt...imperitarunt:** the verse,
framed by the two weighty and sonorous verbs, has an Ennian ring
(Fraenkel 1957: 191 n. 5; Müller 1974: 763). On the scansion *occiderunt*
see 84–6n. *prodiderunt*; and on the frequentative *imperitarunt* see 350–3n.
nominitamus.

1029–33 ille: Xerxes, who built a bridge of boats across the Hellespont; he
need not be named since his feat was unique. That in death the rich and
mighty were equal with the poorest was and is a commonplace of proverbial wisdom: N–H on Hor. *C.*1.4.14. So Shirley:

> Sceptre and crown
> Must tumble down,
> And in the dust be equal made
> With the poor crooked scythe and spade.

Xerxes is similarly instanced in verses by an unnamed poet quoted by
Plutarch, *Cons. ad Apoll.* 15.110d, which L. may have had in mind; and
in the last stanza of a drinking song preserved in a papyrus of the first
century AD (Page 1950: 512–13).   **strauit** 'calmed and paved', 'laid a
smooth road', playing on different senses of *sterno* (*OLD* 3, 6b); cf. 1.315,
4.415 *strata uiarum.*   **iterque...ire** 'and gave his legions a road to tra-
verse over the deep'; *iter* does double duty as direct object of *dedit* and
internal accusative with *ire* (*OLD eo* 1e).   **dedit** 'made available' (*OLD*
15).   **ac pedibus...lacunas:** the verse was condemned by Lachmann
for its 'molesta ac prorsus intolerabilis abundantia'; the case against it
is presented more temperately by Deufert (1996: 252–3). It is not however merely a paraphrastic repetition of line 1030: the high-flown diction
and the paradoxical *pedibus* reinforce the rhetorical impact of the description and point up the insolence of Xerxes' feat, to walk on water, a pre-
rogative of deity: cf. Hom. *Il.* 13.19–20, 20.229; Mosch. *Europa* 114 and
Bühler ad loc.; Apul. *Met.* 4.31.4; Matthew 14: 25–31.   **salsas...lacunas**
[= 5.794] 'salt lakes', an epicizing periphrasis for the sea, modelled on
Ennius' *salsas...lamas* (*Ann.* 370 Sk., q.v. ad loc.); cf. *Neptuniae lacunae*,
objected to by the author of the *Ad Herennium* (4.10.15). The spelling
lucunas is also offered by the MSS at 6.538, 552; it should probably be
ascribed to copyists rather than L.   **super ire:** the early correction to

superare, eliminating the inartistic repetition of *ire* from the preceding verse, perhaps deserves more respect than it has hitherto enjoyed. Lucretian usage requires that it be taken = 'conquer', not 'pass over' (*OLD* 1b), a sense otherwise unattested in the *DRN.*   **insultans:** both 'trampling' and 'insulting' (*OLD* 1a, 3a): here too the language emphasizes hybristic defiance of the *murmura ponti,* Poseidon's indignant protest. **lumine adempto:** cf. 1025 *lumina…reliquit;* for the metre cf. 35–7n. *sub fin.*   **animam…fudit** 'he was emptied of his spirit', literally 'he poured out his spirit'; but he did not will his death: cf. 487–91n. *extentat neruos.*

1034–5 Scipiadas, belli fulmen: cf. Virg. *Aen.* 6.892–3 *duo fulmina belli,* | *Scipiadas. Scipiades* is a hybrid patronymic like *Memmiades* (1.26); the nominative form in *-as* is attested by Lucilius (1139 M.). It is probably P. Cornelius Scipio Africanus Major who is meant rather than the younger Africanus: it was the Second Punic War and the Carthagininian invasion of Spain and Italy that was critical for the future of Roman power in the Mediterranean (cf. 833–7 and nn.).   **fulmen** 'thunderbolt', but also 'stay', 'support'. This latter sense is not recognized by *OLD*; but cf. Ov. *Am.* 1.6.15–16 and McKeown ad loc. on the bilingual pun on the family name exploited by L. here: σκηπτός = *fulmen,* σκῆπτρον = *scipio,* 'staff'. Cf. also Munro's note and Skutsch 1956/1968.   **proinde ac famul infimus esset:** an old commonplace, the uncertainty of human affairs, the declaimer's *locus de Fortuna,* is given a new twist; for the image cf. Shirley (1029–33n.). L. is evidently echoing a corrupt and difficult fragment of Ennius (*Ann.* 312–13 Sk., q.v. ad loc.), the only other place where the form *famul* for *famulus* is attested. It seems to have been an arbitrary abbreviation by Ennius, possibly suggested by *famel,* 'slave', in Oscan, his native tongue (Gell. 17.17.1).

1036–8 repertores: inventors then as now attracted great kudos or opprobrium according to the nature of their inventions (N–H on Hor. *C.* 1.3.12). L. singles out philosophers and artists, but significantly makes no mention of the 'culture-heroes' who are prominent in Greek mythology, dismissing later in the poem the achievements of Hercules with withering sarcasm (5.22–41). Their discoveries we could have survived without; the true *solacia uitae* are due to Epicurus and to him alone (5.13–21). Thus the invention of fire is not ascribed to Prometheus but to man's observation and exploitation of natural phenomena (5.1091–1104); and in his summary of other cultural advances (5.1447–57) L. emphasizes that this was a slow and gradual process made up of many small steps.   **leporum** 'graceful arts' (Munro), complementing *doctrinarum;* used of the charm of poetry at 1.28 *aeternum da dictis, diua, leporem,* 934 *musaeo contingens cuncta lepore,* and of the delights of autumn at 3.1006.   **Heliconiadum comites:** in the

Prooemium to Book 1 L. had allusively but unambiguously rejected the poet's traditional allegiance to the Muses (Kenney 1970b: 375–7/2007: 308–9). On the other hand he uses traditional poetic terminology when he refers to his poem as *carmen Pierium* (1.946 = 4.21); and his invocation of Calliope at the beginning of Book VI adroitly exploits traditional imagery to make a literary point (Kenney 2007: 108). No irony is intended here. This grandiloquent phrase, however, with its echo of Hesiod, *Theog.* 1 Μουσάων Ἑλικωνιάδων, 100 Μουσάων θεράπων, 'servant of the Muses', carries the ironic implication: 'for all that they claim a special relationship with deity, poets die like other men'. **quorum unus Homerus | sceptra potitus** 'for all that he was their one and only monarch' (*OLD unus* 8a); for the concessive nuance cf. 117–20n. *detracto corpore multo*; and for the accusative after *potior,* usual in L. (but cf. 1027, 2.13, 50), cf. 730–4n. *fungitur.* On the portrayal of Homer in art with a sceptre see Brink 1972: 551 and n. 20. The 'poetic' plural *sceptra* perhaps by analogy with *regna* (cf. Löfstedt 1942: 52–4, 54 n. 1); the physical and metaphorical senses of the word, the thing itself and the power that it symbolizes (*OLD* 1a, 2), are merged in a single image. **eadem aliis sopitu' quietest** 'he has been sent to sleep in the same repose as everyone else'; *aliis = ceteris* (526–30n. *alios*). For the condensed or compendious comparison with *idem* cf. 4.1174 *eadem facit... omnia turpi* 'she does the same as an ugly woman', Hor. *AP* 467 *idem facit occidenti* 'he does the same as a murderer'. Cf. also 2.919 *animalia* (*sunt*) *mortalibus una eademque,* 'living things are exactly the same as mortal things', i.e. are mortal because living. For the metre of line 1038 cf. 35 (35–7n.).

1039–41 Democritum: though critical of some of his teaching (370–4), L. treats Democritus with respect as the inventor *par excellence* of the atomic theory. **matura uetustas:** according to one account he was 109. **memores motus** 'the movements of memory', the *sensiferi motus.* His awareness of what was happening to him and why is appropriately described using atomic terminology, the point as so often emphasized by alliteration. **sponte sua...ipse** 'went of his own accord to meet his death': according to Athenaeus (2.46a) by refusing food, a classic method of self-ending (Sen. *Ep.* 77.5–9); according to Hermippus (third century BC), cited by D.L. 9.43, he died peacefully of old age. L. is our oldest authority for his suicide. True or not, the story reinforces his argument by the implied contrast between the behaviour of this, one of the wisest of men, and the reluctance of L.'s imagined addressee to accept the inevitable. The passage lends no support to Jerome's canard (Introd. 5–6). **caput obuius obtulit** 'went to offer his life' (*OLD caput* 4a); the expression, as Heinze remarks, is a more vivid version of the more prosaic *morti se offerre;*

this was an act of free will, with *caput* perhaps suggesting that 'Death seems
to be personified in the form of an executioner' (Smith ad loc. in Leonard
and Smith 1965, printing *Leto* in the text.).

1042–4 ipse Epicurus obit: the only place in the poem where he is named,
the terse phrasing contrasting with the foregoing periphrases for 'die'
and driving home the point.   **obît** = *obiit*; cf. 502 *redîtque*. Butterfield
(2008d: 362–3) objects to this interpretation, arguing that at line 502, the
only Lucretian parallel for this contracted form not required by metre, *reditque* 'can readily be taken as present tense in view of what follows'. That
perhaps overstates the case, given *reflexit* preceding in the same verse referring to the same process. More importantly his reasons for eliminating the
name of Epicurus from the poem hardly seem weighty enough to justify
emending the text. Of his two suggested emendations the second, *ipse pater
obiit* (364), is the better, preserving as it does something of the clinching
impact of the first three words of the verse as transmitted; but it is difficult to see how it somehow 'demotes' the authority of Epicurus to name
him here (363).   **decurso lumine uitae** 'when the light of his life had
run its course' (Smith), a remarkable mixed metaphor. 'The combination results naturally [?] from the conception of the sun (to which Epicurus is compared as both lamp and chariot(eer)' (Smith 1992: 271 ad
loc.). For further exploration of the image, figuring Epicurus as Helios,
see Gale 1994: 202–4. The identification with the Sun dates to Colotes
(fourth–third century BC), hailing Epicurus as the Sun displelling darkness (1–2n.). For *lumine* Pius conjectured *limite* (1511, but confined to his
notes), independently suggested by Nisbet (1995: 346). This gives straightforward pedestrian sense: for *limes* = 'course of life' see *OLD* 4c. However,
L. nowhere else uses *limes*; when he refers to the movements of a heav-
enly body, he uses *cursus* (21x); *limes* in this sense is first attested in Virgil
(*OLD* 4a). L. should not be robbed of his vivid and compelling imagery.
qui…superauit: engraved on the base of Roubiliac's statue of Isaac Newton in the antechapel of Trinity College, Cambridge; cf. 15 *diuina mente*,
5.8 *deus ille fuit, deus.* For the metre of the verse cf. 174n.   **omnis |
restinxit…sol:** a well-known epigram of Leonidas of Tarentum (*AP* 9.24
= *HE* 2174–50) had applied this conceit to Homer; and variations on it
by other poets such as Meleager (*AP* 12.127 = *HE* 4420–7; cf. Lutatius
Catulus 2 (*FLP* 76–8)) perhaps suggest that it was something of a cliché.
L.'s transfer of it to Epicurus puts such dilettantism in its place. Similar
comparisons were at home in the tradition of panegyric (Doblhofer 1966:
86–91; Weinstock 1971: 372 n. 2; N–H on Hor. *C.* 1.12.47–8). L.'s use of
terminology also appropriated to celebrate the deified rulers of the Hellenistic world carries the reminder that Epicurus was the only true deity
and Deliverer, Σωτήρ.   **aetherius sol** [= 5.215, 267, 281, 389]: *sol* also

in final place at 6.620. An Ennian touch, which in later poets becomes something of an affectation: Enn. *Ann.* 87 Sk. *simul aureus exoritur sol* and Skutsch 1985: 49–50, q.v. also ad loc.

1045–52 So far from being aggrieved at the prospect of death, Epicurus had described the last day of his life as 'blessed', μακαρίαν (D.L. 10.22). Who then are you to complain, when indeed you are to all intents and purposes already dead? L.'s words again recall those of Achilles to Lycaon (Hom. *Il.* 21.106): 'Come, my friend, you must die too; why grieve so?', ἀλλά, φίλος, θάνε καὶ σύ· τίη ὀλοφύρεαι οὕτως; The contrast depicted between Epicurean understanding and the half-dead somnolence of the *stultus* begins a transition to the next topic through a carefully contrived progression: sleep > daydreaming > empty fears > mental confusion.   **mortua ... uita:** cf. Sall. *Cat.* 2.8 *multi mortales, dediti uentri atque somno, indocti incultique uitam sicuti peregrinantes transiere ... eorum ego uitam mortemque iuxta aestumo*, Sen. *Ep.* 60.4 (referring to that passage of Sallust) *horum* [sc. gluttons] *licet in limine ipso nomen marmori inscribas: mortem suam antecesserunt*, 77.18 (again to the address of gluttons) *uiuere uis: scis enim? mori times: quid porro? ista uita non mors est?* eqs., St Paul, 1 Tim. 5:6 'But she that liveth in pleasure is dead while she liveth.'   **prope** qualifies *mortua*, 'as good as dead'.   **iam uiuo atque uidenti** 'while you are still alive and kicking', scornfully colloquial; cf. Cic. *Sest.* 59 *uiuus ut aiunt ... et uidens.*   **conteris** 'use up', 'squander', 'waste' (*OLD* A),   **uigilans stertis:** a vivid variation on the usual *uigilans somniare*, 'daydream'; cf. Ter. *Eun.* 1079 *fatuos est, insulsu', stertit noctes et dies: stertit*: 'one stage worse than *dormit*, not only unaware but vulgarly so' (Barsby ad loc.). The *stultus* is uncouth as well as stupid.   **somnia** 'fantasies', 'daydreams' (*OLD* 2). So in the Prooemium to Book 1 (104–6) the idle tales, *somnia*, concocted by priests and seers, *uates*, are said to have the power to disturb the life of reason, *uitae rationes uertere.*   **geris** 'you are saddled with' (Brown); his mind is figured as an encumbrance to be humped around (*OLD* 3a); that the load carried around is 'empty' (*OLD cassus* 2, 3b) sharpens the satire. The image becomes explicit at 1054 *pondus ... quod se grauitate fatigat.*   **quid sit ... mali** 'what is wrong', genitive of the rubric.   **saepe** qualifies *nec potes* preceding.   **cum | ... urgeris ... | atque uagaris** 'when all the time (what is wrong with you is that) you are wandering a victim of causeless fears and error'; the temporal sense of *cum* predominates over the causal.   **ebrius ... uagaris:** the section began with an image of torpor and ends in one of confusion, suggesting jostling by a crowd, underlined in the final verse by the accumulation of four words connoting uncertainty. *ebrius* = 'distraught' is first attested here (*OLD* 2).   **animi incerto fluitans errore** 'drifting on the wayward tides of impulse' (Smith). Lambinus' *animi* imparts order and elegance; *animo* is due to anticipation of *incerto*

(Reynolds and Wilson 2014: 232–3). Bentley's *incertus*, retaining *animo*, leaves *errore* lacking a complement.

1053–1075

Men are unhappy and restless because they do not understand the cause of their unhappiness: the only remedy for this ignorance is offered by philosophy. Epicurus had taught that a correct understanding of nature was essential to happiness (38–40n. *sub fin.*). The restlessness so vividly described in this passage is the converse of the freedom from disturbance, ἀταραξία, which it was the aim of the Epicurean system to attain; and high among the causes of disturbance is the fear of death and of what it might have in store. At 58–98 L. had argued that it was to that fear that disturbing and destructive passions such as ambition and avarice should ultimately be attributed, and it might therefore be supposed that it should follow that fear and the discontent now depicted are in fact one and the same thing. L. does not make this identification in so many words, but it can be felt in the opening lines of the section, in which both ideas are merged. The vividness and particularity of L.'s treatment smack of the diatribe: for discontent with one's lot, μεμψιμοιρία, as a commonplace of popular philosophy cf. Fraenkel 1957: 92–4; Rudd 1966: 20–2; N–H on Hor. *C.* 1.1.17. The adaptations of the passage by Horace and Seneca (1068–9n.) attest to the impression it made.

1053–9 sentire uidentur 'they evidently feel', though without understanding, *sentire* contrasting with *noscere* following at line 1055.   **mali tamquam moles** 'weight of woe'. The figurative use of *moles* is not uncommon (*OLD* 5–8), and it is not clear why L. should seem to excuse it here with *tamquam*, particularly with *pondus* following almost immediately. **ut...nescire** 'as we generally see (them), each one at a loss to know what to do with himself'. The sense is clear, the construction informal: 'in the *ut*-clause, *eos uitam agere, id est* can be supplied to complete the sense' (Brown). The phrasing and what follows are reminiscent of the Soldiers' Chorus in Ennius' *Iphigenia* (*Sc.* 234–41 V.², 195–202 J.):

> otio qui nescit uti
> plus negoti habet quam cum est negotium in negotio.
> nam cui quod agat institutumst non ullo negotio
> id agit, id studet, ibi mentem atque animum delectat suum.
> otioso in otio animus nescit quid uelit.
> hoc idem est: em neque domi nunc nos nec militiae sumus:
> imus huc, hinc illuc, cum illuc uentum est, ire illuc lubet.
> incerte errat animus, praeter propter uitam uiuitur.

(On the text, which is very uncertain, see Skutsch 1953: 193–210/1968: 157–65.) That soldiers should be brought on to the stage in a tragedy to air this philosophical commonplace testifies to its power. Catullus, in a poem which L. evidently knew (153–8n. *sudoresque . . . artus*), applied it to his own case even more starkly:

> otium, Catulle, tibi molestum est:
> otio exultas nimiumque gestis:
> otium et reges prius et beatas
>   perdidit urbes.   (51.13–16)

See further Fraenkel 1957: 211–13.   **quaerere semper | commutare locum:** that change of place solves no problems was also a commonplace and a favourite theme of Horace and Seneca, summed up in Horace's much-quoted line *caelum non animum mutant qui trans mare currunt* (*Ep.* 1.11.27).

1060–7 L.'s choice of illustration is to the address of his aristocratic readers: 'le spleen est une maladie des riches' (Ernout–Robin). This is a sharply focussed contemporary portrait of a well-to-do Roman, with a large town house and a country estate. In spite of political turmoil and civil war the last century of the Republic was an age of enormous private fortunes and much conspicuous consumption,

1060–2 exit 'He is off': the emphatic placing of the verb in a spondaic first foot signals the suddenness of his decision and departure, to be followed by an equally abrupt decision (1061 *subito*) to return.   **pertaesumst** 'is sick to death': on the emphasis imparted by *per-* see 179–8on.; in the perfect tense only the passive form of *pertaedet* is attested. On the 'quasi-caesura' created by the prefix see 174n.   **reuertit:** Pomponius Laetus' correction (ascribed to Politian) is an easy supplement and has become the editorial vulgate; but any supplement here can only be printed *exempli gratia*, and Orth's *recurrit* deserves consideration as more strikingly descriptive, as does Butterfield's *refert se*, its abruptness picking up that of *exit* at 1060 (Butterfield 2008c: 25–6).   **nilo melius . . . sentiat esse:** sc. *sibi*, 'he feels no better off' (*OLD male* 1b).

1063–7 mannos: Gaulish ponies prized for their speed, driven by Cynthia in her headlong triumphal progress along the Appian Way (Prop. 4.8.15). A common passion among the rich for fast driving is a symptom of the desire to 'escape' themselves.   **praecipitanter** 'hell-for-leather'; the metre breaks into a gallop. On the form of the adverb (attested only here) see 776–8on. *praeproperanter*.   **instans; | oscitat extemplo, tetigit cum limina uillae:** the abrupt change from frantic activity to listless inertia

is imaged in the rhythm of the verse, the three long syllables of *extemplo* suggesting his prolonged yawn and the inverted order of *tetigit cum* (granted
that it is necessitated by the metre): ennui overcomes him the moment he
comes through the door.   **grauis** 'heavily', predicative.

1068-9 'In this way each man tries to escape himself, but in his own
despite [*OLD ingratiis* b] he clings to that self, which we know he cannot succeed in escaping, though he hates it.' Antecedents to *quam*
must be understood, sc. *ei haeret et eum odit*; *et* = *et tamen* (*OLD* 14a).
fugit … effugere 'try to escape … succeed in escaping' (cf. Greek φεύγειν,
ἐκφεύγειν). Madvig's *fugitat* (an interpretation rather than a correction of
the transmitted text: from the second century AD onwards Latin books
were normally written in *scriptura continua* without word division, following Greek practice) spoils this contrast and complicates the syntax. It is
clear that Seneca, who quotes and comments on the passage in the *De
Tranquillitate Animi* (see below) read the words as *fugit, at*. The idea behind
these lines was exploited by Horace with his usual happy concision at *C.*
2.16.18–20 *quid terras alio calentes | sole mutamus? patriae quis exul | se quoque
fugit?* and elsewhere (Lejay 1911: 555); and recurs as a commonplace in
Seneca (*Ep.* 2.1, 69.1, 104.8). He ascribes a similar sentiment to Socrates
(*Ep.* 28.2), but elsewhere seems to associate the idea particularly with L.
(*De Tranqu. An.* 2.14). Similarly Plato had argued that the wicked man
hates and is at odds with himself (*Rep.* 1.352a); and Aristotle in his discussion of friendship had observed that the wicked shun their own society, literally, as in L., 'flee themseves', ἑαυτοὺς … φεύγουσιν (*EN* 9. 1166b.13–14).
Whether or not L. had Aristotle in mind here, his graphic description gives
the conceit a new and effective twist.   **potis est:** see 463–9n. *potis est.*
ingratis: the sense required by the context is 'against his will' (cf. above).
MS *ingratius* introduces an irrelevance, and was probably prompted by a
wish to improve the metre by a copyist confronted with an original spelling
ingratiis; cf. 6.216, where the same corruption occurs. That spelling may
indeed have been L.'s own, the word being pronounced as a trisyllable by
synizesis to reflect current pronunciation.

1070-5 If men understood the causes of their discontents, they would
turn to the only source of enlightenment, study of the nature of things:
what is in question is not the impression the world makes on us now, in
the 'one hour' of this brief life, but the fact that it has gone on and will go
on to eternity without us: when we die, we cease to exist for ever. L. ingeniously – though a captious critic might suggest sophistically – exploits the
rhetorical contrast between *una hora* and *tempus aeternum* to press home
the central theme of the book: death and men's attitude to it.   **tenet**
'grasps', 'understands' (*OLD* 23a).   **aeger** 'because he is sick', predicative.   **unius horae:** one of those that the restless and discontented man

is at a loss to fill. If we fix our attention on these central principles we shall achieve ἀταραξία and boredom will disappear.   **ambigitur status** 'it is a question of the condition...'; but the phrase can also mean 'the question before the court is...' The *status* was the issue on which a case was fought (*OLD* 4); Quintilian devotes a long chapter to it (*IO* 3.6); see also Clarke 1953: 26–7, 67–8; Bonner 1949: index s.v. *status*-doctrine; Russell 1983: 40–1 n. 1. Given L.'s evident familiarity with forensic oratory (Kenney 2007: 92–3) and his use of judicial terminology elsewhere, the ambiguity is likely to be deliberate, harking back to Nature's role as plaintiff in a civil suit (970–1n.).   **in quo sit...manenda** 'in which all the time that remains after death is to be passed by mortals'. *mortalibus* belongs in sense with *manenda*; to insert a comma after *cumque*, as modern editors do, is to mistake the role of punctuation, which is to reflect the syntax, not to impose it.   **quae...cumque:** cf. 550, 940.   **manenda:** Lambinus' correction ascribes to L. a possibly unique instance of *manere* transitive (*OLD* 3b, 4) in the passive mood, but (*pace* Müller 1978: 209 n. 2) the transmitted *manendo* yields unacceptably awkward syntax. Singularity is not in itself cause for suspicion of inauthenticity (Kenney 1999: 399–400), and *manenda* is sardonically pointed: what 'awaits' mortals, what they superstitiously dread as their fate in the vast expanse of future time, is – nothing.

1076–1094

It is a mistake to yearn for long life: it does not confer greater happiness (for Cicero's more nuanced view cf. Powell 1988: 5–6), nor does it make death, when it comes, any less eternal. This final passage has been criticized as providing an inadequate ending to the book. Some of the arguments in it we have admittedly met before, but some are new. L. apparently did not feel a need to round off with a final rhetorical flourish; only Book I, as Heinze points out, ends with anything like a formal epilogue. How Book VI might have ended if L. had lived long enough to revise the poem completely remains matter for speculation (Kenney 2007: 109–10 and n. 68). See Müller 1978: 208–12.

1076–84 This echoes, without repeating in so many words, what Nature said at 931–62.

1076–9 dubiis...periclis ~ 55.   **mala** 'malign', 'noxious' (*OLD* 3b, 4a).   **certa** 'irreversible', fixed by natural causes (*OLD* 1b).   **adstat** picks up the image of 959 *mors ad caput adstitit*: death is never far away (959–60n.).   **nec deuitari...quin obeamus:** the pleonasm underlines the inevitability of what we face.   **pote** = *potest*. The form occurs nowhere else in L.'s MSS; it was restored by Lachmann at 5.836. Elsewhere, as at 468 (463–9n. *potis est*), 1069, he uses *potis est*; but *pote* is not

uncommon in other Republican writers and later colloquial Latin (N–W
II 174–6).

1080–1 uersamur ibidem atque insumus usque 'we constantly pass our
time and dwell in the same place', doing the same things and getting
nowhere. The false hexameter ending after the fourth foot is smoothed
over by the elision (cf. 893, 1033 and nn.).   **procuditur:** literally 'is
forged', 'created' (so of producing children at 5.850, 856), but also 'is
prolonged' (*OLD* 2).

1082–4 The theme is that of 957–60 (n.), men's insatiable craving for an
unattainable satisfaction.   **sed dŭm abest:** an example of the so-called
'prosodic hiatus', in which a long or 'middle' syllable is shortened (better 'lightened') before a vowel, a licence relatively frequent in comedy,
presumably reflecting colloquial speech, rare in hexameter poetry. L. provides ten certain instances; the fragments of Lucilius three; other hexameter poets not half-a-dozen in all (Soubiran 1966: 374). Only a monosyllable occupying the first short syllable of a dactyl is so treated; this licence
is to be distinguished from 'epic shortening', *correptio epica*, of the second short syllable. Both licences are found together at 6.716 *tempore eo*
quī etesiaĕ esse feruntur. For the metre of the verse, with a strong caesura
only in the second foot, cf. 122n.   **post** 'afterwards', 'then', adverbial.   **sitis...hiantis:** a fresh twist to the image of the unsatisfied guest
at life's banquet, also recalling Tantalus.   **aequa** 'the same as ever',
'undiminished'.

1085–6 A proverbial sentiment (Otto 1890: 369 s.v. *vesper*).   **uehat**
'may bring', recalling the title of one of Varro's Satires, *Nescis quid ues-*
per serus uehat, and echoed by Virgil, *G.* 1.461 *quid Vesper serus uehat*. The
mutability of Fortune was a declaimer's *locus communis* (1034–5n. *proinde*
ac famul infimus esset), at home in a *consolatio*.   **instet** 'may loom ahead'
(*OLD* 6a), like an iceberg in a fog; the end may come at any moment out
of the blue.

1087–94 A final twist to the thought memorably expressed at 869 (n.) to
conclude the book: however long a man may live, he will still be dead
for ever. In producing this as his last and clinching argument L. rides
roughshod over human psychology and physiology. The instinct to strive
for survival is 'hardwired' into our brains. Epicurus expected a lot from his
disciples.   **nec...hilum:** cf. 220 (n.).   **minus...diu** 'less long' (*OLD*
diu 1b).   **forte** 'somehow or other', 'conceivably' (*OLD* 1, 3, 4). The
irony is characteristic and effective, the suggested corrections pedestrian.
condere saecla 'see the generations laid to rest'; for the idiom cf. 487–91n.
extentat neruos. L. plays on two senses of both words: *condere* = 'see out' a
period, as in Virgil's *longos...condere soles* (*Ecl.* 9.51–2 and Clausen ad loc.)

and in the technical term *lustrum condere*; and = 'bury' the defunct generations (*OLD condo* 8, 13, 4a; *saeculum* 1a, 5). *uiuendo* contributes to the
word-play.   **mors aeterna** ~ 869 (n.).   **iam** 'from then on' (*OLD* 1b).
ex hodierno | lumine 'from being alive today' (*OLD lumen* 3).   **et** 'than',
complementing *minus*: a usage analogous to *alius ac/ atque*, but a good deal
less common. Cf. 5.1081–2 *longe alias iaciunt . . . uoces | et cum de uictu certant*;
OLD et 19a; *TLL* s.v. 894.4–29.

BIBLIOGRAPHY

1. EDITIONS, COMMENTARIES AND TRANSLATIONS

For a comprehensive list down to 1961 see Gordon 1962/1985.

Avancius, H. Text. Venice 1500.
Bailey, C. Text, translation and commentary. 3 vols. Oxford 1947.
Bernays, J. Text. Leipzig 1852.
Brown, P. M. Book III. Text, translation and commentary. Warminster 1997.
Büchner, C. Text. Wiesbaden 1966.
Creech, T. Translation. Oxford 1682 and frequently reprinted. Text with Latin paraphrase and commentary. Oxford 1695 and frequently reprinted.
Diels, H. Text and German translation. 2 vols. Berlin 1923–4.
Duff, J. D. Book III. Text and commentary. Cambridge 1903 and several times reprinted.
Ernout, A. Text and French translation. 2 vols. Paris 1920 and frequently reprinted.
Ernout, A. and Robin, L. Commentary. 3 vols. 2nd edn. Paris 1962.
Esolen, A. Translation with introduction and notes. Baltimore and London 1995.
Flores, E. Text. Vol. I Books I–III. Naples 2002.
Gifanius, O. Text. Antwerp 1565/1566. 2nd edn. Leiden 1595.
Giussani, C. Text and commentary. 4 vols. Turin 1896–8.
Heinze, R. Book III. Text and commentary. Leipzig 1897.
Kenney, E. J. Book III. Text and commentary. Cambridge 1971.
Lachmann, C. Text and commentary. Berlin 1850. 2nd edn Berlin 1853. Index by F. Harder Berlin 1882.
Lambinus, D. Text and commentary. Paris 1563/1564 and frequently reprinted.
Latham, R. E. Translation. Harmondsworth 1951. Revised edn J. Godwin 1994.
Leonard, W. E. and Smith, S. B. Text and commentary. Madison 1942. Reprinted 1961, 1965.
Martin, J. Text. Leipzig 1934. 5th edn 1963.
Melville, Sir R. Translation with introduction and notes by Don and Peta Fowler. Oxford 1997.
Merrill, W. A. Text and commentary. New York, Cincinnati and Chicago 1907.

Text (University of California Publications in Classical Philology 4).
    Berkeley 1917.
Müller, K. Text. Zurich 1975.
Munro, H. A. J. Text, translation and commentary. 3 vols. Cambridge 1864.
    4th edn 1886, reprinted 1891–3.
Naugerius, A. Text. Venice 1515.
Paratore, H. and Pizzani, H. Selected passages. Text and commentary.
    Rome 1960.
Pius, J. B. Text. Bologna 1511, Paris 1514.
Sinker, A. P. Selected passages. Text and commentary. Cambridge 1937.
Smith, M. F. Text and translation by W. H. D. Rouse revised. First published
    Cambridge, Mass. and London 1924. New version by M. F. Smith 1975,
    reprinted with further revisions 1982, 1992.
    Translation. First published 1969. Revised edn Indianapolis and Cam-
    bridge 2001.
Smith, S. B. See Leonard and Smith.
Stallings, A. E. Translation with Introduction by R. Jenkyns and Notes by
    the translator. London 2007.
Wakefield, G. Text and commentary in Latin. 3 vols. London 1796–7.
    4 vols. Glasgow 1813.

2. WORKS CITED IN SHORT FORM

The works in this list are those cited in the Introduction and Commentary. For general bibliographies of Lucretius see Boyancé 1963; A. Dalzell,
The Classical World 66 (1972–3) 385–427, 67 (1973–4) 65–112, covering
1945–72; Gale 1994; Sedley 1998; Gillespie and Hardie 2007.

Adams, J. N. and Mayer, R. G. (edd.) 1999. *Aspects of the language of Latin
    poetry* (Proceedings of the British Academy 93). Oxford.
Algra, K. A., Koenen, M. H. and Schrijvers, P. H. (edd.) 1997. *Lucretius
    and his intellectual background* (Koninklijke Nederlandse Akademie van
    Wetenschapen Verhandelingen Afd. Letterkunde Nieuwe Reeks 172).
    Amsterdam, Oxford, New York and Tokyo.
Allen, W. S. 1965/1978. *Vox Latina. A guide to the pronunciation of classical
    Latin.* 2nd edn with Supplement 1978. Cambridge.
Amory, Anne. 1969. '*Obscura de re lucida carmina*: science and poetry in *De
    Rerum Natura*', *Yale Classical Studies* 21: 145–68.
Appel, G. 1909. *De Romanorum precibus.* Diss. Giessen. Reprinted New York
    1975.
Arnott, W. G. 1996. *Alexis: the fragments. A Commentary* (Cambridge Classi-
    cal Texts and Commentaries 31). Cambridge.

Axelson, B. 1945. *Unpoetische Wörter. Ein Beitrag zur Kenntnis der lateinischer Dichtersprache* (Skrifter utgivna av Vetenskaps-Societeten i Lund 29). Lund.

Bailey, C. 1947. *T. Lucreti Cari De Rerum Natura Libri Sex.* 3 vols. Oxford.

Beer, Beate 2009. 'Lukrez in Herculaneum? Beitrag zu einer Edition von PHerc. 395', *Zeitschrift für Papyrologie und Epigraphik* 159: 71–82.

Bell, A. J. 1923. *The Latin dual & poetic diction.* London and Toronto.

Bennett, C. E. 1910, 1914. *Syntax of early Latin.* 2 vols. Boston and Leipzig.

Berger, A. 1953. *Encyclopedic dictionary of Roman law (Transactions of the American Philosophical Society* 43, 2). Philadelphia.

Binns, J. W. (ed.) 1973. *Ovid.* London.

Blase, H. 1903. 'Tempora und Modi', 'Genera Verbi', in Landgraf 1903: 97–312.

Bluck, R. S. (ed.) 1981. *Plato's* Meno. Cambridge.

Bonner, S. F. 1949. *Roman declamation in the later Republic and early Empire.* Liverpool.

Boyancé, P. 1963. *Lucrèce et l'Épicurisme.* Paris.

Boyd, Barbara W. (ed.) 2002. *Brill's Companion to Ovid.* Leiden, Berlin and Cologne.

Bramble, J. C. 1969. 'Some considerations of period in Latin literature', *Farrago* (Journal of Cambridge University Literary Society) 5: 3–4.

Brink, C. O. 1972. 'Ennius and the Hellenistic worship of Homer', *American Journal of Philology* 93: 547–67.

(ed.) 1982. *Horace on poetry. Epistles Book II: the letters to Augustus and Florus.* Cambridge.

Brown, P. M. (ed.) 1997. *Lucretius De Rerum Natura III.* Warminster.

Brown, R. D. 1982/2007. 'Lucretius and Callimachus', *Illinois Classical Studies* 7: 77–97. Reprinted in Gale 2007a: 328–50.

Büchner, K. 1936. *Beobachtungen über Vers und Gedankengang bei Lukrez* (Hermes Einzelschriften 1). Wiesbaden.

Buglass, Abigail. 'A note on Lucretius' *De Rerum Natura*, 3.361', *Classical Quarterly*, forthcoming.

Butterfield, D. J. 2008a. 'The poetic treatment of *atque* from Catullus to Juvenal', *Mnemosyne* 61: 386–413.

2008b. 'Lucretiana nonnulla', *Exemplaria Classica* 12: 3–23.

2008c. 'Supplementa Lucretiana', *Arctos* 42: 17–30.

2008d. 'Three Lucretian emendations', *Acta Antiqua Academiae Scientiarum Hungaricae* 48: 351–64.

2009. 'Emendations on the third book of Lucretius', *Euphrosyne* 37: 311–16.

2011. 'Lucretius 1.657: the problem of a *crux cruciata*', in Millett *et al.* 2011: 153–66.

2013. *The early textual history of Lucretius' De Rerum Natura.* Cambridge.

Campbell, G. 2003. *Lucretius on creation and evolution. A commentary on De Rerum Natura Book Five, lines 772–1104.* Oxford.
Camps, W. A. 1969. *An introduction to Virgil's Aeneid.* Oxford.
Canter, H. V. 1930. 'The figure AΔYNATON in Greek and Latin poetry', *American Journal of Philology* 51: 32–41.
Capasso, M. 2003. 'Filodemo e Lucrezio', in A. Monet (ed.), *Le jardin romain: Épicurisme et poésie à Rome. Mélanges offerts à Mayotte Bollack.* Lisle, 77–107.
Catrein, C. 2003. *Vertauschte Sinne. Untersuchungen zur Synästhesie in der römischen Dichtung* (Beiträge zur Altertumswissenschaft 178). Munich and Leipzig.
Cherniss, H. F. 1943/1962. 'The biographical fashion in literary criticism', *University of California Publications in Classical Philology* 12: 279–92. Reprinted in J. P. Sullivan (ed.), *Critical essays on Roman literature.* London 1962, 15–30.
Chilton, C. W. 1971. *Diogenes of Oenoanda. The Fragments. A translation and commentary.* London, New York and Toronto.
Clark, A. C. 1911. 'Lucretius III. 687–690', *Classical Review* 25: 74.
Clarke, M. L. 1953. *Rhetoric at Rome. A historical survey.* London.
  1977. 'Lucretius 3.1–3', *Classical Quarterly* 27: 354–5.
Classen, C. J. 1968/1986. 'Poetry and rhetoric in Lucretius', *Transactions of the American Philological Association* 99: 77–118. Reprinted in Classen 1986: 331–73.
  (ed.) 1986. *Probleme der Lukrezforschung* (Olms Studien 18). Hildesheim, Zurich and New York.
Clausen, W. 1949. 'Three notes', *American Journal of Philology* 70: 309–15.
  1955. 'Silva coniecturarum', *Americal Journal of Philology* 86: 47–62.
  1991. 'Three notes on Lucretius', *Classical Quarterly* 41: 544–6.
Coleman, R. G. G. 1999. 'Poetic diction, poetic discourse and the poetic register', in Adams and Mayer 1999: 21–93.
Conte, G.-B. 1965. 'Il "trionfo della morte" e la galleria dei grandi trapassati in Lucrezio III 1024–1053', *Studi italiani di filologia classica* 37: 114–32.
Copley, F. O. 1956. *Exclusus amator. A study in Latin love poetry* (American Philological Association Philological Monographs 17). New York.
Cornford, F. M. 1950. *The unwritten philosophy and other essays.* Cambridge.
Costa, C. D. N. 1995. Review of Gale 1994, *Classical Review* 45: 28–30.
Coulton, G. G. 1943. *Fourscore years; an autobiography.* Cambridge.
Cox, A. 1969. 'Didactic poetry', in J. Higginbotham (ed.), *Greek and Latin literature: a comparative study.* London, 134–45, 158–60. Reprinted in Classen 1986: 219–35.
Crawley, L. W. A. 1963. *The failure of Lucretius* (University of Auckland Bulletin 66, Classics Series 5). Auckland.

Crook, J. A. 1967. *Law and life of Rome.* London.

Cupaiuolo, F. 1966. *Tra poesia e poetica: su alcuni aspetti culturali della poesia latina nell'età augustea* (Collana di Studi Latini 15). Naples.

Dalzell, A. 1972–3, 1973–4. 'A bibliography of work on Lucretius 1945–72', *Classical World* 66: 385–427, 67: 65–112.

   1996. *The criticism of didactic poetry: essays on Lucretius, Virgil, and Ovid.* Toronto, Buffalo and London.

Deufert, M. 1996. *Pseudo-Lukrezisches in Lukrez. Die unechten Verse in Lukrezens 'De rerum natura'.* Berlin and New York.

DeWitt, N. W. 1954. *Epicurus and his philosophy.* Minneapolis.

Diggle, J. (ed.) 1970. *Euripides Phaethon* (Cambridge Classical Texts and Commentaries 12). Cambridge.

Dionigi, I. 1988. *Lucrezio. Le parole e le cose.* Bologna.

Doblhofer, E. 1966. *Die Augustuspanegyrik des Horaz in formalhistorischer Sicht.* Heidelberg.

Dodds, E. R. 1951. *The Greeks and the irrational* (Sather Classical Lectures 25). Berkeley and Cambridge.

   1965. *Pagan and Christian in an age of anxiety. Some aspects of religious experience from Marcus Aurelius to Constantine.* Cambridge.

Douglas, A. E. (ed.) 1966. *M. Tulli Ciceronis Brutus.* Oxford.

Dover, K. J. 1960. (ed.) *Aristophanes Clouds.* Oxford.

Drexler, H. 1967. *Einführung in die römische Metrik.* Darmstadt.

Duban, J. M. 1979. '*Ratio divina mente coorta* and the mythological undercurrent in the deification of Epicurus', *Prudentia* 11: 47–54.

   1982. 'Venus, Epicurus and *naturae species ratioque*', *American Journal of Philology* 103: 165–77.

Duckworth, G. E. 1969. *Vergil and classical hexameter poetry. A study in metrical variety.* Ann Arbor.

Dudley, D. R. 1938. *A history of Cynicism.* London.

   (ed.) 1965a. *Lucretius.* London.

   1965b. 'The satiric element in Lucretius', in Dudley 1965a: 115–30.

Duff, J. D. (ed.) 1903. *T. Lucreti Cari De Rerum Natura Liber Tertius.* Frequently reprinted. Cambridge.

Dutoit, E. 1936. *Le thème de l'adynaton dans la poésie antique.* Paris.

Ernout, A. and Meillet, A. 1957, 1960. *Dictionnaire étymologique de la langue latine. Histoire des mots.* 2 vols. 4th edn. Paris.

Ewbank, W. W. (ed.) 1933. *The poems of Cicero.* London.

Farmelo, G. 2009. *The strangest man. The hidden life of Paul Dirac, quantum genius.* London.

Farrell, J. 2001. *Latin language and Latin culture.* Cambridge.

   2007. 'Lucretian architecture: the structure and arrangement of the *De rerum natura*', in Gillespie and Hardie 2007: 76–91.

Farrington, B. 1955. 'The meaning of *persona* in *De rerum natura* III 58', *Hermathena* 85: 3–12.

1967. *The faith of Epicurus.* New York.

Feeney, D. C. 1978. 'Wild beasts in the *De Rerum Natura*', *Prudentia* 10: 15–22.

Ferber, M. 1999. *A dictionary of literary symbols.* Cambridge.

Festugière, J.-A. 1968. *Épicure et ses dieux.* 2nd edn. Paris.

Fletcher, G. B. A. 1968. 'Lucretiana', *Latomus* 27: 884–93.

Flores, E. (ed.) 2002–. *Titus Lucretius Carus. De Rerum Natura. Edizione critica con introduzione e versione.* Naples.

Foster, J. 1971. 'Terence, *Andria* 567–8 again', *Classical Review* 21: 170–1.

Fowler, D. P. 1989/2007. 'Lucretius and politics', in Miriam Griffin and J. Barnes (edd.), *Philosophia togata: essays on philosophy and Roman society.* Oxford 1989, 120–50. Reprinted Gale 2007a: 397–431.

2002. *Lucretius on atomic motion. A commentary on De Rerum Natura 2.1–332.* Oxford.

Fowler, D. and P. 1997. Introduction and Notes in Melville 1997.

Fraenkel, E. 1917/1964. 'Das Geschlecht von dies', *Glotta* 8: 24–68. Reprinted in *Kleine Beiträge zur klassischen Philologie.* Rome 1964, vol. I 27–72.

1957. *Horace.* Oxford.

Friedländer, P. 1941/1969/1986. 'Patterns of sound and atomistic theory in Lucretius', *American Journal of Philology* 62: 16–34. Reprinted in *Studien zur antiken Literatur und Kunst.* Berlin 1969, 337–53; Classen 1986: 291–307.

Friedrich, W.-H. 1948. 'Ennius-Erklärungen', *Philologus* 97: 297–301.

Gaertner, J. F. 2007. '*Tum* und *tunc* in der augusteischen Dichtersprache', *Rheinisches Museum* 150: 211–24.

Gain, D. B. 1969. 'The life and death of Lucretius', *Latomus* 28: 545–53.

Gale, Monica R. 1994. *Myth and poetry in Lucretius.* Cambridge.

(ed.) 2007a. *Lucretius* (Oxford Readings in Classical Studies). Oxford.

2007b. 'Lucretius and previous poetic traditions', in Gillespie and Hardie 2007: 59–75.

Garani, Myrto. 2007. *Empedocles* redivivus: *poetry and analogy in Lucretius.* New York and London.

Garton, C. 1993. '*Magnis concede* revisited', *Classical World* 86: 486–7.

Getty, R. J. (ed.) 1955. *Lucani De Bello Civili Liber I.* Corrected reprint of 1st edn 1940. Cambridge.

Giancotti, F. 1989. *Religio, natura, voluptas. Studi su Lucrezio con un'antologia di testi annotati e traditi.* Bologna.

(ed. and tr.) 1994. *Tito Lucrezio Caro. La natura.* Milan.

Gigon, O. (ed.) 1978. *Lucrèce* (Fondation Hardt Entretiens sur l'antiquité classique 24). Geneva.

Gildersleeve, B. L. 1930. *Selections from the Brief Mention of Basil Lanneau Gildersleeve*, ed. C. W. E. Miller. Baltimore and London.

Gillespie, S. and Hardie, P. (edd.) 2007. *The Cambridge Companion to Lucretius.* Cambridge.

Giussani, C. (ed.) 1896–8. T. *Lucreti Cari De rerum natura Libri Sex.* 4 vols. Turin.

Gomme, A. W. and Sandbach, F. H. 1973. *Menander. A Commentary.* Oxford.

Goold, G. 1958. 'A lost manuscript of Lucretius', *Acta Classica* 1: 21–30.

  1969. 'Catullus 3.16', *Phoenix* 23: 186–203.

Gordon, C. A. 1962/1985. *A bibliography of Lucretius.* London 1962. Reprinted with Introduction by E. J. Kenney 1985. Winchester.

Görler, W. 1997. 'Storing up past pleasures, the soul-vessel metaphor in Lucretius and his Greek models', in Algra *et al.* 1997: 193–207.

Gow, A. S. F. 1932. 'Diminutives in Augustan poetry', *Classical Quarterly* 26: 150–7.

Guthrie, W. K. C. 1962, 1965, 1969. *A history of Greek philosophy.* Vols. I–III. Cambridge.

Hadzsits, G. P. 1935. *Lucretius and his influence.* London, Calcutta and Sydney.

Hammerstaedt, J. and Smith, M. F. 2011. 'Diogenes of Oenoanda: the discoveries of 2011 (NF 191–205 and additions to NF127 and 130)', *Epigraphica Anatolica* 44: 79–114.

Hardie, P. 1986. *Virgil's Aeneid. Cosmos and imperium.* Oxford.

  2007. 'Lucretius and later Latin literature in antiquity', in Gillespie and Hardie 2007: 111–27.

Harrison, S. J. 1986. 'Philosophical imagery in Horace, Odes 3.5', *Classical Quarterly* 36: 502–7.

Häussler, R. 1968. *Nachträge zu A. Otto Sprichwörter und sprichwörtliche Redensarten der Römer.* Darmstadt.

Headlam, W. and Knox, A. D. (edd.) 1922. *Herodas. The Mimes and Fragments.* Reprinted 1966. Cambridge.

Heinze, R. (ed.) 1897. *T. Lucretius Carus. De Rerum Natura Buch III.* Leipzig.

Henry, J. 1873. *Aeneidea*, vol. I. London and Edinburgh.

Hense, O. 1909. (ed.) *Teletis Reliquiae.* 2nd edn. Tübingen.

Hofmann, J. B. 1951. *Lateinische Umgangssprache.* 3rd edn. Heidelberg.

Hollis, A. S. 1998. 'Nicander and Lucretius', *Papers of the Leeds International Latin Seminar* 10: 169–84.

Housman, A. E. (ed.) 1937. *M. Manilii Astronomicon Liber Primus.* 2nd edn. Cambridge.

  (ed.) 1938. *D. Iunii Iuuenalis Saturae.* 2nd edn. Cambridge.

Huxley, A. 1928. *Along the road. Notes and essays of a tourist.* First published 1925.

Jacobson, H. 1999. 'Lucretius' hunting souls (3, 726–728)', *Museum Helveticum* 56: 33.

2002–3. 'Lucretiana', *Illinois Classical Studies* 27–28: 131–2.

2004. 'Philo, Lucretius, and *anima*', *Classical Quarterly* 54: 635–6.

2005. 'Lucretius, *DRN* 3.296–322', *Illinois Classical Studies* 30: 31–2; 'Lucretius, *DRN* 3.692 *Aequo animoque agedum magnis concede, necesse est*', ibid. 33.

Jocelyn, H. D. (ed.) 1967. *The tragedies of Ennius* (Cambridge Classical Texts and Commentaries 10). Cambridge.

1982. 'Diatribes and sermons', *Liverpool Classical Monthly* 7: 3–7.

1986. 'Lucretius, his copyists and the horrors of the Underworld', *Acta Classica* 29: 47–9.

Johnson, W. R. 2000. *Lucretius and the modern world*. London.

Jones, W. H. S. 1909. *Malaria and Greek history*. Manchester.

(ed.) 1923. *Hippocrates*, vol. II. London and New York.

Kenney, E. J. 1958 'Notes on Ovid', *Classical Quarterly* 8: 54–66.

1959. 'Notes on Ovid: II', *Classical Quarterly* 9: 240–60.

1966. 'First thoughts on the Hamiltonensis', *Classical Review* 16: 267–71.

1969. 'Ovid and the law', *Yale Classical Studies* 21: 241–63.

1970a. 'Tityos and the lover', *Proceedings of the Cambridge Philological Society* n.s. 16: 44–7.

1970b/1986/2007. 'Doctus Lucretius', *Mnemosyne* 4, ser. 23: 366–92. Reprinted with addenda in Classen 1986: 237–65; with further addenda and added references in Gale 2007a: 300–27.

(ed.) 1971. *Lucretius De Rerum Natura Book III*. Reprinted with corrections and addenda 1984. Cambridge.

1972. 'The historical imagination of Lucretius', *Greece and Rome* 19: 12–24.

1973/2002. 'The style of the *Metamorphoses*', in Binns 1973: 116–53. Reprinted with modifications in Boyd 2002: 56–80.

1974a. '*VIVIDA VIS*: polemic and pathos in Lucretius 1.62–101', in T. Woodman and D. West (edd.), *Quality and pleasure in Roman poetry*. Cambridge, 18–30.

1974b. *The classical text. Aspects of editing in the age of the printed book.* (Sather Classical Lectures 44). Berkeley, Los Angeles and London. Italian translation by A. Lunelli, *Testo e metodo*. Rome 1995.

1977a. 'A question of taste. Horace, *Epistles* 1.14.6–9', *Illinois Classical Studies* 2: 229–39.

1977b/1995. *Lucretius* (*Greece & Rome* New Surveys in the Classics 11). Reprinted with addenda by Monica R. Gale. Oxford.

1981. Review of E. Ackermann, *Lukrez und der Mythos*, 1979, *Classical Review* 31: 19–21.

1985. Introduction in Gordon 1985: i–vii.

1998. Review of Deufert 1996, *Classical Review* 48: 25–7.

1998–9. Review of Dalzell 1996, *University of Toronto Quarterly* 68: 417–19.

1999. '"*Vt erat novator*": anomaly, innovation and genre in Ovid, *Heroides* 16–21', in Adams and Mayer 1999: 399–414.

2003. Review of Catrein 2003, *Bryn Mawr Classical Review* 2003.09.46.

2004. Review of Flores 2002, *Classical Review* 54: 366–70.

2006. Review of Piazzi 2005, *Exemplaria Classica* 10: 360–71.

2007. 'Lucretian texture: style, metre and rhetoric in the *De Rerum Natura*', in Gillespie and Hardie 2007: 92–110.

2009a. 'The *Metamorphoses*: a poet's poem', in P. E. Knox (ed.), *A Companion to Ovid*. Chichester, 140–53.

2009b. 'For we are also his offspring', in D. J. Butterfield and C. A. Stray (edd.), *A.E. Housman: classical scholar*. London, 255–60.

Kinsey, T. E. 1964. 'The melancholy of Lucretius', *Arion* 3: 115–30.

Kirk, G. S., Raven, J. E. and Schofield, M. 1983. *The Presocratic philosophers. A critical history with a selection of texts*. 2nd edn. Cambridge.

Kleve, K. 1989. 'Lucretius in Herculaneum', *Cronache Ercolanesi* 19: 5–27.

1997. 'Lucretius and Philodemus', in Algra *et al.* 1997: 49–66.

Korenjak, M. 2008. '*Iam* exclamativum', *Classical Quarterly* 58: 344–7.

Lachmann, C. (ed.) 1850. *T. Lucreti Cari De Rerum Natura Libri Sex*. Berlin. 2nd edn Berlin 1853.

Landgraf, G. 1903. *Historische Grammatik der lateinischen Sprache, III 1 Syntax des einfachen Satz*. Leipzig.

Latham, R. E. (tr.) 1951. *Lucretius On the Nature of the Universe*. Harmondsworth. Revised edn with Introduction and Notes by J. Godwin, Harmondsworth 1994.

Lattimore, R. 1962. *Themes in Greek and Latin epitaphs*. Urbana.

Laughton, E. 1964. *The participle in Cicero*. Oxford.

Lavagnini, B. 1947. 'Motivi diatribici in Lucrezio e in Giovenale', *Athenaeum* 25: 83–8.

Lejay, P. (ed.) 1911. *Q. Horati Flacci Satirae. Satires*. Paris.

Leo, F. 1912. *Plautinische Forschungen zur Kritik und Geschichte der Komödie*. 2nd edn. Berlin. Reprinted Darmstadt 1966.

1960. *Ausgewählte kleine Schriften*, ed. E. Fraenkel. 2 vols. Rome.

Leonard, W. E. and Smith, B. S. (edd.) 1965. *T. Lucreti Cari De Rerum Natura Libri Sex*. Madison. First published 1942.

Lewis, C. S. 2004. *The Collected Letters of C. S. Lewis*, ed. W. Hooper. 3 vols. San Francisco.

Liddon, H. P. 1893–7. *Life of Edward Bouverie Pusey*, ed. J. O. Johnston and J. Wilson. 4 vols. London and New York.

Lindsay, W. M. 1896. *An introduction to Latin textual criticism based on the text of Plautus*. London.

1907. *Syntax of Plautus*. Oxford. Reprinted New York 1936.

1922. *Early Latin verse*. Oxford.

Löfstedt, E. 1936. *Vermischte Studien zu lateinischen Sprachkunst und Syntax* (Skrifter utgivna av Kungl. Humanistika Vetenskapssamfundet i Lund 23). Lund, London, Paris and Leipzig.

1942 *Syntactica. Studien und Beiträge zur historischen Syntax des Lateins. I Über einige Grundfragen der lateinischen Normalsyntax* (Skrifter utgivna av Kungl. Humanistika Vetenskapssamfundet i Lund 10.1). Lund, London and Leipzig.

Long, A. A. 1974. *Hellenistic philosophy. Stoics, Epicureans, Sceptics*. London.

Long, A. A. and Sedley, D. N. 1987. *The Hellenistic philosophers*. 2 vols. Cambridge.

Longrigg, J. 1970. '"Ice of bronze" (Lucretius i 493)', *Classical Review* 20: 8–9.

Lunelli, A. 1969. *Aerius: storia di una parola poetica (varia neoterica)*. Rome.

MacKay, L. A. 1950. 'Notes on Lucretius', *University of California Publications in Classical Philology* 13 (no. 14): 435–45.

Maguinness, W. S. 1965. 'The language of Lucretius', in Dudley 1965a: 89–93.

Maltby, R. 1991. *A Lexicon of ancient etymology* (ARCA 25). Leeds.

1999. 'Tibullus and the language of elegy', in Adams and Mayer 1999: 377–98.

Marouzeau, J. 1949. *Quelques aspects de la formation du latin littéraire* (Collection linguistique publiée par la Societé de linguistique de Paris 53). Paris.

Martha, C. 1867. *Le poème de Lucrèce. Morale – religion – science*. Paris.

Martin, V. 1959. 'Un recueil de diatribes cyniques Pap. Genev. inv. 271', *Museum Helveticum* 16: 77–139.

Marx, F. 1926. *Molossische und baccheische Wortformen in der Verskunst der Griechen und Römer*. Leipzig.

Maurach, G. 1995. *Lateinische Dichtersprache*. Darmstadt.

Mayer, R. 1990. 'The epic of Lucretius', *Papers of the Leeds International Seminar* 6: 35–43

1994. (ed.) *Horace Epistles Book I*. Cambridge.

Melville, Sir R. (tr.) 1997. *Lucretius on the Nature of the Universe*. With Introduction and Notes by Don and Peta Fowler. Oxford.

Michel, A. 1962. *Le 'Dialogue des Orateurs' de Tacite et la philosophie de Cicéron* (Études et commentaires 44). Paris.

Michels, Agnes K. 1955. 'Death and two poets', *Transactions and Proceedings of the American Philological Association* 86: 160–79.

Mill, J. S. 1924. *Autobiography* (World's Classics edn). First published 1873.

Millett, P., Oakley, S. P. and Thompson, R. J. E. (edd.) 2011. *Ratio et res ipsa. Classical essays presented by former pupils to James Diggle on his retirement*

(*Cambridge Classical Journal, Proceedings of the Cambridge Philological Society* Supplementary vol. 36). Cambridge.

Minadeo, R. 1965. 'The formal design of the *De rerum natura*', *Arion* 4: 444–61.

Moles, J. L. 1996. 'Diatribe', in S. Hornblower and A. Spawforth (edd.), *The Oxford Classical Dictionary*. 3rd edn. Oxford and New York, 463–4.

Moore, J. L. 1891. 'Servius on the tropes and figures of Vergil', *American Journal of Philology* 12: 267–92.

Moritz, L. A. 1968. 'Some "central" throughts on Horace's *Odes*', *Classical Quarterly* 18: 116–31.

Müller, C. W. F. 1908. *Syntax des Nominativs und Akkusativs im lateinischen*. Supplement to Landgraf 1903.

Müller, G. 1978/2007. 'Die Finalia der sechs Bücher des Lukrez', in Gigon 1978: 197–231. Reprinted in Gale 2007a: 234–54.

Müller, K. 1973/1975. 'De codicum Lucreti Italicorum origine', *Museum Helveticum* 30: 166–78. Reprinted in id. (ed.), *T. Lucreti Cari De Rerum Natura Libri Sex*. Zurich 1975: 297–319.

  1974. Review of Kenney 1971, *Gnomon* 46: 756–64.

  1975. *T. Lucreti Cari De Rerum Natura Libri Sex*. Zurich.

Müller, L. 1894. *De Re Metrica Poetarum Latinorum praeter Plautum et Terentium Libri Septem*. 2nd edn. St. Petersburg and Leipzig.

Munari, F. 1965. *Il codice Hamilton 471 di Ovidio* (Note e discussioni erudite 9). Rome.

Munro, H. A. J. (ed.) 1886. *T. Lucreti Cari De Rerum Natura Libri Sex*. 3 vols. Reprinted 1894. Cambridge.

Murley, C. 1939. 'Lucretius and the history of satire', *Transactions and Proceedings of the American Philological Association* 70: 380–95.

Murray, G. 1935. *Five stages of Greek religion*. London. (Thinker's Library edn). First published as *Four stages of Greek religion* 1912.

Nabokov, V. 1967. *Speak memory. An autobiography revisited*. London.

Needham, J. 1959. *A history of embryology*. 2nd edn rev. A. Hughes. Cambridge.

Nicoll, W. S. M. 1970. 'Lucretius iii.658', *Classical Review* 20: 140–1.

Nisbet, R. G. M. 1995. *Collected Papers on Latin literature*, ed. S. J. Harrison. Oxford.

Norden, E. (ed.) 1934. *P. Vergilius Maro Aeneis Buch VI*. 3rd edn. Leipzig and Berlin.

  1958. *Die antike Kunstprosa vom VI. Jahrhundert v. Chr. bis in die Zeit der Renaissance*. 2 vols. 5th edn. Darmstadt.

  1966. *Kleine Schriften zum klassischen Altertum*. Berlin.

Nussbaum, Martha. 1994. *The therapy of desire: theory and practice in Hellenistic ethics* (Martin Classical Lectures n.s. 2). Princeton, NJ.

Ogilvie, R. M. 1965. *A commentary on Livy Books 1–5*. Oxford.

Oltramare, A. 1926. *Les origines de la diatribe romaine*. Lausanne and Geneva.

Orth, E. 1957. 'Lucretiana', *Helmantica* 8: 91–106.

Otto, A. 1890. *Die Sprichwörter und sprichwörtlichen Redensarten der Römer*. Leipzig.

Owen, W. H. 1968–9. 'Structural patterns in Lucretius' *De Rerum Natura*', *Classical World* 62: 121–7, 166–72.

Page, D. L. (ed.) 1950. *Select Papyri*, vol. III. *Literary papyri: poets*. Revised edn; first published 1941. London and Cambridge, Mass.

  1955. *Sappho and Alcaeus. An introduction to the study of ancient Lesbian poetry*. Frequently reprinted. Oxford.

Palmer, L. R. 1954. *The Latin language*. London.

Panayotakis, C. (ed.) 2010. *Decimus Laberius. The fragments* (Cambridge Classical Texts and Commentaries 46). Cambridge.

Papanghelis, T. D. 1979. 'Lucretius III. 961–2 once more', Δημοσιεύματα τῆς Ἑταιρείας Μακεδονικῶν Σπουδῶν 31: 342–9.

Paratore, H. and Pizzani, H. (edd.) 1960. *Lucreti De Rerum Natura. Locos praecipue notabiles collegit Hector Paratore. Commentariolo instruxit Hucbaldus Pizzani*. Rome.

Paulson, J. 1926. *Index Lucretianus*. 2nd edn. Leipzig.

Pearce, T. E. V. 1966. 'The enclosing word-order in the Latin hexameter', *Classical Quarterly* 16: 140–71, 298–320.

Pearcy, L. T. 2012. 'Does dying hurt? Philodemus of Gadara, *De morte* and Asclepiades of Bithynia', *Classical Quarterly* 62: 211–22.

Piazzi, Lisa. 2005. *Lucrezio e i Presocratici. Un commento a* De rerum natura *1, 635–920* (Testi e commenti 1). Pisa.

Platnauer, M. 1951. *Latin elegiac verse. A study of the metrical usages of Tibullus, Propertius & Ovid*. Cambridge.

Postgate, J. P. 1907–8. 'Flaws in classical research', *Proceedings of the British Academy* 3: 161–211.

Powell, J. G. F. (ed.) 1988. *Cicero Cato Maior De Senectute* (Cambridge Classical Texts and Commentaries 28). Cambridge.

Powell, J. U. (ed.) 1925. *Collectanea Alexandrina*. Oxford.

Rand, E. K. 1934. 'La composition rhétorique du troisième livre de Lucrèce', *Revue de philologie, d'histoire et de littérature anciennes*, ser. 3.8: 243–66.

Read, W. M. 1940. 'Spontaneous generation in Lucretius III, 713–740', *Classical Journal* 36: 38–40.

Real, H. J. 1970. *Untersuchungen zur Lukrez-Übersetzung von Thomas Creech* (Linguistica et litteraria 9). Bad Homburg, Berlin and Zurich.

Reeve, M. D. 1980. 'The Italian tradition of Lucretius', *Italia medioevale e umanistica* 23: 27–48.

  2005. 'The Italian tradition of Lucretius revisited', *Aevum* 79: 115–64.

2007. 'Lucretius in the Middle Ages and early Renaissance: transmission and scholarship', in Gillespie and Hardie 2007: 205–13.

Reinhardt, T. 2002. 'The speech of Nature in Lucretius' *De rerum natura* 3.931–71', *Classical Quarterly* 52: 291–304.

2004. 'Readers in the Underworld: Lucretius' *De rerum natura* 3.912–1075', *Journal of Roman Studies* 94: 27–46.

2010. 'Syntactic colloquialism in Lucretius', in Eleanor Dickey and Anna Chahoud (edd.), *Colloquial and literary Latin*. Cambridge, 203–8.

Renehan, R. 1969. *Greek textual criticism. A reader*. Cambridge, Mass.

1976. *Studies in Greek texts. Critical observations to Homer, Plato, Euripides, Aristophanes and other authors* (Hypomnemata 43). Göttingen.

Reynolds, L. D. (ed.) 1983. *Text and transmission: a survey of the Latin classics*. Oxford.

Reynolds, L. D. and Wilson, N. G. 2014. *Scribes and scholars. A guide to the transmission of Greek and Latin literature*. 4th edn. Oxford.

Richardson, N. J. (ed.) 1974. *The Homeric Hymn to Demeter*. Oxford.

Rist, J. M. 1969. *Stoic philosophy*. Cambridge.

1972. *Epicurus. An introduction*. Cambridge.

Roberts, L. 1968. *A concordance of Lucretius* (Supplement to ΑΓΩΝ). Berkeley.

Robinson, R. 1964. *An atheist's values*. Oxford.

Romanes, N. H. 1934. *Notes on the text of Lucretius*. Privately printed. Oxford.

1935. *Further notes on Lucretius*. Privately printed. Oxford.

Ross, D. O. 1969. *Style and tradition in Catullus*. Cambridge, Mass.

Rostovtzeff, M. 1957. *Social and economic history of the Roman Empire*, rev. P. M. Fraser. 3 vols. Oxford.

Rowe, G. D. 1965. 'The *adynaton* as a stylistic device', *American Journal of Philology* 86: 387–96.

Rozelaar, M. 1943. *Lukrez. Versuch einer Deutung*. Amsterdam.

Rudd, N. 1966. *The Satires of Horace*. Cambridge.

Russell, D. A. (ed.) 1964. *'Longinus' On the Sublime*. Oxford.

1983. *Greek declamation*. Cambridge.

Saint Denis, E. de 1963. 'Lucrèce, poète de l'infini', *L'information littéraire* 15: 17–24.

Sandbach, F. H. 1940. '*Lucreti poemata* and the poet's date', *Classical Review* 54: 72–7.

Sanders, K. R. 2008. '*Mens* and emotion. De Rerum Natura 3.136–46', *Classical Quarterly* 58: 362–6.

Santayana, G. 1935. *Three philosophical poets. Lucretius Dante Goethe*. New York. First published 1910.

Saunders, T. J. 1975. 'A note on Lucretius III 240', *Mnemosyne* 28: 296–8.

Schiesaro, A. 2007. 'Lucretius and Roman politics and history', in Gillespie and Hardie 2007: 41–58.

Schmid, W. 1944. Review of Büchner 1936, *Gnomon* 20: 5–10.
    1946. 'Lukrez und der Wandel seines Bildes', *Antike und Abendland* 2: 193–219.
    1962. 'Epikur', in *Reallexicon für Antike und Christentum*. Leipzig and Stuttgart, vol. v 681–819.
Schrijvers, P. H. 1970. *Horror ac divina voluptas. Études sur la poétique et la poésie de Lucrèce*. Amsterdam.
    2007. 'Seeing the invisible: a study of Lucretius' use of analogy in the *De rerum natura*', in Gale 2007a: 255–88 = 'Le regard sur l'invisible: étude sur l'emploi de l'analogie dans l'œuvre de Lucrèce', in Gigon 1978: 77–114. Tr. Monica Gale.
Schulz-Vanheyden, E. 1969. *Properz und das griechische Epigramm*. Diss. Münster.
Scourfield, J. H. D. (ed.) 1993. *Consoling Heliodorus. A commentary on Jerome, Letter 60*. Oxford.
Sedley, D. 1998. *Lucretius and the transformation of Greek wisdom*. Cambridge.
    1999. 'Lucretius' use and avoidance of Greek', in Adams and Mayer 1999: 227–46.
Segal, C. 1970. 'Lucretius, epilepsy and the Hippocratic *On Breaths*', *Classical Philology* 65: 180–2.
    1990. *Lucretius on death and anxiety. Poetry and philosophy in De Rerum Natura*. Princeton, NJ.
Sellar, W. Y. 1889. *The Roman poets of the Republic*. 3rd edn. Oxford.
Shackleton Bailey, D. R. 1947. 'Interpretations of Propertius', *Classical Quarterly* 41: 82–92.
    1956. *Propertiana*. Cambridge.
    (ed.) 1980. *Cicero: Epistulae ad Quintum Fratrem et M. Brutum* (Cambridge Classical Texts and Commentaries 22). Cambridge.
Sikes, E. E. 1936. *Lucretius poet & philosopher*. Cambridge.
Sinker, A. P. 1937. *Introduction to Lucretius*. Cambridge.
Skutsch, O. 1953/1968. 'The Soldiers' Chorus in the *Iphigenia*', *Rheinisches Museum* 96: 193–210. Reprinted in Skutsch 1968: 157–65.
    1956/1968. 'De Fulminum appellatione Scipionibus indita et de locis quibusdam Ovidianis', *Studi italiani di filologia classica* 27/28: 536–40. Reprinted in Skutsch 1968: 145–50.
    1968. *Studia Enniana*. London.
    (ed.) 1985. *The Annals of Q. Ennius*. Oxford.
Smith, B. S. 1965. See Leonard and Smith 1965.
Smith, M. F. 1978. Review of Müller 1975, *Classical Review* 28: 29–31.
    1985. 'Notes on Lucretius', *Sileno* 11: 219–25.

(ed.) 1992. *Lucretius De Rerum Natura.* With an English translation by W. H. D. Rouse, rev. M. F. Smith. Cambridge, Mass. and London. First published 1975.

2000. 'Lucretius 3.955', *Prometheus* 26: 35–40. See also list of *errata*, ibid. 192.

(tr.) 2001. *Lucretius. On the Nature of Things.* With Introduction and Notes. Indianapolis and Cambridge.

Soubiran, J. 1966. *L'élision dans la poésie latine* (Études et commentaires 63). Paris.

(ed. and tr.) 1972. *Cicéron Aratea Fragments poétiques.* Paris.

Stallings, A. E. (tr.) 2007. *Lucretius. The Nature of Things.* With Introduction by R. Jenkyns and Notes by the translator. London.

Stokes, M. C. 1975. 'A Lucretian paragraph: III.1–30', in G. M. Kirkwood (ed.), *Poetry and poetics from ancient Greece to the Renaissance. Studies in honor of James Hutton.* Ithaca, 91–104.

Summers, W. C. (ed.) 1910 and frequently reprinted. *Select Letters of Seneca.* London.

Sykes Davies, H. 1931–2/1986. 'Notes on Lucretius', *The Criterion* 11: 25–42. Reprinted in Classen 1986: 273–90.

Syme, R. 1956. *The Roman Revolution.* 3rd edn. Oxford.

1958. *Tacitus.* 2 vols. Oxford.

Tarn, W. and Griffith, G. T. 1952. *Hellenistic civilization.* 3rd edn. London.

Timpanaro, S. 1960/1978. 'Lucrezio III 1', *Philologus* 104: 147–9. Reprinted in id., *Contributi di filologia e di storia della lingua latina.* Rome, 135–40.

1970/1978. 'Longiter in Lucrezio III 676', *Maia* 22: 355–7. Reprinted in *Contributi* 140–6.

2005. *The Genesis of Lachmann's Method.* Ed. and tr. G. W. Most. Chicago and London.

Tissol, G. 1997. *The face of nature. Wit, narrative, and cosmic origins in Ovid's Metamorphoses.* Princeton, NJ.

Townend, G. B. 1978. 'The fading of Memmius', *Classical Quarterly* 28: 268–83.

Toynbee, A. *et al.* 1968. *Man's concern with death.* London.

Vahlen, J. 1907. *Opuscula Academica.* 2 vols. Leipzig. Reprinted Hildesheim 1967.

Vallette, P. 1940. 'Lucrèce et la diatribe', *Revue des Études Anciennes* 42: 532–41.

Volk, Katharina. 2002. *The poetics of Latin didactic. Lucretius, Vergil, Ovid, Manilius.* Oxford.

Wallach, B. P. 1976. *Lucretius and the diatribe against the fear of death. De Rerum Natura III 830–1094* (Mnemosyne Supplementum 40). Leiden.

Waltz, R. 1949. 'Lucrèce satirique', *Lettres d'humanité* 8: 78–103.

Warren, J. 2004. *Facing death.* Cambridge.

Waszink, J. H. 1954. 'Lucretius and poetry', *Mededelingen der koninklijke Nederlandse Akademie van Wetenschappen.* Afd. Letterkunde. Nieuwe Reeks, Deel 17, No. 8: 243–57.

Watkins, C. 1966. 'An Indo-European construction in Greek and Latin', *Harvard Studies in Classical Philology* 71: 115–19.

Watt, W. S. 1990. 'Lucretiana', *Museum Helveticum* 47: 122–7.

Watts, W. J. 1971. 'The birthplaces of Latin writers', *Greece & Rome* 18: 91–101.

Webster, T. B. L. 1964. *Hellenistic poetry and art.* London.

Weinstock, S. 1971. *Divus Julius.* Oxford.

Weise, O. 1909. *Language and character of the Roman people.* Tr. H. A. Strong and A. Y. Campbell. London.

Wellesley, K. 1974–5. 'Reflections upon the third book of Lucretius', *Acta Classica Univ. Scient. Debrecen.* 10–11: 31–40.

West, D. 1969/1994. *The imagery and poetry of Lucretius.* Edinburgh. Reprinted with Preface and Addenda London 1994.

    1972. Review of Kenney 1971, *Journal of Roman Studies* 62: 211–12.

West, M. L. 1961. 'Lucretius, iii.916–18', *Classical Review* 11: 203–4.

Wilkinson, L. P. 1963. *Golden Latin artistry.* Cambridge.

    1969. *The Georgics of Virgil.* Cambridge.

Williams, G. 1968. *Tradition and originality in Roman poetry.* Oxford.

Willis, J. 1972. *Latin textual criticism* (Illinois Studies in Language and Literature 61). Urbana, Chicago and London.

Winbolt, S. E. 1903. *Latin hexameter verse. An aid to composition.* London. Reprinted Cambridge 2011.

Wingo, E. O. 1972. *Punctuation in the classical age.* The Hague.

Wormell, D. E. W. 1960. 'Lucretius: the personality of the poet', *Greece & Rome* 7: 54–65.

    1965. 'The personal world of Lucretius', in Dudley 1965a: 35–67.

INDEXES

References are to the numeration of the notes

3. GENERAL

metempsychosis, transmigration of
  souls 670–3, 674–6, 741–75,
  741–7
metonymy 221–3
metre
  caesura: 'quasi-caesura' 174, 258,
    612–14, 715–16, 790–3, 794–7,
    956–8, 1060–2; noteworthy
    combinations: 2 w(eak) only 83–4,
    770; 3 s(trong) only 884–7,
    904–8; 4 s only 186, 526–30,
    589–91, 1060–2; 2 q(uasi) only
    790–3, 974–8
  descriptive or emphatic effect of
    6–8, 46–7, 61–4, 174, 190–1,
    196–9, 299–301, 417–20, 478–81,
    487–91, 526–30, 543–5, 546–7,
    652–6, 677–9, 773–5, 794–7,
    889–93, 904–8, 952–4, 956–8,
    1000–2, 1060–2, 1063–7;
  diaereses, effect of 35–7, 186,
    196–8, 200, 251, 350–3, 499–501,
    501–8, 804–7
  elision: of final syllable of cretic
    sequence 339–43; 904–8; of *cum*
    (preposition) 159–60; of *de* 852–3;
    of *nilo* 224–7; of final *-s* 51–4,
    896–9; prodelision (aphaeresis)
    174, 374
  'Golden' lines 344–9, 593–6
  Greek quadrisyllable word ending
    line 130–5
  hiatus of *-ae* avoided 374, 531–2;
    admissible instances of in *DRN*
    374; 'prosodic hiatus' 1082–4
  'lex Marxii' 824–7
  monosyllable ending line 28–30,
    1042–4
  prefix treated as metrically separable
    174, 258
  short open syllable treated as 'long'
    or 'short' *metri gratia* 492–4
  spondaic fifth foot 190–1, 196–9,
    252–5, 417–20, 543–5, 904–8
  spondaic word occupying second
    foot 374
  variation *metri gratia*: w. contracted
    form of verb 344–9, 862–9; w.
    frequentative form 350–3, 502–5
  atque unelided 61–4, 909–11
  -que attached to short *-e* 161–7,
    862–9, 1003–7
  see also enjambment, prosody

Mill, James 935–9
mind, where situated 112–16, 140–2
morphology
  variation (generally *metri gratia*): of
    case-ending ablative *ĕ/ē* 548–53,
    730–4; *ĭ/ī* 130–5, 607–12; dative
    u/ui 970–1; genitive *ae/ai* 83–4,
    130–5; of conjugation 156, 184–5,
    916–18; of verbal termination
    -ērunt/-ĕrunt 84–6, 133–4,
    1027–8
  present infinitive passive in *-ier* 66–7,
    262–3, 440–4
  aeuus masculine 603–6
  aliae genitive 916–18
  alid = aliud 970–1
  cuppedo = cupido 992–4
  famul = famulus 1034–5
  sis = suis 1025–6
  uis = uires 262–5
myth, reinterpretation of 14–15,
  978–1023

Newton, Isaac 1042–4

'only' to be understood 143–4,
  350–3
orthography 186, 196–9, 282–7,
  327–30, 363–7, 406–12, 502–5,
  513–16, 533–9, 634–9, 1029–33,
  1068–9
  of Greek proper names 984–6
Ovid 344–9

parody
  of epic style 832–42
  of language of conventional
    mourning 894–9, 904–8
participle
  comparative forms of 190–1
  functions of: adjectival 190–1,
    331–2, 391–5, 396–7, 403–5;
    causal 170–4, 216, 365–6, 558–62,
    702–8, 754–5, 766–8; concessive
    119, 391–5, 403–5, 847–51,
    1036–8; conditional 440–4,
    548–53, 686–97; temporal/
    conditional 589–91
  perfect, aspect of: contemporaneous
    170–4
Paul, Saint 935–9, 1045–52
periphrastic expressions 6–8, 130–5,
  161–7, 182–3, 184–5, 262–5,